Communication
The Canadian Experience

Thomas L. McPhail
The University of Calgary

Brenda M. McPhail
The McPhail Research Group

Copp Clark Pitman Ltd.
A Longman Company
Toronto

Any request for photocopying, recording, taping, or for storing on information storage and retrieval systems of any part of this book shall be directed in writing to the Canadian Reprography Collective, 379 Adelaide Street West, Suite M1, Toronto, Ontario, M5V 1S5.

ISBN 0-7730-4685-2

Executive editor: Brian Henderson
Developmental editor: Barbara Tessman
Editor: Camilla Jenkins
Design and cover: William Laughton
Typesetting: Marnie Morrissey
Printing and binding: John Deyell Co.

Canadian Cataloguing in Publication Data

McPhail, Thomas L.
   Communication: the Canadian experience

Includes bibliographical references.
ISBN 0-7730-4685-2

1. Mass media - Canada. I. McPhail, Brenda M.
II. Title.

P92.C3M26 1990   302.2'3'0971   C89-090603-3

An honest attempt has been made to secure permission for all material used, and, if there are errors or omissions, these are wholly unintentional and the Publisher will be grateful to learn of them.

Dedicated, with love, to our kids, Colleen, Rebecca, Tara, Ryan.

Copp Clark Pitman Ltd.
2775 Matheson Blvd. East
Mississauga, Ontario, L4W 4P7

Associated companies:
   Longman Group Ltd., London
   Longman Inc., New York
   Longman Cheshire Pty., Melbourne
   Longman Paul Pty., Auckland

Printed and bound in Canada

Contents

Abbreviations

ACTRA	Alliance of Canadian Cinema, Television and Radio Artists
AFP	Agence France Press
AGT	Alberta Government Telephones
AP	Associated Press
AT & T	American Telephone & Telegraph
BBG	Board of Broadcast Governors
BN	Broadcast News Ltd.
CAB	Canadian Association of Broadcasters
Cancom	Canadian Satellite Communications Inc.
CATV	community antenna television
CBC	Canadian Broadcasting Corporation
CFDC	Canadian Film Development Corporation
CFVCO	Canadian Film and Videotape Certification Office
CN	Canadian National
CP	Canadian Pacific
CP/PC	Canadian Press/La Presse Canadienne
CRBC	Canadian Radio Broadcasting Commission
CRTC	Canadian Radio-television and Telecommunications Commission
CTC	Canadian Transportation Commission
CTO	Commonwealth Telecommunication Organization
DOC	Department of Communications
EC	European Community
ENP	electronic newspaper
FCC	Federal Communications Commission
FTA	Free Trade Agreement
IBC	Inuit Broadcasting Corporation
ISDN	Integrated Services Digital Network
ITU	International Telecommunication Union
MATV	master antenna television
MCI	Microwave Communications Inc.
NFB	National Film Board
NIEO	New International Economic Order
NWICO	New World Information and Communication Order
RCC	Radio Common Carriers
RCI	Radio Canada International
TASS	Telegrafnoye Agentstvo Sovietskovo Soyuza
TSN	The Sports Network
TVRO	television-receive-only
UHF	ultra high frequencies
UNESCO	United Nations Educational, Scientific, and Cultural Organization
UPC	United Press Canada
UPI	United Press International
VCR	video cassette recorder
VHF	very high frequencies
WAP	Western Associated Press
WPFC	World Press Freedom Committee

Preface

Canadians enjoy the best of both worlds. Not only do we have our own domestic television networks, radio stations, and magazine, book, and newspaper publishers, but we also have free and unfettered access to the communication products of the rest of the world, particularly the United States. The broad range of media offerings available has clearly been a mixed blessing, however, because imports have at times dwarfed our domestic products. The Canadian response has been a plethora of investigations into the cultural, broadcasting, and public policy issues surrounding the entire Canadian communication sector.

What follows is a description of those investigations and of cultural, media, telecommunication, and regulatory issues in the Canadian communication scene. *Communication: The Canadian experience* discusses Canadian communication from a dual perspective. It begins with an overview of theories of the mass media and mass communication, frequently citing American and European scholars. Second, the text describes specifically Canadian concerns about many issues in the communication sector. The discussion elaborates on Canada's perennial cultural anxiety, and sets it against the background of study by two major Canadian communication theorists, Harold Innis and Marshall McLuhan. Their impressive contributions to our understanding of the link between communication and culture illustrate the enormous significance of this connection.

The book also acquaints the reader with historical and contemporary issues, policies, and facts about communication in Canada. It examines print and electronic media, and the range and impact of new technologies. The work then documents Canadian advances and studies in these areas. It also analyses the unique Canadian approach to communication. Canadian communication traditions represent a distinctive international model, combining both public and private institutions and initiatives.

In addition, this book describes the role and importance of the telecommunication sector. Although the broadcasting sector has received more attention and public exposure, through the media and because of many commissions, the telecommunication sector is largely responsible for the emergence of Canada as an information society. In recognition of this, we take a detailed look at telecommunication, explaining its various dimensions and highlighting current challenges. In doing so, we identify the course of action needed for Canada to be an internationally competitive information society in the future.

Communication: The Canadian experience is designed for people with relatively little knowledge about Canadian communication policies and issues. The approach is interdisciplinary, ranging across several areas in order to present the most comprehensive and up-to-date description and analysis of Canadian communication possible. Ideas are drawn from the work of scholars in many fields: from English (Marshall McLuhan and Donald Theall), political economy (Harold Innis), political science (John Meisel and Frank Peers), sociology (John Porter, Benjamin Singer, and Wallace Clement), history (Paul Rutherford), law (Peter Grant), and from management (Colin Hoskins). The primary focus of the book, however, is on previous policy decisions and present policy options. The result of this approach is a blend of the latest thinking in communication theory and extensive coverage of Canadian contributions, research, and experience in the communication sector from a public policy perspective.

The text also contains a chapter dealing with communication law, produced by Peter Mercer, Dean of the Faculty of Law at the University of Western Ontario. We are indebted to him for his expertise. We are grateful as well to many colleagues at the University of Calgary, as well as others in the communication industry, who provided information, advice, and assistance. In particular, we appreciate the feedback on and fine-tuning of the chapter on advertising, provided by John Francis and Jean Andryiszyn of the firm Francis, Williams and Johnson. Laureen Whyte and Gwen Hill gave research assistance and deserve our thanks. Finally, we would like to thank Sylvia Mills and Lorraine Ellert for their patience and excellent word-processing skills. Since this is a book concerned, in part, with the information revolution, we would like to blame all errors on deficiencies in the word-processing software, but we humbly accept them as our own.

Thomas L. McPhail
Director and Professor
Graduate Program in Communication Studies
University of Calgary

Brenda M. McPhail
President of the McPhail Research Group

Part One

Introduction to
Mass Communication
Theory

COMMUNICATION: A SURVEY OF ITS BASIC ELEMENTS

Virtually everyone agrees that communication is a basic human requirement. All of us are born into societies with established cultures consisting of shared values, assumptions, and symbol systems. Communication is the "social cement" that ensures the maintenance and further development of those societies (Merrill and Lowenstein 1971, 5). The definitions of communication are diverse, however, and no single one is completely adequate. Most focus on the aspects of transfer or sharing inherent in communication. Wilbur Schramm (1954, 3) explains:

> Communication comes from the Latin communis, common. When we communicate we are trying to establish a "commonness" with someone. That is, we are trying to share information, an idea, or an attitude. At this moment I am trying to communicate to you the idea that the essence of communication

is getting the receiver and the sender "tuned" together for a particular message.

Communication, then, involves the transfer of messages—information, ideas, attitudes, or experiences—from one person to another. Moreover, Otto Larsen (1964, 349) contends that the messages transmitted must have meaning: "Communication. . . refers to the process through which a set of meanings embodied in a message is conveyed in such a way that the meanings received are equivalent to those which the initiator of the message intended." It appears that communication can best be explained as a process; and in order to understand mass communication, it is necessary to understand the basic communication process.

The communication process

Communication is a two-way process that involves three fundamental elements: a source, a message, and a destination. The source—the sender or communicator—generates the message and encodes it by using a symbol system such as language or pictures. The message is then transmitted via a communication channel or medium to its destination, the receiver or audience. Provided that nothing interferes with the message, the receiver decodes it and responds, or gives feedback. The process can be illustrated by means of a simple model (see figure 1.1). Yet the reader is warned not to be misled. The components are interwoven into an ongoing process rather than operating as distinct elements.

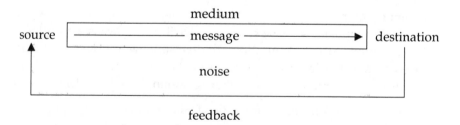

Figure 1.1

The communication process

Noise

Noise is anything that weakens, alters, or distorts the message transmitted from the source to the destination. There are three basic forms of
noise. The first is channel noise, any physical or mechanical problem that
interferes with the physical transmission of the message. Channel noise
may come from a human handicap, such as blindness or deafness, or
mechanical interference, such as broadcast static or blurred print. The
second form of noise is semantic, and it results in the receiver
misunderstanding the meaning of the message. Semantic noise can be
created by a large number of factors, including language, ethnicity, age,
experience, education, or interests. The use of current slang or local collo-
quialisms, for example, can inhibit an outsider's understanding of the
message. Finally, noise can result from an individual's stored experiences, ideas, and values. In this case, the message is distorted or altered
by an individual's use of three universal psychological strategies: selective attention, selective perception, and selective retention.

Selective attention refers to the tendency of individuals to expose
themselves only to the communication they like, want, or need. Only
someone interested in buying or selling a house, for example, is likely to
pay attention to the real estate advertisements in the newspaper.
Moreover, people tend to interpret or perceive messages selectively, in a
way that coincides with their own preconceptions. Their perception of
the real estate market is therefore likely to coincide with their position in
that market as buyers or sellers. Finally, selective retention refers to the
tendency of individuals to remember primarily what they want to
remember. After reading an accurate and neutral report about the real estate market, buyers tend to recall factors that point to a good time to purchase, while sellers remember factors that reinforce their decision to sell.

While there exist several other possible psychological reactions to
messages, many of which are discussed later, these three reduce cognitive
dissonance, the anxiety or discomfort experienced when new information
conflicts with the information, ideas, or attitudes that we already hold
(Festinger 1957). To return to the real estate example, house purchasers
want to believe that they are making a wise decision. By using selective
strategies to create noise in the communication process, purchasers can
modify the messages they receive in order to reinforce their purchasing
decisions and reduce their own anxiety.

Interpersonal communication

The model provided in figure 1.1 can be applied to all sorts of communication. Interpersonal communication, for example, involves face-to-face communication. It may take place at several different levels—one to one, within a small group (three to five people), or in a large group (public speaking)—but the source and destination are always within close proximity of one another. Communication is therefore direct; it uses several sensory channels and moves back and forth rapidly. To return to the model, the source is an individual who uses language or actions (a medium) to encode a message which is transmitted to another individual or group of individuals. On receiving the message, the receiver or receivers may or may not respond with another message. The noise in interpersonal communication can be internal—a sensory experience, a physical impairment, or an emotion—or it may be external, a competing message or a semantic problem.

An example of interpersonal communication is given in figure 1.2. In this case, the source is a student who uses the medium of speech to ask a question. The intended receiver of the message is the professor, who provides feedback to the source by answering the question. It is possible that the message might be distorted, however, if the student fails to speak loudly enough or if the professor is concentrating on something other than the student's question.

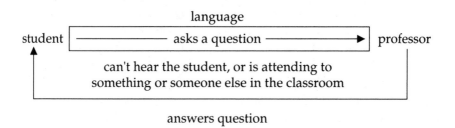

Figure 1.2

Interpersonal communication

Mass communication

Larsen (1964, 348) defines mass communication as "the relatively simultaneous exposure of large heterogeneous audiences to symbols transmitted by impersonal means from an organized source for whom audience members are anonymous." It comprises essentially the same elements as interpersonal communication but a number of differentiating features make it a more complicated process. The most obvious factor is the presence of complex technology. Technology allows a substantial physical distance to exist between the source and the destination. The distance increases the opportunities for noise to interfere with the message, limits the number of sensory channels that can be used to decode the message, and delays and weakens the feedback. As a result, mass communication is not genuinely interactive in the way that interpersonal communication is.

The nature of the actors also differentiates interpersonal communication and mass communication. Both the source and the destination of mass communication are collectivities. The source is a complex media organization composed of many individuals who perform a variety of tasks. The destination or audience is also large and complex. Whereas the destination is always a large number of diverse individuals, however, the source operates as one unified communicator.

The final distinctive feature of mass communication is the presence of *gatekeepers*. John Bittner (1977, 10) defines a gatekeeper as "any person or formally organized group directly involved in the relay or transfer of information from one individual to another through the use of a mass medium." The gatekeeper position is a very powerful one because of its ability to control the messages the audiences receive by limiting, expanding, or interpreting the information transmitted. Examples of gatekeepers include reporters, editors, publishers, and producers.

Despite its distinguishing elements, the mass communication process can be illustrated using the basic model provided in figure 1.1. As figure 1.3 demonstrates, the source in this process is a media organization. Transmission of the source's message is mediated by the technology, in this case the modern daily newspaper. The message consists of "news" that has been selected for publication by a series of gatekeepers, employees of the newspaper organization. The destination of the message is an audience of diverse individuals. They may provide feedback to the source organization in a variety of ways, but the feedback is generally delayed and diffuse, and often measured quantitatively (for example, the number of responses or cancellations generated by a specific message). Finally, there are many opportunities for noise to interfere with message reception: the print may be blurred because of a mechanical failure; an individual may not have the literacy skills required to read the message; or other media may be more successful in attracting audience members.

The model illustrates how complex the communication process is. It is not simply limited to the source and destination. If communication is to be effective, the message must be decoded exactly as the source intended but a number of intervening elements can create noise and distort the message. As the process becomes more complicated, the opportunities for interference increase.

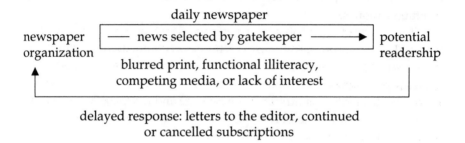

Figure 1.3

Mass communication

Approaches to the study of mass communication

Since the inception of mass media, theorists, scholars, social critics, and analysts have tried in a variety of ways to explain the process of mass communication, the institutions created by mass media, and the role of those institutions in society. Three main theoretical traditions dominate the North American approach to mass communication study: macro-approaches, content analysis, and media impact theories (see table 1.1). The reader is cautioned that the following overview is merely an introduction to these theoretical approaches; suggestions for further reading are provided at the end of the chapter.

Macro-approaches
As table 1.1 illustrates, there are several macro-approaches. Each presupposes a unity of media and society. *Mass society theory* emphasizes the

Table 1.1

Major approaches to the study of mass communication

Macro-approaches	mass society theories
	Marxist or critical theories
	media structure and function theories
	normative theories
Content analysis	traditional content analysis
	structuralism
	semiotics
Media impact theories	media/society autonomy
	media/society interdependence
	societal dominance
	media dominance

interdependence of the institutions of power in a society, institutions such as governments, banks, corporations, schools, universities, and churches. The media, as one of the sources of power and authority, are integrated with others into a complex social system. Society is the source of knowledge, and media content not only emanates from that social system but also reinforces it. The interdependence of institutions of power maintains the status quo, and results in authoritative, or top-down, social control—a recurring theme in mass society theory. Despite its early and consistent support from influential scholars such as C. Wright Mills (1951, 1956), mass society theory remains just that—a theory. It is not open to empirical study.

Marxist or *critical theory*, another of the macro-approaches to mass communication, is based on the writings of the German philosopher, Karl Marx ([1894] 1967), who asserted that the ideologies of the ruling class are the ruling ideologies in any society. According to this view, all social institutions, including the mass media, support the ruling ideologies, thereby inhibiting the development of counter ideologies. The critical or Marxist approach to the study of mass communication is dominated by a concern about power. It attempts to locate and identify the elements in a capitalist system that control the mass media.

Within the framework of critical theory, there are three approaches to analysing power. Each type identifies a different factor as the primary cause of social domination by the ruling elite and their ideologies. The first examines the economic structure of institutions such as the mass media to determine the degree of control exerted by economic elites. It contends that the media's reliance on market forces and financial support from economic elites leads to increased media concentration, reduced journalistic independence, and limited opportunities for media access for those without a recognized power base. Economic imperatives will force the rationalization of any sector, to make it as profitable as possible. The danger is that this may lead to the concentration of media ownership within the hands of a few very powerful corporations.

The second sort of analysis focusses on the content of media messages. It examines the expressions or symbols of the dominant ideology— the manner in which socialist economies are presented in comparison to capitalist ones, for example—and argues that these images are unconsciously assimilated by the masses, thereby shaping mass perception of reality and legitimating the status quo. According to this analysis, therefore, the economic and political elites do not have to impose the ruling ideologies forcibly for those ideologies to hold sway.

The third approach focusses on the media's cultural influence. It argues that the mass media have created a one-dimensional mass culture which integrates divergent interests into the dominant social ideology. In general, Marxist or critical theories tend to view the mass media as somewhat pernicious influences that have distorted our image of reality to ensure the maintenance of the status quo.

Media structure and function theory, like the other macro-approaches, assumes a unity of media and society. It examines the specific functions and structure of the mass media, concentrating on society's media needs and on the role of media in promoting social continuity. The media are seen as connecting elements that integrate individuals into the social structure and its institutions. For example, except for periodic elections, few citizens have direct contact with or control over governments. The media, by reporting and analysing government activities, provide an indirect link between individuals and governments. Unlike the Marxist approach, media structure and function theory does not assume that the media are dominated by a single social group, but both theories suggest that the media encourage social continuity rather than social change.

The final macro-approach is really a subset of the media structure and function theory. It too examines the manner in which the media and society interact but it is more descriptive in its analysis. The *normative theories* offer a series of ideas about how the media operate in different societies, in terms of function, control, and responsibilities. They analyse the given social structure, determine its media needs, and identify the social role of media institutions, governing or regulatory authorities, and audiences. There are four traditional normative mass media theories—authoritarian, libertarian, Soviet totalitarian, and social responsibility—but new ones are appearing to fill in the gaps left by the first four. One of these is development journalism, a normative theory designed to meet the needs of developing countries. It is the best developed of the newer models, and differs from the traditional four in substantial ways. Because of their significant influence on mass media systems, all five will be discussed in greater detail in chapter 2.

Content analysis

The second major theoretical school concentrates on the content of messages disseminated by the mass media.[1] Content analysis examines not only the messages themselves but also the manner in which they are decoded by audiences and the relationship of the messages to the cultural environment. Content analysis takes its emphasis from two basic propositions: that language is rooted in culture; and that the language used by individuals determines their perceptions of reality. When individuals acquire language they not only acquire a way of communicating but also of perceiving, discriminating, and organizing the reality of their cultures and social systems. Language and culture are therefore inextricably linked. When researchers study language or media messages, they are also learning about culture.

Traditional content analysis, structuralism, and semiotics are the primary approaches to the study of media messages. *Traditional content analysis* is a quantitative method that attempts to answer a number of questions. What messages were sent? By whom? How were these messages decoded? Was there an implied message in addition to the explicitly stated one? What does all this tell us about the media, their audiences, and their cultural environment? Generally, content analysis reviews media content, collects data, and analyses them in order to answer the questions posed. It is hard to achieve a high degree of reliability in this kind of analysis, as the results are open to distortion.

An example may help to illustrate the sort of difficulties encountered in this type of research. In a content analysis of prime-time television designed to examine the portrayal of minority groups, several variables must be considered. How does the researcher define "minority"? What minority groups will be included in the study? How will coders know whether or not an individual is a member of a minority or whether a reference is being made to a minority? Must the minority be physically represented to be included in the study or will verbal or other references alone be considered sufficient? Will the analysis include any or all of the following: comments, jokes, implied references, and physical depictions? What cues will coders use to determine whether or not the reference or depiction is positive, negative, or neutral? Problems such as these make it difficult to ensure the validity of the study—that the study actually measures what it is intended to measure. The obstacles are compounded by the need to train all coders to score the same or similar representations in the same way. This is a very challenging task since different coders will perceive the messages they see and hear in very different ways. While statistical methods may be used to determine the reliability of the scoring, there is always a danger that the results will be inaccurate because of systemic coder error.

An alternative approach to content analysis involves two closely linked theoretical methods, *structuralism* and *semiotics*. Based on the writings of Ferdinand de Saussure (1966), Claude Lévi-Strauss (1967), Umberto Eco (1976), and others, both approaches involve the study of signs—words, images, objects, or concepts—which communicate messages. They explore the construction of language systems rather than simply the descriptive meaning conveyed by language, in order to identify the latent cultural meanings of the messages transmitted. For example, a semiotic analysis of a film would seek to reveal its deeper cultural and social meaning rather than the overt content of the film itself. Unlike traditional content analysis, neither semiotics nor structuralism is quantitative; both therefore lack the empirical rigour of other research methodologies. Their main advantage is that they offer a method to analyse non-verbal media messages. As a result, they can be particularly revealing when applied to advertising.

Structuralism is based on the assumption that all manifestations of social activity, from the books we write to systems of kinship and marriage, are systems of communication or "languages." As a method of content analysis, structuralism allows the researcher to go beyond analysis of description, or content, to reconstruct intellectually the logic of the phenomenon under study. This can be done by examining the network of associations between the whole and its parts, and among the parts, in order to make sense of that phenomenon. Structuralism looks at the nature and form of the logical patterns, or structures, that exist below the surface of reality, arguing that "what the observer sees is not the structure, but simply the evidence and product of the structure. On the other hand though, the structure of any activity is not itself what can be seen, it can only be derived from what is seen" (Lane 1970, 15).

Semiotics developed out of structuralism. Although more limited in scope than structuralism, it too involves the study of signification. Within semiotics, signifiers may include a broad range of symbols: words, icons, photographs, films, paintings, sculptures, and even algebraic equations. The meaning of each is interpreted in the context of its specific culture.

It is interesting to note that structuralism and semiotics are not taught within most mainstream communication programs in Canada. They are more frequently found in departments of English, linguistics, or film studies. In Europe, however, semiotics tends to be the dominant mode of research in most media and cultural studies institutes. This contrast reflects the strong American social science bias that predominates in the methodological approaches to media research in Canada.

There are a number of other content-dominated approaches. Some use elements of the foregoing methods in their analysis, while others are less closely associated with them.[2] Content analysis in general can provide empirical and systematic analysis of media content and culture. It can identify trends, traditions, attitudes, and values. It has not, however, solved the enigma of just where the accurate meaning of the message exists: in the language/culture, the source, the destination, or the process of transmitting the message.

Media impact theories

The final school of thought draws together theories that examine the media's effect on their audiences. Taken together these theories hypothesize about the audiences' selection of various media and the consequences of their exposure to them. Denis McQuail (1983, 39–47) has identified four general views of the interrelationship of media and society. The first contends that the two elements exist as autonomous units; change in one element occurs independently of the other. The second describes media and society as interdependent. Neither dominates, but each supports and stimulates the other. The third view presupposes a dominant role for society. Media content, functions, and structures are determined by societal factors. The media therefore do not create social change; they simply reflect it. In the fourth view, the media are perceived as not merely reflecting society, but as moulding and shaping it as well. The media can alter society by promoting changes in mass attitudes, values, or behaviour.

It is important to recognize that attitudes about the relationship of media to society are coloured by basic assumptions about media structure and function. Those who believe that the media are owned and controlled by the dominant economic, political, and ideological elites, who only select content that will legitimate their positions and ensure the continuity of the established social structure, tend to perceive the audience as malleable (Clement 1975; Mills 1956; Porter 1965). On the other hand, those who assume that the media are independent and free to offer competing views on political, economic, or ideological questions in response to the diverse interests in a society are more likely to doubt the ability of media messages to manipulate audiences. Moreover, they are more apt to acknowledge the impact that audiences can have on the media themselves.

Topics in media impact theories will be addressed in greater detail later in this chapter. The treatment here of all three main schools of mass communication theory has been necessarily brief but the content covered in the remainder of this book is derived, in large part, from mass media studies undertaken in response to these theoretical underpinnings.

The mass media

Earlier in this chapter, mass communication was defined as "symbols transmitted by impersonal means from an organized source" (Larsen 1964, 348). The mass media are the organized source, and as such have been described as ubiquitous, pervasive, and persuasive. Together, they undoubtedly act as an important force in modern Western society. Because individual personal experiences are by nature limited, most of what we know about our society and our world is learned through the mass media. The next few pages first provide a general introduction to the structure and functions of the mass media and then describe four typologies that can be used to compare the different mass media.

The structure of the mass media

According to McQuail (1983, 33), "the mass media institution is a distinct set of activities (sending and receiving messages), carried out by persons occupying certain roles (regulators, producers, distributors, audience members), according to certain rules and understandings (laws, professional codes and practices, audience expectations and habits)." This definition identifies at least three significant characteristics of mass media: the media are institutions with definite functions, prescribed roles, and established rules.

In order to fulfil their functions, modern media institutions have developed highly structured, hierarchical organizations. A publisher or station/network manager sits atop the hierarchy, serving as both the ultimate gatekeeper of information and the primary director of the organization's activities. Below this person exists a large bureaucracy responsible for differentiated tasks that require a variety of skills. Each of the individual media employees serves the organization's needs through a sequenced system of control. With respect to content collection, for example, reporters are responsible to desk editors who, in turn, report to senior editors and so on right up to the publisher, and perhaps even the owner of the media organization. A similar organizational chart might be drawn for each of the institution's functions, including production, dissemination, and staff requirements such as payroll and accounting.

Modern media are also big business enterprises whose purpose is to send and receive messages. Gathering or creating, producing, and disseminating content—ideas, information, and cultural products—are therefore their primary tasks. These are expensive undertakings and necessitate intensive capital investment, yet the content remains relatively public. Media distribution systems are informal and anyone with the necessary economic means and cognitive skills generally has access to media products.[3]

Using sophisticated technology to communicate messages from media sources to their destinations enables the mass media to reach large, widely dispersed audiences simultaneously. Despite the heterogeneity of audience membership, mass media facilitate a common exposure to information and ideas never before possible. Messages flow predominantly in one direction, however, and the media are therefore regarded as detached, impersonal communicators.

The functions of the mass media

In their attempt to identify the functions of the mass media, analysts have focussed their attention primarily on the role of media as content providers. A list of these functions makes it clear that each serves a recognized social need.

The most obvious and, perhaps, the most important role of the mass media is to carry information. They communicate news about events at the local, national, and international levels that are outside the personal experience of the audience. The media not only report events but also interpret them. Gatekeepers choose the information and determine how much attention it will be given. In doing so they are also selecting those issues or events that they consider worthy of public attention, thereby determining what the public should know. By selecting particular events for coverage, "the mass media confer status on public issues, persons, organizations, and social movements" (Lazarsfeld and Merton 1948, 95–118). This process is known as *agenda-setting*, and it flows naturally from the gatekeeping process. If the media say that something is news, it becomes part of the public awareness; conversely, without media attention, events or issues are likely to go largely unnoticed.

The second most commonly recognized task of the mass media is entertainment. It is, in fact, the primary objective of some media, such as film and television. The entertainment function serves the audience's need to escape from reality temporarily, to relieve tension or boredom, or simply to while away some pleasurable time. The entertainment and information functions are not fully separable. Entertaining fare may inform and information media may entertain. All of the other media functions also overlap to some extent.

The media's role as persuaders is often the most bitterly criticized. The use of media to influence an individual's choice in everything from toothpaste to political representatives has attracted a great deal of popular attention and professional research. Media persuasion may be either overt, as in advertising or public relations campaigns, or merely implied through information or entertainment.

Socialization, the process by which individuals are integrated into their social system, is a less perceptible media function. It is nevertheless a relevant element of all media genres: information, entertainment, and advertising. By presenting images of social relationships, the media teach individuals about the norms, values, expectations, and behavioural patterns of their own society. They provide models of how to interact with society.

Many media critics and consumers argue that these images, particularly sexual or violent images, are distorted and may have a detrimental effect on the existing social structure. Others worry that mass media reduce social diversity and thereby promote cultural homogenization. Despite these fears, there is general agreement, confirmed by research, that the media tend to promote social continuity and cohesion.

The media are also responsible for the transmission of culture, a role related to their socialization function. They create a record of our culture, from the clothes we wear, food we eat, and games we play, to the political, social, or economic events we experience and our reaction to them. The media disseminate existing cultural products—novels, poetry, music, dance, drama, and art—and promote the creation of new ones. Some critics (Wilensky 1964) differentiate mass culture from high culture, but the role of the media in bringing at least mass culture to audiences is unquestioned. The term mass culture refers to standardized cultural products created solely for the mass market at minimum cost and without attention to excellence. High culture is created by a cultural elite within aesthetic, literary, or scientific traditions and is evaluated by standards independent of consumption. Some media are designed specifically to serve high culture, while others do so only occasionally.

The final role of the media, at least in capitalist societies, is to serve the needs of the economic system. The relationship is an interdependent one. The media sell audiences to advertisers and benefit from advertisers' financial support. The advertisers create a demand for the goods and services provided by their clients, thus maintaining the economic health of the system and benefiting themselves. Because advertisers require specific types of audiences, however, critics argue that their influence on media content can be powerful and detrimental. The potential for influencing content will be discussed in chapters 4, 5, and 12.

To review, media function to inform, to entertain, to persuade, to socialize, to transmit culture, and to serve the economic system. It quickly becomes apparent that different media are best suited to different functions, and that these functions or purposes provide a way to categorize various media. The next section examines other modes of organizing and identifying the media.

Mass media typologies

The following four typologies for classifying media provide frameworks for comparing the complex features of various media. In combination, the typologies outlined here cover most media attributes. The first and most simple is based on the means of production and distribution: whether the medium is print (newspapers, magazines, books), or electronic (radio, television, audio recordings, film, interactive computerized media). The distinction provides only very limited information, but a thorough description of each medium can be achieved by combining this basic typology with others.

Peter Sandman, David Rubin, and David Sachsman (1972, 239) have developed a more detailed typology. It is a concise, easily used tool for classifying media, since it permits rapid comparison of some of the most important attributes of media. When examining and comparing various mass media, Sachsman and his colleagues consider eight physical and cognitive dimensions:

1. *Speed.* How quickly can the medium gather information and distribute it to the public?

2. *Depth.* What depth and comprehensiveness of coverage does the medium provide? (Depth is generally inversely proportional to speed.)

3. *Breadth.* Is the range of topics and interests covered broad or narrow?

4. *Ubiquity.* How accessible is the medium and to what degree is it used by the public in comparison with other media?

5. *Permanence.* What is the opportunity for or likelihood of retaining permanent records of the medium's content?

6. *Locality.* Is the medium local, national, or international?

7. *Sensory involvement.* To what degree does the medium appeal to the senses of its audience?

8. *Credibility.* How believable is the medium in the opinion of the general public?

The third typology focusses on similar media characteristics. John Merrill and Ralph Lowenstein (1971, 18–32) recognize the potential of a medium to shape both messages and the events that prompt the messages. (For example, election campaigns are often organized to suit media deadlines.) From that premise, Merrill and Lowenstein derive five categories of physical and economic elements that can be used to compare the potential effectiveness of different media in structuring messages and reaching their prospective audiences.

1. *Elements of reproduction.* The media record and transmit messages by using different combinations of five distinct elements: verbal symbols, picture symbols, colour, sound, and motion. Merrill and Lowenstein suggest that the greater the number of elements a medium uses, the greater its potential effectiveness. Furthermore, each medium tries to fashion the event covered to suit its own distinctive mix of elements. The electronic media elicit provocative ten-second verbal comments, or "clips"; the visual media arrange the perfect photo opportunity.

2. *Elements of circulation.* The widest possible circulation requires that a medium be portable, simultaneous, and reviewable. In other words, it must be able to reach the audience, to transmit the message as soon as the information becomes available, and to be reviewed at the receiver's convenience. It is in these respects that deadlines and media flexibility become important to the timing and staging of events.

3. *Elements of feedback.* Feedback provides the information a medium requires to adjust to the needs and expectations of its audience. Merrill and Lowenstein identify two kinds of feedback: verbal, such as letters to the editor; and non-verbal, such as broadcast audience ratings. Moreover, they suggest that both the proximity of the audience to the source and the potential for the audience to participate in the medium's activity are important in determining the amount of verbal feedback received. Although feedback is used predominantly to gauge a medium's success in communicating to its audience, it may also influence how future events are presented.

4. *Elements of support.* Merrill and Lowenstein also examine the way that each medium receives its financial support: single sales (books and records), subscriptions (magazines and newspapers), advertising (radio and television), and subsidies (the Canadian

Broadcasting Corporation). Each method is associated with different requisites, and these too can shape events and media messages. A tabloid's reliance on single sales, for example, encourages its management to put a very provocative spin on its coverage in order to peak interest and maximize sales.

5. *Additional elements.* In addition to the four main groups of elements, there are five other features to be considered in any media analysis: the number of available channels, the cost of operation, the complexity of the distribution system, the frequency of publication, and the flexibility of the medium's channel size. The number of channels refers to the number of media opportunities available for disseminating information—the number of editions of a newspaper, the number of newscasts, and so on. Theoretically, any medium that can use a large number of available channels, operate in a cost effective manner, eliminate distribution problems, publish at reasonable intervals, or adjust its channel size to suit the content has a distinct advantage in terms of its ability to shape both events and the images of them transmitted to audiences. Channel size is altered by, for example, increasing or reducing the number of pages of print or the number of minutes on the electronic media.

Denis McQuail (1983, 25–37) has also developed a typology, from what he acknowledges to be "the main component strands in the dominant definitions acquired by the media." In doing so, he recognizes that students of the media are all examining similar elements of similar institutions, regardless of the diversity of their approaches. In his analysis, McQuail identifies five dimensions to media:

1. *Conditions of content, distribution, and use.* The managers and the users of various media control the content, distribution, and use to differing degrees. Analysis of this dimension examines their specific levels of control. Television, for example, is highly controlled; the managers determine what content is to be aired and when. Furthermore, its use is limited to those who are close to a television set. Books, on the other hand, permit the user more flexibility and control.

2. *The political dimension.* McQuail includes in this dimension the degree of regulation imposed on the medium, its importance to political activity, and how liable it is to criticize political authority.

3. *Social and cultural values.* Analysis of this dimension asks whether the medium deals primarily with reality or fiction, serious purposes or leisure, and whether or not its messages are art.

4. *Social relationships.* This dimension includes the social relationships that the medium permits or encourages during its use and degree of involvement or concentration that it requires from the individual. Reading, for example, is a solitary activity because it demands significant attention, while seeing a film is often a social occasion.

5. *Organizational requirements.* The level of technological sophistication required by a medium determines its organizational needs. Examining the technology therefore discloses the medium's organization. It is also necessary to decide which aspect of its activities is the most important: the content, production, or distribution of the message.

Each of the four typologies presented above has practical value for studying the mass media. By applying them either singly or together, we can gain insight into the structure, function, and operation of all the modern mass media. They also allow comparison of media across international boundaries and through time. In subsequent chapters, several mass media will be examined in greater detail, using elements of these typologies. Nevertheless, descriptions of the mass media cover only the source of the communication process. Messages must also be received for communication to occur. The next section examines the character of media audiences.

The audience
Without an audience, the mass media would become useless and cease to exist. The composition and role of audiences and the impact of media on their behaviour are crucial areas of mass communication research. The

concept of the "mass" audience, however, is "one of the great fallacies of mass communication" (O'Hara 1961, 35–36). Audiences exist as groups or specialized publics rather than as masses, a fact that has significant implications for the sorts of content disseminated by specific media.

Mass media audiences do share a number of characteristics. They are physically separated from the source of the message by the intervening technology and the network of distribution. Audiences, in general, tend to be large, heterogeneous, and anonymous. They are composed of individuals who elect to become members of a specific audience. Characteristics such as geography, age, ethnicity, education, occupation, religion, or interests, however, are instrumental in an individual's pattern of media use, and audience members are therefore likely to share these traits. Even so, individual audience members rarely consider themselves part of an audience group. They are aware only of their own unique pattern of media involvement.

Mass communication research has identified several very general trends in the way that individuals use the media and thereby become members of media audiences. People who are above average in their exposure to one medium, for example, are likely to be above average in their exposure to all. This all-or-none principle is probably a function of interest and opportunity. People who enjoy popular entertainment or who seek information are likely to use all available media if they have the opportunity to do so. Conversely, people who are too busy or too absorbed in other activities are less likely to expose themselves to any of the media.

Second, media use is linked to basic demographic variables. As their education and income increase, so does the frequency with which individuals use media. Print, particularly, is more avidly consumed by those who have post-secondary education than by those who do not. This generalization does not apply as well to the electronic media, which have significant appeal for a larger segment of the population. As people age, however, their habits of media use tend to change. Older people use fewer media products than do younger ones and they are more likely to use them for serious purposes than for entertainment.

Finally, certain factors prompt individuals to select one medium as opposed to another. The evidence indicates that people are liable to choose whichever medium will best satisfy their needs with the minimum amount of effort. The time available, the ease of access, individual habits, and the need itself all contribute to their choice of medium.

Given all of the characteristics outlined above, it should be apparent that audiences are amorphous. Their numbers exist in isolated households across vast territories and no two members are exactly alike. Yet advertisers want to reach people with particular characteristics. It is very difficult for media to provide the sort of content that will do that without sufficient information about individual audience members, and even with that information, the differences among members may outweigh the similarities. Even so, in order to satisfy the demands of advertisers, media organizations attempt to analyse their audiences to discover their size, durability, interests, and expectations. Quantitative rating systems, or surveys, can provide some of this information: audience size and durability, and basic audience demographics such as age, sex, level of education, income, and ethnicity. More sophisticated research methods are required to identify the complex psychological characteristics of media audiences, characteristics that provide the media with more reliable and useful data.[4]

We all are exposed to a multitude of media messages daily. If we acknowledge that the information we process influences the type of people we are, it is easy to assume that the media have a significant effect on their audiences. But as Boyd and Jackson (1988, 353) point out, "Mass communication. . . ordinarily serves as an agent of reinforcement for attitudes and behavioural tendencies that individuals already possess. . . and traditionally has not been primarily effective in actual change."

The relationship between media and society

As has been noted, there are four views of the relationship between media and society: autonomy, interdependence, societal dominance, and media dominance. The last approach serves as the focal point for the balance of this chapter.

In his classic review of the effects of mass communication, Larsen (1964, 353–54) identifies eight consequences of mass media consumption:

1. the creation or stimulation of "vast new complexes of activities centering on the manipulation of symbols—e.g., advertising, public relations, entertainment, market research"

2. a larger public with a much broader range of experience and information

3. new patterns of conversation and interpersonal interaction

4. the ability of the media to confer or withhold status, prestige, or authority (agenda setting)

5. an emphasis on the personality of figures in public life

6. altered family patterns

7. an emphasis on material values and the economic sector of society

8. an accelerated process of cultural diffusion and social change

The review was an important benchmark in mass communication studies because it provided the basis for much of the empirical research that was to follow. Although it identifies generalized media effects, however, it doesn't explain the impact of a particular media message on an individual member of the audience. In other words, it doesn't address directly the question posed by Harold Lasswell (1948, 37–51): "Who does what in which channel [or medium] to whom with what effect?" One of the first answers was provided by Bernard Berelson (1948, 172): "Some kinds of *communication* on some kinds of *issues*, brought to the attention of some kinds of *people* under some kinds of *conditions*, have some kinds of *effects*."

Berelson's statement is accurate, but it has little predictive value. The number of ungovernable variables in the communication process prevents research from being more specific. It is difficult, for example, to separate the effect of the mass media message from other elements of an individual's identity such as age, sex, education, religion, prior experience, physical environment, and interpersonal relationships. Nor can one medium effectively be separated from another. Because people are constantly exposed to many messages from a variety of media, there is no way to determine which particular medium or message has had an effect. Moreover, researchers are hard pressed to find a representative control group, the same as the experimental group in all respects but without any exposure to media. Finally, researchers must determine whether the message is the cause or the effect of social change.

Despite these complexities, it has been determined that three conditions must be met for a message to have an effect. The receiver must attend to the message, understand it as the source intended it to be understood, and respond (Larsen 1964, 350). Joseph Klapper (1960, 278)

identifies five theoretical "directions of effects," or types of impact. Although his scheme has some shortcomings in terms of its application to empirical research, it does provide a basic organizational framework.

Klapper first identifies the creative effect: the media can create an attitude or opinion in individuals who previously did not have one. He excludes from this group individuals whose opinion is one of neutrality towards the given issue. The creative effect is difficult to demonstrate empirically because of the problem involved in locating experimental subjects with no opinion. Most of the relevant research has been undertaken with children or has examined how individuals accept new ideas or items. These studies are of particular interest to advertisers.

Second, the media can support or strengthen existing opinions. The reinforcement effect is considered to be the most common one. Based on the concept of cognitive dissonance discussed earlier, it follows from the practices of selective attention, perception, and retention. People want to be reassured and they therefore attend to messages that will strengthen their attitudes or behaviour. Again, the effect is difficult to demonstrate, since it cannot always be determined whether or not a message has had a direct impact.

Third, the media may provoke a minor change in the intensity of an individual's attitude without really altering it. In other words, a positive or a negative attitude may become more neutral.

Conversion is the fourth "direction of effect." For a conversion to occur, the individual must experience a complete reversal in point of view. The likelihood of such an effect is considered slight because human beings have a natural resistance to change. Even so, the media make constant attempts to change audience opinions on a whole range of issues. When a campaign manages to change the opinions of even a small percentage of the audience, it is often considered successful.

Finally, the media may sometimes have no effect. Despite their pervasive nature, it may be that their messages have no power to create, reinforce, or change attitudes and behaviour.

The effects identified by Klapper are among several possible ones. The activation effect refers to the ability of the media to motivate individuals to act. It is measured by audience behaviour, rather than by changes in attitude, and includes, for example, campaigns that prompt people to donate blood, buy a certain breakfast cereal, or get out and vote. Paul Lazarsfeld and Robert Merton have identified the opposite effect, known as the deactivation, apathy, or privatization effect. They

argue that the media can replace active with vicarious or passive participation: "Exposure to [a] flood of information may serve to narcotize rather than energize the average reader or listener. . . . He [or she] comes to mistake knowing about the problems of the day for doing something about them" (Lazarsfeld and Merton 1948, 105–6). The enforcement effect, on the other hand, describes the media's potential for enforcing social norms, attitudes, and behavioural patterns. According to Lazarsfeld and Merton (1948, 499), the media reduce the gap between "private attitudes" and "public morality" by publicly emphasizing prevailing beliefs on right and wrong.[5] This can reduce a society's tolerance for diversity and motivate its members to behave in a similar manner.

The foregoing examination has provided only a cursory review of the potential for media to influence individual attitudes, and behaviour. The impact may be intentional or unplanned, and can be effective over either the short or the long term.

Summary

This chapter began by defining communication and mass communication. It described the basic communication process and identified a number of factors that either limit or distort the reception of messages. A review of the major approaches to the study of communication followed next. By describing the structure and functions of the media, and the various typologies through which the media can be examined and compared, the chapter then provided some general insights into the operation of modern mass media. Finally, it examined the role of audiences and the possible impact of the media and its messages on those audiences.

"Communications, as a subject of study, has moved from marginality to centrality" during the past forty years or so (Schiller 1981, xvii). The amount of literature is growing rapidly as more and more academics, researchers, practitioners, and students realize the pivotal position that communication occupies in our society. This chapter introduced the primary concepts and issues in the communications field. Later chapters will examine the media's impact on political, economic, and social institutions within the Canadian context and, given the policy focus of the text, the impact of those institutions on the media.

Notes

1. Suggested reading for those interested in content analysis includes Barthes (1967), Berelson (1952), Eco (1976), and Hawkes (1977).

2. Other content approaches include the psychoanalytic approach (Kracauer 1949); the study of political language (Edelman 1967); and the political indicators approach (Gerbner 1973).

3. Some media, such as newspapers and magazines, are very inexpensive to use. The initial expenditures required to buy a radio or television are much higher, but the use of these media is almost free if one discounts the advertising costs that are added to most consumer purchases. In addition, the level of cognitive skills required to use different media varies. The functionally illiterate are unable to use the print media, for example, but a number of other media are available.

4. Bittner (1977, 245-67) provides a brief but useful review of types of audience research.

5. Richard Ericson, Patricia Baranek, and Janet Chan (1987) undertook an empirical study of the Canadian media to determine the manner in and degree to which those media "visualize deviance."

References

Barthes, R. 1967. *Elements of semiology*. London: Jonathan Cape.

Berelson, B. 1948. Communication and public opinion. In *Communications in modern society*, ed. W. Schramm, 167–85. Urbana: University of Illinois.

———. 1952. *Content analysis in communication research*. Glencoe: Free Press.

Bittner, J.R. 1977. *Mass communication: An introduction*. Englewood Cliffs: Prentice-Hall.

Boyd, N.T., and M.A. Jackson. 1988. Reducing the risks of pleasure: Responding to AIDS in Canada. *Canadian Public Policy* 14(4): 347–60.

Clement, W. 1975. *The Canadian corporate elite: An analysis of economic power*. Toronto: McClelland and Stewart.

de Saussure, F. 1966. *Course in general linguistics*, trans. W. Baskin. New York: McGraw-Hill.

Eco, U. 1976. *A theory of semiotics*. Bloomington, IN: Indiana University.

Edelman, M.J. 1967. *The symbolic uses of politics*. Urbana, IL: University of Illinois.

Ericson, R.V., P.M. Baranek, and J.B.L. Chan. 1987. *Visualizing deviance: A study of news organization*. Toronto: University of Toronto.

Festinger, L.A. 1957. *A theory of cognitive dissonance*. New York: Row Peterson.

Gerbner, G. 1973. Cultural indicators—The third voice. In *Communications technology and social policy*, ed. G. Gerbner, L. Gross, and W. Melody, 553–73. New York: Wiley.

Hawkes, T. 1977. *Structuralism and semiology*. London: Methuen.

Klapper, J.T. 1960. *The effects of mass communication*. New York: Free Press.

Kracauer, S. 1949. National types as Hollywood presents them. *Public Opinion Quarterly*. 13:53–72.

Lane, M., ed. 1970. *Introduction to structuralism*. New York: Basic Books.

Larsen, O. 1964. Social effects of mass communication. In *Handbook of modern sociology*, ed. R.E.L. Faris, 349–81. Chicago: Rand McNally.

Lasswell, H.D. 1948. The structure and function of communication in society. In *The communication of ideas*, ed. L. Bryson, 37–51. New York: Harper.

Lazarsfeld, P.F., and R.K. Merton. 1948. Mass communication, popular taste and organized social action. In *The communication of ideas*, ed. L. Bryson, 95–118. New York: Harper.

Lévi-Strauss, C. 1967. *Structural anthropology*, trans. C. Jacobson and B. Grundfest Schoepf. Garden City, NY: Doubleday.

McQuail, D. 1983. *Mass communication theory*. Beverly Hills: Sage.

Marx, K. [1894] 1967. *Capital*. 3 vols. New York: International.

Merrill, J.C., and R.L. Lowenstein. 1971. *Media, messages and men*. New York: David McKay.

Mills, C.W. 1951. *White collar*. New York: Oxford University Press.

———. 1956. *The power elite*. New York: Oxford University Press.

O'Hara, R.C. 1961. *Media for millions: The process of mass communication*. New York: Random House.

Porter, J. 1965. *The vertical mosaic*. Toronto: University of Toronto.

Sandman, P.M., D.M. Rubin, and D.B. Sachsman. 1972. *Media: An introductory analysis of American mass communication*. 2d ed. Englewood Cliffs: Prentice-Hall.

Schiller, H.I. 1981. Foreword to *Dependency road: Communications, capitalism, consciousness and Canada*, by D.W. Smythe. Norwood: Ablex.

Schramm, W., ed. 1954. *The process and effects of mass communication*. Urbana: University of Illinois.

Wilensky, H.L. 1964. Mass society and mass culture. *American Sociological Review* 29:173–97.

FIVE CONCEPTS OF
MASS COMMUNICATION

*C*hapter 1 introduced the four basic macro-approaches to mass communication: mass society theories, Marxist or critical theories, media
structure and function theories, and normative theories. This chapter
goes on to examine five normative theories that describe how the media
operate within particular social and political structures.[1] The detailed
review is precipitated by the policy focus of this book. Each normative
theory rests on the assumption that the media take on a form dictated by
their social, economic, and political environment; to understand how and
why different media systems function in different ways, we must examine the basic beliefs of the given societies. These beliefs reveal why
certain types of media policy initiatives are undertaken in some societies
as opposed to others. As the subsequent analysis of Canadian media
policy will illustrate, Canada's media environment is somewhat unusual.
The description of normative concepts given here is intended to provide

historical and philosophical background that will shed light on the motivation of Canadian policy makers with respect to the media.

The five normative concepts of mass communication—authoritarian, libertarian, social responsibility, Soviet totalitarian, and development—each developed at different times in response to different social and political forces. Although each concept is reviewed independently, it is important to recognize that any chosen media system will probably be influenced by a combination of concepts, with one concept predominating. Moreover, media systems can change over time in response to political, economic, physical, technological, or cultural factors. The normative media concepts therefore do not provide pigeonholes into which we may arbitrarily place any given media system. They are instead useful analytical tools to examine and compare media systems in many nations at various times throughout history.

The authoritarian concept of media

Before Gutenberg invented the printing press, communication was limited primarily to the interpersonal level. The population of Europe was for the most part illiterate and the few books that existed were laboriously reproduced by hand for the clergy or the very wealthy. The arrival of the printing press not only made possible the development of the first mass medium but in doing so also created a threat to the established authorities. Their reactions to that threat form the basis of the authoritarian concept of mass communication.

The philosophical environment

According to William Rivers and Wilbur Schramm (1969, 30), "modern communication was born in 1450 into an authoritarian society," a time in European history in which the position of the state was ranked above that of the common individual. Complete political control lay in the hands of monarchs and nobles, who justified their position by the doctrine of divine right; some higher force had endowed them with greater capacity and absolute authority and they were therefore duty-bound to exercise and protect their rights. Religion, too, supported the authoritarian social system. As the recipient of divine revelation, the Church of Rome considered itself responsible for safeguarding God-given truths. By demanding absolute obedience, it sought to protect the masses from heresy and ideological corruption.

Authoritarian systems glorify forms of government in which absolute power resides in the hands of a few selected individuals. Such systems rest on four fundamental philosophical assumptions. First, the state is the embodiment of all that is good and moral, the highest expression of civilized organization. Those who control the state apparatus derive their power from divine guidance in the form of superior intellectual or leadership ability. Second, individuals are limited in their ability to attain their goals independently. Third, it therefore follows that the state and its collective objectives rank above individuals and their private ones. Only by subordinating their interests to those of the state can individuals fulfil their goals. They exist for the state and without it they are incapable of achieving a civilized nature. The final assumption reinforces the first three: truth and knowledge can only be discovered with divine guidance, either through revelation or mental exercise. Since such awareness is unevenly distributed among individuals, those blessed with these divine advantages have a moral obligation to advise and lead, while the rest have a duty to react with absolute obedience (Siebert, Peterson, and Schramm [1956] 1976, 10–11).

Throughout history, authoritarian political systems have had many influential exponents.[2] Plato (428?–347? B.C.), Machiavelli (1469–1527), Thomas Hobbes (1588–1679), and George Hegel (1770–1831) all doubted the ability of individuals to co-operate for social good within a democratic system. Instead, these scholars put the security and interests of the state first and accepted the idea that control of opinion and information is a necessary prerequisite to social peace and order. The list of philosophers and political leaders who have espoused the authoritarian doctrine is a lengthy one, and continues into the twentieth century.[3] Their belief in the four basic presuppositions about the individual, the state, and truth has powerful implications for the type of media system that operates under an authoritarian regime, particularly with respect to the degree of media independence tolerated.

The media system

Siebert, Peterson, and Schramm ([1956] 1976, 10) describe the authoritarian system as one "under which the press, as an institution, is controlled in its functions and operations by organized society through another institution, government."[4] The media are key instruments for disseminating the policies of the state, "tool[s] to promote unity and continuity" (Rivers and Schramm 1969, 33). As such they have no independence; only information or opinions that support the objectives of the government are permitted. The largest problem faced by an authoritarian government, therefore, is determining who has a right to use media and how best to control that use. In most authoritarian systems, the media are privately owned and have elaborate control mechanisms to ensure compliance with government objectives. Legislated codes of conduct, taxation and other economic sanctions or benefits, and government control of editorial appointments, means of production, and imported products have all been used as regulatory mechanisms. In general, control has assumed a negative form, defining what cannot be transmitted and punishing infractions.

The Tudors in sixteenth-century England instituted one of the first control mechanisms. They awarded exclusive patents allowing carefully selected, loyal individuals to engage in printing. The printers were known collectively as the Stationers' Company. Members of the Company, who profited from their monopolistic control of the printing trade, were careful not to publish any material that might offend the government and thereby cause them to lose their privileged and lucrative positions. The Stationers' Company policed its own members and satisfied the demands of the established authorities.

The Company was bolstered by a series of licensing acts, which eventually extended beyond its members. All publications were required to have a licence. Before any material was printed, it had to be submitted for review to state authorities or censors who were familiar with government objectives. Since only material supporting those objectives was granted a licence, the system operated as a form of pre-censorship. Despite the early effectiveness of this mechanism, however, it began to fail as the sheer volume of submitted material grew. The rise of democratic tendencies and increasing complexity of government goals also made it extremely difficult to find censors willing and able to do the job.

By the end of the seventeenth century, however, the system had broken down. As more people learned to read, the demand for printed material grew, and print became an effective way to disseminate new philosophies. In an attempt to increase its own profits, the Stationers' Company had trained large numbers of journeymen, many of whom left the Company and established their own businesses. These new publishers were more than willing to print illegal pamphlets and papers attacking the existing religious and political authorities. As the number of independent publishers grew, the government and its Stationers' Company lost their ability to control the industry.

Censorship of material after publication then developed in the last quarter of the seventeenth century. The authorities began to control the content of the print medium through the judicial system. Charges of treason and sedition were levelled against publishers who printed material that criticized government policies or officials. Treason was defined as any attempt to overthrow the established government and was punishable by death. It was used in only the most serious cases. Sedition was a more frequent and somewhat lighter charge. It was used to punish the publication of any material criticizing the government or a public official in a manner that lessened the affection of the people and thereby reduced the authority of the government or official.

During the eighteenth century, prosecutors continued to bring charges of treason and sedition against errant publishers. However, they found it increasingly difficult to secure guilty verdicts from juries. The democratic ideals of free speech and freedom of the press were gaining a secure hold in Britain and the United States, and the philosophies of a libertarian media system began to overshadow those of the once dominant authoritarian system. Although the traditional control mechanisms continue to be applied in some authoritarian systems, the rise of a free press philosophy has also encouraged the development of more covert methods of control.

As the media have become more sophisticated, so has media control. Threats, bribes, subsidies, and taxation policies are more difficult to identify and therefore harder to oppose and extinguish. Government-supported film and broadcasting companies, complex regulatory systems, controlled access to broadcast receivers, and jamming signals are also used to supervise the electronic media.

It would be a mistake to assume that authoritarian governments and media systems have disappeared. According to the World Press Freedom Committee (WPFC), an organization of journalists committed to preserving and enhancing freedom of expression, "Governments in two-thirds to three-fourths of the nations of the world have a significant or dominant voice in determining what does or does not appear in the media" (Bullen 1982, 38). In addition to the striking findings of the WPFC, there are a number of recent examples of temporary suspensions of press freedom in countries professing libertarian philosophies. Two of the most conspicuous occurred in the early 1980s, when British Prime Minister Margaret Thatcher imposed press restrictions during the war with Argentina over the Falkland Islands, and when U.S. President Ronald Reagan attempted to restrict press coverage of the American invasion of Grenada. In 1987, the British government also blocked publication of Peter Wright's memoirs, *Spycatcher*, which contained allegations of incompetence and subversion in MI–5, the domestic British intelligence service.[5] The most frequently cited Canadian example is the CBC's cancellation, in 1966, of the popular but controversial public affairs program, *This hour has seven days* (Peers 1979, 327–51). Although the occasions for control, the degree, and the mechanisms vary across nations, it is important to note the pervasive nature of the authoritarian media philosophy.

To review then, the authoritarian concept of the mass media developed in sixteenth- and seventeenth-century Europe as an offshoot of the philosophies of divine right and revelation and the absolute power of the state. An authoritarian media system operates according to the following principles:

1. The media exist to support the objectives of government.

2. They are privately owned, but are subject to government control.

3. They must not criticize official policy or offend the dominant social, religious, or political values.

4. Various control mechanisms, including censorship, are employed to enforce the government's will.

The libertarian concept of media

In their review of mass communication, Rivers and Schramm (1969, 35) eloquently noted, "Throughout the sixteenth and seventeenth centuries, a new theory of mass communication struggled to be born, drawing its prenatal strength from the great revolutions of the popular mind and the body politic which characterized western Europe then." The libertarian or free-press theory, like other normative theories, is an outgrowth of philosophical principles underlying the social and political structure within which the media function. It equates press freedom with other individual liberties such as speech and conscience. For most of the twentieth century, a large part of the world has professed adherence to these principles and has put them forward as a model for all to emulate.

The philosophical environment

Four historical developments challenged the philosophy of authoritarianism and created the foundations of liberalism, which involves a profound belief in rational humanism. First, advances in the sciences and geography during the Renaissance challenged traditional knowledge and undermined the established notion of truth. Confidence in the rational and analytical abilities of all individuals grew, while belief in divine revelation and the absolute power of authority diminished. Second, the Protestant Reformation signalled both religious and political change. It opened the doors to freedom of thought and discussion, and independent thinking in all areas of human activity. During the same period, a distinct middle class was emerging for the first time. It was composed of people who firmly believed in the benefits of a capitalist marketplace, a concept that clashed with traditional ideas of special status for aristocrats and unquestioned obedience to authority. Finally, British constitutional reform during the second half of the seventeenth century gradually shifted power from the Crown to Parliament. This political development fostered the new theory of popular sovereignty, in which the people themselves are the rightful locus of power.

All of these trends contributed to the new Age of Enlightenment and a number of influential individuals helped to lay the philosophical foundations of liberalism. John Milton (1608–1674) argued in *Areopagitica* ([1644] 1947) that all individuals can distinguish truth from falsehood by using their powers of reason. To exercise their ability, however, they must have unlimited access to "the open marketplace of ideas." Milton believed that the truth would eventually prevail once all ideas and opinions had been presented and reviewed, and called this "the self-righting process."

John Locke (1632–1704) turned his attention to the role of government in society. In *Second treatise of government* ([1690] 1980), he attacked the principle of rule by divine right and argued instead that individuals are by nature free, equal, and independent, and therefore must consent to be governed. Since governments are conditional and exist to protect the inalienable rights of individuals, citizens have a responsibility to dissolve any government that exceeds its authority. Just as the laws of natural science can be discovered through reason, so, too, there exist discoverable principles of natural law and natural rights governing political arrangements. Freedom of expression is an integral component of those arrangements.

Two centuries after Milton published his treatise on libertarian philosophy, John Stuart Mill (1806–1873) once more approached the problem of freedom of expression. In *On liberty* ([1859] 1975), Mill asserted that liberty was the freedom to act or think as one pleases, as long as no one else is harmed. Society exists to create the greatest happiness for the greatest number of people, and the individual's right to think and act independently is therefore paramount. Mill argued that freedom of expression is absolutely necessary; if even one voice is silenced, the truth and society will suffer.

It is apparent from its philosophical underpinnings that a libertarian society operates under very different assumptions from an authoritarian one. Libertarians regard the individual as a rational, independent being capable of distinguishing truth from falsehood and right from wrong. Individual fulfilment is the overriding social principle, and the state exists merely to enrich its citizens. Government is a useful instrument, created by individuals who freely relinquish some of their natural rights so that society will be able to protect their more important rights. State authority rests with the people, who may withdraw their support at any time. The assumptions of libertarian society are based on the belief that all truth is discernible through reason. Although the capacity for rational thought is not distributed equally, everyone has the inalienable right to express an opinion and indeed, it is only through a free exchange of information and ideas that the truth can be revealed. The critical point here, in terms of the media, is the need for freedom of expression both as a means of intellectual and moral enlightenment and as a safeguard against the abuses of political power.

The media system

According to Siebert, Peterson, and Schramm ([1956] 1976, 3–4),

> In Libertarian theory, the press is not an instrument of government, but rather a device for presenting evidence and arguments on the basis of which people can check on government and make up their own minds as to policy. Therefore, it is imperative that the press be free of government control and influence. In order

for truth to emerge, all ideas must get a fair hearing; there
must be a "free market place" of ideas and information.

It took about two centuries for England and America to shift from
authoritarian to libertarian media systems. The collapse of the licensing
system in England, in 1694, was one of the most significant steps forward
for press freedom. Further inroads were made possible by the emergence
of parliamentary political dominance and the two-party system. In
eighteenth-century America, the media were subject to most of the same
restrictions as in England. Individuals such as Thomas Jefferson advanced the cause of freedom of expression because they recognized its
utility in spreading the message of independence. After the American
Revolution, freedom of expression became an integral part of Americans'
image of their own society, and in 1791, the First Amendment was
ratified to guarantee that "Congress shall make no law. . . abridging the
freedom of speech, or of the press."[6]

As power shifted to responsible, elected governments, a free press became a fundamental social principle. If people are to govern themselves,
they must have access to the information necessary to do so, and as
Thomas Jefferson noted, "If a nation expects to be both ignorant and free it
expects what never was and never will be" (Austin 1964, 56).

The libertarian media has three functions: it must provide both information and entertainment and contribute to the economic system.
Charged with public enlightenment, the media are responsible for giving
the public the information needed to uncover the truth, to make informed
political decisions, and to safeguard individual liberties against government abuse. The role of the media in entertaining the public is perhaps
more obvious in the case of television than of newspapers. Prime-time
schedules are dominated by programs aimed at entertaining ever-larger
audiences in an attempt to satisfy the less overt but equally important
economic function. Not only do the libertarian media seek to make a
profit just like any other private business, but through advertising they
create consumer demand and therefore serve the entire economic system.

Under a libertarian system, anyone is free to own or use the media.
This open system envisages a flexible, adaptable, self-directed media,
which is accountable only to the public that supports it in a capitalist
society. It is assumed that the media will thus convey enough voices to
ensure that the truth eventually prevails. No freedoms are absolute, however, and even in libertarian systems, the media are answerable in the

courts for the consequences of their messages. For example, the purposeful publication of untrue information that causes harm or injury is liable for prosecution and punishment. There are also legal proscriptions against pornography and obscenity. The electronic media present unique problems of regulation because of their ubiquitous and intrusive nature. Handling contentious issues on open-line talk shows, for example, or deciding what degree of media access politicians, parties, or lobby groups should have during political campaigns, provokes issues of media regulation. Although libertarians recognize the inevitability of some government control, they believe that government should intervene as little as possible. Determining the acceptable limits on freedom of the media remains a persistent problem for all societies operating under the libertarian philosophy.

The libertarian media concept, then, developed from the growth of rational humanism and democratic government in England and the United States during the eighteenth century. A libertarian media system operates according to the following principles:

1. The media exist to provide the information that individuals require in their search for truth and their efforts at democratic self-government.

2. Ownership of media publication and distribution facilities is open to any person or organization without government interference.

3. The media are free to publish anything, with the exception of personal attacks or treason.

4. The media are controlled by the self-righting process in a open marketplace of ideas. No prior censorship or restriction on the legal collection or dissemination of information is permitted.

The social responsibility concept of media

The social responsibility concept of mass communication developed in the twentieth century out of "a growing awareness that in some important respects the free market failed to fulfill the promise of press freedom and to deliver expected benefits to society" (McQuail 1983, 90). According to Charles Beard, freedom of the press under the libertarian concept meant "the right to be just or unjust, partisan or nonpartisan, true or false, in news columns and editorial columns" (*St. Louis Post-Dispatch* 1938, 13). That right belonged to those who owned or controlled access to the media's means of production, an increasingly homogeneous group. Many doubted the effectiveness of the self-righting process in correcting the deficiencies of the system. The premise of the new concept therefore rested on the media's responsibility to society:

> Freedom carries concomitant obligations; and the press, which enjoys a privileged position under our government, is obliged to be responsible to society for carrying out certain essential functions of mass communication in contemporary society. To the extent that the press recognizes its responsibilities and makes them the basis of operational policies, the libertarian system will satisfy the needs of society. To the extent that the press does not assume its responsibilities, some other agency must see that the essential functions of mass communication are carried out (Siebert, Peterson, and Schramm [1956] 1976, 74).

The philosophical environment

Peterson suggests that a fundamental difference between the theories of libertarianism and social responsibility lies in the concept of liberty or freedom that each espouses (Siebert, Peterson, and Schramm [1956] 1976, 93–94). For libertarians, liberty is a negative notion—freedom "from." They emphasize the removal of individual restraints. For social responsibility theorists, negative freedom is insufficient unless it is accompanied by positive freedom—freedom "to" or freedom "for." Not only must individuals be free from restrictions but they must also be free to use whatever legal means they require to achieve their goals. Freedom from interference with one's own objectives must not violate the rights of others. Individual freedom therefore carries with it a responsibility for the freedom of all.

The social responsibility concept developed as a result of three trends. Libertarian ideas of natural rights, laissez-faire economics, and the self-righting process gave way to a new intellectual climate as evolutionary theory, social science, and modern economics emerged in the nineteenth and early twentieth centuries. The primacy of the individual was challenged by a more collectivist theory of society.

Second, a technological revolution in the United States after World War II changed society and altered the nature of the media. Innovations increased the speed, effectiveness, and efficiency of existing media and created new, more powerful ones. The technology was very expensive, however, and control of the media became concentrated in the hands of a few economically powerful groups. The media became less pluralistic and more subject to manipulation. Libertarian theorists had never envisaged this situation.

At the same time, a developing spirit of professionalism became evident among publishers and journalists, who recognized that the legally protected position of the press necessitated journalistic responsibility. Codes of ethics and schools of journalism were created to meet the needs of the press and its public. The high standards exhibited by Edward R. Murrow, initially on radio and then on television during the 1950s, exemplified the new professionalism.

The social responsibility concept thus developed amid a somewhat different set of philosophical assumptions than did libertarianism. Although they do not deny the rationality of the individual, social responsibility theorists are sceptical of the idea that everyone is motivated to search for truth. People are more likely to attempt to satisfy their immediate needs and to use their rational capabilities only if prompted. The state exists not only to protect freedom but also to promote it actively. Because neither the individual nor the state dominate, state action to further social goals and values is acceptable even if it limits the freedom of certain individuals. Freedom of expression is valued not for its utility in finding the ultimate truth but because it reveals the plurality of truths that benefits society.

The media system

Denis McQuail (1983, 91) points out that the social responsibility concept of the media tries to reconcile three conflicting principles: individual freedom, media freedom, and the media's obligations to society. It accepts many aspects of the libertarian media concept, including its ideas about ownership, media functions, and restrictions on the collection and dissemination of information. The two begin to diverge when they address the issue of freedom of expression.

Within the social responsibility concept, freedom of expression is a universal, conditional, legal, and moral right, not a natural, absolute one (Hocking 1947, 60–61). All people have a legal and moral right to express their opinions on the condition that they do not use that right to harm others purposely. Despite this, not everyone is entitled to reach the audiences of the mass media. Access is restricted to media owners and to those individuals or groups to whom they give permission.

Growing criticism of media performance and the limited nature of media access led to the establishment of the Commission on Freedom of the Press in the United States in 1947. The Commission report, *A free and responsible press*, and the writings of an individual member of the Commission, William Hocking (1947), provide much of the theoretical and practical analysis of the media that constitutes the social responsibility concept. From the recommendations of media professionals and others, the Commission identified five obligations of the media in contemporary society. They must provide "a truthful, comprehensive, and intelligent account of the day's events in a context which gives them meaning." Fact and opinion should be clearly distinguished. Second, the media should serve as "a forum for the exchange of comment and criticism," carrying information and circulating a broad range of ideas to their large audiences. Closely related to this is the idea that the media must present "a representative picture of the constituent groups in society." Media portrayals should be accurate and sensitive and should avoid perpetuating stereotypes. Fourth, the media are required to educate the public by presenting and clarifying "the goals and values of society." The Commission's final recommendation encompasses the obligations in the first four: the media should provide "full access to the day's intelligence." Only complete, accurate, and balanced accounts can effectively serve the information needs of individuals in a modern, complex society.

Libertarians believe that all these things will evolve naturally, but proponents of the social responsibility concept argue that the libertarian media have failed to fulfil these requirements adequately and that it is therefore incumbent on some other institution to delineate the media's responsibilities and enforce society's standards. In a pluralistic society, however, it is very difficult to determine who should decide what is socially responsible and who should enforce those decisions. Rivers and Schramm (1969, 50) provide one answer: "Social responsibility is defined by various publishers and journalist groups; it certainly is relative, and sometimes nebulous; and no solution that would be widely agreed upon and enforced can ever be reached. In fact, the whole point of social responsibility is that it is defined by journalists and enforced not at all."

Improved performance is therefore essential to socially responsible media and can be encouraged by three groups in society—media professionals, the general public, and governments. Government activity can take the form of legislation to prevent media abuse, financial support of media undertakings, or public media ownership. The public can educate itself to be watchful of the media and to publicize both abusive and admirable media performance. Yet in the long run, it is the media professionals themselves who determine the quality of media fare. Through press councils, codes of performance, and educational and training programs, they can raise their level of professionalism and meet the needs of their society.

To review, the social responsibility concept of the media was first articulated in the mid-twentieth century as society began to recognize the failure of the libertarian media to accept the obligations imposed upon them by their guaranteed freedoms and rights. The social responsibility media operate according to the following principles:

1. The media must accept their social obligations and operate in a manner that improves the general welfare of their pluralistic and diverse society.

2. Media ownership may be either private or public as long as high standards of performance are maintained.

3. Damage to individual or social interests must be avoided. The media is obliged to provide full, balanced, and accurate accounts of the day's intelligence.

4. Self-regulation is the preferred method of control, but community and government action are condoned to secure a socially responsible media system.

The Soviet totalitarian concept of media

Although not developed until after the Russian Revolution of 1917, Soviet totalitarian media theory is based on the earlier writings of the German philosopher, Karl Marx (1818–1883). Although Marx himself had nothing to say directly about the media, his theory provided the foundation upon which others, including Vladimir Lenin and Joseph Stalin, could build the framework of Soviet media theory.

The philosophical environment

In response to overwhelming changes in social patterns, Marx developed a general philosophy of history based on change. More specifically, he argued that an individual's material or economic conditions of life determine that person's ideas. By emphasizing concepts such as freedom and merit, capitalism attempts to convince the working class that its current condition is temporary; hard work and effort will result in success. Yet perpetuating these ideas allows the bourgeoisie to dominate and abuse the working class, or proletariat, in order to benefit itself. The injustice of this situation will eventually be recognized and at that point give rise to revolution; the proletariat will overthrow the capitalist class and create a new, classless society in which the cultural, social, economic, and political structures will be reorganized for the welfare of all.

Once the ideal society has been achieved, the state, according to Marx, will wither away, since it exists merely to allow one class to dominate another. All power will then reside within the people. When the proletariat takes over the means of production (factories, banks, etc.), it ceases to be the proletariat: "The proletariat will use its political supremacy to wrest, by degrees, all capital from the bourgeoisie, to centralize all instruments of production in the hands of the State, i.e., of the proletariat organized as a ruling class; and to increase the total productive forces as rapidly as possible" (Marx [1847] 1947, 518).

It is obvious to even the most casual observer, however, that the Soviet state has not withered away. It is, in fact, larger and more bureaucratic than its prerevolutionary counterpart. Stalin argued that this condition was a necessary consequence of the continuing existence of capitalist power. As long as capitalism is the driving force in other states, the socialist state must maintain a strong government and military presence to prevent any capitalist attempts to overthrow its regime.

Following the 1917 Russian Revolution, Lenin and then Stalin attempted to expand Marxist ideology to create a viable social, political, and economic system. Several elements came to dominate the thinking of the Soviet state but only three, which have particular relevance for media, are noted here: an antagonistic view of private ownership; the unity of the Communist Party; and the idea of a "Bolshevik ideal personality" (Mead 1951). According to Soviet thought, all natural resources and means of production and distribution, including the "means of mental production," belonged to the people as organized into the Communist Party. The Party was united in its goals and its leaders were considered to be infallible. It was a centralized, bureaucratic organization, responsible for dictating the means and ends of the system, including the media; no competing power structures or ideologies were permitted. Finally, the concept of the Bolshevik ideal personality held sway, the person whose "performance is expected to be focussed and meaningful, and. . . [whose] private feelings must be subordinated to the chief goals he [or she] serves" (Siebert, Peterson, and Schramm [1956] 1976, 115). The media, too, was expected to scorn trivial entertainment and be subject to party control.

From the social, economic, and political philosophy just described, the assumptions under which the Soviet totalitarian system has operated become evident. First, the individual has importance only as a member of the collective. Second, the state exists as the self-appointed caretaker of the people and their socialist system. Third, although individuals are subordinate to the collective, they are not subordinate to the state. Individuals and the state work together in a mutually beneficial relationship to ensure the continuation of the classless society. Finally, truth is knowable only through the collective deliberation of the Party. Moreover, there is only one truth—the truth of the people, as expressed by the Party.

From the beginning, the Soviet system has considered the media to be owned and controlled by the people for the benefit of the collective. According to Lenin, the press should be "collective propagandist, collective agitator. . . collective organizer" (Lenin 1927, 4). From this perspective, the media exist to serve serious purposes, primarily the communication of the truth.

Before proceeding, it should be noted that the description that follows is, like the descriptions of other media concepts, based upon historical evidence. Clearly, under Mikhail Gorbachev and his new policy of *glasnost*, the Soviet Union is undergoing transition in all aspects of its social, economic, and political order. There is also growing evidence that *glasnost* will have significant implications for the operation of the Soviet media. In January 1989, for example, the Soviet news agency TASS reported the story of six men who had been rescued from the basement of an apartment building thirty-five days after a devastating earthquake in Armenia. When it became evident that the story was not true, TASS issued an explanation, acknowledging that everyone wants to believe in miracles and good news. Such a turn of events would have been unheard of under the traditional Soviet totalitarian media regime.

The media system

The Soviet media are employed to strengthen the social order by promoting the long-range economic, social, and political objectives of the Party. News is not considered to be a commodity, as it is in the libertarian media, but a tool to educate, socialize, and mobilize the people. While the media are expected to present the Soviet perspective on all matters, criticism of specific actions, individuals, or the means to social objectives is both allowed and encouraged since it uncovers capitalist tendencies and helps to eradicate them. Because all criticism must be guided by the truth as determined by the Party, criticism of state objectives or ideologies is not normally permitted. The Soviets have argued in the past that this is not possible since the Party is the only source of the one truth.

Although the Soviet totalitarian media theory developed as an offshoot of the authoritarian one, there are several crucial differences between them, especially with respect to media control. By removing the profit motive and placing the media under public ownership, the Soviet system transforms media from competitors for state favour into parts of the state itself. Unlike the authoritarian media, which are guided by negative restrictions that promote the status quo, the Soviet media are assigned positive responsibilities to be undertaken for the benefit of the collective. The Soviet media work through, by, and for the Communist Party, serving as advocates for the ruling regime. The authoritarian media are privately owned, and while they must not disseminate information contrary to the ruling position, they are not a part of the governing system.

Despite the degree of state control exerted over the Soviet media, their supporters strongly argue that they are the only free media. For Soviet journalists, media freedom means liberty for the people from "harmful information, debasing entertainment, false teaching" (Rivers and Schramm 1969, 45). Western media freedom, on the other hand, means freedom for those who own the media to advance their own economic and political goals. Such a system intensifies the bondage of the working class rather than promoting liberty.

To review, while the Soviet media are currently in the midst of a transition, the Soviet totalitarian media concept was based on the philosophies of Marx, Lenin, and Stalin. It has operated according to the following principles:

1. The media exist to serve the interests of the Soviet social system by socializing, educating, motivating, and mobilizing the collective.

2. The media are publicly owned adjuncts of the state.

3. The media should provide a complete view of the world from a Soviet perspective, and must not criticize state objectives.

4. Censorship and other economic or political actions are permitted in order to guarantee that the media carry out their assigned roles.

The development concept of media

The seeds of the development concept of communication were sown by the less developed countries of the Third World in international forums such as the United Nations Educational, Scientific, and Cultural Organization (UNESCO) during the 1960s. The concept evolved in response to Third World fears that their increasing dependence on the developed countries for communication hardware, software, and personnel (all of which carry with them foreign norms, values, and expectations) would alter domestic cultures and socialization processes. This relationship of dependence, described as "electronic colonialism," has been compared to the mercantile colonialism of the Industrial Revolution: "Mercantile colonialism sought cheap labour.... Not so with electronic colonialism. Electronic colonialism seeks the mind; it is aimed at influencing attitudes, desires, beliefs, lifestyles, consumer opinions or purchasing patterns of those who consume the imported media fare" (McPhail 1987, 18). Development media theory is only one aspect of a broader development theory designed to restructure current thinking on Third World development in general.

The philosophical environment

During the 1960s and 1970s, the failure of many Third World countries to develop as expected led to a general rethinking of development theory. Until that time, models of development were based on the example of Western progress and therefore defined modernization as a deterministic, inexorable, and universal process. It was measured by a number of economic variables: the degree of industrialization, urbanization, literacy, education, political unification, differentiation and specialization of societal institutions and structures, access to and availability of mass media, and the breakdown of traditions that retard the industrial process.

According to this paradigm, development, or modernization, involves an evolutionary, irreversible progression through a series of logical stages, from traditional society to an age of mass consumption. Despite the vast aid tendered by many developed countries, however, it is apparent that the paradigm is not working. In fact, there is evidence that developing countries are worse off than ever.[7]

Critics were therefore led to question the basic assumptions of the model, especially its emphasis on economic and technological measures of achievement. Alternative models have been developed, and although there is no consensus about criteria for measuring development, many scholars suggest that non-material variables should be the focus of attention. Cultural components are much more difficult to measure than gross national products; they include the accessibility of media and telecommunication, political and social structural changes, social mobility, and individual well-being.

In addition, the earlier model of the development process, which advocated the imposition of change by authorities, has been criticized for its failure to distribute development benefits equally. The new concept of development has identified four prerequisites that strongly contrast with the conditions for development within the economic growth paradigm: the equal distribution of information and socio-economic benefits; popular participation at the village level in development planning and execution; independence from foreign economic control and reliance on local resources; and integration of traditional with modern systems, so that modernization is a blend of old and new ideas (Rogers 1976, 222–23).

Strong criticism of the traditional development model, growing acceptance of alternative paradigms, and awareness in developing countries of their shared interests and power in international forums have together led to calls by these nations for a restructuring of the current world economic and communication systems. Both the New International Economic Order (NIEO) and the New World Information and Communication Order (NWICO) have made demands on the part of developing nations for the world's resources to be shared more equitably. Both orders stress sovereignty, interdependence, and common interest

among all nations, and international co-operation to eliminate the widening gap between developed and developing countries. The orders are alternative models for the functioning of international economics and
communication. Although the NIEO focusses on the socio-economic
aspects of development and the NWICO on the sociocultural, both are
opposed to colonial domination and seek self-determination for all nations.

Out of these debates has emerged a new media theory, development
journalism, which attempts to deal with the needs, strengths, and aspirations of emerging states. It attempts to counterbalance electronic
colonialism and is one element of the NWICO. Applied to development
journalism, the order is an "evolutionary process seeking a more just and
equitable balance in the flow and content of information, a right to national self-determination of domestic communication policies, and, finally, at the international level, a two-way information flow reflecting more
accurately the aspirations and activities of the less developed countries"
(McPhail 1987, 12).

The media system

The media systems of most developing nations are underdeveloped
themselves, with few newspapers, some radio outlets, and perhaps one
television system at most. The demands of an infant press differ substantially from those of a mature press and to impose a model designed to
describe a mature press onto a developing one fails to appreciate the underlying differences. An infant press lacks some of the preconditions for a
mature mass media system: the communication infrastructure, trained
personnel, the cultural and production resources, and the available
audience. It also depends on the developed world for technology, skills,
and software.

The development concept of communication sees the function of the
media as accelerating and assisting progress towards the development
goals of the state. It therefore encourages an engineered press, committed
to priorities and objectives set by the government. The rationale for state-
controlled media is as follows: "All national resources—including the
resource of information—must be directed toward development. If information is allowed to cause dissent or loss of international prestige, it
detracts from the greater goal. By this reasoning, the control of news is
not only a legitimate right but also a national necessity" (Rosenblum
1979, 206).

Development theory rejects the libertarian media values of press freedom, free speech, and the free flow of information with the argument that they cannot afford the luxury of competing media systems and are fortunate to have a single medium, usually radio. High illiteracy rates make a print press an impractical medium in many of these states. Furthermore, the theory argues, if developing countries are to improve their social and economic conditions rapidly, a concerted effort from both government and media is necessary. Competing views are detrimental to the catching-up process.

The development concept also identifies the impact of foreign media on developing countries as a matter of concern. The flow of information from developed to developing countries is essentially one way and has a tendency to homogenize world cultures, emphasize Western goals and values, and create unhealthy dependency. The theory also criticizes the Western "coup and earthquake syndrome" (Rosenblum 1979), which encourages media coverage of the violent, negative, or extraordinary events within a developing country but ignores the slow, undramatic, yet positive aspects of development.

Development journalism encourages the positive use of media to achieve developmental and cultural goals. Collective ends take precedence over individual liberties and certain freedoms are therefore subordinated for the welfare of all. It should be noted, however, that the concept of development journalism need not be limited to less developed nations; all media are, in fact, development media. Every nation has its own preferred social, economic, and political order, and its own unique goals and priorities. Whether or not the imperative is explicitly recognized, media do reflect the dominant ideologies of the societies in which they operate and thereby foster society's objectives.

The establishment and support of the Quebec newspaper, *Le jour*, by the Parti Québécois is an example. Openly committed to the Quebec separatist government's objective of national self-determination, the paper excluded all Canadian federal government advertising. In addition, one could argue that the legal mandates given to the CBC and Telefilm Canada to create a Canadian presence in the electronic media are examples of development objectives.

From a broader perspective, the Western concept of a free press may simply reflect development media that are in favour of a capitalistic social system. They portray values that create a climate favourable to the economic structure of Western nations. The libertarian Western media are not free of values; ideologically, they support an economic system that makes the media a profitable enterprise and maintains the status quo.

The concept of development media originated from the Third World's growing fear of cultural domination by technologically advanced countries, and from their desire for national, self-determined development strategies. The development media operate according to the following principles:

1. The media should contribute to nationally determined development objectives by giving priority to whatever content furthers those objectives.

2. Media ownership may be either public or private as long as the media's responsibilities are recognized and acted upon.

3. Both criticism that could jeopardize the process of development and overabundance of foreign content are rejected in favour of national, pro-development material.

4. The state has a right to interfere in media activity in the interest of development. Censorship, subsidy, ownership, and legislation are all acceptable media control mechanisms.

Summary

This chapter described the five major normative concepts of mass communication. It has demonstrated that each is based on different assumptions about how society should function. These assumptions, in turn, determine the manner in which the mass media operate—their purpose, content, ownership, and mechanisms of control. Table 2.1 provides a brief review of the five concepts. The primary value of the normative theories is their utility for describing, analysing, and comparing individual media systems. Subsequent chapters of this book examine the Canadian media system in detail, revealing how these theories apply in the Canadian context.

Table 2.1

Five concepts of mass communication

	Authoritarian	Libertarian	Social responsibliity	Soviet totalitarian	Development journalism
Purpose	to support government	to provide information and entertainment and support the economic system	to enhance the general welfare	to serve the interests of social system	to contribute to national development
Content	no criticism of government policy or dominant values	broadest possible range of views	full, balanced, and accurate accounts	complete view of the world from a Soviet perspective	pro-development information, no criticism of development policy, reduced foreign content
Ownership	private	private	public or private	public	public or private
Control system	state-controlled negative mechanisms	the self-righting process	self-regulation preferred; state control if necessary	state-controlled positive and negative mechanisms	state-controlled positive and negative mechanisms

Notes

1. Fred S. Siebert, Theodore Peterson, and Wilbur Schramm ([1956] 1976) developed the first four of these normative models. Their book, *Four theories of the press*, remains a classic in the field.

2. Interested students are encouraged to read the original writings of the classic philosophers, including Plato's *Laws*, Machiavelli's *The prince*, and Hobbes's *Leviathan*. A general review is provided by Catlin (1939).

3. Adolf Hitler and Benito Mussolini are examples of twentieth-century political leaders whose published statements and actions "indicate a continuation in a perverted form of the doctrines of authoritarianism....[T]heir treatment of the mass media was entirely consistent with the basic principle of absolutism" (Siebert, Peterson, and Schramm [1956] 1976, 15).

4. For a detailed historical analysis of an authoritarian media system, see Siebert (1965).

5. The British government also tried to block publication of *Spycatcher* in Canada, Australia, and the United States. Some British newspapers defied the government order by publishing excerpts from the book and their editors were subject to jail sentences and unlimited fines. The *News* of London argued, "The people of Britain fought long and hard to achieve a free press and free speech.... We refuse to be silenced by Thatcher's obsessive and increasingly tyrannical government."

6. The 1735 trial on charges of sedition of John Peter Zenger, printer of the *New York Weekly Journal*, was a landmark event in the development of a free press in the United States. Zenger's lawyer, Andrew Hamilton, argued that the law was faulty because it protected the government from legitimate criticism and thereby weakened its responsibility to the people. He asserted that truth should constitute a defence in libel cases. Although the jury agreed with Hamilton and Zenger was acquitted, the libel and sedition laws were not changed until 1790. For a more detailed account of the Zenger case, see Alexander (1963).

7. Information about the widening gap between the developed and developing nations can be found in McPhail (1987, 47–48).

References

Alexander, J. 1963. *A brief narrative of the case of John Peter Zenger*, ed. S.N. Katz. Cambridge: Harvard University.

Austin, A.E. 1964. Codes, documents, declarations affecting the press. Paper. University of North Dakota, Department of Journalism.

Bullen, D. 1982. A free press means better development. In *The media crisis . . . A continuing challenge*. Washington, DC: World Press Freedom Committee.

Catlin, G. 1939. *The story of the political philosophers*. New York: Tudor.

Hocking, W. 1947. *Freedom of the press: A framework of principle*. Chicago: University of Chicago.

Lenin, V.I. 1927. *Collected works*. New York: International Publishers.

Locke, J. [1690] 1980. *Second treatise of government*. Indianapolis: Hackett.

McPhail, T.L. 1987. *Electronic colonialism*. rev. 2d ed. Beverly Hills: Sage.

McQuail, D. 1983. *Mass communication theory*. Beverly Hills: Sage.

Marx, K. [1847] 1947. The Communist manifesto. In *Man and the state: The political philosophers*, ed. S. Commins and R. N. Linscott, 495–532. New York: Random House.

Mead, M. 1951. *Soviet attitudes toward authority*. New York: McGraw-Hill.

Mill, J.S. [1859] 1975. *On liberty*. New York: Norton.

Milton, J. [1644] 1947. *Areopagitica*. London: Oxford University.

Peers, F. 1979. *The public eye: Television and the politics of Canadian broadcasting, 1952–1968*. Toronto: University of Toronto.

Rivers, W.L., and W. Schramm. 1969. *Responsibility in mass communication*. rev. ed. New York: Harper and Row.

Rogers, E. 1976. Where are we in understanding the diffusion of innovations? In *Communication and change: The last ten years and the next*, ed. W. Schramm and D. Lerner, 204–22. Honolulu: University of Hawaii.

Rosenblum, M. 1979. *Coups and earthquakes: Reporting of the world for America*. New York: Harper and Row.

St. Louis Post-Dispatch Symposium on Freedom of the Press. 1938. St. Louis: The *Post-Dispatch*.

Siebert, F.S. 1965. *Freedom of the press in England, 1476–1776*. Urbana: University of Illinois.

Siebert, F.S., T. Peterson, and W. Schramm. [1956] 1976. *Four theories of the press*. Urbana: University of Illinois.

United States. Commission on Freedom of the Press. 1947. *A free and responsible press*. Chicago: University of Chicago.

CULTURE AND COMMUNICATION:
THE CANADIAN PERSPECTIVE

*C*anada has a longstanding ambiguity, unique among modern Western nations, about its culture. We wonder what constitutes our culture and what role government and cultural institutions should play in creating, nurturing, and protecting it.[1] European nations have no similar concern, because their varied and lively cultures have long histories. The United States does not share Canadian concerns either. It dominates international cultural trends—particularly in North America—by virtue of its size and the degree of market penetration achieved by its cultural industries. Canada not only lacks both of these advantages but also has to accommodate five unique types of cultural pressure (Schafer 1976, 20–25).

In his review of Canadian cultural policy, Paul Schafer identifies these five tensions and suggests that the first four have influenced government policy with respect to culture, while the fifth actually shapes our culture. The first tension occurs between French and English cultures within Canada and has prompted the development of bilingualism and multiculturalism as significant political and social concepts. The second tension is created by the proximity of the United States to Canada and the shared language and ancestry of the two countries. These factors have fostered Canadian awareness of the need to assert cultural independence.[2] Different economic and political ideologies contribute to the third tension. The themes of free trade and free enterprise are in conflict with those of public subsidization and protectionist measures. The fourth tension exists between regionalism and federalism: the different provinces have unequal financial resources and there is a struggle among federal and provincial governments for pre-eminence in the cultural policy field. The final tension lies between Canadians and their environment, motivating the artist to create and the audience to appreciate uniquely Canadian culture.

The following pages examine some of the major aspects of culture and communication from a Canadian perspective, including culture's perceived importance to a nation's survival. The discussion then centres on the theoretical contributions of Canada's two foremost communication scholars, Harold A. Innis and Marshall McLuhan, and reviews the work of Wallace Clement, who undertook a critical analysis of the Canadian media. The chapter concludes with a brief description of Canadian government imperatives and objectives in culture and communication policy. Throughout the text, the term "policy" refers to any "course of action or inaction chosen by public authorities to address a given problem or interrelated set of problems" (Pal 1987, 4).

Canadian discourse on culture

The definition of culture, like that of communication, is ambiguous and it is impossible to find one definition that pleases everyone. It is commonly thought to include artistic and creative expression, mores, manners and customs, ethnicity, and social behaviour. Bernard Ostry (1978, 1), in his essay addressing the connection between government and culture, describes culture as our entire awareness of life:

> Culture, however we define it, is central to everything we do
> and think. It is what we do and the reason why we do it, what
> we wish and why we imagine it, what we perceive and how
> we express it, how we live and in what manner we approach

death. It is our environment and the patterns of adaptation to it. It is the world we have created and are still creating; it is the way we see that world and the motives that urge us to change it. It is the way we know ourselves and each other; it is our web of personal relationships; it is the images and abstractions that allow us to live together in communities and nations. It is the element in which we live. Anything so essential and pervasive is easy to overlook.

Others provide more pragmatic definitions. John Meisel (1974, 602), Canadian political scientist and former chairman of the Canadian Radio-television and Telecommunications Commission, distinguishes four groups of meanings. The classical anthropological definition refers to the knowledge, belief, arts, morals, law, customs, capabilities, and habits acquired by people as members of society. The development of the arts, letters, and sciences, Meisel labels aesthetic culture. His third category, political culture, refers to specific political orientations within a society, the attitudes we hold towards political symbols, ideologies, and institutions. Lastly, he identifies leisure culture, which is closely associated with aesthetic culture but is concerned more with avocational pursuits and includes recreational, physical, artistic, media-related, and entertainment activities.

Given the broad spectrum of ideas, values, standards, and behaviours covered by the term, it soon becomes evident that culture "gives people their view of reality" (Tannenbaum 1977, 2). Because the media can in turn act as significant purveyors of culture in all its forms, they have been constant objects of Canadian government policy making. The first media-related policy was undertaken in 1929. The Royal Commission on Radio Broadcasting was established in response to a number of minor irritants that suggested a formal media policy was necessary.[3] The Commission was instructed to investigate the potential impact of American radio programming on Canadian culture. It was the first official body to recommend that a nationalistic protectionist sentiment direct government policies affecting culture and the media. Since that time, there has been growing anxiety among many Canadians that as the media themselves become more pervasive and their technologies increasingly capable of ignoring international boundaries, the existence of a Canadian cultural identity becomes more precarious.

According to Arthur Kroker (1984, 1), Canadians' preoccupation with culture, and the unique historical and geographic conditions of this country, have enabled the Canadian people to develop "a highly original, comprehensive, and eloquent discourse on technology" and its impact on communication media and culture:

> What makes the discourse on technology such a central aspect of the Canadian imagination is that this discourse is situated *midway* between the future of the New World and the past of European culture. . . . The Canadian discourse is neither the American way nor the European way, but an oppositional culture trapped midway between economy and history. That is to say that the Canadian mind is that of the in-between . . . . At work in the Canadian mind is, in fact, a great and dynamic polarity between technology and culture, between economy and landscape. . . . The Canadian mind may be one of the main sites in modern times for working out the meaning of technological experience (Kroker 1984, 1–2).

An examination of the Canadian discourse on technology, communication, and culture should begin with the work of Canada's two most influential communication scholars, Harold Innis and Marshall McLuhan. The value of their contributions lies in their rethinking of the meaning of science and technology, particularly communication technology, in terms of cultural significance. James Carey (1967, 5) writes,

> Innis and McLuhan, alone among students of human society, make the history of media central to the history of civilization at large. Both see the media not merely as technical appurtenances to society but as crucial determinants of the social fabric. For them, history of the mass media is not just another avenue of historical research; rather it is another way of writing the history of Western civilization.

Neither Innis nor McLuhan describe history; rather, they offer a theory of history, or social change, based on technological changes in the communications media upon which society is progressively dependent. Both see communication "as a filter which organizes and interprets our social existence" (Grossberg 1979, 62). Culture, for them, is determined by the dominant communication system.

Harold Innis: Time and space

Harold Adams Innis (1894–1952) was a Canadian economist and historian. Educated at McMaster University and the University of Chicago, he joined the faculty of the University of Toronto in 1920 and at the time of his death was serving as head of the Department of Political Economy and Dean of Graduate Studies. He devoted most of his scholarly efforts to studies of Canada's major industries—the fur trade, cod fisheries, and the Canadian Pacific Railway (CPR). During the last years of his life, however, Innis's focus of interest shifted. He undertook an extensive review of all forms of communication and produced two major works dealing with the subject, *Empire and communications* (1950) and *The bias of communication* (1951).

It has been said that Canadian communication theory began with Innis; that he was the first to acknowledge the unique peculiarities of Canadian life and use them to establish a theory of communication with far-reaching applicability.[4] Innis's initial interest in transportation and economic history aroused his interest in communication. When studying the route of the CPR, he started to examine the migration patterns of European immigrants and came to recognize the role of various communication media in that migration. Settlers followed the routes of rivers or the railway and telegraph in order to establish their new homes in the areas most accessible to communication media. Innis then began to analyse the relationship between communication media and culture by trying to answer two connected questions: What causes changes in cultures and social institutions? and What promotes social and cultural stability? For Innis ([1950] 1972, 5), the answers appeared to lie in the technologies of the predominant communication medium: "It has seemed to me that the subject of communication offers possibilities [for comparing empires] in that it occupies a crucial position in the organization and administration of government and in turn of empires and of Western civilization."

His awareness of the central role of communication technology in determining not only control over communication but also control of consciousness, social organization, and human association made Innis's work unique. He recognized that technological innovation is first applied to communication because communication is valuable to a competitive economic system: new media undercut the existing power structures and create new ones.

The majority of Innis's work examined the kinds of control inherent in communication media. He reviewed the historical forms of communication (speech, writing, print), and the symbol system, tools, and media that each form used. He argued that each of the various stages of Western civilization could be identified by the pre-eminence of a particular medium of communication that influenced the culture and organization of that society. Moreover, he claimed that the rise and fall of successive civilizations or empires resulted from the competition among media for dominance.

The bias of communication

Innis based his theory of competing media on the belief that any given medium of communication is biased in terms of its control over time or space. To describe this belief, he used the terms time-biased and space-biased. Seen as somewhat antagonistic, the terms refer not only to the characteristics of specific media but also to the types of social institutions and cultures that they engender (see table 3.1). As Innis ([1951] 1964, 33) explained, "A medium of communication has an important influence on the dissemination of knowledge over space and over time and it becomes necessary to study its characteristics in order to appraise its influence in its cultural setting. . . . The relative emphasis on time or space will imply a bias of significance to the culture in which it is imbedded."

Time-binding or -biased media include clay and stone. They are durable but difficult to transport or store. Because of these characteristics, time-binding media encourage cultures that emphasize history, tradition, stability, and continuity. Cultural interests in these societies will include religion and magic, the sacred, and the moral; human associations are collective and communal. Time-biased institutions are contractionist and hierarchical, and are concerned with the length of time that they persist. The term contractionist refers to the tendency to operate as small, tightly knit organizations. Innis ([1951] 1964, 33–36) offered the ancient Egyptian empire as an example of a time-biased civilization. He describes the cultural consequences of a monopoly of knowledge centred on stone and hieroglyphics and outlines the challenges presented by the introduction of papyrus, a space-biased medium.

Table 3.1

Time- and space-biased media and cultures

	Time-biased	Space-biased
Primary mode of communication	speech	print
Media	stone clay	papyrus paper
Media characteristics	durable	transportable
Cultural interests	the past the sacred the religious the collectivity	the present the future the secular the scientific the individual
Institutional organization	hierarchical contractionist	bureaucratic expansionist

Space-binding media are less durable but can be easily transported; paper and papyrus permit the accurate transmission of information over large distances. Space-biased cultures focus on the present and future. They are concerned with the secular: economics, politics, geography, science, and technology. Emphasis on the control of vast territories encourages legalistic, bureaucratic, and expansionist institutions. The term expansionist refers to the expansion of authority, bureaucracy, and ideas. It is not necessarily territorial. The ancient Roman empire is an example of a space-biased culture. Papyrus, and later parchment, permitted the establishment of monopolistic bureaucracy determined to codify the law and expand its administrative control of the empire.

Innis did not devote much attention to the electronic media. Although radios were widely available at the time of his death, television was a very new medium. He did recognize, however, that the radio had weakened the bias of print:

> The radio appealed to vast areas, overcame the division between classes in its escape from literacy, and favoured

centralization and bureaucracy. A single individual could appeal at one time to vast numbers of people speaking the same language and indirectly, though with less effect, through interpreters to numbers speaking other languages. Division was drawn along new lines based on language but within language units centralization and coherence became conspicuous. Stability within language units became more evident and instability between language units more dangerous (Innis [1951] 1964, 82).

Moreover, he believed that the electronic media emphasized superficiality, entertainment, and amusement, and that these would be increasingly imposed on the established print media.[5] The impact would destroy time bias in favour of space bias. Finally, Innis ([1951] 1964, 140) suggested that the constant and rapid change in new communication technology is "a crucial factor in determining cultural values..., [increasing] the difficulties of recognizing balance let alone achieving it."

For Innis, the effects of the two dimensions of time and space were best explained by comparing oral and written cultural traditions. Speech is the principal means of communication in oral societies. Its low capacity for travel and storage encourages the development of time-biased societies, which emphasize the oral transmission of history, tradition, and religion from generation to generation. The communal life in these societies focusses on the past and the sacred. Written traditions, however, emphasize the technical and the secular, the present and the future, and the achievements and fulfilment of the individual. Innis recognized an inherent hostility between the two traditions. The introduction of writing meant the end of the oral tradition and signalled a shift from a time-bias to a space-bias. A new monopoly of knowledge was created, which altered the locus of authority.

To answer his first question—What causes change?—Innis looked to the issue of authority. He argued that the predominant medium of communication in any society creates a monopoly or an oligopoly of knowledge and power. Depending on the bias, either technology or the church, religion, and the sacred dominate. The hegemony of one or the other has implications for all institutions and patterns of human association within a society. Eventually, however, the powerless search for and find the means to "compel realignments in the monopoly or the oligopoly of knowledge" (Innis [1951] 1964, 4). Overemphasis on either space or time is the principal reason for the rise and fall of empires.

In his examination of Western civilization, Innis identified a gradual move away from the temporal towards the spatial, which was accelerated by the invention of printing. This produced a shift in authority from the church to the state and a change in interest from the religious to the scientific and secular. The result of overemphasis on the spatial has been rampant nationalism and increased technological complexity and confusion: "The conditions of freedom of thought are in danger of being destroyed by science, technology, and the mechanization of knowledge, and with them, Western civilization" (Innis [1951] 1964, 190).

In response to his second question, then—What promotes social and cultural stability?—Innis ([1951] 1964, 64) argued that stability was possible only through "an appreciation of a proper balance between the concepts of space and time" such as was achieved in Classical Greece. Media favouring both time and space and fostering competing ideas, institutions, and social patterns are necessary for a healthy society. This equilibrium has eluded modern civilization: "The ability to develop a system of government in which the bias of communication can be checked and an appraisal of the significance of space and time can be reached remains a problem of empire and of the Western world" (Innis [1950] 1972, 170).

Based on the implications of his theory, Innis envisioned a unique role for Canada. Poised between the history and tradition of our European past and the expansionist tendencies of our American neighbour, we could mediate between the biases of the two. He also acknowledged our limitations, however, and the effectiveness of the American media that threaten our national cultural lives: "We may dislike American influence, we may develop a Canadian underground movement, but we are compelled to yield to American policy. . . . [T]hey have American dollars" (Innis 1956, 411). Our one chance for national survival, Innis argued, was our ability to exploit the new media of communication to our own advantage. Only then would we find the resources to correct the biases of others.

Innis was the first to undertake a macro-level examination of the link between media and culture. He laid the intellectual foundation for the field and many of his concerns are reflected in Canadian cultural policy debates. His work has been criticized for being too abstract and very difficult to read, but those who have studied Innis in depth have found abundant insights.

Marshall McLuhan: Media and messages

Herbert Marshall McLuhan (1911–1980) was born in Edmonton, Alberta, and educated at the University of Manitoba and at Cambridge in engineering and English literature. He joined the University of Toronto in 1946 as a professor of literature and ended his career there as Director of the Centre for Culture and Technology.[6] During the 1960s, he published a number of books that won him worldwide acclaim. They include *The Gutenberg galaxy* (1962), for which he won the Governor General's Award for Literature, *Understanding media* (1964), perhaps his most influential work, and *The medium is the massage* (1967), which made "McLuhanese" a part of our everyday language.

Like Innis, McLuhan shifted his academic focus to follow a growing interest in communication, a pattern that is more easily understood when we recognize that university departments of communication were very rare during the 1950s and 1960s, especially in Canada.[7] Most communication research was undertaken by isolated academics in a number of disciplines such as economics, sociology, psychology, and English.

It was during the 1960s that McLuhan enjoyed his most resounding fame. He popularized the study of communication and the media and, much to the chagrin of his colleagues and the administration at the University of Toronto, he successfully courted those same media in order to publicize and foster his ideas. He was described as ingenious, imaginative, and eclectic, a guru or prophet of the new media, "a poet of technology" (Carey 1967, 35). John Bittner (1977, 448) described McLuhan's American[8] success:

> For ten years, between 1962 and 1972, Marshall McLuhan's writings and articles written about him filled everything from discussions of the street culture of San Francisco to pages of *The New York Times*. He was the subject of serious broadcast interview programs and popular comedy routines. He was adored, idolized and discarded. Critics called him everything from the greatest original thinker in centuries to a charlatan of intellectual thought.

McLuhan's critics were vehement in their attacks, most of which stemmed from his unwillingness to use the traditional methods of social science. His macro-theories were characterized as poorly formulated, unclear, confusing, inconsistent, illogical, and lacking documentation.[9] Dwight MacDonald's review of *Understanding media* provides an example of such criticism:

> One defect of *Understanding Media* is that the parts are greater than the whole. A single page is impressive, two are "stimulating," five raise serious doubts, ten confirm them, and long before the hardy reader has staggered to page 359 the accumulation of contradictions, nonsequiturs, facts that are not facts, exaggerations, and chronic rhetorical vagueness has numbed him [or her] to the insights ... and the many bits of the new and fascinating information (MacDonald 1964, 206).

McLuhan, however, dismissed the criticism. He saw his role as an initiator of ideas, someone who offers hypotheses designed to make us consider the impact of the mass media on our lives: "I am an investigator. I make probes. I have no point of view. I do not stay in one position. . . . I DON'T EXPLAIN—I EXPLORE" (McLuhan in Stearn 1967, xiii).

McLuhan also characterized his work as an extension of that of Harold Innis, which in many respects is true. Both were technological determinists; they agreed that the media of communication are primary determinants of culture, more important themselves than the messages they transmit. Whereas Innis asserted that communication technology affects social organizations and creates an institutional bias, however, McLuhan argued that each communication technology forces a change in the ratio of the senses that individuals must use to perceive messages (sight, sound, touch, etc.), thereby creating a bias in favour of one form of human perception. McLuhan's explanation of sensory bias with respect to electronic media created his reputation both as a genius and as a fraud.

The media as extensions of the individual

McLuhan began his investigation of sensory bias with the notion that each medium has its own specific grammar which determines the way things are thought about. He argued that media operate like languages: just as the grammar of a language defines reality by giving us a way to categorize it, so too the grammar of a medium structures perception and, therefore, reality.[10]

The grammar of a medium is derived from two related elements: the particular mixture of senses used to receive the medium and the degree of data definition, or clarity of information, provided by the medium. First, according to McLuhan, every medium is biased in favour of a specific mix of senses. In other words, each medium requires us to use one or more of our senses to a greater degree than the others. That sensory bias determines our particular way of knowing by "imposing its own assumption" (McLuhan 1964, 15) on our way of understanding the world. All media are extensions of human sensory capacities. By emphasizing and extending the use of some senses over others, the media can determine what knowledge is and what reality is. A change in the dominant medium changes which senses we use and thereby alters our world view.

The second element of a medium's grammar is the clarity of information provided by a particular medium. McLuhan (1964, 22–32) developed two terms to describe a medium's grammar, hot and cool.[11] Cool media are low in information, or definition. They provide little data, require the use of many senses, and demand high involvement. Television is a cool medium. It uses not only sight and sound, but according to McLuhan, because the television picture is really just a series of lines and dots, viewers must also "mentally touch" television to recreate its picture in their minds. Hot media are high in definition. They provide a lot of data through one sensory channel and require little participation on the part of their users. Photographs, radio, and print are all examples of hot media. The video portion of film, too, is hot, since it provides high-definition visual information. Table 3.2 provides a summary of two examples of McLuhan's media grammar and their cultural implications.

For McLuhan, the medium is the message; it alters the environment, shapes society, and structures thought in a way that its content never can. The medium is also the massage; it encloses and processes us, transforming our way of thinking and understanding:

> All media work us over completely. They are so persuasive in their personal, political, economic, aesthetic, psychological, moral, ethical and social consequences that they leave no part of us untouched, unaffected, unaltered. The medium is the

Table 3.2

Media grammar

	Television	Print
Grammar	• sensory balance: sight, sound, touch • hot • low definition • high involvement	• sensory bias: sight • cool • high definition • low involvement
Perceptual effects	simultaneous perception	sequential perception
Cultural effects	retribalization collectivism co-operation	detribalization individualism competitiveness

massage. Any understanding of social and cultural change is impossible without a knowledge of the way media work as environments (McLuhan 1967, 26).

McLuhan (1964, 57) saw media as "active metaphors" which transmit knowledge and experience. As the dominant medium in any society changes, so does the metaphor, the sensory ratio, and the perception of reality: "Media, by altering the environment, evoke in us unique ratios of sense perceptions. The extension of any one sense alters the way we think and act—the way we perceive the world. When these ratios change, . . . [we] change" (McLuhan 1969, 41).

McLuhan attempted to show how the dominant medium in different eras shaped sensory perception and hence, reality, truth, and knowledge. By examining his review of these eras we can get a better understanding of McLuhan's macro-theory of communication.

He asserts that, although speech was the dominant medium, individuals in the preliterate era could use all the senses equally to relate to experiences. This balanced sensory ratio created a high degree of involvement in the environment. Involvement encouraged co-operation and collectivism among individuals in the society and a communal or tribal village culture therefore developed.

The second stage in communication development involved the introduction of pictoral and written symbols, which shifted the sensory balance to a dependence on sight and visual cues. The invention of the printing press accelerated this shift and created a serious disruption in the sensory balance. Because print uses a discrete, uniform, orderly, and linear arrangement of letters and words on a page, our thinking habits became linear and sequential. Moreover, according to McLuhan, the introduction of print had an "explosive" effect; it broke society and ideas into explicit, uniform, and sequential categories. Trends towards individualism, specialization, privatization, competitiveness, and nationalism are all a result of the sensory shift created by print media. To use McLuhan's words, print "detribalized" society.

The emergence of electronic media, especially television, in the third media era restored the sensory balance of the preliterate era. Television created a social "implosion," bringing individuals and ideas together by removing the constraints of time and space. Because television requires involvement and participation, our modes of thought become "implicit, simultaneous, and discontinuous" (McLuhan 1962, 57). Our perception of reality changes and we are once again concerned about each other and the whole world. The electronic media "retribalize" society into a global village with a collective awareness.

In reviewing McLuhan's theory, Tom Wolfe pinpointed the major shift in perception experienced by the first generation raised in the electronic era:

> The TV children . . . are the new tribesmen. They have tribal sensory balances. They have the tribal habit of responding emotionally to the spoken word, they are "hot," they want to participate, to *touch*, to be involved . . . . The *visual* or *print* man is an individualist; he is "cooler," with built-in safeguards. He has the feeling that no matter what anybody says, he can go check it out. He can *look* it up . . . . The aural man is not so much of an individualist; he is more a part of the collective consciousness; he *believes* (Wolfe in Stearn 1967, 22).[12]

McLuhan looked to many fields to find extensions or examples of his thesis. He argued that education by the textbook and lecture was no longer acceptable in the new media age; that the linear or print-biased compartmentalization of learning is unnatural for the aural students of the electronic media generation. He also predicted a decline in the popularity of baseball, a linear, "one-step-at-a-time" sport, in favour of football because its complex unity and "all-at-onceness" is more perceptually akin to retribalized individuals. Despite the frivolous nature of many of McLuhan's examples, they reveal the essence of his argument; because the media of communication transmit information about the world in a manner that excites a unique sensory ratio, they define knowledge and reality and thereby determine our character. The impact of the communication media on sensory perception influences not only what we think but also how we think.

Wallace Clement: A critical analysis

Wallace Clement (1949–) did not develop a macro-theory about communication media as Innis and McLuhan did. Instead, he undertook an empirical study of the media elite in Canada in order to determine who they were and how they influenced the operations of the media. His interest was sparked by the pathfinding work of John Porter. In *The vertical mosaic* (1965), Porter examined the pervasive inequalities in education, income, and power in Canadian society. He not only addressed the issue of class in general but in particular the role of elites, people who exercise power and control, in various sectors of Canadian society and economy. Part of his analysis looked at the role of media organizations. Here, Porter identified a dual function: the interpretation and dissemination of society's values and ideologies, and the maximization of profits. Because of methodological problems, however, Porter was not able to pursue his findings further to determine whether that dual function implied an overlapping role for economic and media elites and if it did, what the implications were for Canadian society.[13]

Porter's study was Clement's jumping-off point; in many ways he replicated the study, undertaking a detailed analysis of the economic and media elites in Canada. He also reviewed their personal and professional characteristics, the reasons why and the manner in which they control the economy and the media, and the consequences of that control. Finally, he compared the two groups to uncover any overlap between them.

Before presenting his evidence and conclusions, however, Clement grounded them in an analysis of theoretical issues. To begin, he defined ideology as "a framework of assumptions, ideas and values incorporated into the perspective an individual or [a] collective uses to guide analyses, interests and commitments into a system of meaning" (Clement 1975, 270). Based partly on fact and partly on faith, ideologies develop within society and stabilize the social structure. The dominant ideologies of any society are generally those which foster the status quo; they strengthen the existing economic, social, and political institutions by legitimating the value system that supports them. In this way, the function of ideologies is to preserve the power of the social groups that exercise control over those institutions.

We acquire our ideological foundation through the subtle but effective process of socialization. The social environment of an individual dramatically influences that person's perception of society and of the world in general. The family, for example, is one of society's conductors of ideology. As we mature, our ideologies may be altered by the information that we process. As generators and disseminators of ideas and information, educational and religious institutions also transmit ideologies. Given their structure and functions, the mass media, too, have "the potential of being a conductor of ruling ideas par excellence" (Clement 1975, 274).

Critical theorists are very sceptical about the media's ideological impartiality. They argue that the media do not present images, values, and ideas that correspond to the reality of social disparities but instead perpetuate myths about equitable access to social advantages. Because the media elite understand the power of ideological consensus to maintain social cohesion and continuity, and because they are inextricably linked to the other elites in society, they use the media to "reinforce and sustain their hegemonic position" (Clement 1975, 280) by disseminating "ideas and values which affirm rather than challenge existing patterns of power and privilege" (Miliband 1969, 236).

The power of the media elite lies in their subtle control of decisions affecting both the structure of media organizations and the process by which media content is collected and selected. The media elite do not necessarily generate or promote ideologies blatantly, but the gatekeepers who select and interpret the information that is passed on to media audiences operate, whether consciously or not, from their own ideological frame of reference.[14] Because of the pervasive nature of the media, the perspective of the media elite permeates society and is accepted as accurate, fair, and just, thereby legitimating the existing social order.

Clement argued that if the media are to present a balanced picture of reality the media elite must be separate from other elites and must represent all the major groups in society. Only then can the media provide a pluralistic and detached analysis of other elite activity. To discover the degree to which the Canadian media elite meet these criteria, Clement examined media organizations and those who own or control them.

Like the Special Senate Committee on the Mass Media (1970) and the Royal Commission on Newspapers (1981), Clement (1975, 287–90, 306–23) found that concentration of media ownership was a well-entrenched trend in Canada.[15] He then created an aggregate profile of those who own or control these media organizations and found the typical individual to be a man of upper-class origin[16] who attended private school, has a university education, belongs to one or more of the exclusive national men's clubs, and was born in Ontario or Quebec (1975, 325–40). When he compared these findings with his picture of the economic elite, he found extensive overlap. In fact, "together the economic and media elite are simply two sides of the same upper class, [and] between them they hold two of the key sources of power—economic and ideological—in Canadian society and form the corporate elite" (1975, 325).

Because of this finding, Clement also addressed a number of related issues. He examined the questions of access and content with respect to the control exercised by gatekeepers, advertisers, wire services, foreign sources, and the state (1975, 290–306) and concluded that "the mass media in Canada are class institutions run by, for and in the interest of the upper class. More than that, they are instruments of the corporate elite" (1975, 341).

Clement has been criticized for his strong leftist approach to media research and a number of methodological criticisms have been levelled against his main conclusions. Nevertheless, his contribution to our understanding of the way that the Canadian media function is impressive. As a society, we are dependent on "second-hand news" for most of our information. Those who do not agree with Clement's conclusions about ideological manipulation would still concede that he alerts us to the conflict of interest inherent in any monopoly of control over the conductors of news, ideas, values, and information. He forces us to examine the way that news is selected, interpreted, and presented, and its potential for affecting our perceptions of reality. Public awareness can motivate the media to present the diversity of opinions and issues so necessary to the effective functioning of liberal-democratic societies.

Culture, media, and public policy

To complete the review of culture and communication in Canada that this chapter has undertaken, the role of government in this field remains to be examined. In Canada, direct government intervention in support of cultural activities is a twentieth-century phenomenon. As technological innovations have eroded international boundaries, governments have become more concerned with their role in preserving a distinct national culture. Supporters contend that national cultural policies are absolute necessities for social development, economic growth, political stability, and national unity and identity because culture strongly influences "the development of our institutions" and defines our wants "in terms that invite responses by government" (Canada, Federal Cultural Policy Review Committee 1982, 15).

Both government and culture are rooted in and shape society, but an intrinsic conflict exists between their objectives. Government seeks order and predictability; culture thrives on spontaneity and diversity. Any attempt to impose the objectives of one on the other clearly debases the value of both. Despite the danger, each is dependent on the strength of the other (Canada, Federal Cultural Policy Review Committee 1982, 15). Culture needs "wise husbandry" to grow and flourish (Ostry 1978, 2), so that it may "contribute to a sense of belonging and pride among those comprising the state" (Meisel 1974, 606). This nationalistic sentiment is at the core of most Canadian government policies that affect culture.

The Special Senate Committee on the Mass Media identified the perpetual Canadian concern with culture and communication in the opening pages of its report, *The uncertain mirror* (1970, 11). Defining a nation as "a collection of people who share common images of themselves," the report recognizes the valuable contribution of the media in helping us "to define who and what we are." It also acknowledges the obstacles that face the Canadian media:

> Geography, language, and perhaps a failure of confidence and imagination have made us into a cultural as well as economic satellite of the United States. And nowhere is the trend more pronounced than in the media. . . . We are not suggesting that these [American] influences are undesirable, nor that they can or should be restricted . . . . What we are suggesting is that the Canadian media . . . have an interest in and an obligation to promote our *apartness* from the American reality. For all our

similarities, for all our sharing, for all our friendships, we *are* somebody else (Canada, Special Senate Committee 1970, 11).

Cultural nationalism has appeared as a recurring theme throughout the history of Canadian media and cultural public policy making. In the field of mass communication, broadcasting has been singled out as the primary beast of burden for protecting and strengthening the Canadian national identity, but it does not stand alone. Successive governments have established royal commissions, special committees, task forces, cultural agencies, and a variety of ad hoc groups to deal with culture, communication, and our national identity. They have used exhortation, negotiation, moral suasion, direct and indirect expenditures, taxation, loans, public ownership, program development requirements, regulation, and legislation as policy instruments to promote Canadian objectives in many cultural spheres, including visual and performing arts, publishing, audio recording, film, broadcasting, and heritage (museum collections, folk art, and so on).

As in any policy arena, however, Canadian governments must face the imperatives imposed upon them by democratic forms and traditions. It has been said, and often cynically so, that a policy must win more votes than it loses. In other words, "it must yield the most favourable balance of public benefits and must be felt by the public to do so" (Canada, Federal Cultural Policy Review Committee 1982, 17). This requirement places constraints upon the decisions made in any policy area. The government must balance competing public demands against available resources. It must predict the degree of public satisfaction, and dissatisfaction, by anticipating the direct and indirect effects of policy decisions, in terms of both costs and benefits. Furthermore, the process of government involves the interaction of administrative and political institutions and these pursue somewhat different goals. The administrator's chief concern is the machinery and management of government activities, while political actors emphasize policy coherence and accountability. Collaboration is no easier in the cultural arena than in any other.

UNESCO defines cultural policy as "a body of operational principles, administrative and budgetary practices and procedures which provide a basis for cultural action by the State" (Schafer 1976, 33). In Canada, cultural policy development is exercised by all governments and by innumerable agencies within them.[17] In general, they have eight primary objectives:

1. to promote high standards in the creation and performance by Canadians of Canadian material for Canadian audiences

2. to encourage equal access to cultural activities and training opportunities, and to decentralize cultural centres throughout the country

3. to encourage diverse participation in the process of cultural policy, from governments, cultural organizations, and the public

4. to bring international cultural activities to Canadians and to promote the exposure of foreign audiences to Canadian performers

5. to preserve, restore, and protect Canadian heritage

6. to develop new forms of expression worthy of worldwide recognition

7. to establish an effective balance of cultural forces and activities in order to ensure that all interests are considered

8. to encourage the development of a national culture that springs from and strengthens our national identity

The last goal draws the most criticism from those who oppose government intervention in the cultural sector. It is also of deep concern to students of Canadian mass communication, since much of the responsibility for its achievement has been delegated to the mass media. Critics of Canadian cultural policy argue that it is "nothing more than an antipathy towards the 'importation' of U.S. culture" (Globerman 1983, 3). When the Special Senate Committee (1970, 11) acknowledged the influence of American popular culture, it not only praised its "vigor and diversity" but also expressed alarm that it "is close to becoming a world culture." Dallas Smythe (1981, 91–102) has linked U.S. cultural domination with economic domination of this country. He argues that instead of building Canada into a strong, autonomous nation, "Canadian businessmen served as agents of cultural submission" (1981, 98). As a result, "Canada is the world's most dependent 'developed' country and the world's richest 'underdeveloped' country" (1981, 91).

Others contend, however, that Canadian cultural policy is not merely a negative instrument aimed at reducing the impact of American cultural influences, but that it also has strong positive connotations for the well-being of Canada as a whole. When addressing his fellow premiers about the federal government's free-trade initiatives with United States, Ontario Premier David Peterson (in Ostry 1986, 8) warned,

> Nor can we trade away Canada's soul. Cultural sovereignty cannot be separated from political sovereignty. We must maintain our ability to develop and support our own cultural and communication industries. We must maintain our ability to publish books and magazines, produce records and films, and create television and radio programming that help us define our hopes and dreams, our way of seeing ourselves and the world.

Supporters of government intervention in the cultural and media policy arenas believe that if we are to have a country, we need a common identity. The purpose of government intervention is not to restrict access to foreign cultural products but to expand access to similar Canadian products. Ostry (1986, 15) asks, "How can anyone see a barrier in our efforts to make our own voice audible to our own people?"

After reviewing the developments in the cultural sphere during the past three decades, the Federal Cultural Policy Review Committee (1982, 5–6) concluded, "Canadian cultural life can be said to have gained maturity and distinction . . . . Yet cultural policy has not been entirely successful . . . ." Recent statistics back that claim (Canada, Department of Communications 1987). Canadian writers and publishers have never captured more than 27 percent of the Canadian trade book market. Seventy percent of all periodicals sold on Canadian newsstands are foreign. About three-quarters of the film and video distribution revenues earned in Canada go to foreign firms and only 3 percent of screen time in Canada is devoted to Canadian feature films. The eight largest audio recording studios in Canada are foreign owned. Only 28 percent of all English television programming is Canadian in origin, while Canadians spend over 80 percent of their viewing time watching foreign-produced shows. To some, these facts may appear startling; to those who have followed the fortunes of Canadian cultural industries, they are simply more evidence to add to the massive collection of other such disheartening data.

In 1987, the federal Department of Communications published a policy statement entitled *Vital links: Canadian cultural industries*. In it, the

Department outlined the financial problems confronting Canada's cultural industries. Although Canadians are avid consumers of cultural products of all sorts, the Canadian cultural market is abnormal in two important respects: most of the cultural products available here are produced elsewhere; and the revenues generated by their distribution largely flow out of Canada to finance production industries elsewhere. When combined with other financial hurdles, such as the small, dispersed, and diverse market base, the reluctance of financial backers, and the well-heeled competition from large, multinational conglomerates, the outlook for Canadian producers appears bleak. Not only could domestic firms eventually be squeezed out of business but Canadians could suffer even further diminished access to their own cultural products.

According to the Department of Communications (1987, 71), this erosion of our cultural sovereignty "would produce intolerable effects on the cultural well-being of our nation." The Canadian government therefore claims a commitment to the development of a healthy, active, and assertive Canadian culture and has undertaken a number of policy initiatives designed to ensure it.[18] Nonetheless, the decision of Brian Mulroney's federal Conservative government to enter into the Free Trade Agreement (FTA) with the United States has caused many Canadians to question that government's commitment to Canadian culture.[19]

Free trade

In 1988, about 80 percent of the trade in goods and services between Canada and the United States was free of tariffs. The aim of the FTA, one of the most far-reaching economic deals ever negotiated between two sovereign nations, is to increase trade further by eliminating remaining tariffs over a ten-year period. While many Canadians support the idea of free trade, many others reject a number of aspects of this particular agreement. Only those criticisms related to the cultural aspects of the deal will be addressed here.

Prime Minister Mulroney, his ministers, negotiators, and supporters maintain that Canada's culture and Canadian cultural institutions are not at risk. They assert that the cultural sector is explicitly exempted from the FTA. Governments at all levels are free to continue and/or enhance their programs in support of cultural activities. Moreover, their ability to do so will be strengthened by the increased economic prosperity that the FTA is expected to generate. Finally, there is an expectation that Canadian-produced cultural products will be more widely accessible in the vastly larger American market, enhancing both their reputation and their profitability. Supporters conclude: "In general, fears of nationalists that Canada's culture has been sold down the river seem unfounded" (Portman 1987, B8).

The critics of the Free Trade Agreement, on the other hand, see it as the final capitulation of control over the future of Canada's cultural development. They disagree with the reassurances offered by FTA supporters and instead question both the specific terms and general thrust of the deal. With respect to the argument that culture is exempt, critics point to the somewhat contradictory American position, which they sum up as follows: "Canada agrees that future cultural measures will not impair the benefits the U.S. would have otherwise expected from the agreement" (Portman 1987, B8). Since the agreement allows both sides to take "measures of equivalent commercial effect" in any area if and when they find that the other has contravened the principles of the FTA, critics believe that it permits the United States to respond with countervailing penalties to any future Canadian policies that involve subsidies, regardless of whether or not these subsidies are directed solely at cultural industries.

In addition, the suggestion that Canada's opportunities in the American cultural market are enhanced by the FTA is denounced. Mavor Moore (1988, C2), former head of the Canada Council, argues,

> In cultural terms, the main issue is not free trade or no free trade, but the point at which a two-way exchange becomes a one-way throughway for one of the two parties. There is already more free trade in culture between Canada and the U.S. than between any other two developed countries in the world. At the moment the exchange is ridiculously lop-sided: about 90 to 10—and the current pact gives the Canadian partner not a whit wider access to the U.S. culture market than we now enjoy.

Many of those who oppose the FTA argue that not only does it fail to increase opportunities for Canadian cultural products to be sold in the United States, but it also endangers their production and distribution in Canada. These critics contend that Canadian culture already suffers from overexposure to the cultural products of our neighbours to the South; any trade agreement with the United States must therefore recognize this and specifically guarantee Canadians access to their own culture and cultural products. "If it cannot, either the pact or Canada will not work" (Moore 1988, C2).

Many of these criticisms are based upon broad visions of Canada and Canadian culture. Robertson Davies (1989), one of Canada's foremost authors, argues that this sort of opposition rests upon the growing recognition of Canadians that they are different from Americans, that they have a "national soul." In Davies' view, Canadians are not developing a growing anti-Americanism but rather are experiencing greater pride in their own history, efforts, and achievements. The closer economic ties with the United States brought about by the FTA can be seen as the first step in an eventual takeover "not immediately political but cultural and, indeed, spiritual" (Davies 1989, 46).

The FTA is still in its infancy, however, and the debate has just begun. Only time can determine whether the agreement will enhance or erode Canada's domestic independence and international stature.

Summary

This chapter gave a brief introduction to media scholarship and public policy from a Canadian perspective. The theories of Harold Innis and Marshall McLuhan, both of which focus on the cultural impact of communication technology, were reviewed. Wallace Clement's critical analysis of the Canadian media elite and their role in promoting ideologies that preserve the status quo was also outlined. These discussions provided an academic background for the policy discussion that followed.

As was noted, the relationships between culture, public policy, and the mass media are complicated. Culture is an important component of any society and the mass media have a crucial role as purveyors of culture. The chapter identified Canada's unique position vis-à-vis the United States as the main reason for government intervention in culture and communication. Some evidence was provided to demonstrate the weak position of Canadian cultural industries and both sides of the policy debate were reviewed.

During the emerging "information age," the information and service sectors of the economy will continue to outstrip the traditional resource and manufacturing sectors in their contribution to the nation's gross domestic product. If Canada is to play a meaningful role in this international information revolution, it is incumbent upon our legislators to create a coherent and flexible national policy that will safeguard and enhance Canada's information systems for the twenty-first century. The mass media of communication are a single aspect of this policy sector.

Notes

1. This issue is a recurring theme in Canadian mass communication and cultural policy debates. It will be dealt with again in a later examination of the origins and roles of major Canadian cultural policies and industries such as the Canadian Broadcasting Corporation, the National Film Board, and Canadian content regulations.

2. Canadian concerns about national cultural identity were highlighted by the U.S.–Canada free trade discussions. Although the question of free trade is not the focus of this book, the issue has created a heightened interest in Canadian cultural industries and their future.

3. The federal government's first media policy is discussed in detail in chapter 6.

4. Although Harold Innis is now one of Canada's most esteemed scholars, during his lifetime he was almost totally ignored and virtually unknown, in large part because of the ethnocentric nature of academia. His work was not recognized by his colleagues at the University of Toronto, nor by scholars in the United States or Britain. Not only were Canadian academic pursuits considered marginal in international scholarly circles but Innis himself was something of an anomaly. He had shifted his focus of study from economics and transportation to communication. Very few scholars undertook a serious analysis of his contributions. It was not until Marshall McLuhan, the media guru of the 1960s, acknowledged the influence of Innis's work on his own that Innis began to receive the attention he so richly deserved.

5. For a more detailed analysis of the manner in which the electronic media have trivialized culture and media content, see Neil Postman (1984).

6. McLuhan was assigned the directorship of the Centre for Culture and Technology after he was virtually driven out of the English department at the University of Toronto. The Centre itself was nothing more than a place to *put* McLuhan so that he would no longer disrupt the department. McLuhan spent his last years in an abandoned carriage house located in an obscure back lane as a symbol of how Canadian universities perceived communication scholarship. B.W. Powe (1984) wrote an essay describing his experience as a student of McLuhan; in it he discusses the opposition and lack of scholarly respect that McLuhan faced at the University of Toronto. Perhaps the most telling aspect of the Centre's existence was the University's decision to close it down when McLuhan retired in 1980.

7. Even now there are relatively few departments of communication at Canadian universities. Eight currently exist: at Simon Fraser University (British Columbia), the University of Calgary (Alberta), University of Windsor (Ontario), University of Ottawa (Ontario), Carleton University

(Ontario), York University (Ontario), Concordia University (Quebec), and McGill University (Quebec). In addition, there are schools of journalism at University of Regina (Saskatchewan), University of Western Ontario (Ontario), Carleton University (Ontario), King's College (Nova Scotia), and Ryerson Polytechnic Institute (Ontario). By contrast, much of the communication research in the United States emanates from departments or faculties of communication, which exist at almost every major institution.

8. Despite his success in United States, McLuhan, like Innis, faced enormous opposition in Canadian scholarly circles. For the most part, Canadian universities were controlled by British academics, many of whom considered the media unworthy of intellectual study. Many were reluctant to accept the scholarship of Innis and McLuhan because it did not fit within the established disciplines of the university.

9. McLuhan's preoccupation with what some called "cosmic theories" made empirical analysis of his ideas particularly difficult. In order to test McLuhan's hypotheses, one would require massive, cross-cultural, interdisciplinary research studies. However, because many departments of communication exist within social science faculties, doctoral students and other researchers selecting and refining empirical studies have tended more and more towards microlevel analysis. This trend is also reflected in the nature of articles appearing in communication journals published in the United States. As a result, the gulf between American communication research and the theoretical analysis of Innis and McLuhan has grown rather than receded over time.

10. For example, most languages have one or two words that mean snow. The Inuit peoples, however, have several words, each describing a different type of snow. The difference in language is related to the difference in culture. To the majority of people, snow is simply snow; to the Inuit, snow is a vital part of their lives and their language reflects that.

11. The terms hot and cool are perhaps the weakest and most criticized areas of McLuhan's analysis. He used the terms widely to refer to objects, events, cultures, personalities, dances, cars, and art forms. He also warned that certain messages were best transmitted via certain media. He argued, for example, that Americans demanded an end to the Vietnam war because they could no longer tolerate the hot messages on the cool television medium.

12. The authors recognize that McLuhan's theories apply equally to women and men.

13. Porter was unable to compare his data on economic elites with his data on media elites because of a ten-year gap between the collection of those data. He examined the economic elite in 1951 but did not gather data about the media elite until 1961.

14. For Canadian examples of obvious media manipulation, see Hannigan (1983).

15. The issue of concentration in media ownership is examined in detail in part 2 of this text.

16. Clement, following Porter, used a multi-methodological approach to class that included position or occupation of father or other close relative, and attendance at private school. Generally, wealth is the key variable.

17. In Canada, the federal, provincial, and even municipal governments are all involved in the development of cultural policies to varying degrees. At the federal level, several departments, including Health and Welfare, Indian Affairs and Northern Development, Employment and Immigration, Secretary of State, and Communications, are involved in this policy arena. In addition, there are many cultural agencies that are responsible for a variety of specific tasks. Although the agencies are too numerous to list in full here they include, for example, the National Museums of Canada, the Canada Council, the National Arts Centre, the National Archives, the National Film Board, the Canadian Broadcasting Corporation, and the Canadian Radio-television and Telecommunications Commission.

18. In addition to the cultural agencies listed in n. 17, the federal government has cultural policy instruments such as the Canadian Book Publishing Development Program, Telefilm Canada, and the Canadian Cultural Property Export Review Board. For further details, see Canada, Department of Communications (1985, 1987).

19. The November 1988 federal election campaign was essentially a one-issue debate. The FTA swept aside almost all other political concerns. The resulting election of a Progressive Conservative majority government was interpreted by that government as a mandate to conclude the FTA although the majority of the popular votes was cast in opposition to the government's position.

References

Bittner, J.R. 1977. *Mass communication: An introduction.* Englewood Cliffs: Prentice-Hall.

Canada. Department of Communications. 1985. *Canada's cultural agencies: In rhythm with our cultural pulse.* Ottawa: Supply and Services.

———. 1987. *Vital links: Canadian cultural industries.* Ottawa: Supply and Services.

Canada. Federal Cultural Policy Review Committee. 1982. *Report.* Ottawa: Supply and Services.

Canada. Royal Commission on Newspapers. 1981. *Report.* Ottawa: Supply and Services.

Canada. Special Senate Committee on the Mass Media. 1970. *The uncertain mirror.* Vol. 1 of *Report.* Ottawa: Supply and Services.

Carey, J.W. 1967. Harold Adams Innis and Marshall McLuhan. *Antioch Review* 27:5–39.

Clement, W. 1975. *The Canadian corporate elite: An analysis of economic power.* Toronto: McClelland and Stewart.

Davies, R. 1989. Signing away Canada's soul: Culture, identity and the free-trade agreement. *Harper's Magazine* (January), 43–47.

Globerman, S. 1983. *Cultural regulation in Canada.* Montreal: Institute for Research on Public Policy.

Grossberg, L. 1979. Interpreting the "crisis" of culture in communication theory. *Journal of Communication* (Winter), 56–78.

Hannigan, J.A. 1983. Ideology, elites, and the Canadian mass media. In *Communications in Canadian society*, ed. B.D. Singer, 55–61. Toronto: Addison-Wesley.

Innis, H.A. [1950] 1972. *Empire and communications*. Rev. M.Q. Innis. Toronto: University of Toronto.

———. [1951] 1964. *The bias of communication*. Toronto: University of Toronto.

———. 1956. *Essays in Canadian economic history*. Ed. M.Q. Innis. Toronto: University of Toronto.

Kroker, A. 1984. *Technology and the Canadian mind*. Montreal: New World Perspectives.

MacDonald, D. 1964. Running it up the totem pole. *Book Week, New York Herald Tribune*. 7 July. Reprinted in Stearn, G.E., ed. 1967. *McLuhan hot and cool*, 203–11. New York: Dial.

McLuhan, M. 1962. *The Gutenberg galaxy*. Toronto: University of Toronto.

———. 1964. *Understanding media: The extensions of man*. New York: McGraw-Hill.

———. 1967. *The medium is the massage*, with Quentin Fiore. New York: Bantam.

———. 1969. *Counter blast*. Toronto: McClelland and Stewart.

Meisel, J. 1974. Political culture and the politics of culture. *Canadian Journal of Political Science* 7(4): 601–15.

Miliband, R. 1969. *The state in capitalist society*. London: Weidenfeld and Nicholson.

Moore, M. 1988. Ottawa's compromise threatens Canadian culture. *Globe and Mail*. 28 May, p. C2.

Ostry, B. 1978. *The cultural connection: An essay on culture and government policy in Canada*. Toronto: McClelland and Stewart.

———. 1986. Cultural sovereignty and free trade between Canada and the United States. Notes for an address, American Association of Museums annual meeting. 11 June. New York.

Pal, L.A. 1987. *Public policy analysis: An introduction*. Toronto: Methuen.

Porter, J. 1965. *The vertical mosaic*. Toronto: University of Toronto.

Portman, J. 1987. Free-trade deal does little harm to cultural sovereignty. *Ottawa Citizen*. 10 October, p. B8.

Postman, N. 1984. *Amusing ourselves to death: Public discourse in the age of show business*. New York: Penguin.

Powe, B.W. 1984. *A climate charged*. Oakville: Mosaic.

Schafer, D.P. 1976. *Aspects of Canadian cultural policy*. Paris: UNESCO.

Smythe, D.W. 1981. *Dependency road: Communications, capitalism, consciousness, and Canada*. Norwood: Ablex.

Stearn, G.E., ed. 1967. *McLuhan hot and cool*. New York: Dial.

Tannenbaum, E.R. 1977. *1900: The generation before the Great War*. New York: Anchor.

Part Two

The Print Media

THE FOURTH ESTATE:
THE DEVELOPMENT OF
NEWSPAPERS IN CANADA

We begin our examination of Canada's mass media with a review of the newspaper. As the first mass medium and for many years the public's main source of information, the newspaper is in many respects the standardbearer of freedom of expression. Publishers and journalists are adamant about preserving the right to print without state interference, to ensure that the public has access to the information they need to make decisions about self-government.

The newspaper's role in a liberal democratic society is often referred to as the "fourth estate." The term was coined in the early nineteenth century. The three estates, or classes, of the English realm were the clergy, the lords, and the commons. Later the three estates collectively came to represent government, or the state. As "watchdogs" of the state, newspapers take on a policing role on behalf of the public, and in so doing become the fourth estate. In a democratic society, the state must be perceived to be acting in the name of society in order to keep the public's confidence, and it is therefore dependent upon the agencies of cultural production—media, schools, church—to define and maintain its legitimacy. Because journalists see their role as interpreters and investigators of state activities, they too claim to be acting on behalf of the people in protection of the public interest.

This chapter traces the development of the newspaper in Canada, from its beginnings to its future challenges. It examines the editorial and business functions of the press and identifies current trends and problems in the Canadian newspaper industry. Canadian magazines are also discussed.

Chapter 5 analyses the news function of the press in greater detail: the process of news selection, the role of gatekeepers, and agenda-setting. Finally, the section discusses issues facing the newspaper industry which result, for the most part, from the inherent conflict between its news and business functions. The implications of those issues are explored in terms of public policy. Throughout the two chapters, the right of publishers to publish without government interference and the right of the public to be fully informed of the day's intelligence appear as complementary and, at times, as antagonistic themes.

Newspapers: The first mass medium

As the oldest *mass* medium of communication and one of the largest world industries, newspapers broke ground for the media that followed. In the process, they carved a special place for themselves as providers of the day's news and leaders in shaping public opinion. During the "golden age" of newspapers in the late nineteenth and early twentieth centuries, there were general dailies, local weeklies, and specialized newspapers which courted subscribers on the basis of their occupations, interests, and hobbies. George Bernard Shaw called newspapers "the poor man's university." The reading public bought and read them all with enthusiasm.

The forerunner of the modern newspaper[1] can be traced back to Rome in 60 B.C., where each day the *Acta Diurna*, a bulletin of daily events, was published, posted in a public place, and then saved as a record. The publication of the newspaper as we know it became a technical possibility with the invention of the printing press, yet it was more than 150 years later, in 1615 in Frankfurt, Germany, that the first weekly newspaper was published. Within fifteen years, publishers in England,

France, and Italy had printed their first weeklies, but it would be another 120 years before Canada's first newspaper came off the presses.

Unlike their early counterparts, modern newspaper organizations are complex and highly structured. The main functions of newspapers in democratic societies have remained stable over time, however. They collect and report the news in an accurate and balanced manner. In the process, they provide a public agenda for both the governed and the governors, and support the economic system by enabling advertisers to reach consumers. A newspaper's performance is judged by its ability to balance all three functions in a manner that best serves the public interest.

Although newspapers are rarely the first medium to bring news to the public, they do have a number of advantages over the more rapid electronic media. Newspapers can offer more depth of coverage—more detail, explanation, interpretation, and analysis—because they do not share the time and space constraints of the electronic media. Second, newspapers may be examined at the readers' convenience and saved as an account of events. This quality of "reviewability" is essentially absent from the electronic media.[2] Third, newspapers offer readers more choice and control over content than television news broadcasting does. We can scan the paper and read only the information that serves our needs or interests. Finally, unlike the electronic media, which tend to stress national and international news, newspapers are a valuable source of information about local events and issues.

Despite these advantages, the newspaper industry is confronted by several difficulties. As the costs of producing and distributing its product have risen, its circulation figures have declined. Changes in lifestyle and the introduction of electronic media have created a general disinterest in newspapers among the younger audience. The electronic media have also funnelled off some of the newspapers' advertising support. Newspapers have responded by introducing new equipment to reduce operating costs and improve efficiency. They have undertaken extensive surveys of their readers and potential readers in an effort to understand their needs and have begun to publish morning and weekend editions to revive lagging circulation figures. They have also courted advertisers by promoting shopper sections and special inserts. Moreover, the industry as a whole has attempted to rationalize itself; chain ownership and reduced competition have led to higher efficiency and profit levels but reduced diversity in opinion and interpretation.

The problems facing Canadian newspapers are common throughout the modern Western world, and so too is the range of attempted solutions. Examining the historical development of the newspaper in Canada, however, will provide a context for the Canadian perspective on these issues.

The Canadian newspaper industry

Early development

British immigrants brought the printing press to Canada in the 1750s to help colonize the new land and the first publishers were agents of the Crown. Canada's first newspaper, the Halifax *Gazette*, began publication on 23 March 1752, with seventy-two subscribers. The weekly four-page gazettes contained announcements of official government proclamations, foreign news, and a few advertisements. Because the majority of the colony's population was illiterate, however, the first weeklies increased their circulation very slowly. During the War of 1812, the situation changed dramatically. People began to demand more news and information in printed form in order to keep abreast of the war's progress. Small publishers, supported by the Crown, sprang up everywhere and the weekly newspaper became an eagerly awaited commodity.

The official newspaper of the King's Printer gave way to an unsubsidized press during the mid-nineteenth century, when the economic and political elites began to realize the potential power of the press. The new papers had content similar to their official counterparts, but with three differences: they added local news and some entertaining features; the amount of advertising increased to help defray the lost government subsidy; and, most strikingly, they emphasized partisan politics. Political parties used newspapers as extensions of their party apparatus and most communities had two weeklies—one Tory and one Reform.

The francophone press developed along somewhat different lines. French-language newspapers were more learned and more literary in their content. The vitality of the francophone oral culture and determination of French Canadians to preserve it in their newspapers were responsible for the difference. Since French-language papers were slow to include the news function among their priorities, francophone readers relied on the English-language papers for news.

By the end of the nineteenth century, the newspaper had made significant inroads into the collective Canadian consciousness. It was fast becoming an "almost unchallenged . . . superlative vehicle of information and persuasion" (Rutherford 1978, 38). As literacy rates climbed, publishing became one of the leading Canadian industries. There were newspapers for all interests: sectarian and ethnic presses, agrarian, professional, industrial, trade union, and financial papers, journals of opinion, country weeklies, and of course, city dailies.

Dailies, as forerunners of the modern newspaper, first emerged in the 1870s and reached their peak in 1913, when there were 138 daily newspapers in Canada. Paul Rutherford (1978, 48) explains the phenomenon:

> The transformation of the colonial daily into the modern mass newspaper was closely tied to the emergence of industrial Canada. The reading public increased enormously because of the general advance of literacy, the growth of the city population, and above all its apparently unquenchable thirst for news and entertainment . . . . Publishers were able to respond because the new print technology, a plentiful supply of inexpensive newsprint, and a flood of advertising allowed them to mass produce a relatively cheap product.

Newspapers at this time started attempting to increase circulation by appealing to broader audiences. They began to give up their obvious partisan biases in favour of somewhat more objective reporting, although columns and editorials retained much of their political fervour. News reports covered local, national, and international events and trivia, and topics other than politics began to attract the attention of reporters and readers. The early twentieth century was also the era of the scoop; newspapers desperately tried to beat their competitors to publish first accounts of sensational stories.

As editorial content and style shifted, so did the economic objectives of the newspaper industry. Business principles, rather than political ones, began to determine how newspapers would be run. The press standardized its finished product and rationalized its operation and market share as well. Reduced competition meant increased circulation for a single paper within a given area. Most of us consider chain ownership a modern phenomenon, but Canada's first newspaper chain was created in 1897 when Southam Inc., owner of the *Hamilton Spectator*, bought the Ottawa *Citizen*. The company added the Calgary *Herald* (1908), Edmonton *Journal* (1912), Winnipeg *Tribune* (1920), and Vancouver *Province* (1923) to its list of acquisitions long before the Canadian public or its government began to express concern about the move towards concentrated ownership in the newspaper industry.

Current performance

Following World War II, the newspaper industry confronted a number of obstacles. The post-war boom was followed by a decade of high inflation in which production costs soared. The fiscal problems were later exacerbated by the economic recession of the 1970s. In addition, the introduction of the television in the early 1950s posed a dramatic threat to the newspaper industry. Television was an alternative source of news, an additional leisure activity, and a competitor for the pool of advertising dollars. The electronic media threatened to undermine both of the newspapers' traditional sources of revenue: the consumer and the advertisers. Finally, tabloids, with content and format designed to attract the attention of the generation raised on television, gained circulation.

After the initial shock, the newspaper industry took steps in response to the competitive challenges it faced. Higher morning and weekend circulation figures motivated many publishers to shift their afternoon dailies to morning papers and to introduce Sunday papers and larger weekend editions.[3] Many dailies that once emphasized hard news began to include general interest features. These tactics stemmed directly from the industry's fierce determination to increase the circulation figures upon which its vital advertising revenues rested.

Table 4.1 shows the average daily circulation figures of Canada's top fifteen daily newspapers. The *Toronto Star* is Canada's largest daily with an average daily circulation of more than half a million. *Le journal de Montréal* leads the list of French-language papers. The *Globe and Mail*, Canada's national newspaper, achieved an average circulation of 326 000. In all cases where figures are available, highest daily circulation is achieved by a weekend edition (Friday, Saturday, or Sunday).

In an effort to improve cost efficiency and net profits, the industry also began to implement technological innovations at all stages of production. Computerized equipment and telecommunication hardware

Table 4.1

Circulation figures for Canada's top fifteen newspapers, March 1988

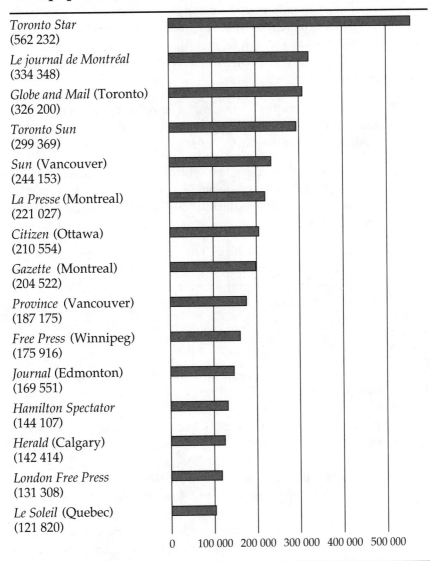

Toronto Star (562 232)	
Le journal de Montréal (334 348)	
Globe and Mail (Toronto) (326 200)	
Toronto Sun (299 369)	
Sun (Vancouver) (244 153)	
La Presse (Montreal) (221 027)	
Citizen (Ottawa) (210 554)	
Gazette (Montreal) (204 522)	
Province (Vancouver) (187 175)	
Free Press (Winnipeg) (175 916)	
Journal (Edmonton) (169 551)	
Hamilton Spectator (144 107)	
Herald (Calgary) (142 414)	
London Free Press (131 308)	
Le Soleil (Quebec) (121 820)	

0   100 000   200 000   300 000   400 000   500 000

Source: *Audit Bureau of Circulation FAS/FAX, March 1988, reported in* Marketing *14 November 1988, 30.*

improved everything from news gathering to delivery of the finished product. It was, in fact, by using these techniques that the *Globe and Mail*, originally a Toronto daily, became "Canada's national newspaper."[4]

The most comprehensive industry response, however, was to rationalize its operation according to the principles of business management. Ownership patterns shifted as the small, independent papers sold out to or shut down in the face of larger, more powerful, and more profitable corporations. By 1980, three ownership trends were contributing to more concentrated control of the industry:[5]

1. Chain ownership. The control of several newspapers by one large corporate owner (e.g., Southam Inc. owns fifteen English-language newspapers in Canada).

2. Cross-media ownership. The control of different sorts of media outlets by one corporate owner (e.g., the Blackburn family holdings in London, Ontario, include both print and electronic media undertakings).

3. Conglomerate ownership. The control of one or more newspapers by large corporations whose primary business is something unrelated to the media industries (e.g., Power Corporation of Canada operates four French-language dailies in addition to its massive interests in insurance, banking, and financial management).

Partly in response to patterns of media ownership, the Canadian federal government undertook two major investigations of the newspaper industry. The first, the Special Senate Committee on Mass Media (1970), is also known as the Davey Committee. Senator Keith Davey proposed the establishment of the Committee in 1968, and also chaired it. Recognizing the pervasive influence of the media and the need for media responsibility and accountability, the Committee set out to "determine whether they [the people of Canada] have the press they need or simply the press they deserve" (Canada, Special Senate Committee 1970, vii). Although the Committee included all forms of mass media within the purview of its study, it concentrated on the print press and the relationship between print and electronic media. A review of media ownership patterns took up about one-quarter of the Committee's report and was strongly critical of concentrated media control.

The Royal Commission on Newspapers, or the Kent Commission, chaired by Thomas Kent, "was born out of shock and trauma" (Canada, Royal Commission on Newspapers 1981, xi). Ten years after the Davey Committee tendered its portentous report, the simultaneous closings of the Winnipeg *Tribune* and the Ottawa *Journal* on 27 August 1980 jolted the federal government into action. It moved rapidly to establish the Commission in September 1980 and gave it a broad and urgent mandate: to investigate the newspaper industry in Canada fully and to suggest remedies for identified problems. The Commission's report covered a wide range of issues, but it paid particular attention to the "shackles" of concentrated ownership which potentially inhibit the operation of a truly free and responsible press.

There have been numerous other committees, commissions, and task forces to examine the media, but these two represent the most intensive and detailed government-sponsored investigations of media ownership in general and the newspaper industry in particular.[6] Much of the data used here is derived from their reports.

The Royal Commission on Newspapers reported that in 1980, three groups controlled nine-tenths of the circulation of French-language dailies and three further groups controlled two-thirds of the circulation of English-language dailies. While some of these conglomerates focussed their interests on communication-related concerns, all of them had businesses outside the newspaper industry. When newspapers are only one of a conglomerate's many types of business enterprise, however, certain issues arise: the priority given the daily newspaper business as opposed to the other businesses, the degree to which other business concerns affect the content, style, and quality of the newspaper, and the extent to which the public's best interest is served.

Two examples illustrate the potential for complications. During 1987–1988, Maclean Hunter Ltd., a mixed-media conglomerate, made a number of changes to its corporate structure. It purchased Selkirk Communications Ltd. and then resold many of its parts, pending approval from the Canadian Radio-television and Telecommunications Commission (CRTC). It began to build a cable infrastructure in Detroit and completed a deal to develop cable television in Britain. It sold the *Financial Post* to one of its own subsidiaries, the Toronto Sun Publishing Corp., with the intention of making the *Post* a daily (*Financial Post* 1988, 15). While there is nothing inherently wrong or unprofessional in this activity, one needs to question what impact it might have on the manner in which the company's newspapers report the news. Did the need for CRTC approval of Maclean Hunter's purchase and resale of Selkirk influence the manner in which stories about the Commission were reported? Does consolidation have positive or negative financial consequences for the company's publishing interests? Indeed, the CRTC approval, in the fall of 1989, of the resale of Selkirk placed some limitations on the transactions that indicated concern about the effects of consolidation.

The dramatic staff reductions made in 1988 and 1989 by Southam Inc. are the second example. Close to one thousand employees, about 7 percent of its work force, were dismissed as the newspaper chain struggled to increase its profitability and appeal for investors. Such a move undoubtedly benefits Southam's shareholders, but its impact on the overall quality of the chain's daily newspapers appears to be of secondary importance. Managerial control of newspaper undertakings has been transferred from journalists who worked their way through the newspaper's ranks, and thereby learned to appreciate journalistic and public interest issues, to accountants and marketing experts who are concerned with net profits. A change of this kind naturally influences the quality of the news product.

Table 4.2 clearly indicates a trend towards chain-owned newspapers across Canada. Not only has the number of dailies decreased but the number of group-controlled newspapers has increased by 11.8 percent over seventeen years.[7] In seven of the ten provinces, the percentage of chain-operated dailies grew between 1970 and 1987. Only New Brunswick showed a net decrease in group ownership. The decrease reflects the introduction of two independent French-language dailies, but all of the English-language dailies are owned by the Irving Group. The Manitoba figures are also misleading. When Southam Inc. closed down its Winnipeg *Tribune* in August 1980, it left Thomson's Winnipeg *Free Press* as the only chain-owned daily in the province. (The Peladeau Group has since introduced a francophone newspaper in Manitoba.) Since the *Free Press* controls 80.2 percent of the total provincial circulation, the effect has been reduced rather than enhanced diversity.

The data in table 4.3 provide an even more striking illustration of the trend towards concentrated ownership. The table reveals that in March 1987, all but 19.6 percent of Canada's newspaper circulation was

Table 4.2

Trend towards group ownership in dailies, 1970–1987

	1970		1980		1987	
	titles	group-owned	titles	group-owned	titles	group-owned
British Columbia	18	83.3	19	94.7	17	100.0
Alberta	7	85.7	9	88.9	9	88.9
Saskatchewan	4	100.0	5	100.0	4	100.0
Manitoba	7	28.6	7	14.3	7	28.6
Ontario	48	62.5	46	73.9	43	83.7
Quebec	14	64.3	11	81.8	11	81.8
New Brunswick	6	83.3	6	83.3	6	66.7
Nova Scotia	6	33.3	7	42.8	7	42.8
Prince Edward Island	3	66.7	3	100.0	3	100.0
Newfoundland	3	66.7	3	66.7	2	100.0
Yukon Territory	0	—	1	—	1	—
Northwest Territories	0	—	0	—	0	—
Canada	116	67.4	117	74.6	110	79.2

Sources: Canada, Special Senate Committee on Mass Media 1970, 17, 20; Canada, Royal Commission on Newspapers 1981, 6–11; and Audit Bureau of Circulation FAS/FAX, March 1987.

controlled by chains. Of the remainder, the *Toronto Star*, Canada's largest independent newspaper, accounts for 9.9 percent, leaving just 9.7 percent of circulation to be shared among the other twenty-one independents. The *Toronto Star* itself is part of the Torstar conglomerate, which has many other media interests in addition to its single newspaper.

Table 4.3

Ownership of daily newspapers, March 1987

Owner	Number of titles	Circulation (as a percentage of the total)
Thomson Newspapers Ltd.	39	20.1
Southam Inc.	15	27.1
Sterling Newspapers Ltd.	9	0.8
Irving Group	4	2.5
Les Publications J.T.C. Inc.	4	5.8
Toronto Sun Publishing Corp.	3	8.3
Bowes Publishers Ltd.	3	0.4
Peladeau Group	3	8.6
St. Catharines Standard Ltd.	3	0.9
Société Media Québec	3	3.5
Armadale Co. Ltd.	2	2.4
Torstar Corp.	1	9.9
Independents	21	9.7
Total	110	100.00

Source: Audit Bureau of Circulation FAS/FAX, March 1987.

The same circulation figures broken down by province reveal that nine of the ten provinces are dominated by chains (see table 4.4). In all but one of these—Ontario—chains control over 85 percent of the daily circulation. Only in Nova Scotia do independents still retain the largest share of circulation.

Table 4.4

Circulation by province, 1987
(as a percentage of total provincial circulation)

Province	Independents	Chains	Owners	Share
British Columbia	0.0	100.0	Southam Inc.	75.0
			Thomson Newspapers Ltd.	19.3
			Sterling Newspapers Ltd.	5.7
Alberta	4.1	95.9	Southam Inc.	57.8
			Toronto Sun Publishing Corp.	30.6
			Thomson Newspapers Ltd.	4.7
			Bowes Publishers Ltd.	2.8
Saskatchewan	0.0	100.0	Armadale Co. Ltd.	87.5
			Thomson Newspapers Ltd.	12.5
Manitoba	7.5	92.5	Thomson Newspapers Ltd.	80.2
			Peladeau Group	12.3
Ontario	34.4	65.6	Thomson Newspapers Ltd.	27.4
			Southam Inc.	21.9
			Toronto Sun Publishing Corp.	12.2
			St. Catharines Standard	2.2
			Société Media Québec	1.7
			Bowes Publishers Ltd.	0.2
Quebec	3.1	96.8	Peladeau Group	37.5
			Les Publications J.T.C. Inc.	28.1
			Southam Inc.	18.0
			Société Media Québec	13.2
New Brunswick	12.3	87.7	Irving Group	87.7
Nova Scotia	75.9	24.1	Thomson Newspapers Ltd.	24.1
Prince Edward Island	0.0	100.0	Thomson Newspapers Ltd.	67.0
			Sterling Newspapers Ltd.	33.0
Newfoundland	0.0	100.0	Thomson Newspapers Ltd.	100.0

Source: Audit Bureau of Circulation FAS/FAX, March 1987.

Revenues and costs

All newspaper undertakings are concerned, to varying degrees, with their profit margins. They all acknowledge that the newspaper industry is among the largest and most profitable in the nation (Canada, Royal Commission on Newspapers 1981, 84). In its business function, the industry really serves two markets — it delivers news and information to its readers and readers to its advertisers. To maintain its profitability it must serve both groups but critics argue that the balance has shifted in favour of the advertisers.

Circulation revenues, as a proportion of total revenues, have declined steadily over the past several decades. They currently account for about 20 percent. The purchase price of a daily newspaper has remained artificially low in order to compete with the "free" electronic media. Newspapers must ensure enough readers to satisfy the demands of their advertisers, who contribute the remaining 80 percent of the newspaper industry's total revenues.

Given its large financial contribution, it is not surprising that advertising influences the format and content of newspapers. Most dailies try to maintain a three-to-two ratio of advertising to non-advertising, or editorial, content. As the amount of advertising increases, therefore, so does the size of the news hole (the space allotted for editorial content), and the overall size of the paper. It is in this way that advertising most overtly affects the editorial function, yet advertisers possess a more subtle but powerful form of influence. Publishers know that their papers must convey the appropriate style and tone to attract and maintain advertising accounts that might otherwise be placed with competing papers or competing media.

Advertisers can also have a substantial impact on the business side of the newspaper industry. For example, many large retailers only place their advertisements in the paper with the largest circulation in the community, which weakens the position of smaller competitors. Such a practice could force small papers to shut down, reducing competition even further.

A newspaper's costs are divided among several categories. Manufacturing or production costs and labour costs in the production, editorial, and administrative departments account for the vast majority of a paper's expenditures. Circulation and distribution, advertising and marketing, capital spending, and the editorial function (collecting the news and other non-advertising content) share the remainder. Although introducing computerized technology and acquiring other newspapers initially stretch capital budgets, over time they tend to reduce overall costs and increase net profits.

The tabloids are organized fiscally in much the same manner as their broadsheet counterparts, but with some significant differences. They receive a considerably larger proportion of their revenues from circulation (about 32 percent) and a correspondingly smaller proportion from advertising (68 percent). Higher manufacturing costs are offset by large savings in circulation and distribution expenses because the tabloids rely less on home delivery and more on newsbox or newsstand purchases. In general, they are more profitable than the traditional broadsheets (Canada, Royal Commission on Newspapers 1981, 80–81).

The Royal Commission on Newspapers devoted part of its investigation to an extensive study of the economic environment of the newspaper industry. Economic conditions had often been blamed for newspaper closures, chain purchases, and deterring the entry of new papers into the market. The Commission concluded, however, that the newspaper industry was earning relatively good profits. In fact, "while the major newspaper owners were telling us at our public hearings that their chief concern was 'survival,' our financial research was telling us that they were surviving quite nicely. For its owners, the Canadian newspaper industry is, so to speak, the Queen Elizabeth of life rafts" (Canada, Royal Commission on Newspapers 1981, 84–85). The finding makes one ask whether concentration has been necessary for the survival of newspapers or whether it merely reflects the international takeover mania that appears to be affecting other business enterprises as well.

Wire services: Bulk news providers

Increased concentration in the newspaper industry is not limited to chain ownership. International and domestic wire services, sometimes referred to as press associations or news services, supply most of the non-local news and information for most mass media. The wire services gather, package, and distribute news to their subscribers for a fee. By pooling their resources, subscribers gain access to more information than would be possible if each acted independently, and at much lower costs. The disadvantage of this practice, from the public's perspective, is that most of the news they receive emanates from one source and therefore lacks a healthy diversity of opinion.

Five international wire services provide the bulk of international news: Associated Press (AP) and United Press International (UPI), both based in the United States; Reuter, the British news service; Agence France Press (AFP) in France; and Telegrafnoye Agentstvo Sovietskovo Soyuza (TASS), the official news agency of the Soviet Union. Collectively, these five dwarf all other news agencies in terms of money, staff, and technology.

In Canada, the Canadian Press/La Presse Canadienne (CP/PC) dominates news collection in both English and French. It provides most of the domestic news carried by the Canadian media and it is doubtful that Canadian newspapers could survive without it or an equivalent service. According to the Special Senate Committee on Mass Media (1970, 229), "Canadian Press pervades the news scene so completely that it has become endowed with a kind of semi-official status as an arm of the public service."

The history of the CP/PC began eighty years ago in Winnipeg, when three local papers launched a battle to break up the monopoly held by the Canadian Pacific Railway (CPR) to distribute Associated Press reports from the United States in Canada. In 1907, the CPR doubled the price of delivering the AP service to the Winnipeg papers. The newspapers responded by creating their own news co-operative, Western Associated Press (WAP), to buy the services of United Press, Publishers' Press, and Hearst News Services. The CPR retaliated by demanding higher rates to carry these services over its telegraph lines. A legal and political battle ensued and eventually the railway was forced to relinquish its AP contract. Canadian Press Ltd. was created in 1911 to take over the distribution of the AP service in Canada and six years later began its own news-gathering service, opening bureaus across the country. The agency was subsidized by an annual grant from the federal government until 1922, when its members took on full responsibility for its financial operation. The French service began in 1951.

The Canadian Press currently operates as a news co-operative. Fees are levied on the basis of each member's circulation figures and any extra services received. All members are expected to supply local news, which the agency then selects, condenses, and distributes to other members, a process that accounts for about 60 percent of the domestic output. In addition, it employs its own reporters to gather news independently of its members.

Although CP/PC staff make the day-to-day newsroom decisions, the publishers of the daily newspapers determine budgetary guidelines and a general philosophy for the enterprise. The Canadian Press management is supervised by a six-person executive board which meets four times a year and reports to the nineteen-person board of directors, which meets semi-annually. This board, in turn, reports to an annual meeting of the members. Proposals made by the executive board are rarely rejected by the membership.

More than half of the agency's members are publishers representing the Southam and Thomson chains, while another quarter belong to the smaller newspaper groups. In a review of Canadian news services, Carman Cumming, Mario Cardinal, and Peter Johansen (1981, 21–28) examined the influence of chain ownership on the CP/PC. They noted that traditionally the members have tried to balance group and regional representation on the executive board and board of directors. In sheer numbers alone, however, the Southam and Thomson groups operating as a bloc have a veto over all CP/PC decisions. Although the chains have rarely used this option, the membership is aware that it exists. Members are also aware that the two chains contribute the bulk of financial support to CP/PC and that this, too, gives them significant influence in its operations. On the basis of their investigation of CP/PC operations from 1911 to 1980, Cumming, Cardinal, and Johansen conclude, however, that in general the chains have not exerted undue influence on the agency's management.

That is not to say that conflict is unknown. Journalists and CP/PC members have directed their major criticisms at Thomson Newspapers Ltd. (Canada, Royal Commission on Newspapers 1981, 119–33). Although the Thomson publishers are relatively inactive in CP/PC committees, there is a belief among members that the Thomson chain's penny-pinching attitude lowers the quality of its editorial contribution to the CP/PC news pool. Thomson publishers argue in return that CP/PC does not exploit their contributions since most of their papers are situated in small communities in which CP/PC has little or no interest.

The uneven quality of its news items and its urban bias are only two of the criticisms levelled against CP/PC. The Royal Commission on Newspapers and some CP/PC members have charged that the agency is dominated by central Canadian interests. Its English bureau is headquartered in Toronto and its French service in Montreal; it has closed some regional bureaus, leaving large areas of the country uncovered; and it has never had a northern Canadian correspondent.

In addition, both the Davey Committee and the Kent Commission identified significant weaknesses in the agency's news coverage. First, it pays slavish attention to "hard" news at the expense of culture, the arts, and the slow processes of social change, and favours discrete, easily identifiable news stories over original and investigative reporting. The result is a "drab uniformity of newspaper reading across the country" (Canada, Special Senate Committee 1970, 231).

Second, the Kent Commission (Canada, Royal Commission on Newspapers 1981, 120) termed the inadequacy of the Canadian Press French-language service "an embarrassment." The French service translates English-language items collected from across the country and reports events in Quebec for the French-language papers. It neither employs any Québécois reporters outside Quebec to report Canadian news from a Quebec perspective, nor provides the perspective of Quebec to the rest of Canada. The CP/PC therefore fails to meet the needs of a bilingual country.

Finally, both investigative committees criticized the quantity and quality of the agency's foreign news coverage. It simply does not have a sufficient number of foreign correspondents. Although they acknowledged the expense involved in achieving a distinctively Canadian viewpoint in international news and analysis, both committees believed that CP/PC could and should do a better job of "reporting the world scene as *Canadians speaking to Canadians*" (Canada, Special Senate Committee 1970, 233).

The Canadian Press is nevertheless a valuable Canadian news asset and most of its shortcomings could be overcome with increased funding and the support of its members. The Royal Commission on Newspapers (1981, 120) found that "CP does an expert, efficient, and conscientious job of covering the news *within the limits of its budget and its mandate*" [emphasis added].

Although there are other services in Canada, none has the scope of CP/PC.[8] Broadcast News Limited (BN), a subsidiary of Canadian Press, provides most of the news to private Canadian broadcasters, in both English and French. United Press Canada (UPC), a private company whose majority shareholder is the Toronto Sun Publishing Corp., provides national and regional coverage to supplement the service of United Press International, its original parent company.

The Southam and Thomson chains both operate news services of their own. Southam News provides background and interpretative pieces for the most part, to supplement CP/PC's basic coverage, and is considered to be of high quality. Thomson News Services focusses more on legislative news with local appeal, staff-written columns, and bulk purchase of syndicated feature columns. (Feature columns appear regularly, cover a given field, such as politics or household hints, and are written by an identified individual.)   There are also two feature syndicates, one operated by the Torstar Corp. (*Toronto Star* Syndicate) and another by the Toronto Sun Publishing Corp. (Canada Wide Feature Service). They not only generate news and entertainment features themselves, but also act as agents for foreign feature services.

Given the specialization of these other services, only UPC currently represents a potential competitor for CP/PC. During the last several years, however, it has suffered a number of setbacks. Numerous newspaper closings during the 1970s and early 1980s and the deteriorating position of UPI have encouraged UPC to concentrate on providing broadcast news services, leaving CP/PC relatively unchallenged in the print sector. UPI has had a number of changes in senior management and ownership that have contributed to difficulties in attracting new clients.

The future of the newspaper

Predicting the future is a risky business generally and no less so in the newspaper industry. Some futurists believe that the newspaper, as we know it, will be replaced by an electronic version by the year 2000. Although it is certainly true that technological innovation is the driving force behind change in the industry, Jon Udell (1980, 191) points out that more sophisticated management techniques and better-trained employees will also play an essential role in the future direction of the newspaper industry.

Three problems are inducing modern newspaper undertakings to change. A general alteration in reading habits has affected the industry. People today do not set aside as much time to read the newspaper as they did in the past. When they do pick one up, they tend to be highly selective, reading only for the sorts of news not readily available from other media. The shift towards "consumer sovereignty" (Smith 1980, 22) means that the newspaper must gear its content to the specialized interests of its readers or risk losing them to other media. Second, the cost of raw materials poses a serious problem. Modern newspapers consume vast amounts of newsprint and ink (a petroleum-based product); the world's supply of both products is shrinking and costs have skyrocketed. Alternatives must be found if the newspaper is to remain affordable and the industry competitive. Third, the industry's most nagging problem is its delivery system. Within a sector so technologically advanced in so many respects, it is somewhat ironic that newspapers are still delivered by hand by ten- to fourteen-year-old neighbourhood carriers. In many cases, this has proven unsatisfactory, especially for newspapers that have switched from evening to morning editions. Hiring adult carriers as a response to the problem is a growing trend. Yet the industry is still dependent on carriers, the postal service, or taxis to get its product to its consumers. Not only are these methods expensive, but they also tend to be unreliable. In an industry that produces such a perishable commodity, a prompt, efficient, and reliable delivery system is vital to its survival.

A range of new technologies can help to meet challenges to the industry by increasing efficiency and reducing costs at all stages. Video display terminals and other computerized applications such as data bases enable staff to gather and compose content and prepare it for production in less time and in a more integrated fashion. The production process itself is cleaner and safer, and results in a higher quality product. New techniques in recycling and paper production may help to offset the high cost of paper. In combination, these innovations can increase the industry's control over the finished product.

The potential impact of technology on the newspaper industry's delivery system sparks the most interest and debate. It is now technologically possible to transfer the contents of a newspaper electronically from computers in the newspaper office to receivers in subscribers' homes. Teletext is the generic term for electronic newspaper (ENP) technology and covers "any method which electronically transmits directly to home terminals information traditionally carried in newspapers" (Ahlhauser 1978, 26).

Although there are no plans to produce an electronic newspaper in Canada in the near future, the groundwork for electronic publishing is being laid. Info Globe, a subsidiary of Thomson Newspapers Ltd., provides a computerized archive for the *Globe and Mail*. It is, however, a much less ambitious venture than Infomart, which is involved in virtually every aspect of electronic publishing. Owned jointly by Torstar Corp. and Southam Inc., Infomart has a virtual monopoly on supplying videotex systems, or teletext, to business and government and is preparing to enter the consumer mass market when the opportunity presents itself.

The Telidon system is another example of electronic publishing. It was developed with the encouragement of the federal Department of Communications, and combined television, computers, and central data bases to allow interactive transmission and display of information. The federal government, recognizing the potential for creating thousands of jobs, committed millions of dollars to the experiment. Yet Telidon failed to capture a meaningful share of the merging interactive electronic data base market. Critics agree that it was too costly—the Cadillac of interactive systems—at a time when consumers were looking for cheaper ways of gaining access to information.

The ENP undoubtedly has a number of advantages. It eliminates problems with raw materials, printing, and delivery and provides fast, on-demand access to a broad variety of information, including news, features, sports scores, weather reports, travel information, entertainment activities, financial news, consumer information, community bulletin boards, and teleshopping (McPhail 1983). As Kenneth Edwards (1980, 219) explains, "Teletext is no gadget. It is a tool for instant dissemination of any information people want to know about." The ENP also has several drawbacks. New hardware and software will eventually overcome its technical limitations but other questions cannot be resolved without much discussion.

The ENP blurs the distinction between print and electronic media and opens the door to myriads of questions about the appropriate roles of the newspapers, broadcasters, and cable operators. Who will decide the content? Who will transmit the messages? Will television sets or computers be used to receive the messages? Will the number of news sources be further reduced?

What role will government play in regulating the new service? Should it guarantee access to the system to anyone who has something to say? Should it treat the ENP as either a print medium or an electronic medium and then regulate it accordingly? Will the courts have to decide which medium teletext and other data services are closest to? International teletext services raise a number of further questions about sovereignty and privacy. Who will control the data? What will it be used for? By whom? Will personal records such as health or financial data be available through these data bases?

Finally, who will finance the system? How can advertisers be encouraged to support the ENP when they might just as well have a channel of their own? Should those who supply content and those who carry it share equally in the costs and profits? What sort of rate structure would be equitable? The ENP will be very expensive to operate and install in homes. What happens to the poor and disadvantaged who will be shut out? Does government have an obligation to subsidize the system so that it will be more affordable for all Canadians?

These and other pressing questions are yet to be resolved. Although most newspaper publishers argue that it will be a very long time before an ENP can compete effectively with the low cost and convenience of traditional newspapers (Canada, Royal Commission on Newspapers 1981, 194–95), others are less certain. They believe that we are undergoing a computer-based information revolution that will transform society (Smith 1980, 3). As a society, we must begin to address these issues to develop appropriate strategies.

The Canadian magazine industry

Canadian magazines have a special cultural significance, as John Van de Kamer (1986, B10) explains:

> They offer Canadians an experience that just isn't available through television, radio or newspapers. They play a vital— and sometimes lonely—role in defining who we are and in building our social fabric the way John A. Macdonald's railway built our economic fabric a century ago. Canadian magazines, written by Canadians for Canadians, aren't just a sweet sentimental idea or a few insert paragraphs on world opinion. I believe they're an invaluable currency, a natural resource but not a renewable one. What's more germane, Canadians actually buy Canadian magazines—in astonishing numbers.

Even so, the domestic magazine industry represents the poor cousin of Canada's print media family when compared with the success and profitability of newspapers. Although *Saturday Night*, *Maclean's*, and *Chatelaine* are venerable Canadian institutions, their successes are the exceptions. A number of economic handicaps have combined to make the history of the Canadian magazine industry a troubled one.

The remainder of the chapter deals primarily with consumer magazines: general interest magazines and magazines with specific subject material that are generally available to the public. Magazines by and for specific groups such as trade unions, medical associations, and so on face challenges similar to those of consumer magazines but are less susceptible to some of the problems because they have a more stable subscriber base.

Consumer magazines are very dependent on the advertising revenue that they generate. Start-up, production, and distribution costs for periodicals are high and only a small percentage is recoverable from subscription and newsstand sales. Yet the relatively small, dispersed Canadian market, the proximity of the United States and its thriving magazine industry, and intense competition from other media such as radio, television, and newspapers combine to make it very difficult for popular, general interest magazines in Canada to attract sufficient advertising revenue:

> Even when a Canadian magazine is genuinely successful in terms of public appeal, it still finds it difficult to make a substantial amount of money .... So reader acceptance—presumably proof of the skills of a magazine's editors, writers and artists—does not guarantee success in Canada. Success can come only when national advertisers feel there is some advantage in spending considerable money in that magazine (Walker 1970, 217).

Early in the history of the Canadian periodical industry, Confederation provided a stimulus by creating a new, national readership but the market was still too small and "precarious and short-lived ventures were the rule" (Litvak and Maule 1974, 17). Attempts at legislation to protect Canadian magazines from foreign competition were coloured by "a mixture of arguments for and against economic protectionism and cultural nationalism, flavored with views about freedom of access to information and expressions of anti-Americanism" (Litvak and Maule 1974, 34). Because of these debates, legislation never provided the degree of protection necessary. Successive governments failed to take a strong stand on the value of the content of domestic magazines because it would mean limiting access to foreign publications, an unacceptable option. The industry was therefore left primarily to its own devices.

By the mid-1950s, conditions had deterioriated to such an extent that there were grave concerns about the survival of the domestic periodical industry. Most Canadian general interest magazines had proven to be financial disasters, together managing to secure only 20 percent of the domestic market (Litvak and Maule 1974, 30–31). Between 1920 and 1960 more than two hundred Canadian consumer magazines had been discontinued or absorbed by others (Ruddy 1971, 120). As a response to the worsening situation, the federal government established the Royal Commission on Publications in 1960, chaired by Grattan O'Leary.

The Commission's report (1961) examined two issues: the threat posed to Canadian culture by foreign periodicals; and the competitive advantages enjoyed by these periodicals. *Time* and *Reader's Digest* were found to be the greatest challenges to the Canadian industry; between them they controlled 52 percent of Canadian magazine advertising revenue (Walker 1970, 213). They were in a very enviable position, as Arnold Edinborough (1962, 27) explained: "*Time* and *Reader's Digest* . . . dump their editorial content into Canada and then solicit advertising to keep the news pages apart. Since their editorial costs have already been paid in the United States, they can run a highly efficient and well staffed advertising department, and can offer . . . deals to big international advertisers."

After identifying the cost and revenue problems of the industry, the Commission made several recommendations to overcome them. The suggestion that had the greatest impact was for the federal government to amend the Income Tax Act to exclude deductions for expenditures on advertising in non-Canadian periodicals, when the advertising was directly aimed at the Canadian audience. The measure was designed to discourage Canadian companies from advertising in foreign, predominantly American, periodicals. It was also hoped that the same companies would re-invest their advertising dollars in the domestic magazine industry.

It was 1966 before Bill C-58 to amend the Income Tax Act was implemented. *Time* and *Reader's Digest* then called on the American government to intervene on their behalf. Since both were publishing Canadian editions, they were exempted from the terms of amendment and Bill C-58 failed to have the desired effect. In fact, by 1970, *Time* and *Reader's Digest* had increased their share of Canadian magazine advertising revenue to 56 percent (Walker 1970, 213).

By 1976, the federal government recognized that its decade-old legislation had failed. It introduced an amendment to eliminate the privileged position of *Time* and *Reader's Digest*. Bill C-58 (1976) declared that 80 percent of the content of the Canadian editions of foreign periodicals must be different from the original in order for advertisers to qualify for tax deductions. As a result, *Time* decided to cease publication of *Time Canada*, but *Reader's Digest* convinced the government that its Canadian edition would be sufficiently different to qualify under the new law.

Bill C-58, in combination with postal subsidies that allow low-cost distribution to subscribers,[9] appears to have achieved its purpose: "C-58 was a law that worked. In Canada, where three out of every four magazines are made in America and where three out of every four television programs are made in America, C-58 has given Canadian publishers a precious freedom: [t]he freedom to compete on fair terms on our own ground" (Van de Kamer 1986, B10). As table 4.5 indicates, there are now more than five thousand magazines published in Canada, producing more than $250 million in annual revenues and covering a broad range of interests. About 30 percent of these titles are French-language magazines. These dominate the Quebec market, accounting for 70 percent of total circulation in the province. Canadian consumer magazines control about 60 percent of the total subscription sales market, up from 37 percent in 1971 (Canada, Department of Communications 1987, 36). Although newsstand sales are still dominated by foreign periodicals, which have a greater number of titles, higher circulation, and higher revenues, table 4.6 illustrates the success achieved by domestic publications. Fully 70 percent of Canada's bestsellers are Canadian.

Table 4.5

Canadian magazines, 1987

Business	2 150
Consumer	1 150
Artistic and literary	650
Religious	600
Scholarly and educational	500
Total	5 050

Source: Canada, Department of Communications 1987, Canadian cultural industries: Vital links, *35, Ottawa: Supply and Services.*

Despite the current success of the Canadian magazine industry, the Federal Cultural Policy Review Committee (1982, 223) notes that challenges remain: "A [Canadian] magazine does not survive just because readers like it. It must also face and overcome at least three orders of problems: capital shortages, distribution difficulties and foreign competition." The Department of Communications (1987, 38) concurs. Although the industry today is "generally healthy, both culturally and economically," it will "continue to require supportive government policies to sustain that health." Canadian publishers and supporters of the domestic magazine industry are of course aware of this, and are suspicious of the Canada–U.S. Free Trade Agreement on precisely these grounds. According to the terms of the FTA, Bill C-58 remains intact for the present, but the postal subsidies currently directed at Canadian publications must either be extended within ten years to American magazines printed in Canada, or removed altogether. The federal government's subsidy for second-class postage has amounted to about $240 million per year but the 1989 budget proposed to cut that figure by $10 million the first year and $45 million the year after that. The long-term effect is yet to be determined.

The federal government supports this move because the American magazines printed in this country provide jobs for Canadians. It argues, moreover, that the change will involve only a few magazines and will therefore not have a negative impact on the Canadian magazine publishing industry (Ottawa *Citizen* 1987, B8). The Canadian Periodical Publishers' Association, however, is not convinced. It believes that the new policy will hurt Canadian publishers in at least three ways: postal costs for Canadian magazines will rise; the present high postal costs for American magazines will be reduced, encouraging new subscription drives; and American magazines might be tempted to solicit more Canadian advertising. Any of these developments would threaten the stability of the domestic industry (*Globe and Mail* 1987, B4).

As with most aspects of the FTA, it will be a few years before the consequences come to be recognized but all parties do appear to agree on the need for continued government support of the domestic periodical publishing industry. Regardless of how successful a Canadian magazine is in the domestic popular market, economies of scale make it virtually impossible for it to compete effectively against its American competitors.

Table 4.6

Canada's twenty largest periodicals based on circulation in 1988

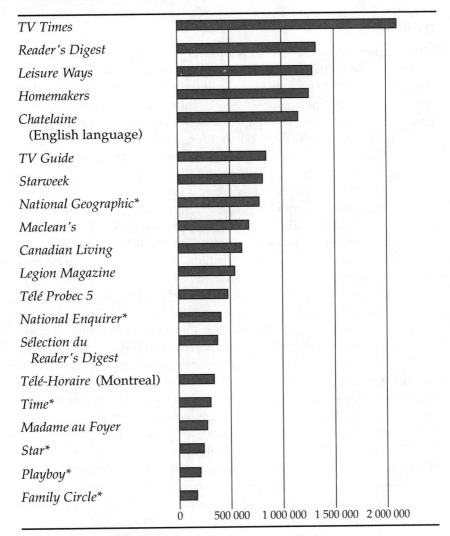

Note: * refers to American magazines.

Source: *Canadian Media Directors' Council Member Agencies*, The Canadian Media Directors'
Council media digest 1988/89, *47-55 (Published by* Marketing *)*.

This irony is one that permeates the Canadian cultural industries sector. It will be examined again in the context of Canadian broadcasting in chapters 6 to 8.

Summary

This chapter reviewed the development of newspapers in Canada. Originally functioning as agents of the Crown, newspapers slowly changed direction to become servants of partisan political interests. Massive economic rationalization in the twentieth century forced another philosophical change as newspapers sought ever larger audiences. They broadened their perspective and took on a mantle of objectivity and balance. Many critics question whether the philosophical position of the newspaper industry reflects actual practice, however.

The chapter also examined the current performance of the Canadian newspaper industry. Several economic factors have encouraged a move towards chain, cross-media, and conglomerate ownership. Both the Special Senate Committee on the Mass Media and the Royal Commission on Newspapers examined present ownership patterns and warned that they have implications for the quality and diversity of news.

Increasing homogenization of newspaper reporting in Canada is also attributable in part to the growing influence of wire services. The Canadian Press/La Presse Canadienne, Canada's main domestic news service, was created in 1911. As a co-operative of Canadian newspapers, CP/PC has come to hold a dominant position within the Canadian news environment but while it does a commendable job in making news available to newspapers across the country, it does suffer from a number of weaknesses. Its French-language service, coverage of Canada's North, and number of foreign correspondents are all inadequate.

The future of the newspaper industry was discussed as well. The industry faces increasing challenges, some of which may eventually be met by the electronic newspaper. The technology for electronic news delivery is available now but issues such as regulation, access, and cost need to be addressed before the electronic newspaper becomes a reality.

Finally, the chapter examined another sector within the Canadian print media — magazines. Magazines face significantly greater economic challenges than newspapers do. High distribution costs and intensive foreign competition make the industry a particularly vulnerable one. As a result of Bill C-58, the last fifteen years have witnessed a resurgence in the domestic magazine industry but analysts are concerned that the FTA will undermine recent successes.

The next chapter discusses news content. News is defined and its characteristics detailed. The primary issues facing the Canadian newspaper industry are then examined again, this time in terms of their consequences for content.

Notes

1. In 1928, German scholar Otto Groth identified five criteria that describe the modern newspaper. It must be (1) published periodically; (2) mechanically reproduced; (3) variable in content; (4) timely, with some continuity of organization; and (5) accessible to anyone who can pay the price (in Bittner 1985, 383).

2. The rising popularity of video cassette recorders is due, in part, to the flexibility that they offer media users. VCRs make it possible for audience members to time-shift—to save television programming to view at their convenience—thereby enhancing the reviewability of television as a mass medium.

3. Indicative of the fierce competition for the Toronto market during the mid-1980s was the circulation "war" between the *Toronto Star* and the *Globe and Mail*. The *Star* started an all-day edition, publishing new editions morning, afternoon, and evening, and the *Globe and Mail* published an early evening edition. Both costs and distribution problems caused cutbacks in these experiments, but they demonstrate the industry's desire to increase circulation and weaken the position of competitors.

4. The *Globe and Mail* transmits its contents by satellite to receivers in various Canadian cities where the paper is printed and distributed to surrounding localities.

5. These trends have led to a geographic concentration of head offices as well. The Royal Commission on Newspapers (1981, 13) reported that corporations controlling 94 percent of the French-language circulation are head-quartered in Montreal, and even more astounding, 83 percent of English-language circulation is controlled from Toronto. It is not surprising, therefore, that Canada's newspaper industry has a centralist bias.

6. Studies of media ownership have also been undertaken by individual scholars. The work of Porter (1965), Clement (1975), and Newman (1975) are examples.

7. The *Financial Post*, under its new owner the Toronto Sun Publishing Corp., became a daily newspaper in tabloid form in 1988. While it adds to the Canadian repertoire of dailies and operates in direct competition with the *Globe and Mail's Report on Business* for circulation and advertising, it is another example of the trend towards concentrated ownership based upon economic principles.

8. Canadian newspapers also purchase news from a variety of American sources, including the *New York Times, Los Angeles Times, Washington Post,* Knight-Ridder, and the *Christian Science Monitor.*

9. As of May 1989, Canadian publishers pay 5.5 to 5.7 cents a copy to mail an average-sized magazine, compared to 7.1 to 7.4 cents for foreign magazines printed and mailed in Canada and 43.5 cents for magazines printed outside Canada but shipped here to be mailed.

References

Audit Bureau of Circulation FAS/FAX. 1987. March.

Ahlhauser, J.W. 1978. Teletext—the electronic newspaper: Four British systems and U.S. editors' assessment of implications. Ph.D. diss., Indiana University.

Bittner, J.R. 1985. *Fundamentals of communication.* Englewood Cliffs: Prentice-Hall.

Canada. Department of Communications. 1987. *Canada's cultural industries: Vital links.* Ottawa: Supply and Services.

Canada. Federal Cultural Policy Review Committee. 1982. *Report.* Ottawa: Queen's Printer.

Canada. Royal Commission on Newspapers. 1981. *Report.* Ottawa: Supply and Services.

Canada. Royal Commission on Publications. 1961. *Report.* Ottawa: Queen's Printer.

Canada. Special Senate Committee on Mass Media. 1970. *The uncertain mirror.* Vol. 1 of *Report.* Ottawa: Supply and Services.

Canadian Media Directors' Council Member Agencies. 1989. *Canadian Media Directors' Council media digest 1988/89,* 47–55. *Marketing.*

Clement, W. 1975. *The Canadian corporate elite: An analysis of economic power.* Toronto: McClelland and Stewart.

Cumming, C., M. Cardinal, and P. Johansen. 1981. *Canadian news services.* Vol. 6 of *Royal commission on newspapers research publications.* Ottawa: Supply and Services.

Edinborough, A. 1962. The press. In *Mass media in Canada,* ed. J.A. Irving, 15–28. Toronto: McGraw-Hill Ryerson.

Edwards, K. 1980. Information without limit electronically. In *Readings in mass communication,* ed. M. Emery and T.C. Smythe, 200–16. Dubuque: Brown.

Financial Post. 1988. MH president predicts year of strong but slower gains. 12 January, p. 15.

Globe and Mail. 1987. Cultural sector in turmoil, torn between hope and despair. 6 October, p. B4.

Litvak, I., and C. Maule. 1974. *Cultural sovereignty: The "Time" and "Reader's Digest" case in Canada.* New York: Praeger.

McPhail, T.L. 1983. The future of Canadian communications. In *Communications in Canadian society,* ed. B.D. Singer, 73–82. Don Mills: Addison-Wesley.

Marketing. 1988. Daily newspapers. 14 November, p. 30.

Newman, P.C. 1975. *The Canadian establishment.* Vol. 1. Toronto: McClelland and Stewart.

Ottawa *Citizen.* 1987. Free-trade deal does little harm to cultural sovereignty. 10 October, p. B8.

Porter, J. 1965. *The vertical mosaic.* Toronto: University of Toronto.

Ruddy, J. 1971. Magazines: Of patriotism and profit. In *A media mosaic: Canadian communications through a critical eye,* ed. W. McDayter, 112–20. Toronto: Holt, Rinehart and Winston.

Rutherford, P. 1978. *The making of the Canadian media.* Toronto: McGraw-Hill Ryerson.

Smith, A. 1980. *Goodbye Gutenberg: The newspaper revolution of the 1980s.* New York: Oxford.

Udell, J.G. 1980. The newspaper of the next decade. In *Readings in mass communication*, ed. M. Emery and T.C. Smythe, 191-202. Dubuque: Brown.

Van de Kamer, J. 1986. Canadian publishing industry must retain its identity and independence. *Toronto Star*. 26 May, p. B10.

Walker, D. 1970. Magazines. In *Good, bad, or simply inevitable?* Vol. 3 of *Report*. Research Studies for the Special Senate Committee on the Mass Media, 209–40. Ottawa: Queen's Printer.

THE CONCEPT OF NEWS:
WHAT ARE THE ISSUES?

*C*hapter 4 concentrated on the structure, function, and development of the print media. Although non-advertising or editorial content was mentioned, the chapter did not discuss the concept of news. All media, to varying degrees, inform their audiences and provide feedback to political, economic, social, and cultural decision makers, but newspapers are the most committed to the news function; news is their central ingredient. This chapter examines news—its definitions and functions, the manner in which it is gathered and selected, and the roles of gatekeepers and agenda-setting. In the process, the chapter explores the current issues and public policy concerns that surround the news media.

What is news?

Any study of news must overcome a basic conceptual hurdle—defining what constitutes "news" and "newsworthiness." There is, in fact, a range of definitions, each of which focusses on a different aspect of news.

Les Brown (1971, 223) defines news by describing its intent: "The purpose of news is not to preserve the status quo but to document change. News is subhistory." Gans (1979, 284), on the other hand, turns to news coverage to arrive at his definition: "News is about the economic, political, social and cultural hierarchies we call nation and society. For the most part, the news reports on those at or near the top of the hierarchies and on those . . . at the bottom who threaten them, to an audience, most of whom are located in the vast middle range . . . . " Others concentrate on value systems. Gertrude Robinson (1981, 118) argues that news is determined by the values inherent in society: "A theory of news values must be couched in economic, political and ideological terms . . . . The values guiding news selection . . . [are] an integral part of the particular socio-economic system in which . . . [the reporter] carries out his [or her] work."

Although it is difficult to define news categorically, it is possible to identify its attributes, the qualities that characterize newsworthiness (McQuail 1983, 139–40):

1. News is timely. It is about recent events.

2. News is perishable. Its value as a commodity relates to its immediacy.

3. News is unsystematic. It deals with discrete, unrelated events.

4. News is concerned with the unusual or unexpected. It covers the unique or the offbeat.

5. News is predictable. Within the realm of the unusual, news centres on those types of events that consistently reappear: conflict, accidents, prominent personalities, politics, and so on.

6. News has relative value for its audience. Its impact depends upon the physical or psychological proximity of the audience to the event.

These six characteristics are generally applicable to all news carried by all media, but events that possess all these qualities must still be selected for coverage before they become "news."

News selection

Each day, the *New York Times* proudly prints its motto on its masthead: "All the News That's Fit to Print." A quick glance through the paper, however, will alert anyone to the exaggerated nature of the newspaper's claim (especially a Canadian, who would be hard pressed to find any coverage about Canada). According to Don Pember (1974, 114), a more accurate motto might be "All the News That Fits, We Print."

Those responsible for selecting the events to be covered and the information to be transmitted by the media are known as gatekeepers. The term gatekeeper was defined earlier as "any person or formally organized group directly involved in the relay of information from one individual to another through the use of a mass medium" (Bittner 1977, 10). All media institutions have many gatekeepers, who are potentially very powerful. They can block, limit, expand, modify, reorganize, or reinterpret the information available to the public. The criteria they use to make decisions may be systematic or random, but in either case their choices control what the public knows.

Social scientists have long been fascinated with the way that news is selected and who selects it. Many studies have looked at the gatekeeping chain of command. At each level of gatekeeping—sources, reporters, wire services, assistant editors, editors-in-chief, and publishers—news may be altered. Each person in the chain has particular responsibilities and each defines news on the basis of values inherent in that position. Sources, for example, define news in terms of their own organizations' interests and characteristics (Ericson, Baranek, and Chan 1989). As one moves up the chain of command, the amount of news under consideration decreases until the final copy is selected.

The second large group of gatekeeping studies examines the factors that influence gatekeepers in the process of selection. There are five sorts of criteria for selecting news: genre-related news values, production-related factors, economic imperatives, socio-cultural pressures, and regulatory and legislative provisions. Some of these are more relevant than others for determining the image of reality that the media transmit to their audiences.

Genre-related news values

Genre-related news values prompt the media to seek out big, clear, unambiguous events that are easy to report, and will be readily recognized and accepted as relevant by audiences (McQuail 1983, 142–43). The varying psychological impact on the audience of the different stories available depends on novelty, proximity, the availability of pictures, the prominence of the actors involved, and the consequences of the event. We can therefore usually expect the news to provide information about people or nations in positions of leadership, power, or wealth, and about negative events. In his study of news in the United States, H.J. Gans's data supports such a conclusion (1979, 8–18). "Knowns," which include people and places of sufficient renown to be familiar to most audiences, dominate coverage, while "unknowns" occupy about 20 percent of available time or space. The majority of unknowns fall into five types: protesters, rioters, and strikers; victims; alleged and actual criminals; voters; and participants in unusual activities such as fads, cults, clubs, or hobbies. Gans found that coverage of governmental and political activity predominated, followed by crime, protest, disaster, innovation, and rites of passage (births, deaths, marriages). Canadian news follows a similar pattern although it is somewhat less preoccupied with violence (Singer 1983).

The predilection of journalists to seek out "bad news" leads them to report social and criminal deviance. While extensively studied in the disciplines of sociology and criminology, deviance as a topic of journalistic interest has received scant attention. A study undertaken by Richard Ericson, Patricia Baranek, and Janet Chan (1987), however, analyses the manner in which journalists, as members of the "deviance-defining elite" (1987, 3), influence our perceptions of order, stability, and change. By systematically examining the way that the media handle deviance as a news item, from initial assignments to depth, amount, and type of coverage, editing, and positioning, the study makes some significant findings about the manner in which news is organized and its impact on the general public:

> Journalists are central agents in the social construction of reality about deviance and control. They shape the moral boundaries and contours of social order, providing an on-

going articulation of our senses of propriety and impropriety, stability and change, order and crises. They underpin the authority of certain control agencies and agents [e.g., courts and police], offering them preferred access and framing events and issues in their terms. They are control agents themselves, using their power of imprinting reality in the public culture to police what is being done in the microcultures of bureaucratic life, including especially the activities of other control agencies. Finally, their own deviance and control processes within the news-media institution play an important part in giving life to their work and shaping how they organize [it] (Ericson, Baranek, and Chan 1987, 359).

Production-related factors

The second group of factors involved in news selection is related to production. These factors are often specific to each medium but the availability of news stories, the size of the news hole, and deadlines are taken into account by all media. The number and type of stories available depend on the wire services and the resources of each individual news medium. Friday, Saturday, and Sunday are traditionally slow days for hard news because governments tend to be relatively inactive on those days. Since there is less available, the media focus more on human-interest, entertainment, and feature pieces.

The size of the news hole—the amount of time or space allotted to news—affects different media in different ways. Under normal circumstances, the electronic media are less flexible than the print media, since they must maintain schedules to accommodate other network programming. Only in the event of major news stories, such as elections, significant parliamentary debates, or international crises, will the electronic media extend their daily news coverage and pre-empt regular programming. The print media are less restricted but they also confront space limitations. Editorial content accounts for about 40 percent of a newspaper's content, and the amount of space available for news therefore depends to a large extent on the amount of advertising.

Certain types of stories, such as political scandals, debates, or decisions, elections, or natural disasters, demand a larger share of the news hole, leaving less room for others. From time to time, important international events dominate the news. The Chernobyl nuclear disaster, the American invasion of Grenada, labour unrest in Gdansk, Poland, and the Mexico City earthquake, for example, all fitted the gatekeepers' criteria for prominent news stories. Stories displaced by more notable ones may be simply discarded, but some are abbreviated and those with a longer shelf-life, such as a story about AIDS research, are set aside to be used at a later date.

All news media tend to prefer stories that fit their twenty-four-hour production schedules. Production deadlines may mean the difference between scooping the competition or being left behind. Gatekeepers must balance the desire for an exclusive story with the possibility of producing an incomplete and perhaps inaccurate report under deadline pressures. These pressures are more acute for the electronic media, which often report fast-breaking stories live without having time to assemble background information.

Media deadlines can also influence news making. During election campaigns, parties orchestrate key speeches, announcements, or public appearances to receive coverage on the nightly news broadcasts. The House of Commons daily Question Period provides a considerable portion of the Canadian news media's political copy. Traditionally scheduled during the afternoon, the Friday Question Period has been shifted to 11:00 A.M., in part to accommodate the media's early deadline prior to the weekend.

Genre-related news values and production-related factors create one kind of bias in gatekeepers' selection of news. Dramatic, immediate types of news are overemphasized and slow, developmental, long-term processes are virtually ignored. In other words, "the doings of the world are tamed to meet the needs of a production system in many respects bureaucratically organized" (Schlesinger 1978, 46). The conventional definition of news based on production requirements can create distortions because "[it] often values speed over completeness, sensation over sobriety, immediacy over perspective, conflict over cooperation, the event over the trend, the entertaining triviality over the difficult but important" (Fletcher 1981, 80).

Economic imperatives

The majority of media in Canada operate as commercial businesses, and their economic imperatives affect the type and content of messages distributed. Up to the time of the Royal Commission on Newspapers in 1981, chain ownership was thought to play a large part in determining content, but existing studies have failed to confirm any systemic negative effect on content, other than dependence on CP/PC for the bulk of news stories (Blais and Crete 1981; Silberberg 1978; Soderlund et al. 1984). Where chain ownership *can* have an impact, however, is on the tone and quality of news coverage, rather than on actual content (Fletcher 1981). A chain reports to shareholders and therefore has a financial imperative to avoid upsetting advertisers, to keep editorial budgets to a minimum, and to select publishers on the basis of their business acumen instead of their journalistic abilities. Finally, the economic incentives that lead to increased concentration can also reduce the independence of journalists. As Robert Lewis (in Fletcher 1981, 39) explains, "Fewer owners means fewer chances to speak out without fear of reprimand."

Fletcher (1981, 38–39) offers examples of economic influences in the industry from his research undertaken on behalf of the Royal Commission on Newspapers. He notes that senior executives in the Thomson chain receive bonuses based upon the profitability of their newspapers and that journalists are well aware of the importance of advertising sales as a criterion for promotion. Without profits, there are no promotions. "Such a scheme may have many virtues but it does not constitute an incentive to put journalistic excellence or the public interest ahead of the interests of advertisers" (Fletcher 1981, 38). Nor does it encourage publishers to spend any more than necessary on their editorial content. James Lamb (1979, 182), a former Thomson publisher, has asserted that "editorial excellence was never a goal of the Thomson group." Instead the chain has attempted to achieve "acceptable levels of news coverage within the framework of a severely limited cost structure" (182). The Southam chain also has financial considerations. Shareholder demands for substantially higher profits have resulted in drastic cutbacks. Layoffs and early retirement incentives are being used to reduce the payroll.

On the other hand, the effects of competition are ambiguous. Theoretically, competition nurtures diverse opinions and investigative journalism because papers attempt to improve their performance and appeal by devoting more resources to news coverage. Yet in their effort to increase circulation, papers may dramatize or trivialize news, or waste time matching the copy of their competition, a phenomenon known as pack journalism. In general, however, Fletcher (1981, 42) concludes that "competition does appear to provide an important check against journalistic abuses and a stimulus to more aggressive . . . reporting."

Advertisers bring additional economic pressures to bear on the process of news selection. Not only does advertising determine the space allocated to news, but it also has some control over the content. Newspapers will frequently publish special supplements or features related to a particular group of advertisers. Travel features, for example, are often supported by airlines, hotel chains, and other travel-related businesses. Although the advertisers do not dictate specific content, they have some power to decide its broad parameters. Finally, advertisers are free to withdraw their financial support if the paper's editorial philosophy or content offends them. The financial implications of angering advertisers are illustrated with the following example. In Calgary in 1988, the *Herald* carried a story about the new 1989 car models, citing the suggested retail prices. Car dealers were so infuriated that they withdrew all advertising for a week in order to demonstrate their economic clout. In this respect, chains are more vulnerable than independents because they stand to lose more advertising.

A newspaper's circulation is, of course, another economic consideration, and plays a part in the paper's style and tone. Many things besides newsworthiness draw our attention to messages in the media. Although certain stories inherently demand notice, others require pictures or headlines to reach their audience. This is especially evident when one compares the front pages of broadsheets and tabloids. Tabloids rely on newsstand sales and must therefore garner sales by the impact of the very first page. Front page stories that attract more attention sell more papers and thereby make the papers more attractive to advertisers. The position of an article on the page, the number of columns, and the attention given the subject by other media are also examples of ways to attract readers' attention.

Socio-cultural pressures

A variety of socio-cultural pressures influence gatekeepers' selection of news. The gatekeepers' personal and professional ethics often underlie their decisions. Ethics are determined to some extent, however, by peer-group pressure. After all, journalists internalize traditional journalistic conventions as they learn their craft.

Similarly, gatekeepers are bound by the news policy or tradition of their various papers, which they learn through a system of rewards and punishments maintained by management. In other words, gatekeepers must select news items that suit the editorial policies of their papers if they are to advance professionally. They also experience a variety of other external pressures imposed by the papers' audiences, the community, and politicians. Regional loyalties, language, and culture can also influence the gatekeepers' decisions.

Regulatory and legislative provisions

Regulatory and legislative provisions are the final category of news determinants. A number of legal restrains limit the ability of journalists to receive or disseminate information: official Cabinet secrecy, parliamentary privilege, the Official Secrets Act, 1939, the Privacy Act, 1982, and the other legislative and regulatory prohibitions against libel, defamation, and obscenity. All of these restrictions are designed to prevent the publication of certain kinds of information. The electronic media are also subject to regulation of their content by the Canadian Radio-television and Telecommunications Commission. It is possible for news stories to meet all of the gatekeepers' criteria but remain unused because of potentially serious legal ramifications.

If audiences understand how news is selected, they will appreciate that "news cannot realistically hope to produce a model which perfectly represents all the contours and elevations of reality" (Epstein 1973, 273). By acknowledging that news does not mirror reality, audiences can better recognize the limited nature of the information they receive from the media and make their decisions on that basis.

Agenda-setting

The agenda of each medium consists of the information that it chooses to present and the manner in which it presents it. Placement, amount of coverage, headline size, pictures, and the number and content of editorials, columns, and letters to the editor reveal the relative importance that a newspaper assigns to its various news stories.

Research has shown that the newspapers initiate an agenda and television then pursues the chosen issues and reinforces them. This sequence is due, in part, to the relatively long tradition of political print journalism, the large editorial staffs of newspapers, and their unrivalled ability to cover issues intensively. Studies indicate that newspapers remain the primary source of public affairs information for top decision makers and the most politically attentive segment of the population at the municipal, provincial, and federal levels (Fletcher 1981, 23).

The most influential agenda-setter in Canada is the *Globe and Mail* (Fletcher 1981, 20). *Le Devoir* plays a similar role in the French-speaking community. Not only is the *Globe* available nationally, but it is also used as a clipping source by most government departments. It is read by almost three-quarters of the country's decision makers at all levels of government. In addition, more than 90 percent of media executives read it regularly (Fletcher 1981, 20). As a result, the *Globe*'s major news stories and features set the agenda for the other media. Even CP wire service takes its cues from the stories and issues that the *Globe and Mail* considers to be important, raising concerns about editorial concentration.

Many studies have shown a substantial correlation between the agenda set by the media and the agenda of the audience—issues that the public perceives to be important—in terms of establishing priorities. In other words the media can determine what we think *about*, but not necessarily what we think (Behr and Iyengar 1985; Carey 1976; Cook et al. 1983; Iyengar and Kinder 1987; McCombs and Gilbert 1986; Protess et al. 1985; Rogers and Dearing 1988; Weaver et al. 1981; Winter and Eyal 1981).

Just as the media can create a public agenda, there is also some evidence that they can influence government priorities (Fletcher 1981, 21–22). The media have little direct impact on decisions made by politicians, economists, and so on in their areas of expertise but they do gauge public reaction to government activities. Although it is difficult for the media to resist the priorities set by government, it is possible. During election campaigns, for example, polls sponsored by various media outlets become part of the media's agenda. Because of the coverage accorded poll results, candidates are forced to respond.[1] During the 1988 federal election, pollsters determined that the Free Trade Agreement was the most salient issue. The media quickly followed by concentrating their coverage on opposing positions on the FTA to the almost total exclusion of other national or local issues. Moreover, the failure of Ed Broadbent, leader of the New Democratic Party, to address the FTA in his opening campaign speech was cited by many analysts as the reason for the NDP's dramatic loss of support.

Another example of the media's ability to resist government priorities occurred during the mid-1980s. Canadian political leaders have traditionally experienced increased prestige and popularity following foreign travel. When Prime Minister Brian Mulroney visited the Pacific Rim nations in 1985, therefore, the main political purpose of his trip was to establish himself as an international statesman and create a positive media image at home. The Canadian press corps travelling with the Prime Minister had a different agenda, however. Reporters were preoccupied with allegations of a conflict of interest levelled against a senior Cabinet minister, which were dominating the headlines at home. Much to the chagrin of Mulroney, his staff, and advisers, his trade talks and diplomatic activities were virtually ignored because the travelling press corps focussed its attention on any comments made about the conflict of interest.

Finally, although the media's ability to influence public attitudes towards public policy issues is still a matter of debate, one thing is clear. If the media tell us nothing about an issue or event, it will remain unknown to us unless we have had personal experience of it. As Eugene Hallman (1981, 5) noted in his report to the Kent Commission, "The reader and subscriber cannot register an effective demand for reports of events not even known to them. This is a significant problem." The relationship between politics and the media is discussed further and at some length in chapter 11.

The last word

What becomes news depends on a variety of factors. News is not fact; it only signals those events or persons considered noteworthy by media gatekeepers. It should be accurate, fair, balanced, objective, and relevant, but selecting news involves values and preferences that are not always explicit. News is not truth, but the news media "can serve as important institution[s] for conveying and circulating information, and signaling changes in the direction of public policy and discourse" (Epstein 1981, 96).

The issues: Freedom of expression, responsibility, and power

An appreciation of the concept of news and news selection is necessary to understand the issues surrounding the newspaper industry today. Those issues focus on two somewhat antagonistic ideas about editorial content: freedom of expression and social responsibility. Freedom of expression is a highly valued media right but carries with it an equally important responsibility to inform the public fully and accurately. Newspapers are business undertakings but they also have a vital and powerful role in the democratic process, as Walter Lippman (1920, 47–48) explained seventy years ago:

> The news of the day as it reaches the newspaper office is an in-
> credible medley of fact, propaganda, rumor, suspicion, clues,
> hopes, and fears, and the task of selecting and ordering that
> news is one of the truly sacred and priestly offices in a
> democracy. . . . The power to determine each day what shall
> seem important and what shall be neglected is a power unlike
> any that has been exercised since the Pope lost his hold on the
> secular mind.

The concepts of freedom, responsibility, and power in news making are of paramount importance. Since World War II, there has been grow-ing concern about the diminishing number of news sources, a phenomenon that has led to an homogenization of reporting on radio and television and in print. Canadians are particularly sensitive to this issue because our news media rely heavily on foreign sources, including AP, Reuter, Agence France Presse, and the three main American television networks.

The balance of this chapter analyses the impact of concentration, the influence of advertisers, current newspaper performance and quality, and future issues. The chapter concludes with some suggestions for using public policy to balance freedom, responsibility, and power in the inter-ests of the common good.

Concentration

The Special Senate Committee on Mass Media (1970, 3) succinctly described the issue of concentrated media ownership in the opening paragraphs of its report:

> The more separate voices we have telling us what's going on,
> telling us how we're doing, telling us how we *should* be doing,
> the more effectively we can govern ourselves. In this sense, the
> mass media are society's suggestion box.... The big trouble
> with this assumption, the notion that media diversity equals a
> higher policy, is that it happens to be in flat defiance of
> economics. More voices may be healthier, but fewer voices are
> cheaper.

The trend towards "fewer voices" is worldwide; even in the United States, the world's wealthiest liberal democracy and strongest advocate of a libertarian press, media diversity is dwindling. In 1987, fewer than 5 percent of American cities had competing newspapers. Just one in five of the 1 657 daily newspapers remained under independent ownership, accounting for about 19 percent of total daily circulation. Only sixteen of those independents had circulations of more than 100 000.

Concentrated ownership began in Canada almost a hundred years ago. In their review of historical developments in press freedom, James Winter and Doris Candussi (1983) trace a philosophic concern about economic concentration back to the beginning of the twentieth century. The governments of the United States and Great Britain first officially identified it as a problem in the newspaper industry during the late 1940s. Canadian government inquiries into the media since 1951 have consistently expressed anxiety about the pattern of ownership.[2] The Royal Commission on Broadcasting (1957, 53), chaired by Robert Fowler, warned media owners that "freedom of the Press is not . . . a right of the publisher to be left free from government interference or control," and subsequent public investigative bodies have recommended government intervention to ensure that the media "achieve accountability beyond the balance sheet" (Ontario, Royal Commission 1976, 61).

Concentration has been documented in all media—book and magazine publishing, radio, television, film, and the new interactive media. Nevertheless, newspapers are often singled out for criticism because they are so instrumental in establishing the public agenda and providing the detailed background of issues of public interest. In other words, debate about economic concentration centres on the implications for editorial content, since the editorial content of newspapers is considered the standardbearer of journalism.

Concentrated ownership makes good economic sense. It allows owners to buy raw material and syndicated copy in bulk, and to sell advertising space at special rates. Chain or corporate ownership can also stabilize and strengthen the industry; it has saved some dailies from closure and contributed to the growth of others. It also has the potential to improve the industry's output by centralizing news collection and permitting newspapers within a chain to exchange ideas and constructive criticism.

In terms of public policy, however, the advantages of concentration are irrelevant (Canada, Special Senate Committee 1970, 6). Economic benefits accrue to media owners, but media audiences are subjected to increased uniformity of news. As the number of independent voices decreases so do the opportunities for access to news. The absence of economic competition may also discourage quality journalism. Once competitive pressures in the industry have been removed, the public must rely on the goodwill or professional ethics of owners and publishers to endure the rigours and expenses of good investigative journalism. Critics point to two modern journalistic trends as evidence that such reliance would be misplaced: market survey journalism and pack journalism.

Market survey journalism depends on audience surveys to point journalists in the direction of higher circulation and profit figures, crucial requirements for newspaper chains. Although responsive media are not by nature purely critical, they do give voice to important social comment. There is a danger that non-competitive media will sacrifice their public service of social criticism to economic objectives. Pack journalism and the closely related parachute journalism both involve the current media practice of focussing on similar aspects of the same news stories. Once an important story appears on the media agenda, all media outlets rush to cover that story, even if that means "parachuting" a reporter into a usually neglected region. It is increasingly rare for a journalist to break away from the pack and investigate the less dominant aspects of a story or to head off in a totally independent direction. These practices, too, reduce media diversity.

Increased concentration also fuels the fear that media owners will use their economic power to control the flow of information in order to protect their own interests or promote their ideological or political convictions. As discussed earlier, concentrated ownership does not usually affect the content of the news directly but it can create an atmosphere that rewards certain perspectives and discourages others.[3]

In his review of media concentration, Ben Bagdikian (1981, 4–8) warns that big media can be just as dangerous as big government. A few large media corporations have more power to mould public opinion than do several smaller undertakings. They are also more susceptible to manipulation by political and economic pressures; pressure on a big media organization will be felt in all its media outlets.[4] Finally, because they are centralized bureaucracies, big media are by nature less responsive to the public. Even though a newspaper or television message is distributed in Halifax, for example, senior management and reporters may live elsewhere, making it difficult for residents of Halifax to get access to those responsible for disseminating the information.

All of these characteristics leave large media undertakings especially open to the problem of news management, subtle government manipulation of public opinion through the media by carefully timed and packaged press releases. At the outset of the Vietnam War, for example, the American media gave blind support to their government's activities. Similarly, the Canadian print media have traditionally supported the two mainstream federal parties, the Liberals and Conservatives, and have presented their views. Both parties have strong connections to the business and legal communities and therefore access to media structures. The New Democratic Party, on the other hand, has values that in many cases differ from those of the primary national media organizations. Its position is consequently not given as much media coverage as that of the other two parties.

Some financial analysts explain the current emphasis on concentrated media ownership as merely an extension of the economic practice of mergers and takeovers in all other economic arenas. There is no indication that the pattern will change. In fact, Conrad Black's Hollinger Inc. purchased thirty-four newspapers in Canada and the United States in 1986, twenty-eight of them dailies, for $130 million. Black also added *Saturday Night*, one of Canada's most prestigious monthly magazines, to his list of acquisitions during the summer of 1987.[5] Maclean Hunter Ltd., a Canadian corporation with a variety of media holdings, announced in January 1988 that it had increased its equity in Toronto Sun Publishing Corp. to 60.5 percent.

The Montreal newspaper market offered a glimmer of hope. Already the most vibrant competitive newspaper market in Canada, Montreal got a new English-language tabloid in 1988. The *Herald* was to be an alternative to Southam Inc.'s Montreal *Gazette*. Analysts predicted fierce competition for readers, advertisers, and even for known and respected journalists (*Financial Post* 1987, 4). Ironically, however, the new paper, a joint venture involving two large media corporations, Pierre Peladeau's Quebecor Inc. and Conrad Black's media conglomerate, folded.

In addition, the *Globe and Mail*'s *Report on Business* faced new competition in 1988 with the transformation of the *Financial Post* from a weekly to a daily. The *Post*'s new owners, the Toronto Sun Publishing Corp., the *Financial Times* of London, and Black's Hollinger Inc. invested between $25 and $30 million in the project and by early 1989, it had surpassed all expectations in terms of circulation and advertising support. The *Report on Business* was enlarged to two sections and major managerial changes were undertaken in response to the competitive challenge.

Advertisers

Another issue of public policy facing us is the degree of control exercised by advertisers. Undoubtedly, advertising is essential to the financial health of media institutions; indeed, it can be argued that today "news is something written on the back of an advertisement" (Clement 1975, 295). Advertisers can influence content in at least three ways—through the advertising copy itself, by linking advertising copy to other content, and by influencing the gatekeeping decisions of owners and publishers. But do advertisers deliberately manipulate the media? As in the case of manipulation by owners, evidence indicates that direct interference from advertisers is rare:

> Broadly speaking the advertisers, their agencies, and the media owners are all the same kind of people, doing the same kind of thing, within the same kind of private-enterprise rationale. There is nothing sinister about it, nothing conspiratorial. Advertiser pressure is not necessary because the influence is there anyway—subtly and by implication (Canada, Special Senate Committee 1970, 245).

It is necessary to be aware of the ideological affinity between owners and advertisers and to acknowledge that it may have significant consequences in terms of setting agendas and public policy. The influence of advertising on media is discussed in further detail in chapter 12.

Performance

Although the subject of performance has arisen in the context of other issues confronting the newspaper industry, it is necessary to examine the topic in a little more detail. The quality of news coverage stands at the crux of all other public policy concerns about newspapers in particular and media in general.

Both the Davey Committee and the Kent Commission found that the Canadian public is generally satisfied with the media's performance. Quality varies greatly, both within and among chains and independents, but both the Committee and the Commission did identify certain weaknesses in the performance of the whole industry.

In the first place, they argue that the industry's definition of news is too narrow. It fails to take into account many events, people, trends, and ideas that have relevance in a modern society. For example, Randy Shilts (1987) details the failure of the media to cover the spread of AIDs adequately prior to the death of Rock Hudson in 1985. The phenomena of pack and market survey journalism narrow news content even further. The problem, according to the Kent Commission, is that newspapers are "neglecting their undoubted power to influence the intellectual tone of the community" (Canada, Royal Commission on Newspapers 1981, 172). They should be providing a forum for public debate on a range of issues.

Newspapers have also made little effort to recruit and train specialists who can keep abreast of developments in highly technical fields. The industry needs more staff like the qualified financial analysts and columnists on some papers, who report complicated economic news in an understandable manner. Failure to keep on top of developments in areas such as medicine, technology, environmental sciences, and other fields not normally within the journalist's definition of news, has inhibited the ability of newspapers to prepare society for change. People look to newspapers to find out what's important, but the industry has a weak record in spotting trends (Canada, Royal Commission on Newspapers 1981, 169).

Finally, both investigative bodies bemoaned the inadequate quality and quantity of foreign affairs coverage. The way that foreign affairs are reported deserves more attention here because of its influence on public policy and because it illustrates many of the problems under consideration in this chapter.

Foreign affairs coverage

In addressing the problem of establishing a Canadian foreign policy, de Montigny Marchand from the Department of External Affairs emphasized the role of the media: "I think we have now virtually reached the point where no idea, policy or event can enjoy more than the most shadowy existence unless it has been consecrated by the media of mass communications" (Canada, Department of External Affairs 1983, 2). Unless placed on the media agenda, many developments will remain unknown to the public. Marchand also noted that the absence of a Canadian perspective on international affairs inhibits informed debate among governments, regions, and the public in this country. The paucity of international news reported from a Canadian outlook and reflecting Canadian interests has been well documented:

> To an importer of widgets, the nationality and allegiance of his supplier are not especially important. To an importer of news they are crucial. Every reporter has a bias. We think it immensely important that the reporters who give us our picture of the world should reflect the kind of bias that Canadians tend to share, rather than the bias that Americans or Frenchmen or Englishmen tend to share (Canada, Special Senate Committee 1970, 234).

News coverage of events around the world has far-reaching implications: a crisis in one part of the world can precipitate a crisis in another, and "international news coverage of a news event can affect the political impact of the event" (Hachten 1981, 23). For example, rumours about financial wrong-doing by members of government in Japan in 1989 affected stock exchanges across the world. International reaction prompted action in Japan, as Japanese leaders tried to assure the economic community that Japan remained a stable nation and its corporations, sound investments. Although foreign news reporting worldwide generally deals with the same kinds of people and activities as domestic news, it tends to be treated with less objectivity and exhibits "explicit value judgements that would not be considered justifiable in domestic news" (Gans 1979, 31). This is particularly worrisome when the role that the media are said to play in international policy is considered.

Newspapers and other news media act as observers, participants, and catalysts in foreign policy (Larsen 1982, 18). As observers, they provide the information that the public needs to create an image of the world. If that information is distorted, so too is the picture of reality. Observation and participation are closely linked; the media not only inform but they inform selectively. Their ability to determine the amount of coverage an event will receive permits them to influence the effect of that event on their audiences. In addition, the news media tend to promote a nationalistic perspective on foreign affairs, thereby manipulating the public's perception of foreign policy issues to suit the national agenda. The media act as catalysts when they influence the opinion of political and economic elites. By choosing some stories and not others, they can set the foreign policy agenda. Furthermore, it has been observed that governments are increasingly using the media to talk to one other, a practice that may lead to distortion (Karl 1982, 147).[6]

Foreign news, then, does more than just document change or inform the public of the state of affairs around the world. The media play both overt and subtle roles in the management of international affairs. In terms of Canadian public policy concerns, the absence of foreign affairs reporting by Canadians for Canadians is therefore an important issue.

As already discussed, the vast majority of Canadian international affairs coverage is lifted from international wire services, mostly American.[7] It is more convenient and cheaper, and therefore suits the Canadian media's perception of foreign news as "almost . . . a necessary nuisance" (Worthington 1971, 54). The problem, of course, is that by relying heavily on American sources, Canadian news media are allowing others to select both the content and the focus of coverage, to assign priorities to issues, and to provide the interpretation and analysis.

If our foreign policy is to be relevant to the national interest, it should foster national aims and sustain our distinct identity. It should also receive public endorsement. Can it achieve these goals if it must constantly compete with a foreign interpretation of world events?

Remedies and suggestions

Various remedies for the problems confronting the newspaper industry have been offered. Those that attempt to remedy weaknesses in the newspaper's performance tend to involve self-regulation, while those that focus on patterns of ownership involve government intervention.

In 1970, the Davey Committee (Canada 1970, 90) concluded that Canada needed a press council, a permanent self-governing body, to enable the press to monitor its own performance. Funded by member media organizations, press councils are composed of representatives of the media and members of the public. They promote high standards of journalism and open access to information, and challenge any perceived threats to press freedom. Councils also adjudicate complaints about media content levelled against members. Although they render decisions, press councils have no legal or statutory powers to enforce them, and instead must rely on moral censure. Critics argue that press councils limit press freedom, but advocates believe that they enhance public confidence in the press and encourage more professional attitudes among journalists and publishers.

The Davey Committee believed, as did the Kent Commission, that a national council would best serve the public, but for two reasons the idea has not been realized. Canada's regional and corporate diversity render a national press council almost completely unworkable. In addition, print journalists, editors, publishers, and owners alike are very reluctant to become involved with such a council, for fear that it would legitimate government supervision or even censorship of the press. Instead, a number of voluntary press councils with limited membership and power have emerged. The councils have had a sincere intention to address the complaints lodged against the print media but their second motive has been less noble. By establishing local or regional councils with limited scope, the press is able to undercut or co-opt any strong government initiative for a national monitoring agency that might evolve into a body akin to the CRTC.

Canadian newspapers have also established press ombudsmen positions to deal with audience complaints, as another form of self-regulation. Ombudsmen are generally long-time, respected employees of a newspaper, who have much credibility with both the newspaper management and the public. The power and effectiveness of ombudsmen are directly related to the freedom they are granted by their publishers. Similarly, improving professional standards and training is an internal method of combatting weaknesses in performance. The Canadian Daily Newspaper Publishers Association adopted "A statement of principles for Canadian daily newspapers" in 1977 in another effort to govern its own membership.

Government intervention is a different approach, specifically designed to limit concentrated ownership. The Special Senate Committee (1970, 71–78) recommended the establishment of a press ownership review board with the power to approve or disallow mergers and acquisitions of media undertakings that operate in the public interest. It also suggested the creation of a government fund to subsidize new or endangered publications. Both recommendations elicited bitter criticism from owners and publishers as potential threats to press freedom. Any such board or fund, regardless of how innocuous, limited, or positive in its intent, may represent the beginning of government control.

The Royal Commission on Newspapers reiterated some of the recommendations of the Special Senate Committee but went further. It proposed legislation "designed to secure for the press of Canada the freedom that is essential to a democratic society from coast to coast" (Canada, Royal Commission on Newspapers 1981, 237). The proposal included not only prohibitions on further concentration and incentives for broader ownership patterns but also provisions for correcting existing situations deemed contrary to the public interest. The Commission suggested, for example, that the Thomson chain be required to divest either the *Globe and Mail*, at least its national edition, or the rest of its chain of newspapers. The recommendations were denounced savagely by the press as dangerous encroachments on the freedom of the press.

Although many of the Commission's suggestions were modified and incorporated into proposed legislation by the federal Liberal government of the day, the bill was never passed by Parliament. Many newspaper owners and publishers believed that when the bill died on the *Order Paper*, so did the furor over their activities. Yet the issue of press freedom remains salient. The enactment of the Canadian Charter of Rights and Freedoms in 1982 and the subsequent legal challenges brought forward in its wake may shift the debate about newspaper performance and ownership from the legislatures to the courts. Many issues could arise to embroil the print media in pivotal court battles.[8] The media's right to protect their sources, and their access to information, are two examples. Should the print press win a number of higher court victories, its traditional role will be reinforced; should it lose, the press of the future might find the principles of social responsibility enforced by interests outside the media themselves.

Summary

Defining news is not an easy task, but this chapter identified several of its features. Gatekeepers use these features, in conjunction with criteria such as economic, regulatory, and production imperatives, to determine media content. News selection is important because it enables the media to influence the public's agenda, and therefore raises the issues of freedom of expression and social responsibility.

As the chapter reviewed the quality of news coverage in Canada, it discussed concerns about the media's narrow definition of news, the practices of pack and market survey journalism, the industry's proclivity for generalists rather than specialists, and its failure to prepare the public for the future. In addition, the negative effects that concentrated media ownership and advertising can have on media content were identified. These deficiencies are particularly visible in media coverage of foreign affairs.

To date, most attempts to improve the quality of news coverage have relied upon the voluntary co-operation of newspapers and their publishers, but any observed reluctance on their part may lead to more obtrusive regulatory options. The industry's surest path for protecting its liberty appears to lie in recognizing and accepting its responsibilities and obligations.

Notes

1. For a more detailed analysis of polls, the media, and elections, see Frizzell and Westell (1985).

2. See Canada, Royal Commission on National Development in the Arts, Letters and Sciences (1951), Royal Commission on Broadcasting (1957), Royal Commission on Publications (1961), Special Senate Committee on Mass Media (1970), and Royal Commission on Newspapers (1981); and Ontario, Royal Commission on Violence in the Communications Industry (1976).

3. For a more detailed analysis of this concept, see Clement (1975, 270–306).

4. Charles King (1987, 10) argues, for example, that Southam Inc., under new president John Fisher, has set new financial goals for its papers, expecting a higher return on investment at the expense of quality journalism.

5. When Conrad Black took over *Saturday Night*, its respected editor, Robert Fulford, resigned fearing editorial interference from his new boss.

6. The government practice of using the media is not restricted to foreign policy initiatives. Marshall McLuhan (1964, 203–4) alluded to this problem when he referred to "government by newsleaks." He argued that governments purposely leak policy positions in order to gauge the public response before the decision is irrevocably taken. The "trial balloon" is now almost institutionalized as a method for government to test certain initiatives in advance via the media.

7. For a more detailed review of Canadian newspaper sources, see Kariel and Rosenvall (1981, 1983).

8. An example of a potential electronic media challenge based on the Charter of Rights and Freedoms is described in McPhail (1986).

References

Bagdikian, B.H. 1981. The media monopolies. In *Mass media issues, analysis and debate*, ed. G. Rodman, 4–8. Chicago: Science Research Associates.

Behr, R.L., and S. Iyengar. 1985. Television news, real-world cues, and changes in the public agenda. *Public Opinion Quarterly* 49(1): 38–57.

Bittner, J.R. 1977. *Mass communication: An introduction*. Englewood Cliffs: Prentice-Hall.

Blais, A., and J. Crete. 1981. La presse et les affaires publiques au Québec. Research study for the Royal Commission on Newspapers. Public Archives of Canada.

Brown, L. 1971. *Television: The business behind the box*. New York: Harcourt Brace Jovanovich.

Canada. Department of External Affairs. 1983. Statements and speeches no. 83/20, Foreign policy and the public interest. Ottawa: Department of External Affairs.

Canada. Royal Commission on Broadcasting. 1957. *Report*. Vol. 1. Ottawa: Queen's Printer.

Canada. Royal Commission on National Development in the Arts, Letters and Sciences. 1951. *Report*. Ottawa: King's Printer.

Canada. Royal Commission on Newspapers. 1981. *Report*. Ottawa: Supply and Services.

Canada. Royal Commission on Publications. 1961. *Report*. Ottawa: Queen's Printer.

Canada. Special Senate Committee on Mass Media. 1970. *The uncertain mirror*. Vol. 1 of *Report*. Ottawa: Supply and Services.

Carey, J. 1976. Setting the political agenda: How media shape election campaigns. *Journal of Communication* 26(2): 50–57.

Clement, W. 1975. *The Canadian corporate elite: An analysis of economic power*. Toronto: McClelland and Stewart.

Cook, F.L., T.R. Tyler, E.G. Goetz, M.T. Gordon, D. Protess, D.R. Leff, and H.L. Molotch. 1983. Media and agenda setting: Effects on public, interest group leaders, policy makers, and policy. *Public Opinion Quarterly* 47: 16–35.

Epstein, E.J. 1973. *News from nowhere*. New York: Vintage.

———. 1981. Journalism and truth. In *Mass media issues, analysis and debate*, ed. G. Rodman, 90–96. Chicago: S.R.A.

Ericson, R.V., P.M. Baranek, and J.B.L. Chan. 1987. *Visualizing deviance: A study of news organization*. Toronto: University of Toronto.

———. 1989. *Negotiating control: A study of news sources*. Toronto: University of Toronto.

Financial Post. 1987. Peladeau and Black go for a new daily. 20 April, p. 4.

Fletcher, F. 1981. *The newspaper and public affairs*. Vol. 7 of *Royal commission on newspapers research publications*. Ottawa: Supply and Services.

Frizzell, A., and A. Westell. 1985. *The Canadian general election of 1984: Politicians, parties, press and polls*. Ottawa: Carleton University.

Gans, H.J. 1979. *Deciding what's news*. New York: Vintage.

Hachten, W.A. 1981. *The world news prism: Changing media, clashing ideologies*. Iowa: Iowa University.

Hallman, E. 1981. *The newspaper as a business*. Vol. 4 of *Royal commission on newspapers research publications*. Ottawa: Supply and Services.

Iyengar, S., and D.R. Kinder. 1987. *News that matters: Television and American opinion*. Chicago: University of Chicago.

Kariel, H.G., and L.A. Rosenvall. 1981. Analyzing news origin profiles of Canadian newspapers. *Journalism Quarterly* 58(2): 254–59.

———. 1983. United States news flows to Canadian newspapers. *American Review of Canadian Studies* 13(1): 44–64.

Karl, P.A. 1982. Media diplomacy. *Proceedings of the Academy of Science* 34(4): 143–52.

King, C. 1987. Readers lose in spending spree. *Sunday Herald*. 14 June, p. 10.

Lamb, J.B. 1979. *Press gang: Post-war life in the world of Canadian newspapers*. Toronto: MacMillan.

Larsen, J.F. 1982. International affairs coverage on U.S. evening network news. In *Television coverage of international affairs*, ed. W.C. Adams, 15-41. New Jersey: Ablex.

Lippman, W. 1920. *Liberty and the news*. New York: Harcourt, Brace, and Rowe.

McCombs, M., and S. Gilbert. 1986. News influence on our pictures of the world. In *Perspectives on media effects*, ed. D.D. Nimmo and D. Zillmann, 1–16. Hillsdale, NJ: Lawrence Erlbaum Associates.

McLuhan, M. 1964. *Understanding media: The extensions of man*. New York: McGraw-Hill.

McPhail, B.M. 1986. Canadian content regulations and the Canadian Charter of Rights and Freedoms. *Canadian Journal of Communication* 12(1): 41–53.

McQuail, D. 1983. *Mass communication theory: An introduction*. Beverly Hills: Sage.

Ontario. Royal Commission on Violence in the Communications Industry. 1976. *Violence in print and music*. Vol. 4 of *Report*. Toronto: Queen's Printer.

Pember, D.R. 1974. *Mass media in America*. Chicago: S.R.A.

Protess, D.L., D.R. Leff, S.C. Brooks, and M.T. Gordon. 1985. Uncovering rape: The watchdog press and limits of agenda setting. *Public Opinion Quarterly* 49(1): 19–37.

Robinson, G.J. 1981. *News agencies and world news in Canada, the United States, and Yugoslavia: Methods and data*. Switzerland: University of Fribourg.

Rogers, E.M., and J.W. Dearing. 1988. Agenda-setting research: Where has it been and where is it going? In *Communication Yearbook 11*, ed. J.A. Anderson, 555–94. Newbury, CA: Sage Publications.

Schlesinger, P. 1978. *Putting "Reality" together, BBC News*. Beverly Hills: Sage.

Shilts, R. 1987. *And the band played on: Politics, people and the AIDs epidemic*. New York: St. Martin's Press.

Silberberg, T. 1978. Ownership as a factor in news content determination: An analysis of coverage of labour's day protest in seven chain-owned newspapers. MA thesis, York University.

Singer, B.D. 1983. Violence, protest, and war in television news: The United States and Canada compared. In *Communications in Canadian society*, ed. B.D. Singer, 192–96. Toronto: Addison-Wesley.

Soderlund, W.C., W.I. Romanow, E.D. Briggs, and R.H. Wagenberg. 1984. *Media and elections in Canada*. Toronto: Holt, Rinehart and Winston.

Weaver, D.H., D.A. Grabner, M. McCombs, and C. Eyal. 1981. *Media agenda-setting in a presidential election: Issues, images and interests*. New York: Praeger.

Winter, J., and D. Candussi. 1983. Kent and the new press freedom: An historical perspective. Paper presented to the annual conference, Canadian Communication Association. June. Vancouver.

Winter, J.P., and C. Eyal. 1981. Agenda setting for the civil rights issues. *Public Opinion Quarterly* 45: 376–83.

Worthington, P. 1971. Foreign affairs: The irrelevant beat. In *A media mosaic: Canadian communications through a critical eye*, ed. W. McDayter, 54-83. Toronto: Holt, Rinehart and Winston.

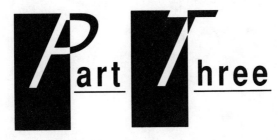

Part Three

The Electronic Media

THE CANADIAN
BROADCASTING SYSTEM

*S*ince its inception, broadcasting has been imbued with special power:

> Like education, broadcasting is, . . . and will remain, an essen-
> tial element of democracy. Broadcasting is not just an element
> or section of culture. It is today the most powerful manifesta-
> tion or mirror of culture. It is the principal theatre, the prin-
> cipal disseminator of news, the principal vehicle of
> entertainment. It has become the national performance stage,
> and the national forum of information and debate (Juneau
> 1986, 4).

The broadcasting media are recognized as important and influential actors in the socialization process. They convey social norms and beliefs in
such a pervasive and persuasive manner that they can shape our mental

picture of reality (Gerbner, Gross, and Melody 1973, 563). Consequently, broadcasting has been a perennial and often troubling public policy issue in Canada for the past six decades.

For the most part, the challenges and dilemmas have changed very little. There are, in fact, three recurring, interconnected themes in the history of Canadian broadcasting: nationalism, economics, and technology. Broadcasting has been charged with the responsibility for promoting the national identity, an obligation that places financial strains on the industry. It is also increasingly affected by technological change. Other factors, such as American television penetration and Canadian geography, complicate all three themes.

This chapter traces the development of broadcasting in Canada within a legislative and regulatory framework and identifies the main participants in this policy arena. It describes the various elements of the Canadian broadcasting system today and examines their current status. (Legal analysis of broadcasting regulation and legislation appears in chapter 13.) Chapter 7 then turns attention to broadcasting delivery systems, identifies current and future technological trends, and briefly assesses their impact. Finally, chapter 8 discusses the policy issues introduced in chapters 6 and 7, particularly Canadian content regulations, and examines the policy guidelines that form the foundations of Canada's proposed new broadcasting legislation. Throughout, the three themes—nationalism, economics, and technology—will reappear frequently.

Radio comes of age

Wireless telegraphy was invented by Guglielmo Marconi in 1895, and with the 1906 invention of the vacuum tube, voice transmission first became possible. Initially used for military purposes, radio was not introduced as a mass medium until after World War I. By the end of the 1920s, it had become a popular source of entertainment and information for large audiences and began to set the stage for television.

Today, radio remains more widespread than television. More people own more radios than ever before. As radio content and format have specialized, listening has become a highly selective activity that appeals to local, fragmented audiences. In other words, there are different audiences for the different kinds of programming available. For the most part, however, radio use is a secondary or supplementary activity; we listen to the radio while we drive, work, study, and so on. Radio caters to our need for entertainment and information when watching television or reading the newspaper are impossible or inappropriate.

Wireless telegraphy was first subject to legislation in 1905 in Canada. The Department of Marine and Fisheries was delegated responsibility for radio and maintained control until 1932 except during the war years, when the Department of Naval Service assumed authority. The Radio Telegraph Act of 1913 defined radio, instituted a licensing procedure, and granted the minister the power to take possession of any station temporarily for the good of commerce or business. The Act included as radio any wireless system for conveying electric signals or messages. It also bestowed on government the power that is "at the root of all regulation": the power to grant or withhold licences and thereby assure control over broadcasters (Blakely 1979, 22).

This did not deter development, however, and the first private radio station intended for a mass audience was established by the Marconi Company in Montreal in 1919. The station represented an effort to boost sales of the company's receiver sets. During the next twenty years, economic problems slowed the expansion of radio. Large distances separated the population and broadcasters lacked the funds to pay for programming production as well as expensive transmission costs. Programming therefore consisted primarily of American material imported from the more financially successful U.S. stations.

Sir Henry Thornton, president of Canadian National Railways, is credited with the creation of public broadcasting in Canada. He equipped some of the trains' parlour cars with radio receiving sets and established a network of stations across the country. Thornton believed his radio network could make rail service more appealing and attract tourists and settlers. He saw radio as a significant unifying force, and according to his biographer, "as a direct result of Sir Henry's ability to see the possibilities inherent in a new medium of expression, the railway did for Canada what she was too apathetic to do for herself" (Marsh 1935, 115).

During this early period, the government had not yet developed a national policy for broadcasting:

> When broadcasting began in Canada, the political leaders did not realize the implications for public policy, or the kinds of decisions and political controversies that must follow. Their procedure, following the line of least resistance, was to make use of an existing radio act, and to undertake as little regulation or control as they could get away with (Peers 1969, 14).

As a result, the granting of licences was tainted with political patronage and the system of allocating frequencies was chaotic. At the same time, Canadian sovereignty was threatened; an estimated 80 percent of the programs Canadians listened to were of American origin (Prang 1965, 4). Canadians tuned in American stations and Canadian stations used increasing amounts of foreign programming.

A crisis erupted in the spring of 1928 when P.J.A. Cardin, Minister of Marine and Fisheries, refused to renew the licence of the International Bible Students Association. They, like others, had been using radio to disseminate their views but Cardin had received many complaints about the "hateful" messages of the Association, messages he termed "unpatriotic and abusive" (Canada, House of Commons 1928, 1951). The House of Commons debated the issue arising from the minister's action and concluded that a consistent and coherent policy was required to avoid arbitrary or partisan decision making.

The Royal Commission on Radio Broadcasting (Aird Commission) was established on 6 December 1928 to determine how radio broadcasting could most effectively operate in the national interest. The Commission was to make recommendations regarding administration, management, control, and financing. The commissioners, Sir John Aird, Charles A. Bowman, and Augustin Frignon, held hearings in Canada and also visited a number of European countries, Great Britain, and the United States. They concluded that "Canadian radio listeners want Canadian broadcasting" and warned that continued reception of foreign programming had "a tendency to mould the minds of the young people in the home to ideals and opinions that are not Canadian" (Canada, Royal Commission on Radio Broadcasting 1929, 6). Because broadcasting could cultivate the national identity, a publicly owned and operated system would best serve Canadian interests.

To this end, the Commission recommended the creation of the Canadian Radio Broadcasting Commission (CRBC), to be financed initially by an appropriation from Parliament. Annual expenditures were to be covered by revenues derived from licence fees, rental of time for indirect advertising,[1] and a federal subsidy. The Aird Commission also recommended against the continued existence of privately owned stations. Control should remain with the Department of Marine and Fisheries, and the primary purpose of the service should be "to give Canadian programs through Canadian stations" (Canada, Royal Commission on Radio Broadcasting 1929, 10).

Although Parliament never fully implemented these recommendations, its response to the Aird Commission continues to influence Canada's broadcasting system. A publicly owned national network was eventually established but the private stations were allowed to survive. (As a result, the sectors still compete with each other for frequencies, audiences, and advertising revenues.) A persistent shortfall in funding left the public sector dependent on the private broadcasters to extend its national service, and a system of private stations affiliated with the public network developed. Despite the intentions of the Aird Commission, the resultant system solved neither the problems of sovereignty nor of economic viability.

Following the Aird Commission report, the provinces unsuccessfully challenged Ottawa's authority in this public policy arena, in both the Supreme Court of Canada and the Judicial Committee of the Privy Council in Great Britain. Broadcasting was not specifically enumerated in the British North America Act. The provinces saw it as a local concern, one that was limited to activities within a province. They also argued that provincial jurisdiction over education gave them control over broadcasting. The legal ramifications of the court cases are discussed in greater detail in chapter 13. One of the most significant aspects of the decisions against the provinces was the reiteration of a national role for broadcasting:

> It is scarcely necessary to give in detail the extent and importance of the service now rendered to the whole people of this and other countries by radio communication. The broadcasting service is one most familiar to the masses of people, and is useful to them as a means of enjoyment, of information and education (*Re regulation and control of radio communications in Canada* [1931] S.C.R. 541, 572).

Parliament reacted to the judicial decisions by establishing the Special Committee on Broadcasting in 1932 to review the situation. The Committee concluded that Canada owed a great debt to private broadcasters and that they should be allowed to continue to serve their local audiences until such time as the national service was complete. This left private broadcasters in a very awkward position, not knowing when or if their stations might be expropriated or forced to cease operations. Most station owners were reluctant to expand or modernize their undertakings and although no stations were ever closed, the private broadcasters never knew how far the government was prepared to go.

The subsequent Canadian Radio Broadcasting Act, 1932 was significant in two respects. It gave the CRBC power not only to carry on the business of broadcasting but also the authority to license and regulate all private stations. Private broadcasters were therefore dependent on their competitor for regulatory control, a situation they actively opposed until the creation of the Board of Broadcast Governors in 1958. Second, it officially recognized the airwaves as a national resource. Prime Minister R.B. Bennett made this clear in a speech in the House of Commons:

> First of all, this country must be assured of complete control of broadcasting from Canadian sources, free from foreign interference or influence. Without such control radio broadcasting can never become a great agency for communication of matters of national concern and for the diffusion of national thought and ideals and without such control it can never be the agency by which national consciousness may be fostered and sustained and national unity still further strengthened.... The use of the air . . . that lies over the soil or land of Canada is a natural resource over which we have complete jurisdiction under the recent decision of the Privy Council [and] I cannot think that any government would be warranted in leaving the air to private exploitation and not reserving it for development for the use of the people (Canada, House of Commons 1932, 3035–36).

After winning the 1935 federal election, the new Liberal government established another special committee. The resulting legislation, the Canadian Broadcasting Act, 1936, replaced the CRBC with the newly created Canadian Broadcasting Corporation (CBC). The CBC Board of Governors was regionally representative, and the Corporation had more autonomy than its predecessor. The position of the private broadcasters was strengthened as well, however, since the CBC was required to seek the prior consent of the governor-in-council before acquiring private stations. This stipulation was crucial: by ensuring the private sector a place in the single Canadian broadcasting system, the Act committed all broadcasters to the task of encouraging national unity.

Finally, the Act carefully redefined broadcasting to include "the wireless transmission of writing, signs, signals, pictures and sounds by means of Hertzian waves, intended to be received by the public either directly or through the medium of relay stations." The redefinition was vitally important for the future. Television was a known technology. Although still experimental, it had been the subject of discussion during the sessions of the Special Committee on Radio Broadcasting, 1935–1936. After considering both the high costs of talent, equipment, and production, and the technological intricacies of the medium, the government decided that television was not an economically feasible medium in the Canadian market at that time.

The introduction of television

Television combined the audio qualities of radio with the video of film and brought them into the family's living room. As a medium of communication, it is highly complex, expensive, and intrusive. Television's ability to provide "an electronic magic carpet that transports millions of people each day to faraway places" (Agee, Ault, and Emery 1976, 274) has resulted in its present power and ubiquity.

It was 1948 before the CBC decided to introduce a television service in Canada, and then only to large cities. The Cabinet, recognizing the negative political ramifications of such a proposal, refused to allocate the necessary funds to support a project that would not benefit all Canadians. Instead, it created the Royal Commission on National Development in the Arts, Letters and Sciences (Massey Commission) to review the entire Canadian cultural situation and to investigate how best to develop television nationally.

The Commission's report concluded that broadcasting was developing as it should. It described broadcasting as "one of the great forces in our country in promoting Canadian unity and Canadian cultural life" (Canada, Royal Commission on National Development in the Arts, Letters and Sciences 1951, 295). It recommended strengthening the role of the CBC but recognized that private broadcasters had played and should continue to play a part within the single national system.

An official government policy on television developed from the report, advocating a single channel scheme: only one television broadcasting licence would be allocated in any given community, and private stations could be established in those areas not served by the CBC. They would be obliged to carry CBC programming, however, thus establishing a system of CBC television affiliates. The policy allowed less costly and more rapid expansion.

Meanwhile, the CBC had begun television undertakings in Montreal, Toronto, and then Ottawa. The 1953 coronation of Elizabeth II was an incentive to provide television services rapidly to Canadian viewers, and the CBC proudly demonstrated its broadcasting capability by transmitting the coronation film before it was available on an American network. By 1955, Canada had twenty-two private and six public stations. These stations had succeeded in drawing a significant portion of the audience away from available U.S. channels by scheduling the popular American programming in prime time and surrounding it with Canadian productions. As the broadcast day grew longer, however, the percentage of Canadian programming decreased because the additional hours were filled with foreign programming. Table 6.1 shows the percentage of time devoted to Canadian programming, live or recorded, on Canadian television stations in the mid-1950s.

Table 6.1

Proportion of Canadian programs on Canadian television stations, for the week of 15 January 1956

Class of station	Percentage of broadcasting time
CBC French	87
Private French	76
CBC English	45
Private English	44

Source: *Canada, Royal Commission on Broadcasting 1957, 65.*

The decreasing proportion of available Canadian programming disturbed government decision makers, who believed that television should foster national goals. Yet debate over effective broadcasting regulation and an appropriate system of paying for television remained unresolved.

To find answers, the government established another royal commission on broadcasting in 1955. Its chairman was Robert Fowler.

The Fowler Commission was asked to review CBC television broadcasting policies and finances, the measures necessary to provide an adequate proportion of Canadian programs, and the licensing and regulation of private stations. Two hundred and seventy-six briefs were received. Many dealt with the problem of regulation and criticized the CBC's dual role as cop and competitor, but no direct examples of abuse were cited. When its report was tabled in March 1957, the Commission restated the central proposition advanced by Aird, that

> as a nation, we cannot accept, in these powerful and pervasive media, the natural and complete flow of another nation's culture without danger to our national identity.... Assuming, as we must, that their broadcasting system is satisfactory and suitable for Americans, this is no basis for thinking it is desirable for Canadians (Canada, Royal Commission on Broadcasting 1957, 8).

Acknowledging the cost of a national system, the Fowler Commission supported the CBC in its efforts to expand service and admonished the private stations for their lack of Canadian programming. Nevertheless, it further recommended that broadcast hours and geographical coverage be extended and that second stations be allowed to enter the market. Instead of allowing only a single broadcasting licence in a community, the government would permit a second station, which would produce its own domestic programming and thus increase the total supply. For those who believed that the system was already failing in its attempts to provide a Canadian alternative, the recommendations were a grave concern. More broadcast hours might mean the importation of more foreign programming to fill them.

The Commission was less clear on the subject of regulation. Despite announcing that a new regulatory board should be instituted, the report argued against "any fundamental change in the arrangements for regulation and control of Canadian broadcasting that have existed in the past" (Canada, Royal Commission on Broadcasting 1957, 91, 136). Scholars and analysts have assumed that the Commission recognized the failings of the existing regulatory authority but was reluctant to advocate a two-board policy since it would, in effect, destroy the single-system concept.

In the 1958 general election, the Progressive Conservatives won a massive majority. Despite having created the CRBC almost three decades earlier, the Conservatives had become very critical of the public network and more supportive of private interests. They gave notice that they planned to reorganize the broadcasting system and promised in the throne speech to create a new regulatory agency.

The Board of Broadcast Governors (BBG), created by the Broadcasting Act of 1958, was delegated regulatory power over the CBC and the private stations but was not responsible for the management of the public sector. That task remained with the CBC Board of Governors. Chaired by Andrew Stewart, the BBG consisted of three full-time and twelve part-time members selected on the basis of regional representation. The staff included a technical adviser, legal counsel, researchers, secretaries, and clerical workers. The Board was financed by parliamentary appropriations and was required to submit an annual report, through the minister of transport, to Parliament.

The BBG was an independent regulatory agency and political influence was controlled by the terms of the Broadcasting Act. Cabinet had the power to appoint board members, to approve the issuance and revokation of licences, and to set aside specific BBG decisions on appeal. Parliament, on the other hand, by amending the Broadcasting Act, could provide the BBG with general policy directions. No other political interference in the activities of the Board was permitted. The BBG had direct regulatory power to enact, amend, and enforce regulations pursuant to sections 11 and 13 of the Act.[2] With respect to licensing, however, its role was advisory: it would make recommendations to the transport minister after holding a public hearing to consider the licence application.

The general mandate of the BBG was stated in section 10 of the Act:

> The Board shall, for the purpose of ensuring the continued existence and efficient operation of a national broadcasting system and the provision of a varied and comprehensive broadcasting service of a high standard that is *basically Canadian in content and character*, regulate the establishment and operation of networks of broadcasting stations, the activities of public and private broadcasting stations in Canada and the relationship between them and provide for the final determination of all matters and questions in relation thereto [emphasis added].

This was perhaps the most debated, most amended section of the bill, but it still provoked conflict between the BBG and the CBC Board of Governors. The move to separate the regulatory and broadcasting roles of the CBC was a fundamental change in Canadian broadcasting policy, and the two boards each interpreted the Act to suit their own interests. The BBG believed that it had regulatory control over the CBC exactly as it had over private stations. The CBC argued that it had priority when it came to determining its own operations and content.

Before the bill was enacted into law, the CBC had been the dominant force in Canadian broadcasting. Under its tutelage, television had grown more rapidly in Canada than anywhere else in the world (Canada, Royal Commission on Broadcasting 1957, 217). The CBC live-production output also surpassed that of any other network (Peers 1979, 174). The government's decision to finance television expansion in the most inexpensive manner possible, however, left the CBC outnumbered five to one by the private stations by 1958. The Corporation was also under increasing pressure from its affiliates to schedule American programming during peak viewing hours. (CBC affiliates were privately owned television stations operating under agreements with the Corporation over network programming.) The imminent introduction of second stations after 1959 would increase competition for advertising revenues and the affiliates did not want to lose their predominant position. It was becoming increasingly difficult for the CBC to provide Canadian programs for Canadian audiences.

The primary result of the Broadcasting Act, 1958 was to equalize the public and private sectors, placing them both under the authority of a single, separate regulatory board. Once the private broadcasters had succeeded in their struggle for an independent regulator, they then set about the task of convincing the BBG that economic factors—such as the cost of transmission and programming, and profit margins—should be given more consideration in broadcasting-related decisions. The BBG was eager to act. Second stations were licensed and the CTV network was permitted to begin operation.

The Board's prime objective, however, was ensuring the Canadianization of the airwaves, and hearings were held in November 1959 to address the issue of proposed Canadian content quotas. The Board agreed with the conclusion of the Fowler Commission (Canada, Royal Commission on Broadcasting 1957, 153), that "free enterprise had failed to do as much as it could in original program production and the development of

Canadian talent, not because of a lack of freedom, but because of a lack of enterprise." The BBG feared that the new CTV network would tend to import American programming. It also recognized that without a performance criterion the industry would continue to be guided only by the financial dictates of the marketplace. The Board therefore imposed a 55 percent Canadian content quota as of 1 April 1962. According to BBG chairman Andrew Stewart (unpublished, 40-41), "the regulations were designed to ensure the quantitative participation of Canadians in the broadcasting service." Further, they were "part of the broad policy of directing broadcasting in Canada toward the achievement of 'national purposes,'" as outlined in section 10 of the Act.

Of the initial undertakings of the BBG, new licensing procedures drew the most criticism. The review process for licences was time consuming and a backlog developed. In addition, the Board lacked the authority to revoke licences and was therefore powerless to enforce its own regulations. It could recommend revokation but Cabinet had the real authority. Cabinet, however, was consistently reluctant to revoke a licence and leave a community—and therefore voters—without a television station. The inability of the BBG to resolve such persistent issues stimulated criticism from both the public and private sectors.

When the Liberals returned to power in 1963, an informal committee known as the Troika was appointed to tender advice on a future regulatory framework. Its three members were unable to reach a consensus and each tabled a separate report. One week later, the Advisory Committee on Broadcasting was established, to be chaired by Robert Fowler.[3] It was directed to suggest improvements to the existing regulatory structure. This indicated a change in the broadcasting policy of the Liberals. Originally opposed to the two-board system that separated the management of the public sector from the regulation of broadcasting in general, the Liberals now exhibited a new willingness to accept it. The dual supervisory system was supported by some influential Liberal advisers, but more importantly, the party could not afford to ignore the growing size, profitability, and influence of the private broadcasters.

The Committee's report (1965) emphasized programming. It stated that although the CBC had paramount responsibility for maintaining a distinctively Canadian broadcasting system, the private sector must share in these objectives. In any dispute between the two sectors, however, the interests of the CBC were to prevail. The Committee also recommended the return to a single-board regulatory system through the creation of an independent public regulatory agency, responsible to Parliament and entrusted with the complete control of broadcasting in Canada, including the management of the CBC. It further directed the government to state clearly, in statute, its objectives for the broadcasting system.

The November 1965 federal election overshadowed the Fowler Committee's report but it is doubtful that many of its recommendations could have been implemented. It was met with unified opposition. The single-board proposal was criticized by the Conservatives, who had initiated the two-board system, the Canadian Association of Broadcasters, which had fought for thirty years for an independent regulatory body, Andrew Stewart of the BBG, who had recommended the continuation of the two-board system, and the CBC, which feared that the proposed board would be much too powerful.

In December 1965, Prime Minister Pearson announced that he would head a special Cabinet committee to study the Fowler Committee's report and produce a white paper for submission to Parliament. That document served as the basis for a debate that led to the passage of the Broadcasting Act, 1968. The white paper had two themes: it reiterated the place of broadcasting in maintaining Canadian unity; and it recognized that the system must be able to adjust readily to demands placed upon it. To these ends, the white paper made several points. It acknowledged the historical role of the CBC in providing Canadian programming, the positive contribution of Canadian content quotas, and the need to strengthen the regulatory body. It also recommended that cable television be included as part of the national broadcasting system and be subject to regulation. The paper recognized the three recurrent themes of nationalism, economics, and technology and tried to incorporate them into a coherent policy.

The 1968 Broadcasting Act defined the framework for broadcasting within which the system currently operates. For the first time, a statute clearly enunciated a broadcast policy and in doing so invested all elements of the system, including the private sector, with socio-cultural responsibility. Section 3 of the 1968 Broadcasting Act reads as follows:

Broadcasting Policy for Canada

3. It is hereby declared that:

   (a) broadcasting undertakings in Canada make use of radio frequencies that are public property and such undertakings constitute a single system, herein referred to as the Canadian broadcasting system, comprising public and private elements;

(b) the Canadian broadcasting system should be effectively owned and controlled by Canadians so as to safeguard, enrich and strengtnen the cultural, political, social and economic fabric of Canada;

(c) all persons licensed to carry on broadcasting undertakings have a responsibility for programs they broadcast but the right to freedom of expression and the right of persons to receive programs, subject only to generally applicable statues and regulations, is unquestioned;

(d) the programming provided by the Canadian broadcasting system should be varied and comprehensive and should provide reasonable, balanced opportunity for the expression of differing views on matters of public concern, and the programming provided by each broadcaster should be of high standard, using predominantly Canadian creative and other resources;

(e) all Canadians are entitled to broadcasting service in English and French as public funds become available;

(f) there should be provided, through a corporation established by Parliament for the purpose, a national broadcasting service that is predominantly Canadian in content and character;

(g) the national broadcasting service should

(i) be a balanced service of information, enlightenment and entertainment for people of different ages, interests and tastes covering the whole range of programming in fair proportion,

(ii) be extended to all parts of Canada, as public funds become available,

(iii) be in English and French, serving the special needs of geographic regions, and actively contributing to the flow and exchange of cultural and regional information and entertainment, and

(iv) contribute to the development of national unity and provide for a continuing expression of Canadian identity;

(h) where any conflict arises between the objectives of the national broadcasting service and the interests of the private element of the Canadian broadcasting system, it shall be resolved in the public interest but paramount consideration shall be given to the objectives of the national broadcasting service;

(i) facilities should be provided within the Canadian broadcasting system for educational broadcasting; and

(j) the regulation and supervision of the Canadian broadcasting system should be flexible and readily adaptable to scientific and technical advances;

and that the objectives of the broadcasting policy for Canada enunciated in this section can best be achieved by providing for the regulation and supervision of the Canadian broadcasting system by a single independent public authority. *Reproduced with the permission of Communications Canada and the Minister of Supply and Services Canada, 1989.*

Apart from including cable as part of the broadcasting system, most changes set out in the 1968 Act were incremental in nature; they represented minor modifications to existing policies rather than dramatic new policy directions. A new regulatory agency, the Canadian Radio Television Commission (CRTC)[4] was created with authority over all public and private broadcast undertakings and cable television distributors. Its mandate is still in force today and includes administrative regulation, the promotion of the national interest, and the advancement of social and cultural values, as did the BBG mandate that it superseded. The Commission is also required to base its decisions on the broadcast policy enunciated in section 3 of the Act.

The Commission consists of nine full-time and ten part-time members appointed by governor-in-council. The executive committee, which has nearly exclusive decision-making power, consists of the full-time members. The part-time members, who represent the various regions, must be consulted with respect to issuing or revoking licences but are unable to overturn a decision made by the executive committee.

In order to maintain control over the CRTC, Cabinet has the power to review the agency's decisions and issue policy directives on broad issues. In addition, anyone who believes that a CRTC decision is contrary to the intent of the Broadcast Act may appeal to the governor-in-council. Although the Commission respects the position of the government in this regard, it argues that such actions undermine the integrity of its dealings with the industry.

The Commission develops regulations based upon the information it receives during public hearings, where it encourages sources with differing views to have a voice. It also acknowledges that its decisions can often be characterized as "policy" rather than "regulation" (Meisel 1983, 4). During his appearance before the House of Commons Standing Committee on Communications and Culture on 20 May 1987, André Bureau, then CRTC chairman, outlined the Commission's objectives:

Commitment of the CRTC for 1987

The commitment of the CRTC, the federal communications regulator, is to preserve and enhance communications systems in Canada in the interests of the Canadian public. In carrying out this commitment, the CRTC will foster an environment characterized by a wide diversity and availability of Canadian services and facilities offered by adequately resourced entities. Furthermore, in pursuit of this commitment, the CRTC will act in an efficient, pro-active and adaptive manner supported by the fullest possible public participation.

Broadcasting Goals

Within the context of the objectives, policy elements and directives contained in the existing legislation, the Commission will, as intermediate term goals:

1. foster quality, quantity and diversity of Canadian programs, and the development of Canadian talent;

2. foster the equalization of viewing and listening opportunities for all Canadians;

3. expand program choice for all Canadians;

4. facilitate the ability of the Canadian broadcasting system to perform successfully;

5. ensure regulation is responsive to cultural, social and other public concerns; and

6. ensure regulation continues to reflect the evolution of new technology.

Telecommunications Goals

Within the context of the objectives and policy elements contained in the existing legislation, the Commission will, as intermediate term goals;

1. ensure the provision of efficient, justly and reasonably priced telecommunications services;

2. ensure universal accessibility to basic telephone services;

3. ensure that telecommunication carriers do not unfairly take advantage of their monopoly or dominant market positions in dealings with subscribers, other carriers, or competitors;

4. ensure that telcos [telephone companies] are financially viable and able to provide basic services of adequate quality to meet subscriber needs; and

5. determine where regulation could be eliminated, reduced or made more flexible and, in particular, where regulation could be replaced/supplemented by reliance on market forces (Bureau 1987). *Reproduced with the permission of the House of Commons.*

The passage of the Broadcasting Act, 1968 and the establishment of both the CRTC and a House of Commons Standing Committee on Broadcasting and the Arts did not bring to an end disagreements over broadcasting in Canada. Indeed, the debate simply entered a new and more vigorous phase. The newly instituted CRTC held hearings in April 1970 to review the Canadian content regulations. Despite continued opposition from private broadcasters, the Commission retained the quota system established by the BBG and in fact attempted to reinforce it.

Meanwhile, the Special Senate Committee on the Mass Media released its report in 1970. It was very complimentary about the CBC's Canadian program content, taking into account the persistent funding problems, but severely criticized the private sector. Despite their profitability, private broadcasters achieved only the minimum content required by law (Canada, Special Senate Committee 1970, 205). They were making no real effort to achieve the nationalistic objectives of broadcasting.

The changing environment

The years following the enactment of the 1968 broadcasting legislation saw various studies undertaken to examine broadcasting. The lack of Canadian programming emerges as a consistent theme.

In 1978, the CRTC commissioned a special study to review the state of broadcasting in Canada over the previous decade. The report included a statistical review of the economics of broadcasting, the state of Canadian programming, and the interaction of the two. It concluded that broadcasters were able to comply with the minimum regulatory requirements with as little expense and effort as possible and that there must be "a renewed determination to produce high quality Canadian programming which will be watched by Canadian audiences" (Canada, CRTC 1979, 103).

The same trend was also noted by the Consultative Committee on the Implications of Telecommunications for Canadian Sovereignty. Established by the minister of communications in 1978, the Committee was directed to make recommendations on the future of the Canadian telecommunication system in relation to new technologies and foreign competition. Special attention was to be paid to the role of broadcasting in preserving Canada's sovereignty. The Committee concluded that the Canadian broadcasting system was not achieving the objectives of the Broadcasting Act. Broadcasters provided the minimum Canadian programming at the lowest possible cost; few resources were directed at producing good domestic programming.

In response to this and its own study, the CRTC declared its intention to review the Canadian content policy once again and hearings were held in December 1981. Before it could announce its new regulations, two further sets of policy recommendations were made, one by the Federal Cultural Policy Review Committee and the other by the federal Department of Communications (DOC).

The Federal Cultural Policy Review Committee produced a comprehensive review of federal cultural institutions and policies in 1982. The government was anxious both to ensure better control of the allocation of resources and to achieve policy coherence and accountability. To that end, the Committee made several recommendations about both the CBC and private broadcasters. It warned that technology was complicating the issue of Canadian programming on Canadian television by destroying international boundaries and suggested that new broadcasting legislation be brought forward to buttress the position of the CRTC.

To deal with new technologies such as satellite-delivered programming, the Department of Communications issued a statement in February 1983, reiterating the obligation of broadcasting to maintain the national identity. Four important new policies were outlined in the statement, two of them dealing specifically with programming and regulation: to establish a fund for assisting private television producers and to grant directive power over the CRTC to the Cabinet. In addition, eight proposals were advanced for further discussion. The policies and proposals together had three fundamental goals:

1. To maintain the Canadian broadcasting system as an effective vehicle of social and cultural policy in light of a renewed commitment to the spirit of the broadcasting objectives set out in the 1968 Broadcasting Act.

2. To make available to all Canadians a solid core of attractive Canadian programming in all program categories, through the development of strong Canadian broadcast and program production industries.

3. To provide a significantly increased choice of programming of all kinds in both official languages in all parts of Canada (Canada, DOC 1983b, 5).

The CRTC then held a series of consultative meetings with the Department of Communications and industry representatives to clarify the definition of "Canadian content." A point system was established in April 1984 that clearly delineated the criteria to be applied. In an effort to encourage development, the new definition was made identical to the one used by the Canadian Film and Videotape Certification Office of the DOC for funding film production. In addition, the CRTC awarded a 150 percent time credit for Canadian dramas carried by a licensee, if the dramas met the specified criteria.[5]

In May 1985, the newly elected Progressive Conservative government established the Task Force on Broadcasting Policy. Co-chaired by Gerald Caplan and Florian Sauvageau, the Task Force was required to make recommendations on "an industrial and cultural strategy to govern the future evolution of the Canadian broadcasting system through the remainder of this century, recognizing the importance of broadcasting to Canadian life" (Canada, Task Force 1986, 703). The findings are discussed in greater detail in chapters 7 and 8. For now, it is enough to recognize that the Task Force (1986, 5–6) was struck by two important perceptions: the Canadian broadcasting system "mostly works"; and the current issues are essentially the same ones that have plagued this policy arena from the beginning.

The Task Force also recognized that dramatic technological changes in the delivery, production, and reception of broadcast programming threaten the system by undermining regulation even as they enhance quality and choice. It therefore attempted to put forward recommendations that would maintain the integrity of the system. Like its many predecessors, it concluded that the Canadian broadcasting system "should offer, so far as possible, a truly Canadian service for those millions of Canadians who have demonstrated their belief in one" (Canada, Task Force 1986, 21).

The system today

Canadians are voracious consumers of electronic media products. With 514 originating radio stations, 114 television stations, and a multitude of rebroadcast transmitters, virtually every Canadian has access to radio service and all but 1 or 2 percent of the population can receive at least one television station.[6] In 1984, the average Canadian spent 23.6 hours per week watching television and 19.9 hours per week listening to the radio (Canada, Task Force 1986, 85). While radio audiences make very selective, individual decisions about the programming they listen to, the overwhelming choice of television viewers is drama, followed by news and public affairs. (Drama includes all live-action, story-telling types of programming.) As table 6.2 illustrates, this trend is consistent for English- and French-language television.

Table 6.2

Types of television programs viewed, 6 A.M. to 2 A.M., Monday to Sunday, 1984

Program type	English language (percentage of total viewing)	French language (percentage of total viewing)
News	12	13
Public affairs	6	12
Sports	12	12
Drama	48	36
Variety/music/quiz	19	21
Other	3	6
Total number of program hours available	51 900	20 700

Source: Canada, Task Force on Broadcasting Policy 1986, 91–92.

Canadians choose programs from three different sources: the public broadcasters, the private broadcasters, and the American broadcasters whose signals are available either off-air or via cable systems. The third sector is discussed in chapter 7 as part of the examination of cable television, but the discussion turns now to Canadian providers.

The Canadian Broadcasting Corporation

The Canadian Broadcasting Corporation is a federal Crown corporation responsible for national public broadcasting. Established by statute in 1936, the CBC reports annually to Parliament through the minister responsible. The CBC currently operates according to the Broadcasting Act, 1968. It is required to offer services in both English and French, which should be extended to and serve the needs of all parts of Canada.

It must also balance information and entertainment for people of different ages, interests, and tastes, and promote cultural and regional exchange. Finally, it must contribute to the development of national unity and the continuing expression of Canadian identity. Not a small chore!

Although it has been described as "the flagship and cultural guardian of the system" (Canadian Conference for the Arts 1980, 121), the CBC is the object of frequent and bitter criticism. Its bureaucratic and complex organization, its management and fiscal decisions, and its programming content and format have all been the subject of vociferous public debate. As Don Jamieson (1966, 145) once wrote,

> Practically everyone in Canada has an opinion on what ought to be done with the CBC. Few subjects generate more controversy or stronger feelings, and the remarkable fact is that the Corporation has succeeded in arousing the displeasure of friend and foe alike. Both groups agree on the need for changes, but there is no unanimity on the form the changes ought to take.

Despite its weaknesses, the CBC has been extremely successful in providing a variety of services to Canadians from coast to coast. Programming on all CBC services is overwhelmingly Canadian. Its radio services are highly distinctive and offered without commercials. The CBC owns and operates thirty-one originating television stations and sixty-eight originating radio stations (see table 6.3). It has affiliate arrangements with thirty-one television stations and a number of radio stations to deliver portions of CBC programming to areas where it has no stations of its own. With seventy-five production sites and sixteen hundred rebroadcast transmitters, the CBC spreads its signals into smaller communities. In addition, it operates an international short-wave service—Radio Canada International—and northern service for radio and television. The CBC also delivers to cable operators, via satellite, the House of Commons debates in both English and French and an English-language all-news specialty channel, for a total of twelve separate and distinct services.[7] It is not surprising, therefore, that the CBC is the largest single employer of Canadian performing and writing talent. These facts not only give some indication of the size of the CBC's operation, but they also suggest the importance of the Corporation to the federal government's cultural policy. They are, in part, the reason why the Task Force on Broadcasting Policy (1986, 269) identified the CBC as "the centerpiece of our broadcasting system . . . our largest and most important cultural institution."

Table 6.3

CBC stations operating in June 1986

	Television	Radio
English	18	31 mono 16 stereo
French	13	15 mono 6 stereo
Total	31	68

Source: Canada, Task Force on Broadcasting Policy 1986, 274.

Despite the glowing commendation, the CBC is facing a crisis. The federal government cut the Corporation's budget by $85 million between 1984 and 1989. Then in April 1989, Finance Minister Michael Wilson announced the government's intention to slash another $140 million from the CBC's parliamentary appropriations over the next five years. The Corporation claims that the real value of the cut is $380 million when extra taxes, increased costs of unemployment insurance, and lack of protection from inflation are taken into consideration (Austen 1989, 17). The cuts are a severe challenge for the public network and have a number of implications for its operations. Its plan to increase Canadian content from 80 to 95 percent is jeopardized. Plans to open new stations will probably be scrapped and some smaller stations may be forced to close. Radio Canada International may be forced to shut down and the northern service could experience cutbacks. Former CBC president Pierre Juneau believes, moreover, that about five hundred CBC employees will lose their jobs and warns, "There is a possibility that this is the beginning of the end. If the CBC stops doing the things that people feel make it indispensable, it starts a vicious cycle with more people saying it's not worth it" (in Austen 1989, 17).

The private broadcasters

To the private broadcasters, broadcasting is a business—a commercial, profit-making enterprise, financed through the sale of audiences to advertisers. They therefore often find themselves at odds with the government and the regulator over the conditions imposed upon them in return for the privilege of a broadcast licence. According to the Canadian Association of Broadcasters, "Private broadcasters undoubtedly form the chief, if not the only group in this country, which can be said to have a real thorough knowledge of the practical aspects and of the day to day challenges of broadcasting in this country" (Canada, CRTC 1970, 535).

The Association is a voluntary, non-profit national trade association whose members are people associated with broadcasting, and federally licensed individuals or companies operating television and radio stations or networks. Canada's private broadcasters are a heterogeneous group. Some are independent operators who own one or two small radio or television stations; others operate in much larger market areas. Members of networks that share the costs of producing and buying programming make up another group of television station owners. The main private English-language television networks are CTV and Global Television; French-language television network services are provided by TVA and Quatre Saisons. The CTV Television Network Ltd. is Canada's largest private television network, with eleven affiliated stations and $135.4 million in revenues in 1986 (*Financial Post* 1987, 7).[8] Each member station is obliged to sign an affiliation agreement that defines the ownership of the network and the relationships among the participants (one affiliate, one vote). The agreement stipulates the programming responsibilities of each party and the methods of sharing revenue. When the CRTC renewed the network's licence for five years in the spring of 1987, it demanded that CTV revise its 1976 affiliation agreement to encourage more Canadian content production. A serious struggle resulted between the network's two most powerful stations which has weakened, at least temporarily, CTV's once enviable position in the broadcasting arena.

Private radio stations are also a significant element of Canadian broadcasting. As illustrated in table 6.4, there were 446 originating private radio stations in Canada in 1984. Although the majority operate on the AM band, FM is quickly becoming the preferred medium and the number of FM stations has almost doubled since 1960. Private radio derives 97 percent of its total revenues from advertising, and spends 36 percent of its operating budget on programming. Although the overall profitability of radio has slipped over the past fifteen years, FM stations and AM stations in large metropolitan centres have increased their profits.

Table 6.4

Originating private radio stations, 1984

	AM	FM	Total
English-language	261	100	361
French-language	63	19	82
Other	2	1	3
Total	326	120	446

Source: Canada, Task Force on Broadcasting Policy 1986, 392.

Private radio and television undertakings approached revenues of $1.5 billion in 1984 and advertising accounted for the vast majority of that figure. Advertising is, in fact, vital to the success or failure of individual broadcast stations and to the maintenance of the whole system. Over the past twenty-five years, the electronic media's share of the total advertising revenue available has grown. Radio's portion has remained relatively stable, while television's has almost doubled its proportion at the expense of the daily newspaper.

Radio operates as a predominantly local medium and television tends to function on a national level. Of the eighty-one private originating English- and French-language television stations, all but ten are affiliated with networks and carry the network feed—the programming transmitted to the broadcasters by the network (see table 6.5). As in radio, advertising provides television stations with the largest share of their operating revenues. Revenues vary from station to station and are determined by each station's audience share. The relationship between audience share and revenues accounts, in large part, for the private broadcasters' programming patterns. Not only is it cheaper to buy foreign (mostly American) programming than to produce domestic fare, but such programming also attracts a larger audience and therefore a larger share of available advertising revenue.

Table 6.5

Private television stations, 1984

	English-language	French-language
Independents	10	0
TVA affiliates	0	10
CTV affiliates	29	0
CBC affiliates	27	0
Radio-Canada affiliates	0	5
Total	66	15

Source: Canada, Task Force on Broadcasting Policy 1986, 419.

Table 6.6 illustrates the programming expenditures of the private television broadcasters and the CBC. Not only do the private stations spend less in general on programming than the CBC does, they also spend considerably less on the production of domestic programming. Although this pattern holds true for the industry as a whole and for the anglophone stations in particular, it is not as characteristic of the French-language stations, which spend a high proportion of their programming budgets on Canadian material. Moreover, the pattern of program expenditures differs between English- and French-language stations in another respect. English-language stations devote a larger proportion of their domestic production budgets to local, regional, and national news and public affairs, products unavailable from foreign producers. They prefer, however, to rely on foreign producers for the majority of their entertainment programming. Because French-language stations do not have the option of purchasing a large variety of foreign-produced entertainment programs relatively cheaply, they must produce their own. A larger proportion of their budgets is therefore directed towards entertainment productions than towards public affairs programming, since entertainment is more expensive.

The failure of private anglophone television broadcasters to do more with respect to domestic programming, especially drama and children's

Table 6.6

Programming expenditures (in $ millions), 1984

	Private stations	CBC	Total
Canadian programming	$292	$540	$832
Foreign programming	$142	$ 23	$165
Total	$434	$563	$997

Source: *Canada, Task Force on Broadcasting Policy 1986, 429.*

shows, has been the most criticized aspect of the industry. Television has remained a consistently lucrative business during the last ten years, with average before-tax profits of between 17 and 20 percent. Many critics argue that the broadcasters have a responsibility to put a little more back into the system to enhance and strengthen it. This issue will be dealt with in more detail in chapter 8.

Educational broadcasting

Broadcasting is a federal responsibility, but education falls under the purview of the provinces. Educational broadcasting was therefore a disputed issue in Canada until 1969, when the jurisdictional debate was settled by a compromise. Each province was permitted to establish an independent authority to produce and transmit educational programming, loosely defined as programming that provides a continuity of learning opportunities for the members of the audience.

To date, four educational networks have been established. Radio-Québec, the Ontario Educational Communication Authority (TV-Ontario), and the Alberta Educational Communication Authority (ACCESS) are all federally licensed and each produces, purchases, and transmits programming. British Columbia's Knowledge Network is funded by the province, but since it merely transmits programs rather than producing them, the provincial government defines it as a telecommunication service. The network therefore does not require federal licensing. The other six provinces have begun to develop educational networks but none has yet reached the level attained by the first four.

The Task Force on Broadcasting Policy (1986) was very supportive of the educational networks and recommended that they be encouraged to participate fully in the Canadian broadcasting system by selling more of their programming, both to the CBC and to private stations, especially in provinces without educational networks. They supply indigenous programming of all sorts and are particularly valuable sources of programming for children, an audience sorely underserved by the existing system.

Other broadcasting services

In addition to the broadcasting services outlined above, there are several others that, although small in scope, are nonetheless important elements of the Canadian broadcasting system. They are directed to community interests, native peoples, official language minorities, and a variety of multicultural minorities.

In the past, technical impediments such as limited spectrum space and the challenges of geography restricted the provision of these services. However, advances in transmission and delivery techniques, including cable and satellite technologies, have eased the difficulty of providing the services. Yet like all other broadcast undertakings they remain expensive to operate. Substantial programming costs and the need for a fairly high degree of technical expertise reduce the number of potential alternative services. Both the federal and provincial governments have assisted several groups seeking access to the broadcasting system, as has the cable television industry. Despite their inherent value in preserving cultural heritage and promoting a sense of community, however, these services remain on the fringe of broadcasting.

Quebec: Pas comme les autres

Broadcasting in Quebec is distinctive. Its special flavour springs from a linguistic and cultural heritage that has acted as a lively creative force within the province. In addition, the government of Quebec has steadfastly involved itself in the communication policy arena since the Aird Commission in 1929. Relying on its jurisdictional control of education and culture, the provincial government has taken a number of steps to ensure that its presence is felt. It established Radio-Québec, a provincial Department of Communications, the Société de développement des industries de la culture et des communications, and the Société générale du cinema, and in doing so has created an extensive network of support for film and television production.

Because there is little suitable French broadcast programming available from foreign sources, Quebec's public and private broadcasters are obliged to produce their own. Although they began by imitating the formats of popular American fare, Quebec productions soon took on a unique character. Variety shows featured francophone performers and created several new stars, but the most popular genre of programming was, and still is, the "téléroman" or television novel. Based on both the literature of Quebec's foremost novelists and new scripts, these weekly half-hour serials met with great success. *La famille Plouffe*, one of the first teleromans produced, attracted a faithful audience in both English and French and remains one of Radio-Canada's most successful production ventures. *Des dames de cœur*, a recent hit, is merely an updated version of the traditional genre. Although the francophone production industry has clearly been successful and its Canadian programming has proven very popular with the francophone audience, this lively sector is currently facing a variety of threats.

As in English Canada, the slick production values of American programming are attracting more and more viewers in Quebec, especially those in the younger age groups. The trend can be attributed to the inadequacy of financial resources for Canadian productions. It currently costs about CDN$100 000 to produce one hour of drama for francophone television. English-language drama productions, which compete more directly with American-produced shows, cost about CDN$250 000 per hour. On the other hand, it is not unusual for the American networks to spend CDN$1 000 000 to produce hour-long episodes of their most popular programs. With such disparities, it is not surprising that Canadian viewers find themselves attracted to high-budget American broadcast fare.

The increasingly competitive nature of the francophone broadcasting market is another factor undermining indigenous programming. Each time a new broadcast service enters the market, the amount of American programming available in that area increases. New domestic stations rely on foreign programming to reduce costs and increase revenues. Purchasing and dubbing American productions is cheaper than producing domestic fare; and American programming attracts a larger audience and more advertising revenue. American services that are transmitted via cable or satellite broadcast also increase competition in the broadcasting market and fragment the available audience. What is more, their programming has almost 100 percent foreign content. Whether or not a new service is Canadian, then, it increases the total hours of foreign programming available and therefore diversifies the already small audience and dilutes the limited advertising base.

The international predominance of American productions creates another somewhat ironic dilemma for French Canadian film and video producers. The shared language of Quebec and France naturally encourages co-production agreements, but Quebec film producers are becoming more and more frustrated with this arrangement. Some of their European counterparts prefer to shoot their films in English to enhance their appeal in the American market and then have them dubbed in French for home audiences. Unless Canadian producers agree to these conditions, they are obliged to look elsewhere for financial partners.

The unique challenges confronting francophone broadcasting have been recognized by both the federal and provincial governments. Quebec is fiercely protective of its control over cultural affairs, carefully guarding this policy arena from federal encroachment. Yet a growing awareness of the industry's problems encouraged the province to enter into an agreement with the federal Department of Communications in February 1986, in order to co-ordinate the development of French-language television in Quebec and across the country. The joint undertaking is a milestone in the effort to revitalize francophone broadcasting services.

Broadcasting in the North

Although Canada's North remains physically isolated, the electronic media have brought the rest of country and indeed the world into the homes of northern residents. As Andra McCartney (1984, 15) notes, "It is impossible for the North to be isolated as in the past when the news is now shown several times a day. . . . Residents of the Terrorities are aware of all that happens in the world, through the eyes of the commercial media."

Northern broadcasting began in 1958 with a tape-delayed short-wave radio service[9] instituted by the newly created Northern Service of the CBC. Fifteen years later, the Corporation began its drive to bring television services via satellite to all communities of five hundred or more residents. Today, the Northern Service provides over one hundred hours of television programming per week, Canadian Satellite Communications Inc. (Cancom) delivers a full satellite-to-cable service of radio and television broadcast channels,[10] and northerners themselves operate close to two hundred smaller broadcasting services. These impressive gains, however, have not been without financial and cultural costs.

During the latter half of the 1970s, the federal government seriously addressed the issue of broadcasting quantity, quality, and content in the remote and underserved areas of the country. Satellites were judged to be "an ideal technology for overcoming the tyranny of distance and population dispersion" (Department of Communications 1983a, 1). In 1973, under pressure from the government of the day, the CBC began to make significant investments in the Anik-series satellite program, providing regular CBC programming to remote and underserved areas. The service was very successful in its own right, but it was not enough to satisfy the demands of broadcast consumers. More and more individuals, communities, and cable companies began to receive and distribute American satellite signals, a practice unauthorized by the CRTC and the owners of those signals.

Policy makers found it increasingly difficult to respond to the demands of the underserved communities. Establishing satellite broadcasting infrastructures was expensive, especially when calculated per capita. Citizens in the heavily settled regions of the country were also making demands for more and better electronic services. In response the CRTC established the Committee on Extension of Service to Northern and Remote Communities (1980), chaired by Réal Therrien, to provide advice about the general expansion of television services.

On the recommendation of the Therrien Committee, the CRTC called for applications from private entrepreneurs to provide a national satellite service and subsequently licensed Canadian Satellite Communications Inc. Cancom began its service in 1981 with authorization to carry eight radio and four television channels. In 1983, it was granted permission to transmit each of the four American networks. Cancom provides radio signals at no charge, but individuals who want access to the scrambled television signals must either own their own satellite receivers and rent decoders from Cancom, or subscribe to a local cable service.

In addition to the services of Cancom, which now reach close to one million households, northern and remote viewers can also get access to satellite-delivered Canadian pay-television and specialty channels,[11] and to a number of unauthorized American satellite services. Undoubtedly this represents a dramatic increase in the range of available services, yet certain issues remain unresolved: copyright infringement, the high cost of the services, the paucity of available French-language services, and the cultural impact of imported broadcasting on northern native peoples.

In Canada's North, as in other regions of the country, the influence of broadcasting is pervasive. Almost all northern native households have radio, between 88 and 96 percent have television, and 20 to 40 percent have video cassette recorders (Stiles and Litvak 1988, 42). Initial efforts to bring broadcasting services to the North were directed at non-indigenous residents, however, not native peoples. Although the first Inuit-language radio program was broadcast in 1960, English-language programming produced in southern Canada or the United States has always clearly predominated in northern broadcasting. Furthermore, it can be argued that "northern communication policy . . . evolved on an ad hoc basis, . . . in response to a technological policy determined to make Canada internationally competitive in the aerospace industry" (Roth 1983, 43). The federal government and the broadcasters themselves ignored native needs for the most part throughout the first ten to fifteen years of northern broadcasting.

By the mid-1970s, it was becoming very apparent that the available broadcast programming posed threats to the Inuit culture and way of life:

> Television service . . . was greeted with mixed emotions in native communities, ranging from curiosity to contempt. Soap operas like *The Edge of Night* and *All My Children* proved so popular that work hours and community activities had to be scheduled around them.
>
> Children in many parts of the Northwest Territories were habitually late for school after watching late-night movies on television. Many communities were concerned about the gratuitous violence, the exploitation, and the consumerism of southern TV (Stiles and Litvak 1988, 22).

In response to growing concerns about the decreased cohesiveness of native communities and the personal identity crises faced by many youths, native people began to demand more say in northern broadcast services.[12] They wanted programming in their native language, about their traditional lifestyles and values. They insisted that they had a right to participate in program production and that they be consulted about northern communication services.

In 1981, the CRTC licensed an Inuit television network to share satellite transponder space[13] with the CBC and with a satellite radio network jointly operated by the Yukon Indians and the Dene.[14] The radio network was designed to offer programming in several aboriginal languages. Yet these measures were merely a stopgap until the federal government could devise a detailed policy for northern broadcasting. After consultation with native peoples, the government announced its northern broadcast policy in 1983. Its objective was to maintain native language and culture through relevant programming produced by aboriginal groups themselves. To this end, the government directed existing northern broadcasters, including the CBC and Cancom,[15] to distribute native-language programming, and established the $40 million Northern Native Broadcast Access Program to train and assist native northerners to produce their own radio and television broadcast programming.

The Inuit Broadcasting Corporation (IBC) began transmission in January 1982. By 1986, there were thirteen independent native societies producing about 10 hours of television and 150 hours of radio programming per week, most of it in native languages (Task Force 1986, 516). Although native broadcasting has improved significantly, much remains to be done. Native broadcasters want a satellite uplink of their own, to eliminate their dependence on other service providers. An uplink would permit them to transmit their own signal to their own satellite transponder. They also require more funding in order to increase the amount of programming they can make available, and want legislated recognition of aboriginal broadcasting rights. Both the Task Force on Broadcasting Policy (1986) and the Standing Committee on Communications and Culture (1988) were sympathetic to these demands:

> All Canadians should take pride in the remarkable achievements of native broadcasting. Aboriginal broadcasting in our northern regions is a uniquely Canadian success story and serves as an example to the rest of the world . . . . Our recommendations are designed to place aboriginal broadcasting, especially native-language broadcasting, on a firm foundation that will enable it to continue to flourish in Canada's North and expand to meet the needs of the native populations elsewhere in Canada (Standing Committee 1988, 275).

Film

Film developed as a mass medium during the first two decades of the twentieth century. It combines good quality sound and video to create a high-involvement medium that reaches many different audiences. Although it has many possible functions, film is most often used as an entertainment medium and is chosen as such by millions of people, especially in the younger generation.

Canada's film industry began in 1939, when the federal government established the National Film Board (NFB) with a mandate requiring it to interpret Canada to Canadians. Led by John Grierson, the NFB pioneered the documentary film genre and over the past fifty years has established an enviable international record. Canadians, however, are less appreciative of the NFB. The Board produces an average of ninety films a year but few are ever exhibited to large audiences. Neither TVA nor CTV use much NFB material in their schedules and although the CBC exhibits more, most of the films are used as fillers and have low audience appeal. The exceptions are films co-produced by the CBC and NFB, which generally get reasonable air play. Two recent examples are *Canada's sweetheart: Hal Banks* and *Final offer: Bob White and UAW*. Generally though, the networks argue that most NFB films are unsuitable for television. They are reluctant to replace profitable American programming with unproven and financially risky NFB films.

In 1968, the federal government created the Canadian Film Development Corporation (CFDC) to develop a private film production industry in Canada as an alternative to the NFB. The CFDC stimulated the industry by assisting independent film makers financially, and by 1979 there were almost as many movies made in Canada as in Hollywood (Knelman 1985, 136). Some of these films reflected Canadian life and received critical acclaim in domestic and international film circles, but the vast majority were American movies made with Canadian money in Canadian cities.[16] Some of them were so bad that they were never released.

By 1983, the bubble had burst and Minister of Communications Francis Fox announced a number of changes to the government film development policy. The CFDC became Telefilm Canada. Not only was Telefilm required to support a film production industry but it was also obliged to administer the newly created $254 million Canadian Broadcast Program Development Fund for television programming. The criteria for funding were tightened to ensure that Telefilm was supporting Canadian productions rather than subsidizing the American industry. The new Canadian Film and Videotape Certification Office (CFVCO) rated all applications by a point system to determine their acceptability.

Following some changes to its initial funding arrangements, Telefilm has been very successful. During its first three years of operation the Broadcast Fund was partially responsible for increasing the number of hours of Canadian drama on English-language television by 49 percent, from 5.4 percent of the total to 8 percent. Telefilm has helped the CBC to produce such recent successes as *Anne of Green Gables*, *Love and larceny*, and *Danger Bay*, and the CTV network to create *Night heat*, *Bell Canada playhouse*, and *The Campbells*. In addition to receiving domestic acclaim, many of these productions have attracted highly sought-after foreign sales.

Despite its successes, Telefilm Canada has recently come under attack for its lack of a strong, coherent policy that would take the future of the industry into account. Failure to spend all of its annual budget, to accept all of the projects presented to it, and to achieve a reasonable degree of regional equality in distributing financial grants has placed Telefilm in the midst of controversy. In combination with the unpredictability of long-term funding, these factors threaten the continued success of this cultural agency.

Perhaps the most significant hurdle to the establishment of a profitable Canadian production industry is the distribution system. Access to Canadian and foreign theatres and to the revenues they generate is still very restricted. In Canada, as elsewhere, foreign gatekeepers, mostly American, control the distribution companies. Canadian films are given only about 3 percent of available domestic screen time (*Globe and Mail* 1987, C1). Over 80 percent of Canadian theatrical distribution revenues go to distributors owned and operated by the large Hollywood production companies, which tend to flood the market with their own films (Canada, DOC 1984, 37). When and if they exhibit a Canadian film, they do so only in a limited number of theatres for a short time, retaining the lion's share of the exhibition revenues.

The federal Department of Communications has recognized the severity of the problem. In 1987, it drafted legislation designed to give Canadian film distributors more control over distribution and a bigger share of the lucrative market, but although it was not a part of the FTA, the Cinema Bill fell victim to the free trade negotiations with the United

States. When the American film industry lobby exerted its powerful clout in Washington, Ottawa was forced to shelve the impending legislation in order to keep the FTA discussions on track. The situation therefore remains unchanged. Without access to movie theatres at home and abroad, and to the revenues they generate, the future for the Canadian production industry is bleak.

Summary

This chapter detailed the development of radio and television broadcasting and the film production industry in Canada. Special attention was paid to broadcasting in Quebec and in the North. Throughout, the chapter emphasized the recurrence of three themes—nationalism, economics, and technology—that have marked the history of the electronic media in Canada. Broadcasting has been selected by federal policy makers as the primary medium for transmitting Canadian ideals, values, and culture: "No cultural industry is more central to the Canadian public consciousness than broadcasting; none captures as much of our leisure time. For these reasons, the Canadian Broadcasting System, in both its private and public elements, has long been recognized as one of the principal instruments for our cultural expression" (MacDonald 1987, 10).

Domestic broadcasters are confronted by many economic challenges, however, that make accomplishing that task difficult. The relatively small and widely dispersed population and the existence of two official languages make broadcasting an expensive undertaking in Canada. Broadcasters also face competitive threats from the well-financed, highly popular American networks. New and powerful technologies have compounded the challenges facing broadcasting by removing international boundaries as a barrier to communication. Chapter 7 examines these innovations with particular emphasis on the new delivery systems and the services they make possible.

Notes

1. There are two general classes of advertising. Direct advertising involves, for example, a car manufacturer renting a short amount of broadcast time to extol the virtues of an automobile. Indirect advertising, on the other hand, permits the manufacturer to rent a large block of time, produce a program, and announce before, during, and after the show its name and the fact that it contributed to the program.

2. The BBG could regulate matters with respect to its own rules of procedure, the amount of time reserved for broadcasting network programs, program standards, advertising, political broadcasts and advertisements, public interest broadcasts, conditions of station operation, and the information required from licensees. It could also use regulation to promote and ensure the greater use of Canadian talent by broadcasting stations.

3. Robert Fowler chaired two investigations into broadcasting in Canada. The first was the Royal Commission on Broadcasting from 1955 to 1957. The second was the Advisory Committee on Broadcasting in 1965. Care must be taken to avoid confusing the two.

4. The CRTC's title and mandate were altered in 1976 when the Commission was delegated responsibility for telecommunications and was renamed the Canadian Radio-television and Telecommunications Commission. Until that time, telecommunication issues were regulated by the Canadian Transportation Commission (CTC) under the terms of the Railway Act. It became evident, however, that the expertise required suited the CRTC more than the CTC. Since 1976, the CRTC has divided its bureaucracy into two sections. In addition, when the CRTC sits in public hearing, two essentially distinct panels review either broadcasting or telecommunication issues.

5. A broadcaster who has been granted a 150 percent time credit for a given program can count one and a half times the actual length of the program towards the Canadian content time quota. A two-hour Canadian movie, for example, could be counted as three hours of Canadian content.

6. Originating stations produce and transmit programming; rebroadcast transmitters merely help to transmit the signals produced by originating stations.

7. The CBC's twelve services are, in both English and French, AM radio, FM radio, television, Northern Services, and Parliamentary Channels, and in English only, Radio Canada International and the all-news television specialty channel, Newsworld.

8. The number of CTV affiliates recently dropped to nine when two stations withdrew because the network could not resolve the issues of ownership and control.

9. Tape-delayed programming is aired some time after it is first taped.

10. Cancom transmits radio and TV signals via satellite. The cable operators who receive the signals then deliver them via cable to subscribers.

11. Pay-TV and specialty channels are all owned and operated independently but their delivery is contingent upon individual agreements with home-service suppliers such as cable companies.

12. Gail Valaskakis (1983, 1986, 1988) provides a detailed analysis of Inuit broadcasting development and related issues.

13. Every satellite has several transponders, each assigned to a single broadcaster or telecommunication carrier. The transponder receives the signal

transmitted by the broadcaster and then sends it back down to a large area of the earth's surface.

14. The cost of operating the network was subsidized by the federal Department of Indian and Northern Affairs.

15. While Cancom distributes the radio programming of two native communication societies, it has neither provided a video uplink for native-produced programming nor included ten hours per week of native-produced television programming on its schedules. Both of these requirements are a condition of its licence.

16. One of the challenges to the Canadian production industry is explained by Robertson Davies (1989, 40), who recalls "being offered publication in the United States on the condition that I make a few alterations that would transfer the scene of my novel to the United States. To this day that is virtually a condition of having a motion picture made of a Canadian novel."

References

Agee, W.K., P.H. Ault, and E. Emery. 1976. *Introduction to mass communications.* 5th ed. New York: Harper and Row.

Austen, I. 1989. The clouded CBC picture. *Financial Times of Canada.* 22 May. pp.17–18.

Blakely, S.W. 1979. Canadian private broadcasters and the re-establishment of a private broadcasting network. Ph.D. diss., University of Michigan.

Bureau, A. 1987. Address to the House of Commons Standing Committee on Communications and Culture. 20 May. Ottawa, Ontario.

Canada. 1936. *Canadian Broadcasting Act, 1936.* Ottawa: King's Printer.

———. 1958. *Broadcasting Act, 1958.* Ottawa: Queen's Printer.

———. 1968. *Broadcasting Act, 1968.* Ottawa: Supply and Services.

Canada. Advisory Committee on Broadcasting. 1965. *Report.* Ottawa: Queen's Printer.

Canada. Canadian Radio-television and Telecommunications Commission (CRTC). 1970. *Public hearings.* Vol. 1. 14–22 April. Ottawa, Ontario.

———. 1979. *Special report on broadcasting, 1968–1978.* Vol. 1. Ottawa: Supply and Services.

Canada. CRTC. Committee on Extension of Service to Northern and Remote Communities. 1980. *The 1980s—A decade of diversity: Broadcasting satellites and pay-TV.* Ottawa: Supply and Services.

Canada. Department of Communications. 1983a. *Direct-to-home satellite broadcasting for Canada.* Ottawa: Supply and Services.

———. 1983b. *Towards a new national broadcasting policy.* Ottawa: Supply and Services.

———. 1984. *The national film and video policy.* Ottawa: Supply and Services.

Canada. Federal Cultural Policy Review Committee. 1982. *Report.* Ottawa: Supply and Services.

Canada. House of Commons. 1928. *Debates.* 16th Parliament.

———. 1932. *Debates.* 17th Parliament.

Canada. House of Commons. Standing Committee on Communications and Culture. 1988. *A broadcasting policy for Canada.* Ottawa: Supply and Services.

Canada. Royal Commission on Broadcasting. 1957. *Report.* Vol. 1. Ottawa: Queen's Printer.

Canada. Royal Commission on National Development in the Arts, Letters and Sciences. 1951. *Report.* Ottawa: King's Printer.

Canada. Royal Commission on Radio Broadcasting. 1929. *Report*. Ottawa: Edmund Cloutier.

Canada. Special Senate Committee on Mass Media. 1970. *Report*. Vol. 1, *The uncertain mirror*. Ottawa: Queen's Printer.

Canada. Task Force on Broadcasting Policy. 1986. *Report*. Ottawa: Supply and Services.

Canadian Conference for the Arts. 1980. *A strategy for culture: Proposals for a federal policy for the arts and the cultural industries in Canada*. Ottawa: Canadian Conference for the Arts.

Davies, R. 1989. Signing away Canada's soul: Culture, identity, and the free-trade agreement. *Harper's* (January): 43–47.

Financial Post. 1987. CTV power struggle darkening. 16 November. p. 8.

Gerbner, G., L.P. Gross, and W. Melody. 1973. *Communications, technology and social policy*. New York: Wiley.

Globe and Mail. 1987. The great Canadian screen test. 10 October. p. C1.

Jamieson, D. 1966. *The troubled air*. Fredericton: Brunswick.

Juneau, P. 1986. Remarks to the annual conference of the International Institute of Communications. 11 September. Edinburgh, Scotland.

Knelman, M. 1985. Whatever became of our film industry? *Toronto Life* (November): 78, 136, 138.

McCartney, A. 1984. Letter from Yellowknife. *border/lines* (Fall): 15–20.

MacDonald, F. 1987. Address to the Canadian Cable Television Association. 5 May. Montreal, Quebec.

Marsh, D. 1935. *The tragedy of Henry Thornton*. Toronto: MacMillan.

Meisel, J. 1983. Address to the Canadian Association of Members of Public Utilities Tribunals. 7 September. St. John's, Newfoundland.

Peers, F.W. 1969. *The politics of Canadian broadcasting, 1920–1951*. Toronto: University of Toronto.

———. 1979. *The public eye; Television and the politics of Canadian broadcasting, 1952–1968*. Toronto: University of Toronto.

Prang, M. 1965. The origins of public broadcasting in Canada. *Canadian Historical Review* 46(1): 1–31.

Re regulation and control of radio communications in Canada [1931] S.C.R. 541.

Roth, L. 1983. Inuit media projects and northern communication. In *Communications and the Canadian North*, 42–66. Montreal: Department of Communications, Concordia University.

Stewart, A. (unpublished mimeograph). Alternative television service.

Stiles, M.J., and W. Litvak. 1988. *Native broadcasting in the North of Canada: A new and potent force*. Ottawa: Canadian Commission for UNESCO.

Valaskakis, G. 1983 Communication and control in the Canadian North: The Inuit experience. In *Communications in Canadian society*, ed. B.D. Singer, 237-47. Don Mills: Addison-Wesley.

———. 1986. Restructuring the Canadian broadcast system: Aboriginal broadcasting in the North. In *Canadian broadcasting: The challenge of change*, ed. C. Hoskins and S. McFadyen, 53–57. Edmonton: University of Alberta.

———. 1988. Television and cultural integration: Implications for native communities in the Canadian North. In *Communication Canada: Issues in broadcasting and new technologies*, ed. R.W. Lorimer and D.C. Wilson, 124–38. Toronto: Kagan and Woo.

FACING THE
TECHNOLOGICAL CHALLENGE

*T*he consequences of technological change were identified in chapter 6 as a recurring theme in Canadian broadcasting. Although technological progress helps Canadians to communicate with one another across this vast country, it also threatens our cultural sovereignty. Routinely, the arrival of each advance in communications technology has been greeted eagerly by the private sector and the general public but with anxious uncertainty by governments and regulators. New technologies create demands for new cultural products, and domestic cultural industries are ill-equipped to keep pace. Successive governments have therefore tried to delay implementation of technological innovations, for fear that foreign-produced software will dominate the new hardware. By the time governments respond to public demand, audiences have become accustomed to a steady flow of foreign cultural products and resist attempts to curtail or modify it. The traditional solutions have been to impose Canadian content guidelines and to use financial incentives to boost domestic production. This cycle has repeated itself for several decades.

The introduction of television, a medium requiring both expensive new hardware and programming content, provides a clear example of this pattern. While the Canadian government studied the new technology, its citizens, particularly those living close to the American border, were buying television receiver sets and large rooftop antennae to gain access to the television programming available in the United States. By the time the CBC was permitted to undertake television broadcasting, the domestic audience had become familiar with the production and content of American programming. Canadians were reluctant to accept the new and different programming of their national broadcasters, and began demanding more foreign content on domestic stations. Because of the economic benefits, many broadcasters were willing to oblige, and Canadian governments and regulators continue to look for ways to enhance the domestic presence on the nation's airwaves.

From the developments in electromagnetic broadcasting to the digital and laser innovations of today, the impact of technology on communication and culture has been profound. It has helped to create cultural industries, such as the recording industry and the film production industry, and has made cultural products accessible. Yet because technology respects no boundaries, it has also increased the potential for one culture to dominate another.[1] What is more, the newest technologies are challenging the existence of older ones:

> New communications technology is radically changing the basic fabric of the traditional cultural industries: print and electronic media. It is giving birth to new variants such as videotex and videodisc; it is substantially altering the electronic cultural industries of radio and television; and it is causing great uncertainty about the continuing viability of other established cultural industries, such as newspapers, film and publishing (Lyman 1983, 1–2).

Peter Lyman (1983, 14–19) identifies four effects of technology on the evolution of cultural industries. Technology not only provokes changes within a particular medium, it also forces changes in other media as they attempt to adjust to the altered environment. Again, the introduction of television illustrates the point, since it forced both radio and newspapers to re-evaluate their content. Radio dramas have virtually disappeared and newspapers now emphasize their own visual content, using photographs, illustrations, and colour. Second, technology shapes the form, content, and consumption of media products. New media initially imitate the programming of their predecessors. (Television was first treated as radio with pictures.) The media soon create their own formats and patterns of consumption, however, based on the imperatives and potential of the technology that they use. Third, the impact of technology is difficult to predict. We tend to overestimate the early effect of a new technology and to underestimate its consequences over the long term. Finally, once a new technology is successfully introduced, it enables new media products and service to follow rapidly. When cable television service first became available, for example, it spawned various new services such as pay-TV and specialty channels.

Lyman (1983, 19–24) also predicts four future media trends based on the evolution of existing technologies: convergence, segmentation, home consumption, and globalization. Convergence refers to the blurring of media boundaries. To the consumer, movies, television, pay-television, and video cassettes are virtually interchangeable entertainment media. Segmentation occurs as more specialized services—such as specialty television and radio channels—become available. Specialized products segment the mass audience by catering to very specific interests. Third, the home is fast becoming the centre for both information and entertainment media. As telecommunication develops, component media centres will incorporate a greater variety of elements (see figure 7.1) and people will be able to use more and more services at home. Finally, media production and distribution can be expected to become increasingly global in scope. Although globalization gives the advantage to large, multinational hardware and software interests, there is still potential for smaller producers, like those in Canada, to reach international and specialized markets.

This chapter reviews the technological developments that have created challenges for Canadian policy makers, analyses the public policy responses to these innovations, and examines future issues and solutions from a Canadian perspective.

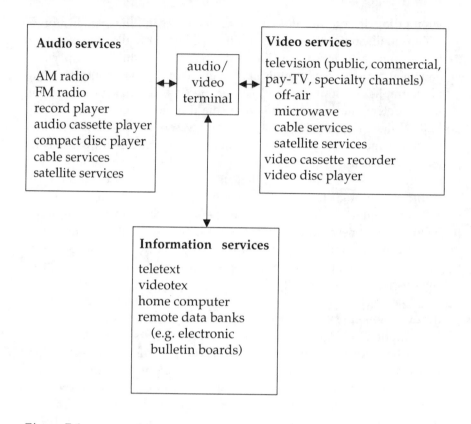

Figure 7.1

The component home media centre

Radio: AM and FM

Since its invention almost a hundred years ago, radio broadcasting has experienced many technological improvements to the strength and fidelity of its transmitted signal. In recent years, the FM transmission mode has gained popularity over AM. The shift marks an important development in the quality and fidelity of radio signals.

AM and FM radio signals are distinguished by two technical features: frequency and modulation. A radio transmitter produces electric waves called carrier or radio frequency waves, and combines them with the electric waves produced from the sound of the particular radio program. AM (amplitude modulation) and FM (frequency modulation) are the two different methods of combining the carrier waves and the program signal in order to transmit the sound. AM signals are transmitted by varying the *amplitude* of the carrier waves (their height, or strength) to match variations in the electric waves from the program. FM signals, on the other hand, vary the *frequency* of the carrier waves—the number of times they vibrate per second. (See figure 7.2.) AM signals occupy medium frequencies along the electromagnetic spectrum[2] and FM signals operate at very high frequencies. Because of their different methods of transmission, AM and FM radio signals have different characteristics. FM can carry more information and is less susceptible to static than is AM. As a result, FM radio delivers a high-fidelity sound. AM signals, however, can travel much greater distances.

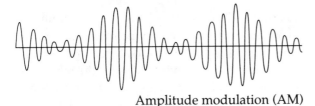

Amplitude modulation (AM)

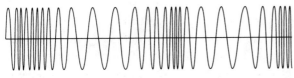

Frequency modulation (FM)

Figure 7.2

Amplitude and frequency modulation

FM radio in Canada has always been subject to detailed CRTC regulation designed to protect the markets of AM radio stations. FM is considered a medium for catering to specialized audiences, while AM radio retains its general appeal. FM stations are therefore subject to stringent format regulations, which not only limit direct competition between AM and FM stations but also ensure diversity in radio services. AM stations, on the other hand, are subject to only two basic regulatory requirements: they must conform to a 30 percent Canadian content quota for musical selections and they must maintain logs or diaries and logger tapes—tapes of programming.

Canadian policy makers generally support differentiation between AM and FM services and continued regulation to preserve the distinctive nature of the Canadian radio broadcasting industry. The regulations are intended to meet the needs of the audiences without restraining broadcasters' creativity. In other words, the difference that the regulations uphold between FM and AM programming is in the degree of flexibility they allow: "It is a matter of à-la-carte programming for AM and table-d'hôte programming for FM" (Task Force 1986, 406).

Over-the-air television

Television, like radio, was originally transmitted over the air from the television station to receiving antennae perched on the rooftops of many homes. This mode of transmission is limited by distance and terrain. Television signals travel in a straight line, leaving those on the other side of a hill or down in a valley without access to the signal. The signals are also restricted to very high (VHF) and ultra high frequencies (UHF), and are therefore subject to interference from the weather and other electromagnetic energy.[3]

Direct over-the-air transmission was eventually supplemented by microwave relay stations. (The term microwave refers to the wave path used by these transmissions.) The originating station sends out the signal to a transmitter about fifty kilometres away, where it is received, amplified, and transmitted to the next relay station, and so on until the signal reaches its destination. The initial capital expenditures are very high but once in place, the technology is not only cost effective but also highly efficient. It is limited, however, to receivers within a fifty-kilometre line-of-sight radius from the relay stations.

Over-the-air and microwave transmission techniques were very useful in extending the broadcast signals of local Canadian broadcasters, both public and private, but they did not satisfy the demands of the Canadian public for access to signals from the American border stations. By delaying the introduction of television in Canada until 1952, the Canadian government had inadvertently encouraged Canadians living along the Canada–U.S. border to become accustomed to programming from nearby American stations. When Canadian television stations failed to provide that programming, or at least enough of it, consumers looked for other means to satisfy their programming appetites. Cable television distribution systems provided the answer.

Cable systems

The Caplan/Sauvageau Task Force (1986, 551) describes community antenna television (CATV), or cable as "a unique component of the broadcasting system." Cable systems began as a means of improving the over-the-air transmission of local broadcast signals, since cable could provide a more clearly defined picture without static or interference. During the 1960s, CATV systems were increasingly used to import the broadcast signals of American border stations. Today, over nine hundred systems deliver a wide range of broadcast signals, both domestic and foreign, to over five million Canadian homes.

Cable technology has three elements: the head-end, a device to capture the broadcast signal and amplify it; a trunk line, which connects the head-end to the delivery system; and the delivery system itself, which carries the signal to each individual subscriber. A collection of trunk lines makes up a trunking system. The lines are made of coaxial cable.[4] Although the cable has the potential to carry about fifty channels, including two-way communications, the system's length and capacity are both limited in order to maintain the clarity of channel signals.

Coaxial cable has about three hundred times the capacity of the paired copper wire traditionally used in telephone lines but it is outshone by the newest transmission medium—optical fibre. Optical fibres are very thin strands of glass capable of carrying large amounts of information in very little space. With laser technology, signals travel further and with less interference through optical fibre than they do via coaxial cable. The new technology is slowly replacing both paired copper wire and coaxial cable in the trunking systems of telecommunication carriers but it will be some time before it is used to transmit information directly to households.

Although Canada is the second most cabled nation in the world (after Belgium), CATV delivery systems are not at present available to all Canadians; nor do all Canadians with access to cable service subscribe to them. Cable subscribers tend to be younger, better educated, and more affluent than non-subscribers. Table 7.1 indicates that although 80 percent of Canadians have access to CATV systems, only about 76 percent of those subscribe, leaving the total penetration rate at about 61 percent.

Subscription levels also vary by province. While its coverage and penetration levels have probably peaked, cable remains the preferred distribution system for most Canadians.

Table 7.1

Availability of cable, and subscription levels, 1984

	Households in cabled areas (as a percentage of total households)	Cable subscribers (as a percentage of households in cabled areas)	Cable subscribers (as a percentage of total households)
Newfoundland	49.1	74.4	36.5
Prince Edward Island	45.0	88.9	40.0
Nova Scotia	62.0	85.6	53.1
New Brunswick	58.1	87.2	50.7
Quebec	79.6	59.6	47.5
Ontario	82.4	82.3	67.8
Manitoba	76.5	83.4	63.9
Saskatchewan	59.4	68.2	40.6
Alberta	85.4	72.6	62.0
British Columbia	92.5	88.0	81.4
Canada	80.0	75.9	60.8

Source: Canada, Task Force on Broadcasting Policy 1986, 553.

Each CATV system in Canada operates as a monopoly within its licensed distribution region. Cable companies differ widely in terms of their subscriber base: about 80 of the 940 cable operations claim fewer than 200 subscribers, and Canada's 7 largest cable companies serve almost 2.5 million subscribers (Canada, CRTC 1986, 13; Canada, Task Force

1986, 564). Similarly, revenues and profitability vary considerably. Because cable companies operate as monopolies, their rates for basic service are regulated by the CRTC but rates for discretionary services, such as pay-TV, are not. The CRTC reviews each cable company separately and rates vary across the country, depending upon the size of system.

Approximately 84 percent of the cable industry's revenues come from its basic service, which also accounts for about 82 percent of expenses and 88 percent of the profits derived from providing the service (Canada, Task Force 1986, 558). These profits are substantial, ranging between 29 and 44 percent of revenues. After depreciation and interest expenses, however, before-tax profits average 9.5 percent (Canada, Task Force 1986, 561).

Although this is a very respectable figure, it does not reflect the range within the industry. Two-thirds of Canada's cable companies have fewer than five thousand subscribers each, and together they account for only 7 percent of the industry's revenues and 6 percent of its total subscriber base. Over 80 percent of the corporations that reported a loss in 1984 were among this group. Of the companies with more than fifty thousand subscribers, fewer than 4 percent reported a loss (Canada, Task Force 1986, 563–65). In the cable industry, it really does appear that bigger is better.

The size of individual cable undertakings, however, does not affect the overall impact of cable on the Canadian broadcasting system. Because CATV systems import U.S. broadcast signals directly, they have increased the proportion of American television programming available to Canadians. Cable has also increased the likelihood that *Canadian* broadcasters will offer American programming in their efforts to compete more successfully for audiences. The result has been a drop in the amount of Canadian content exhibited, especially in prime time. As well, cable has weakened the economic stability of Canadian broadcasters by fragmenting their audience. As more channels become available, a smaller percentage of the total viewing audience will watch any one channel, since the absolute size of the audience remains the same. Reducing the size of each broadcaster's actual audience also reduces that broadcaster's potential attractiveness to advertisers, causing revenues to fall. Cable operators are free to use the broadcast signals of individual stations without paying any compensation. They argue that the value of the broadcast undertaking is enhanced by its inclusion in the cable system. Ironically, however, cable can also lessen the value of the broadcaster's operation by weakening the revenue base.

Prior to 1968, cable systems were regulated in only the technical aspects of their operations, as opposed to, for example, rate structures or the order of priority in which the systems should carry different channels. During the debates leading up to passage of the Broadcasting Act, 1968, legislators became increasingly aware of the potential cultural and economic impact of cable technology on broadcasting. The White Paper on Broadcasting (Canada, Secretary of State 1966, 19) identified the need for an adaptable broadcasting system capable of harnessing the "new forces" of technology to work towards "the essential goal of Canadian unity." To this end, CATV systems were incorporated as part of the single Canadian broadcasting system, subject to the same objectives as broadcasters under section 3 of the 1968 Broadcasting Act (see chapter 6). The newly created CRTC was given the authority to regulate cable undertakings to ensure that they met policy objectives: "The CRTC realized, after assuming office in 1968, that unless cable television were regulated closely, as an instrument of national policy, the broadcasting system laboriously developed in the preceding thirty-five years might come tumbling down" (Peers 1979, 90).

Without any precedents to follow, the CRTC held public hearings in 1968 and 1969 to discuss regulatory options. When the Commission announced its cable television policy in May 1969, two objectives were paramount: to protect the economic position of the Canadian broadcasters; and to minimize the cultural inroads made by American programming and stations. With minor alterations, the regulations have remained much the same during the past two decades.

The CRTC requires all cable undertakings to be licensed. During licensing hearings, the Commission reviews ownership, the conditions of licence, and the applicants' promises of performance. Local ownership is preferred. Common carriers and broadcast undertakings are not allowed to own cable services, and networking is not permitted.[5] The conditions of licence include the rate structure, the provision of a community channel, and the practice of commercial deletion or substitution.[6] The Commission is able to tailor the conditions to suit each market area.

The CRTC also established a tiered system for carrying cable signals which gives priority to local Canadian broadcasters. A CATV system is required to carry television services in the following order of precedence:

1. Basic service
   - all local television signals
     French- and English-language CBC
     provincial broadcasters
     private broadcasters (network and independent)
   - regional stations
   - a community channel

2. Converter service
   - any priority stations not carried on the basic service
   - the parliamentary channel
   - optional stations, including other Canadian stations, the three commercial American networks, and American public television

3. Discretionary service
   - Canadian pay-TV
   - Canadian specialty programming services
   - foreign services (a maximum of five)

4. Non-programming service
   - security monitoring
   - computer-assisted services (e.g., teletext)
   - other (e.g., telebanking)

When cable service began, its only function was to carry signals; today it acts as carrier, programmer, and provider of non-programming services. As its influence on Canadian broadcasting increased, so did the concern of legislators and regulators: "The technology, enhanced by cable, is at hand. But broadcasting cannot survive by technology alone. The most perfect electromagnetic signal into every Canadian home is without value unless it bears a message" (CRTC 1971, 47). There is still no clear definition of cable's role in the Canadian broadcasting system today. The Task Force on Broadcasting Policy (1986, 577) recognized this and suggested that the cable system should serve as "a carrier of *Canadian* radio and television broadcasting services, both public and private" (emphasis added). It therefore made a series of recommendations designed to ensure that cable would promote Canada's broadcasting policy. These are discussed further in chapter 8.

Satellites: A proliferation of services

Satellites have a tremendous, unrealized potential to provide broadcast services. They are particularly well suited for one-way, point-to-multi-point services since neither the distance nor the number of earth stations receiving the signals affects the cost of transmission. Satellites can transmit television programming to a widely dispersed population and are capable of sending many signals simultaneously. Because they reach such large audiences, satellites make it feasible to carry channels with highly specialized content.

High frequency broadcast signals are transmitted from ground stations to the satellite (uplinks). When these signals reach the satellite, each is placed on one of twenty-four transponders, or channels. The signals are then transmitted back to earth (downlinks) where they are received by parabolic antennae or "dishes."[7]

Canada played a leading role in the development of satellite technology. Telesat Canada, established in 1970, is jointly owned by the federal government and Canada's largest telecommunication carriers. It operates as a monopoly and leases satellite capacity to approved carriers and broadcast undertakings. Telesat launched its first Anik satellite in 1972,[8] and for several years, the CBC was its main broadcast customer. In 1981, Canadian Satellite Communications Inc. was licensed to provide residents of remote or underserved areas, where cable systems were prohibitively expensive, with a basic package of broadcast signals: four Canadian and four American television channels and eight radio superstations.[9] Cancom leases capacity from Telesat. In addition, pay-television and specialty services are now transmitted by satellite and the CTV network is expected to use satellite transmission in the near future.

The proliferation of satellite services makes broadcasting more competitive in at least three ways. First, satellite technology makes a great many more stations available to individuals. It is legal in Canada for individuals to own television-receive-only (TVRO) satellite antennae and Canadians buy a lot of them. The dishes enable their owners to receive 80 to 120 channels, most of them American. This situation prompted Donald Coxe (1983, 134) to quip, "The dish is a large wok that threatens to cook the goose of the entire Canadian broadcast industry. . . . "

Second, many large apartment or hotel complexes use satellite receiver units. These master antenna units (MATV) pick up satellite signals that are then transmitted to individual units within the complex.[10] Normally the systems are used to get access to American satellite signals.

Such behaviour not only threatens the economic stability of the local cable operator, it also undermines the regulatory authority that promotes the Canadian broadcasting system. In an attempt to counteract the growing illegal reception of American television signals, the CRTC licensed Cancom. Cancom would provide broadcasting services via satellite to remote and rural areas and thereby reduce people's wish to pirate signals. As part of the same effort, the Parliamentary Standing Committee on Communications and Culture has recommended amendments to the Radio Act to give all discretionary services, including American ones, the private right to take legal action against unauthorized reception, or pirating, of their broadcast signals.

Third, satellites are being used in conjunction with cable television systems to provide pay-TV and specialty services that have been licensed by the CRTC. The services increase both the number of competitors in the Canadian broadcasting system and the relative proportion of American programming available to Canadian viewers. Undoubtedly, satellites widen the broadcast consumer's range of choice but their signals also fail to remain within national borders, making the job of regulators and policy makers increasingly complex. The new generation of satellite technology—more powerful signals, smaller and cheaper receivers—raises even stronger doubts among cultural nationalists about the chances for preserving a unique Canadian system.

Pay-television and specialty services

Pay-television and the specialty television services are delivered via satellites to the cable operators who then, for an additional charge, deliver them to the subscriber. Whereas pay-TV is designed for the mass audience, the specialty services, as their generic name suggests, are targeted to attract special-interest audiences in areas such as sports, religion, health, news, children's programming,[11] and arts and culture.

The CRTC first examined the pay-TV option in 1972 but waited until 1981 to call for applications to provide the service because it feared a disruptive impact on the existing Canadian broadcasting system. As it reviewed the proposals of the twenty-eight applicants, the Commission attempted to achieve the three basic objectives it had established for pay-TV in 1978: to strengthen the Canadian broadcasting system; to enhance the diversity of available programming; and to provide new opportunities and revenue for indigenous production (Canada, CRTC 1978).

In March 1982, the CRTC licensed six of the hopeful applicants and determined that pay-TV would be offered as a discretionary, cable-delivered service with rates set by the pay-TV and cable operators. The pay-TV operators own the pay-TV licences and channels. They buy and produce programming, just as other broadcasters do. The cable operators, who deliver the programming, and the pay-TV operators negotiate contracts together to set rates. They both then realize revenues from the sales to subscribers.

The Commission also set Canadian content quotas for both programming time and revenues. All pay-TV services were to devote at least 30 percent of their total program schedules and also of their prime time schedules to Canadian content. That quota was to rise to 50 percent by 1984. Moreover, the Commission expected drama to account for at least half of the Canadian programming provided. Pay-TV operators were also required to expend 45 percent of their revenues and 60 percent of their programming budgets on Canadian programming. This represented a new twist in the Commission's attempts to strengthen indigenous Canadian production efforts.

Within months things started to fall apart. The expected rush of subscriptions never materialized; operators needed a 10 percent penetration level to break even, but they barely achieved 5 percent. C-Channel (the arts and culture service) and Star Channel (the Atlantic regional service) both declared bankruptcy and folded. First Choice, the national pay-TV service, scandalized some potential subscribers when it negotiated a programming deal with the American *Playboy* channel. Its action not only hurt pay-TV's reputation as a family medium but also incensed the cultural community. As well as exhibiting existing *Playboy* programming, First Choice planned to meet a portion of its Canadian content requirements by co-producing *Playboy* programming that featured Canadian Playmates.

After one and a half years of operation, the pay-television industry had lost about $50 million and in the summer of 1984 the remaining operators applied to the CRTC for relief. The Commission decided to restructure the Canadian pay-TV market base; instead of having one national and several regional operators, it now divided the national market among three undertakings. First Choice and Superchannel merged operations. The former served subscribers from Ontario eastwards; the latter covered the four western provinces and northern Canada. Super Écran was licensed to serve Quebec and the francophone market in eastern

Canada. There was no francophone service in the West. The Commission also permitted the creation of the "Canadian Pack" marketing package, which included one Canadian pay-TV service, the two Canadian specialty services—MuchMusic and The Sports Network (TSN)—and three American services. Almost all cable companies decided to offer the package. Finally, the CRTC reduced the Canadian content requirements for pay-TV operators. The resulting system was very far removed from the one originally proposed.

Following the restructuring, pay-television has experienced slow but steady growth, although all three undertakings are still experiencing financial difficulties. Analysts blame the failure of pay-TV on the popularity of VCRs and TVROs, the lack of quality programming, high connection charges, and poor marketing techniques. The pay-television operators are quick to blame the CRTC and its "unreasonable" Canadian content regulations. Even after the merger, the president of Superchannel, Douglas Holtby, remarked "We can't make it. It just isn't feasible. Under these rules, the thing is not going to turn around. It's not viable" (*Financial Post* 1986, 12). In his critical review of Canadian broadcasting, however, Herschel Hardin (1985, 293) claims that the pay service "never made Canadian sense" since the small size of the Canadian market inhibits domestic production and makes pay-TV dependent on American programming.

According to Lyman (1983, 85), the primary contribution that pay-TV has made to Canadian broadcasting is a forced upgrading of the cable system. Once again, technology has overshadowed content:

> The outcome of the CRTC pay-TV decision is likely to be a strong encouragement to the delivery system rather than a means of stimulating Canadian content. . . . This spur to cable should convert it to a more aggressive, marketing-oriented industry, with the capacity to deliver several user-pay services. This result could be of strategic importance in the face of the future delivery technologies. . . .

Cable's upgraded technological infrastructure now means that it can provide sixty or more services to subscribers. Where once the industry concentrated on the engineering aspects of its business, it must now turn its attention to marketing and customer relations, to convince people to buy the additional services. Pay television, and eventually pay-per-view programming, must succeed if cable operators are to fill their excess capacity and increase their profits. Otherwise, new delivery technologies such as direct broadcast satellites could threaten the survival of cable.

The pay-TV fiasco is a clear example of the Canadian cycle of technological implementation. After delaying the introduction of new technology and allowing consumers to develop a taste for foreign services, the regulator licensed Canadian applicants who promised the moon, but delivered much less. In the end, the regulator backed down, and government stepped in with the offer of financial incentives to bolster indigenous program production.

The growing number of specialty services makes it difficult to predict the future of pay-television. In November 1987, the CRTC announced its decision to license nine new specialty services that the individual cable operators have the option to distribute on the converter service tier.[12] It also licensed The Family Channel to broadcast family programming, including some from the American Disney Channel, as a discretionary English-language pay-television service. Finally, the Commission placed TSN and MuchMusic on the converter service, removing them from the discretionary tier. CRTC chairman André Bureau justified the Commission's decision by explaining the positive effect it will have on the Canadian broadcasting environment:

> The broad range of newly licensed specialty services should offer high quality, attractive, entertaining and informative programming of a specialized nature designed to appeal to different audiences and meet the distinctive needs and interests of Canadians in both francophone and anglophone markets. These new specialty services will complement and diversify existing broadcasting services and will provide new outlets for Canadian creative expression, new stages for Canadian talent and new exhibition windows and sources of funding for Canadian program production (Canada, CRTC 1987, 1–2).

The cable industry is very much in favour of filling its excess capacity with specialty channels and thereby increasing its overall profitability. Adding specialty channels to the cable menu challenges the existing system in two ways, however. General entertainment broadcasters, particularly those in the private sector, worry about the level of competition. When they consider the relatively small size of the market and the existing number of video alternatives, broadcasters fear that the new services can only fragment their audiences further while siphoning off a significant proportion of available advertising revenues. They argue that such inroads on their fiscal stability threaten their continued existence. Second, subscribers, consumer advocates, and the general public are all concerned about where the new channels are placed on the cable band and who pays for them. Because these services have been put onto the converter cable band, all subscribers have to pay for them. Given that they are special-interest channels, this appears to contradict their mandate. To place them on the discretionary service band, however, would jeopardize their chance for lasting economic viability. Over time, some new channels will find a strong source of revenue from advertising, others will survive as pay-per-view systems, and the remainder will fail.

The CRTC specialty services hearings raised fundamental questions about the structure and function of the Canadian broadcasting system and about how broadcast policy is determined in this country. Many observers are critical of the Commission's decision to proceed with the licensing hearings before establishing policy guidelines for specialty services. More importantly, however, critics also question the role of the CRTC in establishing any broadcasting policy. The CRTC decision to consider applications before proposed new federal legislation to restructure the Canadian broadcast system is tabled appears to undercut the government's policy-making mandate. This failure to await political direction may have serious implications for the Commission, specialty licensees, and the broadcasting system as a whole. When the provisions of a new broadcasting act become a matter of public record, they may alter the direction of current broadcasting policy, leaving broadcasters vulnerable to increased competition or the CRTC open to greater political involvement with its activities.

Video cassette recorders: The consumer in control

Video cassette recorders (VCRs) and video disc players have also made an impact on Canadian broadcasting in recent years. About half of Canadian households have a VCR and that number is rising. VCRs have penetrated the market faster than have pay-television services, partly because of cassette rentals.

Video cassette technology developed in the 1950s, but it was not until 1974 that Sony introduced a model for the consumer market. Capable of recording video signals and playing prerecorded tapes, VCRs come in two incompatible formats—Beta and VHS. VHS is fast becoming predominant. Video discs are the latest video technology. Discs about the size of a 33 1/3 rpm record are prerecorded using laser technology. They are fully digital with enormous capacity and versatility, and very high-fidelity sound and pictures. They can record film, music, and data. They cannot be used to record television programming, however, and to date, penetration levels have been low.

Like cable subscribers, VCR owners are younger, better educated, and have higher incomes than average, and are more likely to be professionals. VCRs suit their desire for increased choice in and control over what they watch. As an integral part of the home component communication centre, VCRs cater to specialized viewing habits by enabling viewers to time-shift[13] and to watch programming of their own choosing.

The VCR industry is virtually unregulated. Prerecorded tapes are subject to customs inspection when they enter this country and some are turned away, but otherwise the market determines patterns of usage. The use of VCRs raises two issues of concern to regulators and policy makers: copyright and access.

Copyright law protects, supports, and encourages the creation of intellectual and entertainment material. VCRs make it possible to reproduce television programming, which is subject to copyright protection, but detection, enforcement, and prosecution of illegal copying are extremely difficult. Artists, producers, and the government have suggested that a special entertainment tax or royalty be levied on VCRs, blank tapes, and cassette rentals. The proposal is based on the assumption that VCRs are used to infringe upon the copyright provisions and that the proceeds from a tax or royalty of this sort should therefore be put towards the domestic production industry.

Uncontrollable access to foreign programming on video is another issue confronting Canadian policy makers. Since it is not possible to impose a quota to deter the VCR user from consuming a steady diet of foreign videos, policy makers realize that the only real option is to make a greater number of high-quality, entertaining Canadian productions available. Yet, as in the past, neither policy makers nor the Canadian production sector can keep up with technology. Funds, facilities, and software are all inadequate to meet public demands.

The consequences of technology

Each successive generation of broadcasting technology has held forth the promise of higher quality, greater choice, and more flexibility, just as it has also created or reinforced certain public policy concerns. The most obvious problem is the increasing foreign domination of Canadian broadcasting. Canadians want American programming available on all the new services, but unfettered importation will fragment the audience, raise Canadian production costs, and limit the ability of domestic broadcasters to profit from the services they offer. As more channels become available, it is likely that the proportion of Canadian content will decrease and that programming will become more homogenized as a consequence. The question of equitable access is also a concern. Many of the new technologies are affordable only to people in the higher income strata of Canadian society, a situation that fuels fear of a society divided in the future into information and entertainment haves and have-nots. Finally, the new technological environment challenges the theoretical underpinnings of regulation. Government control has traditionally been defended because of the limited nature of the radio spectrum, which had to be carefully allocated to prevent chaos and abuse. Technologies now available can bypass the radio spectrum and offer an almost limitless number of channels.

Some critics argue that governments and the industry have placed too much emphasis on new types of hardware and too little on the need for increased production of Canadian software to fill the newly available channels. Both private entrepreneurs and public policy makers need to strike a balance or they will create a lopsided system that fails to meet the objectives established for it in Canada's broadcast policy.

In his review of the new communication technologies, Lyman (1983, 26–32) notes that in Canada, "technology has always been the ally of the foreign content producer." He believes that the country must seize the opportunities provided by new technologies to foster an indigenous production industry, and argues that Canada's protective cultural strategy should be replaced by aggressive production and domestic and international marketing. Only by combining strong cultural and economic policies can Canadian objectives be realized: "In order for the country to know itself, Canadian culture needs to be attractive to Canadians and properly marketed and distributed to take advantage of the efforts of artists and producers. Competitive cultural expression needs to extend beyond the parochial or the amateur and to be of potential interest to a national and international audience" (Lyman 1983, 32).

Summary

This chapter briefly described a number of broadcasting technologies, from radio to video, and identified their different implications for the Canadian broadcasting system. Technological development interacts with the two other predominant concerns in Canadian broadcasting: economics and cultural nationalism.

All of the technologies described present difficulties to Canadian policy makers. The introduction of FM radio, cable- and satellite-delivered television, and VCRs has threatened the economic viability of the Canadian broadcasting system by segmenting its relatively small audience and adding to the number of media undertakings that compete for a share of the available advertising revenue. New recording technologies have also encouraged the importation of foreign programming. Regulators have attempted to address these issues but every innovation makes their task more difficult, and in some cases the nature of the technology makes regulating content next to impossible.

These problems are not uniquely Canadian, although their consequences are particularly significant for Canada. Other countries, too, recognize the globalization of broadcasting. Yet the future of the domestic industry need not be considered hopeless. As broadcast channels proliferate, it will become very difficult for the industry in any one country to produce enough programming to fill them all. The objective for Canada, and others, is to produce high-quality programming capable of entertaining international audiences. In this way, the national production industry may not only save itself but also achieve its elusive goal, the development of a faithful domestic audience: "The appropriate objective for public policy in the face of the technological challenge from American television is to offer all Canadians compelling home-made alternatives so that they will choose to resist the foreign seduction" (Canada, Task Force 1986, 76).

Chapter 8 addresses the issue of Canadian broadcast programming in more detail as it examines the predominant public policy issues in the broadcasting environment.

Notes

1. The connection between communication and cultural domination is not dealt with here in great detail, and the interested reader is directed to Mc-Phail (1986), Rogers (1976), Schiller (1976), and Schramm (1964). Grant (1965) and Smythe (1981) review the issue from a Canadian perspective.

2. The electromagnetic spectrum consists of a whole range of wavelengths, or frequencies, of electromagnetic waves capable of carrying signals. The frequencies range from "very low" to "extremely high" and are measured in kilohertz and megahertz. One megahertz is equal to a thousand kilohertz, which is equal to a thousand hertz, or vibrations per second. The higher the frequency, the more vibrations per second there are in the pattern of electromagnetic waves. Frequencies have a variety of different uses. For more information, see Gross (1986).

3. The mid-range frequencies within any given section of the spectrum experience virtually no interference, while those at the extreme ends of that section will receive interference from services in the next section. In households that rely on over-the-air television transmission, turning on another electrical appliance, such as the vacuum cleaner, can interfere with the reception of the television signal.

4. Coaxial cable contains an insulated copper core, surrounded by a copper or aluminum tube. Each cable may contain several concentric copper conductors capable of working separately or in combination.

5. Common carriers, such as telephone and satellite companies, simply carry messages without making any changes to them; broadcasters, on the other hand, decide what content to carry. Broadcast networks are groups of broadcasters who share programming. Cable networks operate in much the same way as broadcasting networks, but rather than sharing programming they share stations.

   Under a system that allows networking, a few selected stations are available to all subscribers of the cable network. For example, a network might offer Toronto's Global station, Ottawa's English-language CBC station, Montreal's French-language CBC station, and Calgary's CTV station. All subscribers, regardless of where they live, could then receive these stations, and only these stations, through their cable service. The implications of networking are profound indeed. Such an arrangement would make it difficult for subscribers to watch their local stations and the size of both audiences and advertising revenues would therefore decrease. A privileged few broadcast undertakings would become superstations, because national advertisers would concentrate their advertising efforts on the few stations carried by the cable network. Local stations might be forced to close and broadcast networks would probably dissolve as a result of disputes between the cable-selected affiliates and those not carried by the cable networks. A broadcasting oligopoly could develop.

6. Commercial deletion and substitution provisions require the cable operator to delete or substitute the advertising segments of non-local broadcast stations delivered via cable if they carry the same programs as local stations.

This practice is intended to protect the advertising revenue base of the local stations.

7. Communication satellites circle the earth in a geostationary orbit, 31 200 km above the equator. In this position, satellites orbit the earth at the same speed at which the earth itself rotates. As a result, satellites appear to remain stationary. This is important to ensure that the satellite's "footprint," the area covered by the signal, remains constant.

8. It is interesting to note that future Anik launches will be undertaken by the Ariane (French) launching system. This reflects not only Canada's growing partnership with the European Space Agency, but also the inability of NASA to launch commercial satellites since the January 1986 shuttle disaster. NASA launched all earlier Canadian satellites.

9. Superstations are available well beyond their local, territorial base because of their distribution arrangements.

10. Entire towns have also established MATV systems in an effort to receive broadcast signals that would otherwise be unavailable. For examples, see Harbourne (1985) and McPhail and Downey (1984).

11. The Task Force on Broadcasting Policy (Canada 1986, 351) did not support the idea of a channel dedicated exclusively to children. While it recognized the need for more quality children's programming, it argued that the Canadian system simply does not have adequate resources to accommodate such a channel. Instead it suggested that existing stations and the proposed TV Canada/ Télé-Canada service increase their contributions to this sector.

12. The new English-language specialty channels are: CBC Newsworld (all-news channel), Vision-TV (a multi-faith service), YTV (a youth and children's channel), and MeteoMedia: Weather Now (a national weather service). The new francophone services are: Le Canal famille (a youth and children's channel), Le Réseau des sports (RDS, a twenty-four-hour sports channel), Musique plus (music video programming), TV-5 (an international French service), and MétéoMedia: Media Météo-Instant (a national weather service).

13. Time-shifting refers to the practice of taping broadcast programming to watch at a more convenient time.

References

Canada. Canadian Radio-television and Telecommunications Commission (CRTC). 1971. Public announcement, The integration of cable television in the Canadian broadcasting system. February. Ottawa: CRTC.
———. 1978. Report on pay television. March. Ottawa: CRTC.
———. 1986. Public notice, CRTC 1986-27. 13 February. Ottawa: CRTC.
———. 1987. News release, More Canadian programming choices. 30 November. Ottawa.
Canada. Secretary of State. 1966. White paper on broadcasting. Ottawa: Queen's Printer.
Canada. Task Force on Broadcasting Policy. 1986. *Report*. Ottawa: Supply and Services.

Coxe, D. 1983. Francis Fox and the satellite invasion: He can dish it out, but can he take it? *Canadian Business* (October): 134.

Financial Post. 1986. Pay-TV promise a fading dream. 9 August. p. 12.

Grant, G. 1965. *Lament for a nation: The defeat of Canadian nationalism*. Princeton: Van Nostrand.

Gross, L.S. 1986. *The new television technologies*. 2d ed. Dubuque: Brown.

Harbourne, D. 1985. Communications infrastructures: The Alberta experience. In *Communication in the 80s*. rev. ed., ed. T. McPhail and S. Hamilton, 123–30. Calgary: University of Calgary.

Hardin, H. 1985. *Closed circuits: The sellout of Canadian television*. Vancouver: Douglas and McIntyre.

Lyman, P. 1983. *Canada's video revolution: Pay-TV, home video and beyond*. Ottawa: Canadian Institute for Economic Policy.

McPhail, T.L. 1986. *Electronic colonialism: The future of international broadcasting and communication*. Beverly Hills: Sage.

McPhail, T.L., and B.M. Downey. 1984. Community broadcasting: High-tech represents a new twist. *Canadian Journal of Communication*. 10(3): 47–64.

Peers, F.W. 1979. Tension over communications. In *The future of North America: Canada, the United States and Quebec nationalism*, ed. E.J. Feldman and N. Nevitte, 87–100. Montreal: Institute for Research on Public Policy.

Rogers, E. 1976. *Communication and development: Critical perspectives*. Beverly Hills: Sage.

Schiller, H. 1976. *Communication and cultural domination*. White Plains: Sharpe.

Schramm, W. 1964. *Mass media and national development*. Paris: UNESCO.

Smythe, D.W. 1981. *Dependency road: Communications, capitalism, consciousness and Canada*. Norwood: Able.

BROADCAST POLICY: CONFRONTING THE ISSUES

*T*he government of Canada formally recognized the potential benefits and risks of broadcasting for the first time in 1928, when it established the Aird Commission. Its concern was prompted by a need for technical administration to prevent misuse of the airwaves, a desire to isolate broadcasting from partisan politics, anxiety over the intrusive effects of American broadcast signals, and a vague but growing awareness of the possibilities offered by broadcasting for advancing national objectives. After considerable debate about the appropriateness of government intervention in the broadcasting arena, fear of American domination eventually persuaded even the most ardent critics that an official public response was required. As MP J.S. Woodsworth argued, "I may be afraid of handing power to any one government, but I would rather trust our own Canadian government than trust these highly organized commercial companies in the United States" (Canada, House of Commons 1928, 3622).

The first broadcasting legislation in Canada, the 1905 Radio-Telegraph Act, had required that all radio-telegraph equipment be licensed, but although it had stipulated the conditions of licence, they were so general that they contained few restrictions on licence issuance. The Canadian Radio Broadcasting Act, 1932, attempted to redress this weakness by creating the Canadian Radio Broadcasting Commission (CRBC) to provide a national service in the interests of Canadians. The Commission would also regulate the industry. The Act rested on the premise that the airwaves are public property and that broadcasting stations are licensed to operate as temporary monopolies in the public interest.

The establishment of the CRBC removed broadcasting regulation from the direct control of political actors. Subsequently, the Canadian Broadcasting Corporation (1936), the Board of Broadcast Governors (1958), and its successor, the Canadian Radio Television Commission (1968), were each created by statute as an independent agency, and charged with the task of regulating broadcasting. In each case, the agency's authority was limited by a mandate established by Parliament and all its regulatory decisions were subject to Cabinet review. This still holds true for the CRTC. The issue of political accountability has always been an important aspect of the Canadian parliamentary system, yet in practice the Cabinet rarely overturns agency decisions. Regulatory agencies have traditionally been permitted to generate policy as the need arises, leading Richard Schultz (1977, 342) to suggest that they are the most important structures within the Canadian bureaucracy.

Recently, however, the federal government has made moves to repoliticize the regulatory function. The minister of communications would use more directive power than at present, especially with respect to broad policy decisions. (Currently, the CRTC is responsible to Parliament rather than to the minister and adheres to directions outlined in legislation.) Many observers applaud this intention because the change would ensure that democratically elected representatives establish and remain accountable for broadcasting policy, and it would promote a coherent, unified cultural and communication policy. Others worry, however, that involving politicians further in broadcasting and cultural policy will inhibit journalistic, artistic, and creative freedom.

The Task Force on Broadcasting Policy (1986, 697) endorsed the right of the government to provide general policy directives to the CRTC and suggested that the government "indicate in no uncertain terms that the CRTC must not only assign specific responsibilities to each part of the [broadcasting] system but also ensure that those responsibilities are carried out." On the other hand, the Task Force also wanted the government to provide appropriate safeguards in future broadcasting legislation, to keep the CRTC independent.

Undoubtedly, the ultimate responsibility for broadcasting policy rests with Parliament; it is not limited to proposed legislation. Parliamentarians have periodically established committees to discuss issues relevant to broadcasting, and in 1964 a permanent Standing Committee of the House of Commons was created to review matters concerning broadcasting, film, the arts, culture, and communication. Although ministerial responsibility for broadcasting has frequently been shifted or shared among various government departments,[1] each has consistently emphasized the value of broadcasting as an agent of national unity.

This chapter looks at the most significant and persistent issues in Canadian broadcasting. It begins with an analysis of the purpose and scope of Canadian content regulations. Next, it examines the reports of the Task Force on Broadcasting Policy (1986) and the House of Commons Standing Committee on Communications and Culture (1987a, 1987b, 1988). Bill C-136, the federal government's legislative response to these reports, is reviewed, and the chapter ends with a brief analysis of the impact of the Free Trade Agreement.

Canadianizing the airwaves

In 1965, the Fowler Committee on Broadcasting (Canada, Committee on Broadcasting 1965, 3) concluded, "The only thing that really matters in broadcasting is program content; all the rest is housekeeping." Programming persistently resurfaces as a thorn in the side of the entire Canadian broadcasting system. Despite Canadians' rapid acceptance of television as a news and entertainment medium, the national production industry has failed to grow accordingly. The lacklustre performance of Canadian broadcasters can be directly related to the success of the American television industry: "High cost, professionally produced, lavishly publicized American programmes attract large viewing audiences in

Canada. The challenge for Canadian networks, with far less money and smaller resources, is to create programmes and schedules to compete for the Canadian audience" (Hallman 1977, 2).

Since more than half of Canadian households are within direct reach of broadcast signals from the United States, Canadian audiences are accustomed to the glossy production values of programming that is American in content and design. Although Canadian broadcasters spend substantially less than their American counterparts do on indigenous productions, to station owners and network executives the expenditures represent a considerable portion of revenues. These gatekeepers recognize that they can maximize their profits by purchasing foreign programming at low cost;[2] not only is it less expensive than original production but it also attracts a larger audience and thus a larger share of advertising revenues.[3] As is quickly evident, the factor with the greatest effect on a station's profitability is the amount of Canadian programming broadcast.

When the BBG was established in 1958, it undertook to create a system of regulations that would encourage Canadian program production and distribution. The resulting Canadian content quota, initially limited to television programming, was intended to quantify the Board's mandate: to ensure that the national broadcasting system was "basically Canadian in content and character" (Canada, Broadcasting Act, 1958, s. 5.10). Although the Board recognized the limitations of the regulations, it believed that they were consistent with the government's policy of directing broadcasting in the service of national purposes. Adopting a broad definition of "Canadian" programming, the Board originally set a minimum Canadian content quota of 55 percent, to be phased in gradually. The regulations were essentially economic, as opposed to cultural or content-oriented, and required stations to invest in Canadian production facilities and talent.

During the first decade of implementation, every aspect of the regulations was attacked but three issues continually resurfaced: the definition of Canadian content was so broad that credit was granted to many programs not really Canadian in content or character;[4] the quota system did not improve quality; and the regulations did not encourage broadcasters to employ Canadians. Although the BBG acknowledged that the regulations required a thorough review, it was reluctant to proceed without a clarified and fortified mandate from Parliament.[5]

In the 1968 Broadcasting Act, Parliament reaffirmed the concept of a single Canadian broadcasting system operated "to safeguard, enrich and strengthen the cultural, political, social and economic fabric of Canada. . . . " The newly created CRTC, which superseded the BBG, decided to retain the basic quota system but improve the definition of "Canadian" content, the quotas themselves, and the measuring period. The measuring period is the time during which the content quota can be met. A measuring period of a year, for example, enables a station to broadcast all of its Canadian material during the summer, when few people are watching. A measuring period of four months eliminates this problem. The Commission extended the content regulations—in order to include radio broadcasters—and clarified their purpose. The regulations were intended to increase the options available to Canadian audiences by encouraging high-quality, entertaining domestic programming. At no time were the regulations to be used as an instrument of censorship: "The Commission has never said and will never say that programmes from other countries and from the United States in particular should be kept out of Canada. For one thing, this would be impossible. It is also undesirable" (CRTC 1971, 12).

Despite the laudable intentions of the CRTC, it amended and eased the regulations over time. Private broadcasters argued that they could not meet the quotas as outlined and still produce quality programming. The financial investment required to fill the existing quota also prevented broadcasters from extending their service to all Canadians, another objective of the Commission.

In 1978, the CRTC undertook a special study of broadcasting in Canada. It discovered that the Canadian delivery system was among the best in the world. Ninety-eight percent of Canadians living outside Quebec received CBC television, and 95.5 percent could receive at least one other signal (CRTC 1979, 13). Cable television was available to over 71 percent of Canadians, two-thirds of whom subscribed to a cable service (CRTC 1979, 19).

The status of the Canadian production sector, however, was considerably less encouraging. American television stations had captured about one-quarter of the English-language Canadian audience (Audley 1983, 312). Between 77 and 85 percent of the total time that Canadians spent watching television was devoted to viewing foreign programming

(Canada, DOC 1983, 8). Although the CBC had, since 1968, increased the amount of Canadian programming it exhibited during prime time (7:00 P.M. to 11:00 P.M.) to about 68 percent, both the CTV and Global networks had reduced the amount of prime-time Canadian content they carried by approximately half, to about 6 percent and 23 percent respectively (CRTC 1979, 48). The bulk of the Canadian programming scheduled in prime time was sports, news, and information (Hoskins and McFadyen 1984, 28). Finally, only 2.9 percent of all the prime-time hours of television programming available to Canadians in 1983 was filled with Canadian drama (Starowicz 1984, 18).

The CRTC was fully cognizant of the trend indicated by these statistics and in December 1979 announced its intention to revise the regulations. After seeking advice from a variety of sources, including the broadcasters themselves, the Commission released its official policy statement on Canadian content on television, in 1983.[6] The statement admitted that Canadian content had a poor record and addressed some of the economic, technological, and political conditions that contributed to the problem. The proposed new regulations featured quantitative requirements, as the old regulations had, and a definition of "Canadian" based on a point system. As was noted in chapter 6, the Commission also created the Dramatic Programming Credit, which awarded a 150 percent Canadian content credit to domestic drama programs that conformed to the specified requirements. The Department of Communications reinforced the incentive when it created the Canadian Broadcast Program Development Fund in 1983, to help finance production.

This two-pronged approach, using regulation and incentive, is a novel one in broadcasting policy. It recognizes the need for a co-operative partnership of the private sector, the CBC, the DOC, and the CRTC to provide Canadian content on television. Although it is still too early to evaluate the strategy, it does not appear to have made any significant changes to the daily menu of programming available on Canadian television. The private broadcasters, including pay-television, still decry the burden imposed by regulation and claim that they simply cannot afford to meet the requirements. The CBC, while valiantly struggling to develop a distinctively Canadian service, is faced with massive financial cutbacks. It appears that little has changed since the publication of the Aird Commission report in 1929. More than half a century later, the main objective of the Canadian broadcasting system is still to promote a national identity within an ever-advancing technological environment, and broadcasters are still consistently more concerned with the bottom line on their balance sheets than with the stated national goals of government.

The problems faced by Canadian broadcasters

A number of arguments have been offered to explain the failure of Canadian broadcasting to develop a vigorous indigenous presence. The one perhaps most widely noted is the absence of financial commitment to production.[7] As Robert Babe (1975, 259) noted, "From the time of the Aird Commission to the present, Canadian programming has been and continues to be antithetical to the financial interests of the broadcasters (it costs more and earns less)."

Undoubtedly Canadian broadcasters face economic challenges. The vast expanse of this country makes the technical aspects of broadcasting expensive. The potential national audience is only one-tenth the size of the U.S. market and the small audience base is divided by competing programming from American stations, cable- and satellite-delivered services, and home video. Broadcasters also have to cope with the expense of high-quality, in-house production and demands from advertisers to deliver large audiences.[8]

Table 8.1 contains the programming costs borne by Canadian broadcasters for the year ending 31 August 1985. It indicates that for both private and public stations and for English- and French-language broadcasters, the greatest program expenditures are on Canadian productions. Yet the table does not show three crucial considerations. First, most of the Canadian expenditures are devoted to news and public affairs programming; less than 5 percent is spent on features or series and less than 3 percent on children's programming, two of the areas in which the lack of Canadian content is most keenly felt. Second, a dollar spent on foreign programming actually buys more program hours than a dollar spent on Canadian production, allowing broadcasters to fill their broadcast day more cheaply. Finally, the revenue generated by foreign shows, especially entertainment, far exceeds the revenue from Canadian programs. In other words, broadcasters get "a lot more bang for their buck" by exhibiting foreign material. It is these factors, according to many analysts, that

Table 8.1

Canadian television program costs for the year ending 31 August 1985 (in $ millions)

	Canadian		Foreign	
	$	%	$	%
English stations				
CBC	336.5	95.6	15.6	4.4
Private	225.9	63.0	132.9	37.0
Total	562.4	79.1	148.5	20.9
French stations				
CBC	203.6	96.4	7.6	3.6
Private	65.8	88.0	9.0	12.0
Total	269.4	94.1	16.6	5.8

Source: Canada, Task Force on Broadcasting Policy 1986, 434–35.

most hinder television from promoting a Canadian cultural identity. The cultural priority conflicts with private broadcasters' desire for profits.

The second argument advanced for the failure of Canadian television to achieve its cultural objectives is that content quotas do not work. Quotas simply fail to acknowledge either the quality, nature, and distinctiveness of specific programs or the amount of money spent on them: "Television programs are a completely different type of product [from other goods]. No two are alike. If they are good they reflect something vital, insightful, and dramatic about their subject . . . . In the realm of culture, Canada cannot import Canadian products . . . . If Canadians do not produce their own writing, music, theatre, films and television programs, no one else will" (Canada, Federal Cultural Policy Review Committee 1982, 288).

Wayne Stacey (1986, 13), former executive vice-president of the Canadian Association of Broadcasters, argues that "private and public broadcasters should be freed from the necessity of producing programs on a 'tonnage' basis to meet fixed hourly quotas. We should stop worrying that there are more U.S. programs available than Canadian, and instead concentrate on producing a more attractive product." Although some critics question his assertion that Canadian broadcasting services can never be "predominately Canadian," they agree that new policies and regulations are needed "to ensure that the Canadian component of our broadcasting system remains clearly visible and relevant as we move into the 1990s" (Stacey 1986, 13).

The third explanation for the absence of high-quality Canadian entertainment programming is the low priority that broadcasters give to indigenous cultural products for television. In an indictment of the Canadian broadcasting system, and the CBC in particular, Robert Fulford (1987, 6) claims that "Canadian television puts drama last on its list of priorities, and very seldom gets to the bottom of the list." He suggests several reasons for the weakness.

The first reason is political. Politicians want to be seen advancing their policies; news and public affairs programming are the best vehicles for doing this, and entertainment and drama are perhaps the least effective. Politicians, who depend on public support, have also emphasized the extension of service over the production capabilities of the system. All of them want basic broadcasting services for their constituents, regardless of the cost. The second reason is financial. The initial investment for dramatic productions is substantial and the risk of failure is higher than for other program genres.[9] Third, the cultural composition of this country influences production priorities. Canada is "essentially a political gathering of several quite different cultures rather than a cultural entity with shared tastes, myths and beliefs" (Fulford 1987, 8). Canadians and their broadcasters therefore prefer fact over fiction. We have not yet committed ourselves to the idea that drama is as important to our national identity and interests as are news and information. Although Fulford, and others like him, recognize the cultural contributions of our artistic communities, they mourn that these have not translated into success on television.

The final argument put forward to explain the difficulties of creating a truly Canadian broadcasting system focusses more explicitly on political realities than do the others just outlined. Supporters of this view assert that the political will to bring the broadcasting system completely under Canadian control has gradually dissipated since it was first given voice in the 1932 Canadian Radio Broadcasting Act. Despite the rhetoric of successive governments, "we have mortgaged our cultural sovereignty and become part of an electronic melting pot" (Starowicz 1984, 11).

Critics such as Mark Starowicz believe that Parliament and the regulators share responsibility for a broadcasting environment very different from the one envisaged by Sir John Aird and Prime Minister R.B. Bennett. By failing to exert sufficient political determination, they allowed, and to some extent encouraged, the Americanization of the Canadian system without giving a sufficient boost to domestic production. Canadian governments have permitted cable carriers to distribute the four American networks, licensed growing numbers of private stations, pay television, and specialty channels to import a large number of American programs, and failed to support the public broadcaster either financially or morally.

The explanations advanced for the failure of government to vigorously pursue the objectives of successive broadcasting acts are many and varied. Government has been unwilling to apply effective sanctions for fear of negative political ramifications;[10] it has given insufficient attention to the appointment of regulators; it has been guided by policies of economic and fiscal restraint; and it has allowed a long-standing preoccupation with national unity in the political sphere to colour its decisions about broadcasting. The love–hate relationships among the public, politicians, and the CBC have also played their part. Regardless of the reasons for it, the contradiction between policy and action has left the Canadian broadcasting system incapable of fulfilling its social and cultural mandate.

In May 1985, therefore, the long process of devising a strategy to guide the Canadian broadcasting system into the twenty-first century began. The first step was the creation of the Task Force on Broadcasting Policy.

The Task Force on Broadcasting Policy

When the Task Force on Broadcasting Policy offered its report to the minister of communications in September 1986, it presented the government with the most extensive review of broadcasting policy since the Fowler Committee report in 1965. The year-long study concluded that "Canada has evolved a radio and television system that, like the country itself, mostly works" (Canada, Task Force on Broadcasting Policy 1986, 5). It also noted, however, that the broadcasting system is plagued by precisely the same problems as the Royal Commission on Radio Broadcasting identified in 1928: not enough Canadian programming or high-quality programming; insufficient drama programming by the private sector in English Canada; lack of attention paid to information and public affairs programming by the private sector in Quebec; and a general reluctance to give priority to the social and cultural goals of the broadcasting system. According to the Task Force (1986, 691), the reasons for these persistent problems are clear: "The public sector, which must be the chief purveyor of quality Canadian programming, is inadequately scaled [in size and distribution of broadcasters across the country] and funded; the private sector, which should complement the public sector at least to the extent of contributing to the social objectives of the Broadcasting Act, is not contributing enough."

The report placed the blame squarely at the feet of successive governments, which have refused to provide adequate funding, and of the regulator, which has failed to implement the *Broadcasting policy for Canada* detailed in the Broadcasting Act. The Task Force recommendations are for the most part designed to address these two problems and to ensure that Canadians receive high-quality Canadian programming. The next few pages review the conclusions of the study in the following policy areas: the basic assumptions and provisions that should be included in new broadcasting legislation; the Canadian Broadcasting Corporation; the private sector; the distributors; the Canadian Radio-television and Telecommunications Commission; and TV Canada.

Recommendations for broadcasting policy and legislation

The Task Force recommended that new broadcasting legislation contain a statement of the fundamental principles, similar to section 3 of the 1968 Broadcasting Act, upon which to base policy decisions.[11] The statement should reaffirm the principle of Canadian ownership and control, and the public trustee concept—the idea that frequencies are public property and that all persons authorized to use them are trustees of the Canadian public. The Task Force argued that it is also necessary, however, to recognize the composite nature of the Canadian broadcasting system, in particular the distinct characters of English- and French-language broadcasting. The legislation could then address the specific responsibilities that each sector of the broadcasting system has towards the objectives of the whole. Moreover, the definitions of broadcasting and related concepts should be broadened in order to encompass new technological aspects of the system.

The Task Force (1986, 152) reiterated that the overarching goal of the broadcasting system is to provide "a continuing expression of Canadian identity" to "safeguard, enrich and strengthen the cultural, political, social and economic fabric of Canada." It also added the requirement that the system "serve the special needs of the geographic regions and actively contribute to the flow and exchange of information and expression among the regions." Programming should be varied, comprehensive, balanced, and of high quality, "based on recognized professional standards" (Canada, Task Force 1986, 164).

As well, the report recommended the inclusion of three public rights in any new legislation:

1. the right of Canadians to receive broadcasting services (as opposed to particular programs on that service) in French and English, to be implemented by means of concerted legislative, regulatory, or corporate action in the public sector if necessary; the right of aboriginal peoples to receive services in native languages, where numbers warrant and as funds become available; and a consideration for the needs of hearing impaired people

2. the right, for all Canadians, of access to the broadcasting system, and recognition of the role of community broadcasting in this regard

3. the equal right of women and minority groups to gain employment within, make decisions about, and have access to the broadcasting system

Finally, the Task Force (1986, 157) advised that new legislation ought to accommodate the principle of federal–provincial consultation. Intergovernmental co-operation can strengthen broadcasting policy but should not interfere with the autonomy of broadcasters or regulators.

In general, most of the recommendations for legislation altered existing policies instead of replacing them, and proposed changes in light of technological developments that have occurred since the enactment of the Broadcasting Act, 1968. The main change to the present system would be an official recognition of the composite character of the broadcasting system and the diverse needs of the various regions. The overriding purpose of the recommendations is to fortify the social and cultural objectives of the Canadian broadcasting system.

Recommendations for the CBC

The Task Force (1986, 693) described the Canadian Broadcasting Corporation as the "major instrument of Canadian culture, but also of culture in Canada." It also noted that the CBC cannot be expected to solve all the country's programming problems alone. The report therefore suggested that the requirement for the CBC to contribute to the development of national unity be replaced by a requirement to contribute to the development of a national "consciousness." By changing this one word, the legislation would free the Corporation from a constraining attachment to a political order and permit it to engage in a more broadly defined pursuit of national culture (Task Force 1986, 284–85).

Although the Task Force advised easing the restrictive demands placed on the CBC, it also wanted new legislation to reaffirm "that the national broadcasting service be predominantly Canadian in content and character, and that the service provide for a continuing expression of Canadian identity." In order for the national service to achieve this lofty mandate, the report further recommended requiring the CBC to cover the whole range of Canadian programming and the best of international programming *not* normally available,[12] extending the service to all parts of Canada and expanding the scope of services as needed, permitting the Corporation to allow the English- and French-language services to develop differently as needs dictate, and encouraging it to create an English-language all-news and information channel.[13] Moreover, in the event of conflict over licences for particular services, the CBC should be given "paramount consideration" over private interests.

As outlined in chapter 6, the CBC currently operates a number of services, some of which are stipulated by the Broadcasting Act, 1968, others of which it has chosen for itself. The Task Force proposed that three of these non-mandatory services—the Northern Service, the Parliamentary Television Network, and Radio Canada International—be incorporated into new legislation to ensure that they continue and to give them official recognition. The Corporation would also be relieved of the financial burden of operating two of these services. The expense of the parliamentary network would be borne by the Speaker of the House of Commons, who would also determine the nature and scope of the coverage. The costs of operating Radio Canada International would be assumed by the Department of External Affairs, which would then define the scope of the service but not interfere with its journalistic independence.

Perhaps the most far-reaching recommendations of the Task Force were those concerned with funding the national service. The report advised that CBC radio services "be spared any further budget cuts," and insisted that some stability in funding was needed for the entire Corporation. Money should match the services demanded of the CBC. The Task Force strongly suggested that the government provide a clear indication of the funding it intends to provide, before hearings are held on CBC station and network licence renewals. That way, the Corporation could outline plans that are consistent with its budget and the CRTC could attach realistic conditions to the licences it issues. In addition, the CBC should be expected to live within its means, regardless of unexpected shortfalls in revenue or fluctuations in the cost of carrying out its business.

The Task Force made other recommendations as well but all of them are designed, like the principle ones outlined here, to strengthen and expand the role of the CBC in providing Canadian broadcasting content. The report attempted to promote a stable and secure environment in which the national service can most effectively carry out its mandate.

Recommendations for the private sector

As it addressed the issue of private broadcasting, the Task Force (1986, 381) was mindful of a persistent dilemma:

> Private broadcasters in Canada have long agreed that in return for the genuine—and often lucrative—privilege of being granted a broadcasting licence, they are obligated to perform certain services for the system that are not necessarily in the best immediate self-interest of their enterprise. The question has always been, however, the balance that should be struck between their private needs and their public responsibility.

When it studied private radio, the Task Force reinforced the importance of having a healthy radio sector and praised it for its genuine efforts in the face of a range of problems. The report suggested retaining regulation to promote both diversity and Canadian content and resources, but recommended applying more flexible regulatory tools, such as conditions of licence for content and format, to ensure that the regulation is appropriate to the individual needs of each station. The majority of the recommendations for radio are a matter of fine-tuning in the balance between cultural and industrial objectives.

The Task Force was much less sympathetic to the private television sector which, it argued, had essentially failed to contribute as much as it could to quality Canadian programming. The Task Force recognized that regulation should protect the markets of private television broadcasters, but stressed the need for continued Canadian content regulations in terms of both quotas and expenditures. Moreover, the Task Force suggested holding licence renewals for the CTV network and its affiliated stations at the same time, to allow regulators to undertake a thorough financial review of the whole enterprise and then impose suitable conditions of licence. Similar recommendations tying content requirements to financial health were made for pay-television and specialty services in an attempt to protect the services from foreign competitors and make certain that they produce and exhibit Canadian programming.

In general, the Task Force (1986, 468) promoted a policy that would "establish a Canadian presence on television through programs that are made by Canadians, chiefly for Canadians and good enough to attract Canadian viewers." Its primary purpose was to encourage the regulator to ensure that objective.

Recommendations for the distributors

The Task Force clearly discerned the significant potential of new distribution technologies, including CATV and satellite systems, to expand the range of available broadcasting services. It emphasized the need to take technological development into account when considering how broadcasting can best achieve its cultural objectives. As an example, cable could be used to provide a French-language service where none exists off air.

As a first step, the Task Force considered it necessary to define cable systems clearly as undertakings that receive and retransmit signals, distinct and separate from undertakings that create, assemble, and market programs. Community channels would then have to be independently licensed and operated. They are currently operated by cable companies, which determine schedules and assist with production. As carriers, it is also important that cable systems give priority to Canadian services, and it may be necessary to restructure the existing cable tiers to ensure this objective.

Since cable systems operate as monopolies within their given geographic areas, the Task Force proposed that the CRTC continue to regulate the rates for basic services, determining them from a full financial disclosure of each system. Rates for discretionary and non-programming services, which may be provided as long as the cable operators meet their programming obligations, were to be negotiated between the cable companies and the owners of the discretionary services.

The Task Force also advocated using satellites as carriers of broadcast signals and developing policies to delineate the roles of Telesat Canada and Cancom. As in other areas, the report suggested changes to bring the distribution sector in line with the objectives of the proposed new broadcasting legislation, and therefore focussed on creating a more clearly defined regulatory framework.

Recommendations for the CRTC

The Task Force report was generally critical of the CRTC. It argued that the Commission often made ad hoc decisions that did not actively support the broad objectives of the *Broadcasting policy for Canada*. Moreover, the Commission had failed to ensure that licensees complied with its regulations and conditions of licence. The report also noted the many charges laid against the regulator by public and private broadcasters, consumers, and politicians. The CRTC has been accused of, among other things, being a captive of the industry, reacting too slowly to industry innovations, holding too many costly hearings, not covering enough during the hearing process, promulgating too many complex regulations, and not regulating with sufficient vigour.

The Task Force observed that in order to develop effective policies, politicians and regulators must co-operate with one another. It is the responsibility of Parliament to articulate, through legislation, the fundamental principles and obligations of broadcasting. One of the tasks of the CRTC is to issue policy statements delineating its own objectives. Just as the two bodies share responsibility for establishing broadcasting policy, both have a role in selecting the most suitable means to put policy into effect. The CRTC assumes primary responsibility for implementing the decisions and making sure that broadcasters comply with them. Evaluating the results most frequently falls to special committees, royal commissions, and task forces.

Underlying the Task Force recommendations for the CRTC is the principle of ministerial responsibility, or accountability, an essential part of parliamentary government. Parliament can assign the dominant responsibility for guiding the development of broadcasting to a regulatory agency that operates independently of partisan politics, but the government or more specifically, the Cabinet, ultimately remains responsible for the decisions of the agency. The Task Force recommended that one of two methods to preserve this principle be adopted, but not both. Cabinet should decide either to reserve the right to set aside Commission decisions or refer them back to the agency for revision, or to issue general directives for the Commission to interpret and implement. Although the Task Force preferred the second option, it emphasized that such directives should be used in moderation, only after Cabinet has sought public advice from broadcasters, cable companies, the public, performers, and so on, and should not interfere with the day-to-day operation of the Commission.

After looking at the operational structure of the CRTC, the Task Force suggested broadening the powers and duties of the regional offices and appointing a public advocate for each region, to ensure that the agency is responsive to the public. The new arrangement would eliminate the need for part-time commissioners, who cannot, in any case, keep abreast of developments in the complex arena of broadcasting policy. In addition, the public hearing process should be changed both to allow interested parties to use cross-examination more freely in order to address issues effectively, and to amend the current confidentiality practices since they hinder public evaluation. The report recommended as well that both the federal and provincial governments financially support the efforts of representative citizen groups to monitor the activities, hearings, and decisions of the Commission.

The study concluded that new legislation should sustain the extensive power of the CRTC to regulate all matters within its jurisdiction. All regulations should be clearly drafted in both English and French, and simplified and updated by a regular review. Moreover, the Task Force encouraged the CRTC to apply tailor-made conditions of licence, such as requiring different licensees to spend predetermined amounts for specific purposes. Finally, and perhaps most significantly, the report insisted that the Commission adopt a strategy to guarantee that it costs licensees less to comply with regulations than not to comply.

In general, the Task Force recognized the need to balance conflicting objectives. Regulation must be flexible, yet has to uphold the legislative objectives effectively. Journalistic and creative independence must be protected, yet the system has to accommodate political accountability. The Task Force report (1986, 697) noted in conclusion, "The CRTC will continue to have great power over the world of broadcasting; indeed it is a veritable parliament of broadcasting. Like other parliaments, it must remember that its mandate requires it to represent the general interests of *all* Canadians and not primarily the interests of the giant industry it regulates."

TV Canada/Télé-Canada

As a means of redressing the current predominance of American programming on Canadian television, the Task Force on Broadcasting Policy proposed the creation of two new services—TV Canada (English) and Télé-Canada (French)—to distribute television programs made specifically for Canadians. As public, non-commercial, satellite-to-cable basic services they would offer children's and educational programming, documentaries, performing arts broadcasts, and the best programs of other Canadian broadcasters, particularly regional productions. They would not carry sports or English-language news and public affairs programs.

The new services would operate as a consortium of all public broadcasters: the CBC, provincial broadcast authorities, independent producers, the NFB, and Telefilm Canada. The Task Force recommended funding the services by a direct charge on cable operators, which they would in turn pass on to their subscribers. The charge would create a fund of between $45 million and $90 million.[14] With a predictable source of revenue and without large and expensive production infrastructures, the services could finally offer Canadians a truly indigenous alternative. They would ensure the availability of existing Canadian programming, some of which is not currently telecast, or is telecast only in limited regions.

The Task Force suggested that Télé-Canada could use some of the resources of TV5, an international francophone network that exhibits programming from France, Belgium, Switzerland, and Canada via satellite to Europe and North Africa. Coincidentally, in September 1987, then Minister of Communications Flora MacDonald announced that a favourable CRTC ruling had paved the way for TV5 to become available in Canada, through a project jointly funded by the federal and Quebec governments. Although TV5 offers francophones excellent French-language programming, it currently exhibits only six hours of Canadian material per week. The Canadian programming is prepared by a consortium that includes Radio-Canada, Radio-Québec, Télé-Métropole, Télévision Quatre Saisons, the NFB, TV Ontario, FilmSat Inc., and Cogéco Inc. Whether importing the TV5 network will increase the opportunity for Canadian participation remains to be seen.

Conclusion

The Task Force recognized that enabling the Canadian broadcasting system to fulfil the stated social and cultural objectives will take money. It estimated that the recommendations in its report would require additional expenditures of about $75 million initially, rising to $270 million with full implementation. The Task Force (1986, 687) asserts that these costs are not extravagant and that there are many potential sources of revenue, such as government, cable television, advertising, and private broadcasters: "In a real sense, then, paying for the new system is the easy part of the problem. The more difficult question is whether we have the will, whether we care enough about the role Canadian broadcasting plays, to do so."

The Standing Committee on Communications and Culture responds

The Task Force on Broadcasting Policy report was tabled in Parliament on 29 January 1987 and referred to the Standing Committee on Communications and Culture at that time. The Committee was instructed to review the report and respond by accepting, rejecting, amending, or adding recommendations as necessary. As it did so, the Committee considered the historical development of broadcasting in Canada and concluded that a new broadcasting act, reaffirming the cultural and social objectives of broadcasting, should be drafted for Parliament's consideration as soon as possible.

Recommendations for broadcasting policy and legislation

The Committee agreed with the Task Force that the act should include a statement of policy to serve as the basis for decisions by governments and regulators. It approved the majority of the Task Force recommendations in this area, and made changes primarily to clarify, broaden, or strengthen the principles set down in the report.

The Committee acknowledged the reality of the composite system, but emphasized that it should be regulated by a single agency to ensure that each part contributes to the stated objectives. Ownership of all broadcast undertakings must be at least 80 percent Canadian and no single foreign shareholder should be allowed to control more than 10 percent. As well, each undertaking must be effectively controlled by Canadians.

The Committee rejected the Task Force proposals to define program quality by accepted professional standards and to guarantee access to the system. It did not see the value of adding a more specific criterion for broadcasting quality to the act and it believed that rights of access were adequately covered in other, more general provisions.

The changes made by the Committee reflect its concern for the programming objectives of any new legislation. It argued that the language of both the Broadcasting Act, 1968 and the Task Force recommendations was for the most part too general. Its own recommendations are more specific and, by its own estimation, more meaningful. They are also a clear signal to broadcasters of the government's objectives for the system as a whole. They are included here because of their vital, comprehensive nature:

Recommendation 21

The Act should provide that the Canadian broadcasting system should serve the needs and interests of both sexes.

Recommendation 22

The Canadian broadcasting system should play an active role in stimulating a Canadian consciousness and should serve the special needs of each geographic region and both official language groups. By contributing actively to the exchange of information and expression among the regions, and between French- and English-speaking Canadians, the system should acquaint all Canadians with the traditions, values, practices and aspirations of each region of Canada.

Recommendation 23

The Canadian broadcasting system should encourage the development of Canadian expression, providing a wide range of programming that reflects Canadian attitudes, opinions, ideas, values and artistic creativity, displaying Canadian talent in entertainment programming, and offering information and analysis concerning Canada and other countries from a Canadian point of view.

Recommendation 24

The programming carried by the system should provide a balanced representation of Canadian society, reflecting its multicultural and bilingual realities, its aboriginal peoples and the composition of its population with respect to sex, age, race, national or ethnic origin, colour, religion and mental or physical handicaps.

Recommendation 25

The Canadian broadcasting system should offer a range of programming that is varied and comprehensive, providing a balance of information, enlightenment and entertainment for people of different ages, interests and tastes (Canada, House of Commons, Standing Committee on Communications and Culture 1987b, 38–39). *Reproduced with the permission of the House of Commons.*

Recommendations for the CBC

In its *Fourth report* (1987a, 3), the Standing Committee on Communications and Culture noted that the CBC "remains essential to Canadian life." It also confronted the financial problems that plagued the Corporation during 1986 and prevented the auditor general from completing an audit of the Corporation's books. There was no evidence of misappropriation of funds, but the absence of a reliable accounting of public moneys raised substantial concerns. The Committee also offered recommendations to balance financial accountability with journalistic and programming independence. These included plans for restructuring CBC management. The communications minister accepted the recommendations and promised to table legislation as soon as possible.

The Standing Committee (1987b, 71) saw the need for "a greater degree of rationality and predictability in CBC funding." While it accepted the Task Force recommendation that the government precede CBC licence renewals with a statement outlining proposed funding during the term of the licence, it also realized that Parliament was not bound by its prior decisions. The Committee therefore suggested that new legislation incorporate an indication of future funding. Although the statute could then be amended by Parliament, the decision to do so would require public debate. It was hoped that this safeguard would substantially reduce the Corporation's financial uncertainty.

In terms of programming, the Committee concurred with several of the Task Force recommendations. The CBC should be required to cover the whole range of Canadian programming but released from the directive to contribute to national unity. CBC programming ought to satisfy both regional and national needs with productions that reflect the diversity of unique regions to other parts of the country. The Committee disagreed, however, with the Task Force suggestion to limit CBC foreign programming to material unavailable from other sources, arguing that the Corporation should be free to exhibit the best foreign programs possible.

Finally, the Committee assented that the parliamentary, international, and northern services should be entrenched in any new legislation. In doing so, it conceded the failure of the Corporation to make full use of its parliamentary channel and agreed that the Speaker of the House of Commons should assume both the cost of the service and responsibility for determining its scope and nature. The Committee was reluctant to assign responsibility for funding Radio Canada International to the Department of External Affairs, however, for fear that such a move would endanger journalistic independence. Instead, it suggested that Parliament allocate RCI funds separately within the overall budget for the CBC, thereby ensuring sufficient financial resources without draining the Corporation's domestic budget.

In general, the recommendations put forward by the Standing Committee are intended to strengthen the position of the CBC within the Canadian broadcasting system and to increase the Corporation's financial accountability without damaging intellectual and creative freedom.

The recommendations take into account the role of the CBC as the primary source of domestic programming, and obligate the Corporation to provide a full and balanced range of Canadian programming.

Recommendations for the private sector

The Committee did not address issues bearing on private broadcasters until the minister of communications responded to its initial deliberations by calling for further study. In its 1988 report, the Committee then examined both private radio and television. Like the Task Force, it was generally pleased by the efforts of private radio broadcasters and seconded most of the recommendations to maintain "distinctive, varied and Canadian private radio programming" (Canada, Standing Committee on Communications and Culture 1988, 59).

Private television broadcasters, however, were chided for "making an insufficient contribution to achieving the goals of the *Broadcasting Act*" (Canada, Standing Committee on Communications and Culture 1988, 150). Pointing to the financial strength of the conventional television broadcasters, the Committee (1988, 173) examined various types of performance incentive programs, "in light of the high profits achieved by private broadcasters and the feeling that the Commission (CRTC) has not asked broadcasters to do enough in return for their use of a scarce public resource. . . . " Among the incentives is a plan requiring broadcasters that fail to meet the Canadian content conditions of their licences to contribute financial resources to Canadian programming, through a performance fee levied by the CRTC. The fee is essentially a fine. The Canadian Association of Broadcasters, not surprisingly, opposes this idea. It prefers positive incentives, arguing that some broadcasters may be tempted to buy their way out of Canadian content obligations. While this concern would need to be addressed before the plan is implemented, the CRTC does not, in any event, currently possess the authority to undertake such a scheme. The Standing Committee therefore suggested that new legislation contain a provision permitting the Commission to take such action if necessary.

Generally, the Committee confirmed Task Force recommendations aimed at protecting the advertising base of television broadcasters, strengthening Canadian content regulations, and increasing the commitment of broadcasters' financial resources to Canadian programming through specific conditions of licence.

Recommendations for the distributors

Like the Task Force on Broadcasting, the Standing Committee devoted a great deal of attention to the place of CATV systems and other distributors, such as satellite systems, within the broadcasting system. It recommended giving their hybrid nature—as both common carriers and content providers—unique status within legislation. A new broadcasting act would recognize their role as integral components of the system and impose obligations upon them. The Committee was nevertheless reluctant to apply a narrow definition to cable services that would prevent them from providing community channels. Unlike the Task Force, the Standing Committee saw no need to license and operate community channels separately. The Committee was opposed to cross-ownership and vertical integration[15] of cable undertakings and pay or specialty services, because they involve inherent conflicts of interest, but it did not object to integrated ownership of cable and conventional broadcast undertakings. Pay and specialty carriage are determined by contractual agreement between the carrier and the service, but the CRTC decides which conventional stations a cable outlet must carry and so no opportunity for preferential treatment exists.

The Committee reaffirmed the findings of the Task Force that both channel priority and rates for basic services need continued regulation, noting that the regulatory powers should be explicitly outlined in the legislation. Non-programming services ought to be permitted, as long as their costs are kept separate, excess channels are available, and the services are clearly defined to avoid overlap with regular programming services. In conjunction with the existing legislative provisions within s. 3 of the Broadcasting Act, 1968, these changes should improve the ability of CATV undertakings to strengthen the Canadian broadcasting system.

Recommendations for the CRTC

The Standing Committee on Communications and Culture addressed the criticisms levelled against the CRTC by advising government to reinforce both its own power to control the general direction of the Commission and the agency's mandate. CRTC decisions must be firmly grounded in a clear but broad policy because it is the Commission that implements legislation. To this end, the Committee made three recommendations. Government objectives for the broadcasting system should be stated comprehensively in the act, as should the Commission's responsibilities for achieving them. Second, the government may issue policy guidelines to the CRTC as the need arises, as long as public review is ensured by tabling directions in the House of Commons and clearing the Standing Committee process. Third, the government may set aside CRTC decisions not consistent with broadcasting objectives or refer them back to the Commission for revision. These recommendations are clearly contrary to those of the Task Force, which argued in favour of enhancing directive power only and leaving the appeal of individual decisions to the judicial system.

On the other hand, the Committee reaffirmed, as the Task Force did, the CRTC's power to regulate all matters within its jurisdiction. The Committee also encouraged the use of conditions of licence, such as provisions obliging licensees to spend specific amounts for specified purposes, and recommended that failure to comply with a condition of licence be included as an offence under the act and subject to fines. The Standing Committee argued as well that the CRTC could encourage licensees' respect for the regulations by issuing short-term licences more frequently and calling for new applicants at the licence renewal hearings of non-compliant broadcasters.

In terms of structural and procedural changes to the CRTC, the Standing Committee agreed with the Task Force that if the Commission were to be made more responsible to the public, part-time commissioners would no longer be effective. It proposed appointing twelve full-time commissioners, one for each of the regional offices. Each commissioner would be involved in all decisions related to the assigned region and would supervise regional licensees. The plan was very similar to that of the Task Force, except that the commissioners would not act directly on behalf of their regions. The Committee applauded the public hearing process but agreed that cross-examination and confidentiality practices ought to be altered as the Task Force recommended. The Committee neither approved of funding provisions for public interest groups that wish to intervene in the hearings, however, nor of creating regional public advocates.

With respect to policy, the Committee believed that for the CRTC to be accountable, consistent, and effective, it was essential that it have the power to issue policy statements. The Standing Committee report therefore recommended awarding the Commission statutory power to develop policy. Moreover, the CRTC should be required annually to interpret its mandate, to describe how it will achieve its objectives, and to evaluate its past activities. Under no circumstances, however, should the Commission be required to justify individual licensing decisions.

Conclusion

Although the Standing Committee on Communications and Culture did not agree with all the Task Force recommendations, it did reaffirm the same basic social and cultural objectives for the Canadian broadcasting system. It identified the same issues and also recognized their increasing complexity. Furthermore, the Committee agreed that the time had come to effect positive changes in the system, to ensure that Canadian broadcasting can finally fulfil the goals set for it almost sixty years ago.

The government position: Bill C-136

Minister of Communications Flora MacDonald tabled her response to the initial reports of the House of Commons Standing Committee on Communications and Culture on 26 August 1987. Concerned about the inadequacies of the various reports, especially with respect to private broadcasting, she sent the Committee back to consider further options, reiterating the objectives of the exercise:

> As the government moves to conclude its fundamental review of broadcasting policy, its hope is to ensure that whatever strategy we ultimately adopt for the future of the Canadian broadcasting system is indeed a strategy for the future; one which has contemplated all the options, including far-reaching ones, before committing to any particular path. There is one over-riding goal, . . . to ensure that Canadians have an adequate choice of Canadian programming before them. The improvement of the quantity, and quality, of programming is central to national purposes (MacDonald 1987, 4).

Reaction to the tenor of the minister's statement was swift and bitter. The cultural community feared that the minister had lost her willingness or ability to act and wondered if her nationalistic statements were made simply to pacify them in the face of the on-going free trade talks. Broadcasters argued that they could not plan for the future amidst such uncertainty. William Roberts (1987, D1), senior vice-president of the Canadian Association of Broadcasters, quipped "If we're aiming to have an act to take us into the twenty-first century, then we should have it introduced before the twenty-first century." Jeffrey Simpson (1987, A6), columnist for the *Globe and Mail*, remarked that "apart from an abiding dislike for the Canadian Broadcasting Corporation, not much else is clear about the Conservatives' attitudes towards broadcasting." Other critics wondered whether the minister had a good grip on her portfolio or whether she had any power in Cabinet to push her proposed legislation through the system.

Even Edmonton Conservative MP Jim Edwards, who chaired the House Standing Committee, expressed disappointment with the minister's response. He stressed that her initial sense of urgency had prompted the Committee to hold marathon hearings and submit its report in segments so that the DOC could begin drafting the new legislation. He was upset by the brevity of the minister's response and her challenge to the Committee to begin a new policy chase. He was also frustrated that her decision to delay left policy making in the hands of regulators, rather than elected politicians.

Despite the anxiety and confusion, the Standing Committee on Communications and Culture returned to its deliberations and submitted the *Fifteenth report: A broadcasting policy for Canada* in June 1988. This time, the minister was ready to proceed and she introduced Bill C-136 in the House of Commons on 23 June 1988. The 1988 broadcasting bill focussed on four separate but related areas—programming, fairness and access, technology, and operations and administration—and tried to meet seven objectives:

1. To give primacy to Canadian programming, so that Canadians may always be able to find Canadian images among the myriad of choices available.

2. To ensure continued reflection of the linguistic duality of Canada and the different cultural and economic realities of the French and English broadcasting industries.

3. To provide for a new television programming service oriented to minority interests and needs not met effectively by mass audience commercial television.

4. To ensure that the broadcasting system reflects Canadian culture, tastes and realities, both in its programming and operations.

5. To provide all Canadians with reasonable access to a wide range of radio and television signals.

6. To be technologically neutral so as to be able to accommodate any and all technological changes that may occur over time.

7. To ensure that the Government's key institutions, the CBC and the CRTC, are efficiently managed and responsive to the needs of Canadians (Canada, DOC 1988, 61).

Bill C-136 confirmed the role of the CBC as a vital instrument of cultural policy and supported its Canadian content goals. Following the recommendations of the Task Force and the Standing Committee, it altered the mandate of the Corporation from fostering national unity to contributing to national identity. The proposed legislation also strengthened administrative accountability. It granted Cabinet authority to issue broad policy directives to the CRTC *and* upheld Cabinet's right to set aside or refer back Commission decisions. At the same time, it enhanced the power of the CRTC, especially its power to monitor the programming performance of private broadcasters. The CRTC would continue to regulate cable and was also assigned responsibility for mediating between traditional cable distribution service and the newly authorized cable programming service, to prevent conflicts of interest. In addition, the government announced its intention to amend the 1988 Copyright Act, to require cable operators to pay copyright fees for the right to transmit broadcasters' signals.

The bill also provided a financial framework that would improve the ability of the CBC to plan over the long term. The government planned to spend a total of $250 million over four years to help broadcasting achieve the goals set for it in the bill. The CBC was to receive budget increases of $35 million annually, Telefilm about $18 a year, TV5 more than $2 million a year, and the CRTC about $6 million. The government would also underwrite the cost of a satellite distribution system for aboriginal programming in the North and the cross-Canada National Broadcast Reading Service for visually impaired people.

Bill C-136 contained several other elements of note. It introduced new definitions for cable undertakings, to suit the changed technological environment in broadcasting. It required the industry to reflect the nature of Canadian society in its programming by representing the various regions of the country and the roles of women, disabled people, and native peoples. The bill also offered legislative protection for journalistic, creative, and programming independence. Finally, Bill C-136 contained a unique provision: for the first time, differences between English- and French-language broadcasting were recognized in law.

The proposed legislation met with mixed reviews. The communication minister hailed it as "a comprehensive and fundamental redrafting of the blueprint for broadcasting in Canada ...[providing] new tools and resources to help broadcasters produce more and better Canadian programming" (MacDonald 1988, 4–5). Most observers applauded the legislation's rhetorical emphasis on increasing and improving Canadian content but criticized the absence of concrete measures. Critics argued that the CBC had been assigned additional responsibilities without sufficient resources to accomplish those it already shouldered: "The CBC's function as a national catalyst is confirmed, so long as the corporation never demands enough money to fulfill it properly" (Moore 1988, C3). Private broadcasters welcomed the incentives to produce Canadian programming but railed against the proposed performance bond requirement. Stations would be required to post a bond at the time of licence renewal. Failure to meet the conditions of licence and quotas would result in forfeit of the bond. Cable operations expressed concern about the increased regulatory power of the CRTC. Public interest groups, scholars, and broadcasters worried that Cabinet's new directive power, in combination with its capacity to set aside or return CRTC decisions, would make the regulator vulnerable to political interference.

Finally, those who were already concerned about the future of Canadian cultural industries in the face of the FTA, found nothing to reassure them in the proposed legislation:

> The omission in the bill of a clear requirement that the programming of Canadian broadcasters be predominantly Canadian is considered by many to be a Machiavellian stroke on the part of the government. It is a reflection that the government has, privately, concluded that the Canadian broadcasting system will become "North Americanized." Why did the government adopt its unequivocal policy "not to restrict access to foreign services"? The current perception in the industry is that the Prime Minister did not want to adopt any new provisions which would contravene the FTA. The

concern is great that if the Broadcasting Bill is passed in its present form, and the FTA is implemented, Canada will have foregone the freedom in the future to maintain and develop a separate Canadian broadcasting system, one that can grow and respond to Canadian needs in a period of rapid technological change (Bernstein 1988, 16).

In the end, however, none of this mattered. The House of Commons passed Bill C-136 on 28 September 1988, but after the call for a general election, it died on the Senate's order paper. Minister of Communications Flora MacDonald was not re-elected in November, and the Cabinet vacancy was filled by Marcel Masse. Masse had held the portfolio previously and had initiated seven task forces and policy review committees to examine broadcasting and telecommunication. He therefore brought with him considerable familiarity with the issues of the portfolio.

Summary

The precise nature of any future legislation is not clear. The delay has provided various interest groups, particularly the private broadcasters, with ample time to seek significant alterations to Bill C-136. At the same time, the CBC is having to contend with reduced fiscal resources that could diminish its role in the future and make some aspects of the original bill meaningless. No timetable has been determined for introducing new legislation but one thing is clear: delay in drafting and tabling a broadcasting act will not strengthen the Canadian presence in the Canadian broadcasting system.

Notes

1. Ministerial responsibility for broadcasting has rested with a variety of departments and been governed by two separate pieces of legislation. Responsibility for the implementation of the Radio Act, initially passed in 1905, has been handled by the Departments of Marine and Fisheries (1905–1914, 1922–1936), Naval Services (1914–1922), Transport (1936–1939, 1948–1969), and Communications (1969–), and by the Prime Minister between 1939 and 1948. The Broadcasting Act, first passed in 1932, has been the responsibililty of the Departments of Marine and Fisheries (1932–1936), Transport (1936–1939), National War Services (1941–1945), National Revenue (1945–1963), Secretary of State (1963–1972), and Communications (1972–), and of the Prime Minister (1939–1941). To complicate things still further, the power to issue broadcast licences has also shifted frequently to

include the Minister of Marine and Fisheries (1905–1914, 1922–1932), the Minister of Naval Service (1914–1922), the CRBC (1932–1936), the CBC (1936–1958), the BBG (1958–1968), and the CRTC (1968–).

2. The American networks recover their costs and make a reasonable profit by selling their programming to their own domestic stations. They then dump their programming in foreign markets at markedly lower costs, usually less than 5 percent of what it costs to produce them.

3. Advertising rates are determined by the size of the audience that the broad-caster can deliver, based on the ratings each program achieves. Ratings are very powerful tools that measure market trends and tastes. Supporters of the rating system claim that it stimulates better quality programs. Critics argue that it simply reinforces the "tyranny of the majority," since popularity does not always equal quality. What is more, ratings compare only what is available; they do not recognize the choices between available programming or nothing, or available programming and something better.

4. For example, the BBG awarded Canadian content credit to stations that covered the 1963 assassination and funeral of American president John F. Kennedy, on the grounds that they were of general interest to Canadians.

5. The BBG placed most of the blame for the failure of the content regulations on the ambiguous nature of the Broadcasting Act, 1958. Austin Weir (1965, 357) claimed that it lacked clarity and definition. In all cases in which the Board's regulations were referred to the courts, the BBG was totally unsuc-cessful in defending its right to impose limitations or requirements. Moreover, it lacked the power to suspend or revoke licences in order to en-force its regulations. Only Cabinet had that right, and it was reluctant to be-come involved with such potentially contentious political decisions.

6. The Commission did not alter the radio regulations because it believed that they were achieving the desired results.

7. The CTV network, which has borne the brunt of this criticism, responded by producing a new drama series entitled *Mount Royal* at a cost of $800 000 per one-hour episode. The series was cancelled after its first season.

8. The Task Force on Broadcasting Policy (1986, 432) does indicate, however, that broadcast undertakings are profitable enterprises in Canada, with an average before-tax profit of about 18 percent.

9. An ambitious and expensive CBC production during the 1971–1972 season, entitled *The Whiteoaks of Jalna* and based on the books of Canadian author Mazo De La Roche, was a vivid example of the risk involved in producing dramatic programming for television. The Corporation hired Canadian writers, actors, producers, and other skilled personnel. Having produced a high-quality, well-publicized product, the CBC expected large audiences, rave reviews, and profitable international sales. None of these materialized. Not only did the Corporation lose a considerable sum of money on the project, both its pride in and enthusiasm for similar projects suffered.

10. No broadcast station has ever had its licence revoked for failure to abide by the broadcasting regulations or its own conditions of licence. Many critics

argue that neither Cabinet nor the government of the day are willing to face constituents' anger over the loss of a television station.

11. Section 3 of the Broadcasting Act, 1968 is included in chapter 6.

12. One effect of this recommendation would be to prevent the CBC from broadcasting the programming of the three major American networks, since it is already available in its entirety via cable and in part on private Canadian stations. It would also prohibit the exhibition of major foreign films for the same reason.

13. The Corporation has already acted upon this recommendation.

14. The Task Force proposed an initial surcharge of 75 cents per subscriber rising by 25 cents annually to $1.50, thereafter determined by inflation. Its estimates were based on five million subscribers nationally.

15. Cross-ownership, in this context, is ownership of a range of cable and broadcasting services; vertical integration is ownership of production, broadcast, and distribution facilities.

References

Audley, P. 1983. *Canada's cultural industries: Broadcasting, publishing, records and film.* Toronto: Lorimer.

Babe, R.E. 1975. *Cable television and telecommunications in Canada: An economic analysis.* East Lansing: Michigan State University.

Bernstein, C. 1988. Broadcasting future threatened. *Financial Post.* 10 November. p. 16.

Canada. 1958. *Broadcasting Act, 1958.* Ottawa: Queen's Printer.

———. 1968. *Broadcasting Act, 1968.* Ottawa: Supply and Services.

Canada. Canadian Radio-television and Telecommunications Commission (CRTC). 1971. Policy statement on cable television, Canadian broadcasting, [and] "A single system." 16 July. Ottawa: CRTC.

———. 1979. *Special report on broadcasting, 1968–1978.* Vol. 1. Ottawa: Supply and Services.

———. 1983. Public notice 1983–18, Policy statement on Canadian content in television. 31 January. Ottawa: CRTC.

Canada. Committee on Broadcasting. 1965. *Report.* Ottawa: Queen's Printer.

Canada. Department of Communications. 1983. *Towards a new national broadcasting policy.* Ottawa: Supply and Services.

———. 1988. *Canadian voices, Canadian choices.* Ottawa: Supply and Services.

Canada. Federal Cultural Policy Review Committee. 1982. *Report.* Ottawa: Supply and Services.

Canada. House of Commons. 1928. *Debates.* 16th Parliament.

———. 1958. *Debates.* 24th Parliament.

———. 1988. *Bill C-136: An Act respecting broadcasting and to amend certain Acts in relation thereto and in relation to radiocommunication.*

Canada. House of Commons. Standing Committee on Communications and Culture. 1987a. *Fourth report.* 17 February.

————. 1987b. *Sixth report*. 6 May.

————. 1988. *Fifteenth report: A broadcasting policy for Canada*. Ottawa: Supply and Services.

Canada. Task Force on Broadcasting Policy. 1986. Report. Ottawa: Supply and Services.

Fulford, R. 1987. Stage fright. *Saturday Night* (April): 5–8.

Hallman, E.S. 1977. *Broadcasting in Canada*. Don Mills: General Publishing.

Hoskins, C.K, and S. McFadyen. 1984. International competition in television broadcasting. Paper prepared for the Academy of International Business meeting. June. Singapore.

MacDonald, F. 1987. Government response to the fifth and sixth reports of the House of Commons Standing Committee on Communications and Culture. 26 August.

————. 1988. Notes for a statement at a news conference to announce a new broadcast policy and legislation. 23 June. Ottawa, Ontario.

Moore, M. 1988. It's not what the Broadcasting Act says but how it came to say it. *Globe and Mail*. 16 July. p. C3.

Roberts, W. 1987. Whatever became of super-Flora? *Globe and Mail*. 29 August. p. D1.

Schultz, R. 1977. Regulatory agencies and the Canadian political system. In *Public administration in Canada: Selected readings*, ed. K. Kernaghan, 333–43. Toronto: Methuen.

Simpson, J. 1987. Broadcasting limbo. *Globe and Mail*. 8 September. p. A6.

Stacey, W.A. 1986. Why the magic 50 percent will never happen. *border/lines* (March): 13.

Starowicz, M. 1984. Slow dissolve: How Canada will lose its broadcasting sovereignty. Address to the Graduate Programme in Communications Studies, University of Calgary. 27 November. Calgary, Alberta.

Weir, A.E. 1965. *The struggle for national broadcasting in Canada*. Toronto: McClelland and Stewart.

Part Four

Telecommunication and the Information Economy

TELECOMMUNICATION: THE CANADIAN ENVIRONMENT

*T*elecommunication is a complex and rapidly expanding economic sector, the backbone of the emerging world information economy.[1] An information economy is one in which large numbers of people are employed in organizations whose primary responsibilities are handling, manipulating, transmitting, or storing information. People in information-based economies either work directly with computer hardware and software or rely on information technologies to conduct their work. The world information economy therefore takes in a vast array of jobs, ranging from data entry to space science. Although telecommunication began as a rather simple undertaking, involving first the delivery of telegraph and then basic telephone service, today it encompasses fibre optics, satellites, microwave, "intelligent telephones," "smart buildings," and "smart homes."[2] Telecommunication is a broad term and refers to "any transmission, emission or reception of signs, signals, writings, images and sounds or intelligence by wire, radio, optical or other electromagnetic systems" (International Telecommunication Union 1986, 5). The telecommunication sector is sometimes referred to as the "telecom" industry.

This chapter and the one following examine the major aspects of the Canadian telecommunication environment, focussing on two types of policy issues: conventional communication policy and information policy. The first type of policy deals with the information infrastructure, the second with the application of telecommunication and information technology in other sectors of society. Policy makers can no longer ignore or underrate the impact of technological advances on existing economic, social, and political systems if these innovations are to benefit Canadian society.

The evolving information economy is held together by and dependent upon the speed, reliability, competitiveness, and sophistication of telecommunication systems that transmit data of all types—voice, video, and computerized information bases. Just as Harold Innis identified the significant changes that oral and print media made to culture, so once again we find ourselves about to move into a new era, the information era.[3] This era provides unparalleled opportunity for expansion in the information-based service sector of the Canadian economy.

While the telecommunication revolution has been sweeping Canada, Canadian regulators and politicians alike have been slow to perceive its significance and adjust their policies. This is not totally surprising; telecommunication developments are driven by technology and market demand, not by policy. In fact, there is a general tendency for public policy and legislation to lag substantially behind both sophisticated technological realities and the marketplace adaptations to them. As three Canadian telecommunication authorities, Janisch, Rawson, and Stanbury (1987, vii), point out, "The Canadian telecommunications industry has undergone a profound transformation in the past decade. A largely monopolistic industry structure has been transformed to one characterized by vigorous and sustained competition in a growing number of market segments. Regulation has, as a result, become far more fragmented and complex than it ever was under monopoly."

Technological forces have, in many ways, usurped the power of the regulatory authorities and political leadership, both of which have failed to understand or to come to grips with the information revolution. The Canadian telecommunication environment consists of a patchwork of regulatory systems with inconsistent objectives at both the provincial and national government levels. What has emerged is a series of ad hoc decisions that, to varying degrees, have attempted to control the impact of telecommunication technologies on Canadian society. While each, isolated regulatory decision has appeared justified at the time it was made, taken together they have unintentionally distorted the natural market forces in the Canadian telecommunication scene. Whether critics have turned their attention to the proliferation of satellite dishes, to the failure of broadcasters and telecom carriers to make full use of Canadian satellite systems, or to the collapse of Telidon, they have given the Canadian policy track record in the telecommunication sector mixed reviews.

The origins and development of telecommunication in Canada

Since the dawn of civilization, communication has been vital to survival and progress. Distance limited the means by which our ancestors could communicate but they developed a number of ingenious methods, using smoke and fire, drums, horns, mirrors, and various other signals to transmit information. Fleet-footed messengers also carried oral messages. Not only was this a risky business but it involved delays and errors in the transmission of information.

When writing and later print were introduced, culture and civilization advanced. The written word made it possible to transmit messages accurately through both space (large geographical distances) and time (down through the centuries). In recent years, however, our attention has focussed on another facet of communication—speed. Modern inventions have accelerated the communication process. Whereas it once took months, days, or hours to relay messages to distant receivers we, in the Western world at least, can now transmit information in a very few seconds.

The telegraph and telephone

Centuries after the first attempts to relay messages across vast distances, scientific knowledge of electricity and magnetism advanced to the point at which it could be applied to practical purposes, and the first telecommunication service was developed. The initial attempts to use electricity in long-distance communication took place in the early eighteenth century. They included many variations of the pith ball, spark, electrolysis, charged-wire, litmus, chronometer, and needle telegraphs.[4] Each of these systems suffered from some fault that made it impractical for regular use. The coding and transmission system invented by Samuel Morse during the mid-nineteenth century made it possible to develop the telegraph we know today. Shortly after Morse's successful demonstration of his new code, the first Canadian telegram was sent from the mayor of Toronto, Ontario, to the mayor of Hamilton, Ontario, in December 1846.

During the next fifty years, many telegraph companies sprang up in Canada. Most were small and designed to serve limited geographical areas, and amalgamation was therefore inevitable. As well, many of these smaller companies were controlled by American parent interests. Because the Canadian federal government perceived a danger in allowing this vital national service to be controlled by foreign interests, it decided to grant commercial telecommunication franchises to the Canadian railways. By 1915, only three major telegraph companies were still operating in Canada: Canadian Northern, Grand Trunk, and Canadian Pacific, the company that had provided the first all-Canadian continental telegraph service in 1886. In 1920, the federal government took over the Canadian Northern and Grand Trunk railways and created the new Canadian National Railway. Canadian National Telegraph was established to provide service to the rail company and the public. By the 1930s then, only two telegraph companies remained, Canadian National (CN) and Canadian Pacific (CP). These two began joint operations in 1947 but the partnership was not formally sealed until 1 January 1980, when the new corporation became known as CNCP Telecommunications.[5]

About thirty years after the transmission of the first Canadian telegraph message, Alexander Graham Bell built and began testing his model of the telephone. It was designed to transmit speech by using the principles of electromagnetism. On 10 March 1876, with Bell's famous message, "Mr. Watson, come here. I want you," the age of the telephone began. A year later, Alexander turned over 75 percent of his Canadian patents to his father, Melville Bell, who founded the Bell Telephone Company of Canada in 1880. During the next few years, the Canadian telecommunication environment underwent dramatic changes: telephone exchanges were established in various parts of the country; the Niagara Falls telephone convention adopted "Hello" as a standard telephone salutation; the first public pay phones were introduced (users paid an attendant); and the Bell manufacturing shops were established, functioning as the forerunner of Northern Electric. Despite the hectic pace of this activity, it was another fifty years (1931) before the Canadian transcontinental long-distance telephone network was completed under the auspices of the TransCanada Telephone System, now known as Telecom Canada.

Over time, a Canadian carrier system evolved that met the demands of the country's fragmented regions. Today, it serves 98 percent of Canadian households and has a technical infrastructure worth more than $20 billion. Moreover, "the telephone is now so entrenched as part of our way of life, so accepted as a social necessity, that its presence in the home and business is largely taken for granted" (Pike and Mosco 1986, 26). Other technological developments also fostered the growth of the telecommunication industry. On 23 December 1900, Canadian Reginald Fessenden achieved the first wireless voice transmission over one mile in distance. Less than a year later Marconi received the first wireless signal from England, at Signal Hill, Newfoundland, ushering in the era of international telecommunication services. By 1933, Canadians had access to telephone links to Europe, Asia, Africa, and Australia and by the late 1960s, to virtually every country in the world. This was thanks to the Canadian Overseas Telecommunications Corporation, which became Teleglobe Canada in 1975.

In addition to large-scale innovation in the conventional telecommunication sectors, a number of new technologies broadened the scope of the industry. Microwave, satellites, and cable extended the range and variety of services available. Broadcast communications and specialized services such as paging, mobile communications, message services, and so on were added to the basic telephone and telegraph services offered by the common carriers. The challenges of Canadian geography—6 400 kilometres from coast to coast, 80 percent of the population strung along the southern border, and more than five time zones—induced the country to lead in both satellite and cable technology. The Anik I satellite, launched on 9 November 1972, became the world's first geostationary, domestic communication satellite. Until recently, Canada also claimed the reputation of the most cabled country in the world, a significant accomplishment considering its huge area and sparse population.

Canadian contributions to the development and refinement of telecommunication technology do not end here. The list is too long to detail but includes work in satellite mobile radio applications, digital communications such as DATAROUTE, DATAPAC, DATALINK,

INFODAT, INFOSWITCH, GLOBETEX, and the Integrated Services Digital Network (ISDN), high-frequency communications, meteor-burst technologies, and Telidon, the Canadian videotex phenomenon.[6]

ISDN, optical fibre applications, and cellular radio are examples of three major new technologies. ISDN is a communication system that relies on digital codes, or signals. These signals are very precise and the resulting video, voice, or data transmissions have almost total clarity and accuracy. Optical fibres, as we saw in chapter 7, are extremely thin strands of glass or plastic that have the capacity to carry a multitude of signals simultaneously. Cellular radio is a mobile telephone technology. A cellular system divides a given area into districts, each equipped with a low-power radio transmitter and receiver. As people using cellular telephones in their cars drive through each district, a computer transfers their phone calls from one transmitter and receiver to the next. Sales and use of cellular phones in North America have surpassed all predictions and the trend continues unabated.

Industry structure

Technology is only one aspect of telecommunication in Canada. Marketing structures and regulation make up the other side of the telecom industry coin. Canadians currently have one of the best telecommunication systems in the world. Service is provided by suppliers in seven categories:

1. The 9 regional telephone companies and over 150 smaller systems make up the key element of the telecommunication sector by providing a monopoly network for local and long-distance public voice transmission. Telecom Canada, an unincorporated association of the largest telephone company operating in each province and Telesat Canada, develops and maintains the Canadian system.[7] Its members voluntarily co-operate with one another to allow calls to be transmitted from one carrier to the next. Although Telecom Canada is an unregulated entity, each of its member companies is regulated. BC Tel (British Columbia) and Bell Canada (Ontario and Quebec) are responsible to the Canadian Radio-television and Telecommunications Commission (CRTC), while the seven other telephone companies are regulated by boards or commissions within their own provinces.

2. Another major telecom supplier is CNCP Telecommunications, which has traditionally offered public telegraph service. During the 1950s, it began to establish a nation-wide microwave network to offer business users both private telephone lines, as an alternative to the public switched network, and data communication services for computer-generated information. CNCP has continued to develop and promote its services, and its rivalry with Telecom Canada has intensified. CNCP operations are regulated by the CRTC. Although the Commission turned down CNCP's application to offer public long-distance telephone service in competition with Telecom Canada, most analysts agree that such a development will be inevitable following the federal government's ongoing telecommunication policy review. CNCP believes that its position as Canada's "only national telecommunications carrier" (Wells 1985, 46) makes it an eminently suitable rival for Telecom Canada. This position has been strengthened, following the Rogers Communications Inc. purchase of 40 percent of CNCP, by the addition of a national cellular telephone service and cable television infrastructure.

3. Telesat Canada was established in 1970. It is Canada's monopoly domestic satellite company. It is jointly owned by the federal government, Telecom Canada members, CNCP Telecommunications, Québéc-Téléphone, and Ontario Northland Transportation Commission. Telesat Canada once functioned solely as a carriers' carrier, but it now also sells satellite capacity directly to end users.

4. Teleglobe Canada was originally established in 1949 as the Canadian Overseas Telecommunications Corporation, to provide Canada with telecommunication links overseas. It also serves as Canada's representative to international telecommunication organizations (INTELSAT, INMARSAT, the International Telecommunication Union (ITU), and the Commonwealth Telecommunication Organization (CTO).)

    Since 1984, the federal Conservative government in Canada has been privatizing a number of Crown corporations. One of the large corporations to be put on the auction block was Teleglobe Canada. Until that time, Teleglobe operated as a highly profitable Crown corporation and an unregulated telecom carrier. Its main customer was Telecom Canada. After a lengthy bidding process, a dark horse, Memotec Data, Inc. of Montreal, won the right to purchase Teleglobe Canada. The final price was less than what the federal government had expected. It is important to note that as part of the sale agreement, the government promised to introduce legislation that would not only bring Teleglobe Canada under the regulatory jurisdiction of the CRTC but would also make it the preferred off-shore international carrier. This move would increase regulatory control over Canadian telecommunication carriers by preventing them from bypassing Teleglobe and using some other international carrier to funnel calls to Europe or the Pacific Rim. In addition, the legislation will ensure that Teleglobe Canada's profit is regulated by the Canadian Radio-television and Telecommunications Commission, and that there will be a series of public hearings before any significant rate increases are approved for international telephone calls. The regulator is particularly anxious to prevent Teleglobe Canada's monopoly from allowing it to raise prices to increase its profits. Some commentators have found it somewhat ironic that a Conservative government elected to reduce regulation of Canadian businesses had, in fact, increased regulation when it sold its major telecommunication Crown corporation.

5. Approximately five hundred cable systems offer services to about 80 percent of Canadian households. Although primarily an extension of the broadcasting industry, the cable sector is beginning to offer a range of interactive telecommunication services and to investigate others. The CRTC regulates the carriage signals and rates of cable companies. (For more detail, see chapter 7.)

6. The Radio Common Carriers (RCCs) constitute a growing sector of the telecommunication industry. First licensed in 1963, RCCs provide a wide variety of services: paging, mobile radio, message forwarding, cellular telephones, alarm monitoring, and digital transmission. Although not directly regulated, RCCs

have the terms of their interconnection with the telephone companies (telcos) controlled in each case by the agency that regulates the given telco. This provision guarantees RCCs fair and equitable treatment by the telcos with whom they compete.[8]

7. The final group of suppliers are non-carriers, such as equipment manufacturers and data processors, who provide both telecommunication hardware and a number of enhanced services. (Enhanced services are services offered over the basic telecommunication network that add value to basic services. Storing and forwarding data are examples.) Although not regulated, non-carriers compete directly with the traditional, established carriers, who also offer both equipment and enhanced services.

In addition to the seven categories of recognized suppliers, a new wrinkle has recently been added to the Canadian telecommunication environment. Unregulated American discounters are entering the market and offering long-distance service to international destinations at cheaper rates than the regulated Canadian telcos.[9] Table 9.1 identifies the territorial market base and ownership classification of Canada's main telecom suppliers, and illustrates the patchwork nature of the system. This brings us to the questions of regulation and competition in the Canadian telecommunication industry.

Regulation

When examining regulation in the telecommunication sectors, two factors are important and should be kept in mind: this is an area in which the economic and political stakes are very high indeed; and it was originally assumed that economies of scope and scale made it imperative to deliver telecommunications through a monopoly. For these reasons, an elaborate regulatory mosaic evolved to monitor the telecommunication infrastructure. While regulation was deemed necessary to prevent abuse under monopolistic conditions, it also furthered three overarching government objectives for the telecom industry: universal access, substantial Canadian ownership, and regional economic development.

Table 9.1

Ownership and territory of major Canadian telephone and telecommunication carriers, 1989

Newfoundland Telephone Co. Ltd.*	private	Newfoundland
Terra Nova Telecommunications	private	Newfoundland
Island Telephone Co. Ltd.*	private	Prince Edward Island
New Brunswick Telephone Co. Ltd.*	private	New Brunswick
Maritime Telegraph and Telephone Co.*	private	Nova Scotia
Bell Canada*	private	Quebec, Ontario, and eastern N.W.T.
Québec-Téléphone	private	Quebec
Télébec Ltée.	private	Quebec
Northern Telephone Ltd.	private	Ontario
Manitoba Telephone System*	public (provincial)	Manitoba
SaskatchewanTelecommunications*	public (provincial)	Saskatchewan
Alberta Government Telephones*	public (provincial)	Alberta
'edmonton telephones'	public (municipal)	Edmonton
BC Tel*	private	British Columbia
NorthwesTel	private	N.W.T., Yukon, and northern B.C.
Cable companies	private	Canada—specified territories
CNCP Telecommunications	private	Canada
Cantel Inc.	private	Canada
CellNet	private/public**	Canada
Teleglobe Canada	private	international
Telesat Canada*	private/public***	Canada

Notes: * a member of Telecom Canada
       ** an association of eleven cellular telephone providers owned by Canadian telephone companies
      *** an incorporated company owned jointly by the government of Canada and the member companies of Telecom Canada

Source: McPhail and McPhail 1989.

Universal access

A number of regulatory policies have been implemented to permit universal access. Regional telcos are required to provide service in both profitable and unprofitable areas. The basic pricing principles have been established—value-of-service pricing and system-wide price averaging—to create a complex system of income redistribution. Value-of-service pricing refers to the principle whereby those who value or need the service more, pay more for it; so business users pay higher basic telephone rates than residential users do. System-wide price averaging refers to the process whereby telephone rates are relatively balanced throughout the system. While it costs significantly more to provide telephone service to rural and remote areas than to urban ones, these costs are averaged out and subscribers in all regions pay approximately the same rate. In combination, these principles mean that business users, urban communities, and long-distance toll charges make proportionately larger contributions to the common telecommunication costs than do residential users, rural residents, and local rates. Any significant shift in rates in one of these domains may affect universality and other government objectives. Although these practices have caused the telcos some financial strain, they have also kept local rates low. This has helped to enlarge the size of the public network, thereby increasing the value of the telecommunication system for its users.

Regulation also attempts to ensure that the technology itself promotes universal access and serves the Canadian public interest. It recognizes that the selection of technologies is not neutral—that it involves questions of equity. Basic copper-wire and microwave technologies, for example, allow costs to be distributed among all users, whereas cellular technology allows larger technology costs to be transferred to the individual user. Regulation sets technical standards and ensures that all the hardware within the system is compatible, in an effort to provide telecommunication and information services to all. Regulators appear to have heeded the warning of John Madden (1980, 36): "Do not . . . assume that the system will automatically ensure that . . . the new technologies [are] put to good use . . . to benefit us all."

Finally, regulation ensures universal access by preventing concentration of control. There is always the danger that special interests will gain control of a monopoly to the detriment of the general public. The aim of regulation is to compensate for the potential excesses of market forces. As an example, regulation ensures that Alberta Government Telephones

(AGT), which has a monopoly in Alberta, allows 'edmonton telephones' to interconnect with AGT subscribers. Theoretically, without regulation AGT could refuse interconnection or charge inflated prices to 'edmonton telephones' subscribers who want to call elsewhere in Alberta.

Canadian ownership

The second objective of the government is to maintain Canadian sovereignty in the telecommunication sector. Fear of foreign domination is reflected in three policy positions. First, successive governments have believed that Canadian ownership and control is essential. A growing societal dependence on information makes the nation increasingly vulnerable to foreign inroads into our culture, economy, and political life. This susceptibility is lessened if regulation requires Canadians to have sovereign control of their own communication system. Control is crucial in areas such as national defence and intergovernmental communication, and has economic and social significance for the nation.

Second, telecommunication technology has raised concerns about information privacy. The role of regulation is to prevent abuses of individual privacy. By determining which organizations are allowed to provide information services, regulators can set limits on what can be done with the information and punish offenders, provided, of course, that an offence occurs in a Canadian data base, in Canada.

Third, government policy reveals the ever-present issue of Canadian cultural identity. The intensification of international, transborder competition influences the degree to which a strong national industry can reflect Canadian values and needs, remain subject to Canadian laws, and respond to Canadian policy objectives. Regulators have the responsibility to develop a framework to ensure these characteristics in the telecommunication sector.

Regional development

The regional development objective is also a broad one. Although specific objectives vary from region to region, telecommunication is integral to any development scheme. Regulation allows governments to impose development responsibilities on the telecommunication sector in order to fulfil broader goals. The employment opportunities that development produces in various regions, for example, are part of the government's motivation to foster the growth of regional telecommunication sources and systems.

Although it is undeniable that regulation promotes laudable goals, the regulatory framework is under severe strain and several issues have become increasingly problematic. The present, regionally fragmented regulatory system defies logical explanation.[10] Federalism, constitutional ambiguity, and rapid technological change make it difficult to achieve a cohesive national policy. The telecom industry believes that a settlement of the jurisdictional entanglement is "an integral and essential component of any effort to rectify or improve telecommunications policy in Canada" (Thompson 1985, 32). The long-awaited national telecommunication policy, along with enabling federal legislation, will be emerging during the early 1990s.

Competition

Many observers now argue that information technology is beyond regulatory control. To date, regulation has not kept pace with technological change or recognized the convergence of communication and computer technology. Not only is monopoly no longer necessary in many sectors, but it may no longer be able to operate effectively. While it is still possible to retain a monopoly in public long-distance service, for example, the monopoly could become dysfunctional. Its existence may encourage private long-distance networks, which draw revenues away from the public system and force increases in public rates. Higher rates increase the desire to bypass the public system, and a vicious circle is created. The monopoly public network could therefore remain intact but its value be destroyed.

The current environment has reduced the ability of regulators to effect change. Regulation, which is necessary under monopolistic conditions, requires consensus, and increased pluralism has made consensus much more difficult to achieve. Preoccupation with possible monopolistic abuse slows innovation and fosters the status quo. Roger Noll ([1979] 1980, 259) argues that regulation has a conservative bias and Richard Schultz (1983, 218) warns that unless the situation is altered, Canadian social, economic, and cultural interests may be left exposed and defenceless. An unchanged regulatory framework may inadvertently leave Canadians with an inadequate telephone service, for example, or ignore issues of privacy raised by new capabilities to transfer data from place to place.

U.S. firms enjoy the benefits of reduced long-distance rates as a result of competition, but Canadian firms continue to pay artificially inflated long-distance rates. Although CNCP has applied to the CRTC for regulatory permission to provide long-distance service at rates lower than those currently available, the Commission maintains that approval of the application would cause a significant increase in local rates as other telcos seek compensation for lost long-distance revenue. This decision is clearly regulatory, not technical, because the technology does exist to permit competition in long-distance traffic.

In addition, the carriers believe that regulation prevents them from operating their businesses in the most efficient manner possible. Regulatory restrictions slow the adoption of new technologies and inhibit flexible responses to market demands. Furthermore, regulation is costly in terms of both time and money. The regulated carriers claim that consumers are bearing the heavy burden of continued regulation and that the economy will suffer for it. Their argument is that higher telecom rates under regulation impose higher costs of doing business on Canadian companies. This increases the cost of goods and services produced, which in turn both increases the cost of living in Canada and makes the goods and services less attractive on international markets.

Finally, another important issue is emerging. As other nations allow market forces to determine prices and corporate success in the telecommunication sector, some critics of Canadian regulation maintain that Canadian telecommunication firms are reluctant to engage in substantial research and development, for fear that their innovations will not receive swift regulatory approval. The incentive for Canadian telecommunication firms to develop new product lines is low compared to their aggressive global competitors.

At present, there is widespread support for reform of the regulatory system, to make it more adaptable, anticipatory, and reflective of current technological realities (McPhail and McPhail 1985). Opponents and proponents alike are aware of the limitations of regulation. Its tools are limited; its process, adversarial; its time frame and bureaucratic requirements, a burden. Currently, regulation is a blunt instrument. Regulatory decisions are most often incremental in nature and therefore fail to deal with the substantial policy issues involved. According to John Dealy (1982, 31), regulation should begin to address society's changing needs, not its own past principles.

Competition within the telecommunication sector involves three industries once considered distinct—telecommunication, data processing, and office products. The boundaries between them are blurring as the market expands and diversifies. The industry is increasingly volatile and there is worldwide pressure for change. Whereas protected monopolies were once considered necessary for telecommunication infrastructures to function efficiently, that assumption is being challenged. Many now argue that monopoly is nothing more than the ability to manipulate prices and eliminate competition unilaterally.

In addition, technology has increased flexibility and individualization in the telecommunication services available. Consumers, especially business users, are becoming more sophisticated in their needs and are demanding services at lower prices. In doing so, they are influenced by developments in the United States, since the Canadian and American systems have traditionally offered similar services and adopted common technologies. Canadians, aware of the proliferation of services in the U.S. market, are frustrated by limitations at home.

A competitive market offers several economic advantages. Prices are forced closer to costs and consumers benefit. Competition also encourages innovation and quality control. The number of services and suppliers increases and customers have expanded choice. Furthermore, competition can have positive effects on a country's economy by strengthening its position in the world market. If a company tailors its telecommunication services and products to its customers' needs, rather than to regulatory demands, and at the same time, lowers its overall telecom costs, it can pass savings onto consumers by way of lower prices or improved products. A number of people believe that only a competitive telecommunication environment can provide these advantages. To date, competition in the Canadian market has been limited and controlled by the various different federal and provincial regulators. Although criticism of the fragmented regulatory structure in this country is valid, full deregulation—the complete absence of regulation—is an unlikely option. Reregulation, which would revise regulatory control, is more feasible.

The debate over telecommunication competition focusses on the question of rate rebalancing. At present, regulation guarantees the application of the two basic pricing principles already noted: value-of-service pricing and system-wide price averaging. While these principles have fostered universal access and regional development, critics contend that the result is an inefficient, inequitable, and unresponsive system that fails to acknowledge its cost for all sectors of the Canadian economy in terms of international competitiveness. Rate rebalancing would bring an end to the application of these principles by aligning rates and costs.

If rate rebalancing and competition are introduced, local basic rates for individual consumers are expected to rise. Many fear that the increase will place ordinary telephone service beyond the reach of many Canadians and exaggerate the discrepancy between "haves" and "have-nots." As Pike and Mosco (1986, 32) note, "Access to electronic technology will be essential for daily life. Will we be so mystified by the fantasies of a computer society that we lose sight of the many people who cannot afford the basic price of admission to the Information Age?"

Various solutions to this problem have been offered, such as direct government subsidies, multi-party service, and life-line rates. Life-line rates are very low rates for basic connection only. Any use of the system would be subject to additional rates. Whatever the solutions, regulators are aware that rate rebalancing creates the impression of inequality. Business users will experience dramatic savings as average subscribers confront higher rates. On the other hand, it is argued that competition can benefit the national economy by reinforcing its position in the domestic and world markets. Dale Orr, Bell Canada's chief economist, argues, "It's not enough to look at your phone bill. Consumers can be winners due to growth in the economy and because prices of many goods and services will be lower" (in McKendry 1986, 12).

It is clear that telecommunication is big business in Canada. It currently employs over 100 000 Canadians and the gross domestic product in the telecommunication services sector is growing at a higher rate than the GDP for the overall economy. Yet the importance of this sector cannot be determined solely on the basis of industry assets and revenues. It provides essential services to the information-based and high-technology industries—two of the fastest growing sectors of the economy. Telecommunication is therefore vital to the overall future health of the Canadian economy.

The international sweepstakes

It is important to bear in mind that Canada is only one of a number of nations attempting to position themselves as frontrunners in the evolving information age. Clearly the United States and Japan lead the world in information technology, but several other nations are also attempting to benefit from the movement to information-based economies. West Germany, France, Great Britain, Australia, Singapore, South Korea, and Sweden are all expanding their domestic information industries and their export of telecommunication products and services around the world. In fact, the European Community (EC) has launched a major research and development campaign, known as Esprit, as a means of catching up with Japan and the United States in the telecommunication field and ensuring that European nations do not become the technological serfs of other countries in the future. The EC also plans to establish standard telecommunication rules across Europe by 1992. This will create the type of single mass market needed for EC high-technology firms to have a large volume of equipment sales. Foreign firms from Canada, Japan, and the United States will probably encounter great trading barriers when they try to sell to the EC after 1992.

Canada, rather than launching a similar research and development drive, has been relying upon a mix of public and private initiatives to establish itself as an information-based economy. Northern Telecom and Spar Aerospace, for example, are private companies involved in telecommunication development. Public initiatives by the federal Department of Communications and studies such as those undertaken by the Science Council of Canada, on the other hand, are examples of governmental attempts to maintain a substantial presence for Canada in the telecommunication field.

In Canada today, several telecommunication entities come under the federal regulatory umbrella. Some are there by historical accident and others because of deliberate policies to ensure that the federal presence is maintained. Another group is regulated by provinces or municipalities. A series of new telecommunication services and suppliers is emerging, however, with no restrictions or conditions placed upon their market behaviour. These include foreign telcos, domestic manufacturers, and suppliers of services such as cellular phone service and computer-enhanced services. They are the representatives of a free-enterprise model in which the dynamics of the marketplace determine successes and failures. Regulated telecommunication carriers and suppliers, on the other hand, must work through a maze of requirements and suffer delaying and expensive public-hearing processes which inhibit market realities.

The future of telecommunication in Canada revolves around two distinct possibilities. The first is a single network relying primarily on fibre optic technology. Myriads of services would be provided by one dominant carrier and many ancillary service providers. In many respects, this reflects a more technologically sophisticated extension of the traditional system. The second possibility is to have a much more competitive environment, in which both the technologies and services available are offered by a broad range of carriers and suppliers, many of whom may be foreign owned and operated. Such a system would reflect an attempt to accommodate a rapidly changing, dynamic industry. Canada is in a good position to adapt to the first situation but would face more difficulty with the second. Our research and development position is weak compared to our international competitors, and our main carriers, suppliers, and manufacturers are currently ill-prepared to face the onslaught of well-organized foreign competition.

The telephone is now the gateway to a world of information, and telecommunication policy serves as the central nervous system for the emerging information economy. If the federal government and others fail to direct the telecommunication system in the right direction, the consequences could be politically, socially, and economically devastating.

Summary

This chapter reviewed the telecommunication sector in Canada. The role of technological advances was examined in relation to public policy. The fragmented Canadian regulatory system was described, as was its impact on the industry structure. Competition and rate rebalancing were identified as major regulatory and policy issues.

Canada has been a leader in the telecommunication field and has a long and substantial record of technological innovation. Even with its current problems, the Canadian telecommunication sector is of a very high calibre. Resolving the issues that plague us will, however, have significant implications for all sectors of the Canadian economy. The next chapter examines in more detail the efforts of successive Canadian governments to make sure that Canada develops as a modern, information-based economy.

Notes

1. Chapters 9 and 10 draw on *Telecom 2000* (McPhail and McPhail 1985), a research report prepared for the Department of Communications (DOC), as well as a paper, "The history of telecommunications" (McPhail 1986), presented at a DOC conference in November 1986.

2. Smart buildings and homes reflect the state of the art in terms of wiring and microprocessor technology. Buildings in the future will have wiring designed for a multitude of services, ranging from computer connections to intelligent machines. The machines will do everything from making coffee to warning householders about faulty wiring.

3. For further information about Harold Innis, see chapter 3.

4. Although a full explanation of each of these inventions is beyond the scope of this book, brief descriptions follow:

   a) The pith ball telegraph had twenty-six wires and pith balls, one for each letter of the alphabet. When a charge was applied to the wire, the corresponding ball would move, indicating the letter being transmitted.

   b) The spark telegraph functioned in much the same way, except that a jumping spark would indicate which letter was being transmitted.

   c) The electrolysis telegraph had thirty-five wires (twenty-six letters, nine numerals) that led to electrodes immersed in water. When the line was charged, bubbles appeared, to indicate which symbol was transmitted.

   d) The charged-wire telegraph reduced the number of wires to ten. The message was received by an individual who placed his or her fingers and thumbs on a metal plate and received an electric shock on the appropriate digit when the wires were charged.

   e) With the litmus telegraph, litmus paper was placed at the ends of the wire. Discoloration of the paper indicated a charge and the letter transmitted.

   f) The chronometer telegraph had a disc marked with the letters and figures. The disc would rotate to reveal the transmitted letter in response to an electric charge.

   g) The needle telegraph used the principle of compass needle deflection in response to electrical charges to transmit coded messages.

5. CN sold its share of CNCP Telecommunications to CP in 1988. Less than a year later, 40 percent of the company was purchased by Rogers Communication Inc. The final deal is still pending, awaiting CRTC approval.

6. For a detailed review of the significant contributions of Canadians to the field of telecommunications, see McPhail and Coll (1986). Their book has

chapters on satellite, mobile, fibre optic, and digital communications, and innovative research projects.

7. The member companies of Telecom Canada are as follows: BC Tel, Alberta Government Telephones, Saskatchewan Telecommunications, Manitoba Telephone System, Bell Canada, New Brunswick Telephone Co. Ltd., Maritime Telegraph and Telephone Co., Island Telephone Co. Ltd., Newfoundland Telephone Co. Ltd., and Telesat Canada (which joined in 1977).

8. For a more detailed review of Radio Common Carriers, see Batten (1985).

9. Discounters are not telephone companies themselves. They reroute Canadian long-distance calls through American networks. Examples of American discounters include Longnet, ETI Telecom International Inc., and Cam-Net. Savings amount to as much as 35 percent.

10. The regulation of telecommunication carriers in Canada is a complex issue. The following list enumerates some of the major carriers and the responsible regulatory authority for each:

Newfoundland Telephone Co. Ltd.	provincial authority
Island Telephone Co. Ltd.	provincial authority
New Brunswick Telephone Co. Ltd.	provincial authority
Bell Canada	federal authority
Québéc-Téléphone	provincial authority
Télébec Ltée.	provincial authority
Northern Telephone Ltd.	provincial authority
Manitoba Telephone System	provincial authority
Saskatchewan Telecommunications	provincial authority
Alberta Government Telephones	provincial authority
'edmonton telephones'	municipal authority
BC Tel	federal authority
CNCP Telecommunications	federal authority
Telesat Canada	federal authority
Cable companies	federal authority
Teleglobe Canada	federal authority

References

Batten, M.C. 1985. Competition in provision of communication services. In *Communication in the 80's.* rev. ed., ed. T.L. McPhail and S. Hamilton, 38–46. Calgary: University of Calgary.

Dealy, J.F. 1982. Telecommunications: Policy issues and options for the 1980s. *The Brookings Review* 1(2): 30–33.

International Telecommunication Union. 1986. *Information, telecommunications and development.* Geneva: ITU.

Janisch, H.N., S.G. Rawson, and W.T. Stanbury. 1987. *Canadian telecommunications regulation bibliography.* Ottawa: Canadian Law Information Council.

McKendry, D. 1986. Ringing change: A new way of setting phone bills will soon make basic service a lot less affordable. *Canadian Consumer* 16(5): 10–14.

McPhail, T.L. 1986. History of telecommunications. Paper presented at the Conference on Telecommunications and Economic Development. 10–12 November. Ottawa, Ontario.

McPhail, T.L., and D.C. Coll, eds. 1986. *Canadian developments in telecommunications: An overview of significant contributions.* Calgary: Graduate Programme in Communications Studies, University of Calgary.

McPhail, T.L., and B.M. McPhail. 1985. *Telecom 2000: Canada's telecommunications future.* Calgary: Graduate Programme in Communications Studies, University of Calgary.

———. 1989. *Telecom 2001: A strategic forecast.* Calgary: MRG Ltd.

Madden, J. 1980. Julia's dilemma. In *Gutenberg two,* ed. D. Godfrey and D. Parkhill, 13–38. Toronto: Porcépic.

Noll, R.G. [1979] 1980. Regulation and computer services. In *The computer age: A twenty-year view,* ed. M. L. Dertouzos and J. Moses, 254–84. Cambridge: Massachusetts Institute of Technology.

Pike, R., and V. Mosco. 1986. Canadian consumers and telephone pricing: From luxury to necessity and back again? *Telecommunications Policy* 10(1): 17–32.

Schultz, R.J. 1983. Regulation as Maginot Line: Confronting the technological revolution in telecommunication. *Canadian Public Administration* (Summer): 203–18.

Thompson, E.D. 1985. Competition in provision of communication services. In *Communication in the 80's.* rev.ed., ed. T.L. McPhail and S. Hamilton, 28–33. Calgary: University of Calgary.

Wells, D. 1985. Competition in provision of communication services. In *Communication in the 80's.* rev. ed., ed. T.L. McPhail and S. Hamilton, 46–52. Calgary: University of Calgary.

TELECOMMUNICATION AND PUBLIC POLICY

*T*oday, the information sector of the Canadian economy . . . is a 35 billion dollar business. It accounts for about eight per cent of the gross national product and is larger than our traditional staples—agriculture, forestry, and fishing—combined (MacDonald 1986).

The preceding chapter detailed the main actors in the Canadian telecommunication environment. This chapter first reviews the major Canadian studies of the telecommunication sector and then discusses both current concerns about the information economy and the entire question of Canada's future in the international information scene. On the one hand, our proximity to the United States is a tremendous benefit because of the opportunities, experience, and markets it represents, but at the same time it tends to dwarf Canadian initiatives and Canadian opportunities. This geographical reality must be kept in mind when we examine Canada's public policy position with respect to telecommunication and the information economy.

Background studies

With the creation of the first federal department of communications in 1968, the government pulled together a number of previously unconnected activities in the field of communication—specifically cultural, broadcasting, and telecommunication activities. The newly created department was eager to get a handle on its policy area and sponsored a series of telecommunication studies. The Science Council of Canada also pursued several studies of its own. Before describing the findings of some of the most important studies, we should point out that although Canada has an excellent track record in studying the telecommunication sector, it has a relatively poor record in legislating for this crucial area. Many foreign nations hold Canada in high regard for its research in and understanding of the role of telecommunication, and Canadian advice is frequently sought out by foreign delegations. Nevertheless, the actual, day-to-day legal, regulatory, and legislative aspects of the Canadian telecommunication policy environment leave much to be desired.

Instant world

In September 1969, Canada's first federal minister of communications, Eric Kierans, announced the intention of his department to undertake a comprehensive telecommunication study to be known as the Telecommission. Its purpose was to provide the government with advice about policy for the main issues and problems in the entire field of telecommunication, ranging from technical to social aspects. More than forty individual studies were undertaken and a major research publication, *Instant world* (Canada, Telecommission 1971), resulted. To a large extent, *Instant world* was recognized as a landmark study. Canada was one of the first industrialized nations to undertake a systematic examination of telecommunication and its potential impact on all sectors of society.

The various Telecommission studies and the final publication examined six areas:

1. the historical development of telecommunication and the main participants in the field

2. the technological dimensions of telecommunication and the potential problems confronting regulators as a consequence

3. social issues such as individuals' right to access, participation, and privacy, and intellectual property

4. future concerns such as improved service, access, and the linkage of computers and telecommunications

5. the governmental role in protecting and overseeing the public interest, regulating telecommunication rates, and so on

6. policy options for both the telecommunication industry and federal and provincial governments to consider

The green paper

Neither an official policy paper on communication nor any substantive legislative action followed the completion of the Telecommission study. As the debate continued during the 1970s, various position papers were produced by successive ministers of communication. One of the earliest, green paper entitled *Proposals for a communications policy for Canada*, a appeared in March 1973. It dealt with both the industry structure and public policy concerns. This position paper was not exhaustive; rather it put forward a number of issues to serve as a basis for meaningful public discussion.

The green paper began with a statement emphasizing both the importance of the public interest in telecommunication and the nation's considerable reliance on telecommunication to pull itself together along the east/west axis. East/west connections are essential to counteract the strong north/south flow of data and telecommunication links:

> The existence of Canada, as a political and social entity, has always been heavily dependent upon effective systems of east/west communications. This is the historical reason for the successive development of the routes of the voyageurs, coast-to-coast railways, telegraph and telephone systems, broadcasting services, airlines, the Trans-Canada Highway and, most recently, a domestic satellite-communications system. These systems, counterbalancing the strong north/south pull of continentalism, have been essential for industrial and resource development, for the transmission and dissemination of

information, and for the expression and sharing of social and cultural values (Canada, Department of Communications (DOC) 1973, 3).

The paper went on to discuss these issues in more detail and concluded with suggestions for the development of a national telecommunication policy. It gave particular emphasis to providing solutions to some of the complex issues facing Canada and offered six proposals:

- a positive commitment to, and the development of mechanisms for, consultation and collaboration among federal and provincial governments and regulatory bodies in the formulation and implementation of national policy objectives;

- a commitment to the principles of broadcasting policy as enunciated in the Broadcasting Act;

- the development of means to ensure that technological advances, such as coaxial-cable and satellites are used to contribute to the capability of the Canadian broadcasting system to fulfill its responsibilities to the people of Canada;

- a revision and consolidation of federal legislation relating to telecommunications;

- a provision for more effective regulation of telecommunications carriers subject to federal authority; and

- the establishment of a single federal agency to regulate both broadcasting and the operations of the carriers subject to federal authority (Canada, DOC 1973, 35).

These proposals were received with considerable scepticism by both the industry and provincial governments alike. One item dominated the policy debate during the 1970s—the contentious relationship between federal and provincial objectives, activities, and roles in the field of telecommunication. Although friction between the federal and provincial spheres had appeared to be a minor irritant during the 1960s, it took the form of serious policy and political differences during the next decade. The strain on federal–provincial relations plus the rapid changes in telecommunication fuelled by technological innovation left many doubtful not only about the ability of the federal government to create an enlightened national policy, but even about the necessity of an increasing federal role in the development of the telecommunication industry.

The grey paper

In April 1975, a grey paper entitled *Communications: Some federal proposals* was released by the federal Department of Communications. Since the green paper had not prompted any legislative enactments, the grey paper set about to define areas of interest and concern more precisely. Once again, federal–provincial conflict dominated the rhetoric:

> The Government intends to give full recognition to provincial and regional objectives and priorities, while continuing to fulfill its responsibility for this essentially national dimension. Thus, there is an urgent need for agreement on cooperative arrangements that will enable better account to be taken of provincial concerns while avoiding the fragmentation of Canadian telecommunications systems and protecting the interests of Canada as a whole (Canada, DOC 1975, 4).

The grey paper then set out a series of telecommunication objectives very similar to those embodied in the Broadcasting Act, 1968, including developing the telecommunication sector in order to strengthen the economic, cultural, and political fabric of Canada as a modern state. Issues such as the role of computers and satellites were glossed over, while the bulk of the paper dealt with applying the Broadcasting Act to telecommunication and placating the provinces by dealing with their concerns. The grey paper contained a single major conclusion:

> The principal conclusion to be drawn from all the studies of communications in Canada that have been undertaken in recent years is that all forms of telecommunications have both national and local aspects, and that these aspects cannot be separated on the basis of the technological character of the facilities involved. Legalistic questions as to which aspect predominates in a particular situation are much less important than a mutual determination to ensure that the people of Canada have access to the best communications services that the country can afford. This objective can best be achieved if the federal and provincial governments can agree upon effective means of harmonizing their policies and priorities so as to

arrive at the best results for the Canadian public. It is in this spirit that the Federal Government, after discussion with the Provinces and careful consideration of their views, has elaborated the arrangements described in this paper as a basis for further discussion with the Provinces and the enactment of federal legislation (Canada, DOC 1975, 17).

The call for provincial co-operation fell on deaf ears. Moreover, the problem has been exacerbated lately. In fact, a federal–provincial meeting in Calgary, Alberta, in the mid-1980s nearly disbanded before it began because of the hostility between the provincial representatives and the federal officials.

The Clyne report

When then Minister of Communications Jeanne Sauvé appointed the Consultative Committee on Implications of Telecommunications for Canadian Sovereignty on 30 November 1978, she provided it with the following terms of reference to guide its deliberations. The Committee was requested

> to produce specific recommendations on a strategy to restructure the Canadian telecommunications system to contribute more effectively to the safeguarding of Canada's sovereignty; and to make recommendations on the future of the Canadian telecommunications system in relation to new technologies and the need for Canadian software and hardware resources to meet foreign competition, with particular reference to the role of broadcasting in contributing to the preservation of the sovereignty of Canada, including:
>
> a) the use of communications satellites to the best advantage of Canada;
>
> b) the status of the cable companies in relation to broadcasting and to the common carriers in the provision of new services;
>
> c) the importation of foreign programming;
>
> d) the framework and timing for the introduction of pay-television nationally (Canada, Consultative Committee 1979, i).

The final report, entitled *Telecommunications in Canada* and commonly known as the *Clyne report*, was extremely critical of the direction that telecommunication was taking in Canada vis à vis national sovereignty and the domestic industry. In particular, the report was concerned about the extensive foreign corporate control—mostly American control—of the computer and data base industries and the emerging public policy problems in transborder data flow. The *Clyne report* (1979, 2) states:

> Canadian sovereignty in the next generation will depend heavily on telecommunications. If we wish to have an independent culture, then we will have to continue to express it through radio and television. If we wish to control our economy, then we will require a sophisticated telecommunications sector developed and owned in Canada to meet specific Canadian requirements. To maintain our identity and independence we must ensure an adequate measure of control over data banks, trans-border data flow, and the content of information services available in Canada. . . . In approaching telecommunications we should realize that its importance demands we view it in a special way. Telecommunications, as the foundation of the future society, cannot always be left to the vagaries of the market.

In its concluding section, the report made relatively strong statements on the future of telecommunication in Canada, particularly when one considers that most government documents are usually either extremely bland or extremely guarded. Such a claim cannot be made about the major conclusion of the *Clyne report* (1979, 5):

> Unless positive action is initiated now, the sovereignty of Canada will be jeopardized in two main fields. First, Canadians are already being swamped with foreign broadcast programming and a new approach to the problem is urgently required; at the same time, there is a danger that foreign interests may achieve a predominant share of the market for data processing services and far too much of the information stored in data banks will be of foreign origin. Second, Canada is heavily dependent on imports in telecommunication technology. In certain sectors, such as communication satellites and information exchange, Canada is in the forefront of competitive technological developments. The exploitation of developments requires

public support that doesn't entail a vast expenditure of public funds; this is an industrial sector that can create jobs and be competitive on an international scale. The timing is important. It may not be possible to do tomorrow what we fail to do today.

Despite the sense of urgency evident in the Consultative Committee's report, once again neither legislative nor regulatory action followed; rather, the government sought further advice.

Planning now for an information society

Another study of Canada as an information economy was produced by the Science Council of Canada. In 1978, it established the Committee on Information and the Canadian Society. The committee was directed to examine recent developments in computers, micro-electronics, data transmission, machine intelligence, and digital transmissions. It was to study the impact of these developments across several sectors, including industry, employment, education, and research, and to determine the possible consequences for individuals. The Science Council of Canada had a long history of interest in the impact of the computer in many areas and at the time the study was conducted, Canada was experiencing a growing trade deficit in electronics of all sorts. These factors lent a broad perspective to the study. Consider the following statement, which emphasizes the vast spectrum of institutions and sectors that will feel the influence of the information age:

> The task is large. Policy makers at all levels need to be better informed about the new technologies, their likely effects and the role that Canadians and Canadian industry can play in future developments. Educational institutions need to re-examine their curricula and priorities to take account of a rapidly changing social and economic environment. Industrial leaders must also ensure that they and the corporations they manage not only understand the new technologies, but also plan intelligently for their introduction into manufacturing and administrative processes in an orderly manner. All of this must take place within a swiftly changing international situation in which foreign governments and large multinational companies are committing vast amounts of money and labour

to ensure their place in a high-technology future (Canada, Science Council 1982, 25).

The report concluded with twenty-seven wide-ranging recommendations concerning governments, the private sector, higher education, and many other areas. Although the bulk of the recommendations were aimed at the federal government, there was also some criticism of the Canadian business sector for failing to recognize and adapt to the tremendous impact of the information economy. The report (Canada, Science Council 1982, 56) states:

> The information society is upon us. The manner in which Canadians choose to participate will have far-reaching implications. The microelectronics revolution, upon which the information society is predicated, presents both threats and opportunities. How we respond will determine the shape of our own lives and Canada's future role in the world economy.
>
> Most advanced nations of the world are preparing to place themselves at the forefront of the information society. Many of the changes described will take place whether we like it or not. The question that remains is whether Canada will be an active or a passive participant.

The Science Council report continued by noting that although Canada participated in the early stages of the global telecommunication revolution, it has not kept pace. Unless we put more money into research and development (R & D), and undertake initiatives such as joint federal–provincial ventures and university research positions, our future is bleak and our country, vulnerable. The demise of industrial activity will mean a loss of jobs and unless high-technology firms locate in Canada, these jobs will not be replaced. Permanently high unemployment rates, compromised personal privacy, and weakened political and cultural sovereignty "would bring Canadians inevitably to a condition of pastoral servitude by the middle years of the twenty-first century" (Canada, Science Council 1982, 56).

Nevertheless, if Canadian governments and businesses muster the political and economic will to address technological challenges, we can still reap the many benefits the new age will bring. The Council (1982, 57) concluded with an exhortation to all sectors of Canadian society:

We have defined the key actors (governments, labour organizations, educational institutions, professional, commercial
and industrial associations), and attempted to alert them to
important facts, trends and problems. It is up to them to play a
role in informing Canadians of the massive changes being
wrought by the mighty chip, and, of course, to frame their
own response to the enormous challenges confronting us all.
No one is exempt.

The uneasy 80s

An initial flurry of media activity in response to the Science Council
report was followed by silence. Whether from confusion, fear of new
technologies, or corporate unwillingness to encourage government involvement in the planning process, neither Canadian business nor government undertook even conservative action on the problems, and no
legislation appeared.[1]

Despite the difficulties it encountered, the Science Council commissioned another report, entitled *The uneasy 80's: The transition to an information society*. In it, author A.J. Cordell examined several topics: carrier
technologies, new products associated with information technology,
robotics, artificial intelligence, privacy issues raised by technology, and
the impact on work of technologies such as office automation. The study
focussed on the impact of change:

> In the transition to an information economy, change becomes
> the new constant. The pace of change today is unprecedented,
> and change itself has become a source of the stress that charac-
> terizes the uneasy eighties.
>
> ... Two factors—the prevalence of change and the
> dominance of the economy by information-related activities—
> combine to give the new information technologies the cumula-
> tive force of a transformative technology. The nature of their
> impact on the economy, society, and politics is difficult to
> predict, but it is safe to say that few areas will be unaffected
> (Cordell 1985, 133).

Cordell enumerated five significant challenges that will confront us
with the advent of an information society:

1. All aspects of Western society will undergo a fundamental transformation.

2. Traditional norms and values related to work will require rethinking.

3. Major changes in the kinds and costs of goods and services produced, marketed, and consumed will place demands on industries to restructure their operations.

4. The more manageable and efficient use of information will provide innumerable benefits but will also raise essential questions about our concept of personal privacy.

5. The whole area of artificial intelligence will force a reshaping of our philosophical framework for "the nature of intelligence, consciousness, and the nature and place of our species in the universe" (Cordell 1985, 134).

Although Cordell recognized that societies do not adapt well to change, he emphasized that there is little choice. Our future well-being rests on acknowledging that information as a resource will soon affect all human activity. Unless we begin now to deal with the transition in a positive and productive manner, we may lose the opportunity forever.

The various studies of the telecommunication sector just described dealt with everything from the classification of different technologies to more contentious policy issues such as traditional monopoly structure and foreign control of equipment. The underlying theme, however, was consistent. The studies all examined the extent to which the telecommunication infrastructure has clear economic consequences for Canada. As was pointed out in *Instant world* (Canada, Telecommission 1971, 7–8),

> One predominant theme emerges from the telecommission studies. The technologies of telecommunications and computers, effectively used in combination, could make a striking contribution to economic prosperity and the general quality of life in Canada; to the development of remote and sparsely populated regions of the country; to the extension of French and English broadcasting services from coast to coast; to the

ability of individuals and groups in Canada to express themselves and communicate their views in the language of their
choice; and to Canadian acceptance of responsibility for participation in the achievement of international objectives, especially the social and economic development of less fortunate
countries in many parts of the world.

The ball had been thrown into the court of the public policy makers.

Structural difficulties in the telecom environment

Telecommunication already plays a vital role in Canada's social and
economic development. It is among the fastest growing sectors of the
Canadian economy; it is an instrument of national unity; and it provides
general benefits to Canadian society. Canada's telecommunication system is technologically advanced, highly reliable, widely accessible, and
universally affordable. Yet as we have seen, many factors are forcing
changes within the sector.

Recent technological developments have increased the efficiency
and speed of telecommunication systems but have also raised new policy
issues. In addition, Canadian business and industry are demanding new
services at lower cost in order to improve their productivity and competitiveness. The structure of the industry itself is therefore being altered as
new services become integrated with the traditional ones. Moreover,
these new services generally fall into the competitive sector rather than
the regulated monopoly sector. As the technological distinction between
computers and telecommunication blurs, a major re-examination of
public policy becomes necessary, and indecisiveness on the part of either
regulatory agencies or governments creates an atmosphere inconducive
to business. Finally, the world telecommunication sector is estimated to
be worth in excess of $100 billion and there is intense competition from
the United States, European nations, and Japan. Canada's telecommunication policies must accommodate the vast potential of the export
market. Canada will lose the advantage if business is unable to benefit
from both domestic and international opportunities. All these forces have
prompted the federal government to undertake a general review of national telecommunication policy.

Before examining the review process, it is important to realize that
the Canadian telecommunication sector faces three significant structural

problems. In the first place, Canada does not have the large defence budget that often provides a country with enormous R & D funds for high technology. Indeed, one could explain the rise of Silicon Valley in California as possible only through the immense number of military contracts held by the various high-technology firms.[2] Partly because of the absence of a large defence budget, Canadian high-tech firms suffer from a chronic shortage of R & D funds.

The second structural problem is demographic. Canada's domestic population of twenty-five million is insufficient to generate the large production runs that reduce average unit costs. Canadian manufacturers must instead rely upon export markets in order to become viable and competitive corporations. Northern Telecom is a clear example of a large Canadian telecommunication firm that has succeeded very well on an international scale.

Third, Canada's proximity to the United States makes the Canadian market a logical extension of American marketing efforts designed for their own domestic products and firms, ranging from IBM to Radio Shack. Canadian firms therefore confront tremendous competition and it is difficult for high-technology companies to enjoy an early period of modest technological and corporate development. Their smaller R & D budgets and equally high start-up costs mean that they produce little compared to their U.S.-based competitors.

In addition, U.S. firms, even those with Canadian subsidiaries, undertake their research and development programs within the United States rather than in Canada. As a result, not only do the Canadian branch plants lag behind but Canadian university graduates in engineering and other high-technology areas have fewer employment options in Canada. Over time this can become a serious problem, if the best young technicians, researchers, and engineers move to the United States in order to pursue their professions. Some Canadian social critics warn that Canada will become a technological serf in the information revolution, if the brain drain is not plugged.

The deregulation option

Deregulation involves loosening regulatory restraints in favour of market-driven forces. The deregulation of telecommunication has moved swiftly both in the United States and in Europe, where some major telecommunication firms have been privatized and government control over others has been loosened. The situation in Canada, however, is clearly different. As mentioned before, applications by CNCP Telecommunications during the mid-1980s to introduce competition in certain long-distance markets were denied by the CRTC. Requests from business users to attach their own telecommunication equipment to public network facilities either met with delay or, when granted, were restricted. The decision to allow private ownership of unlicensed satellite dishes also involved a series of delays. Nevertheless, a significant thrust towards deregulation came in 1987, with the application by both Bell Canada and BC Tel for rebalancing of local and long-distance rates.

These two carriers, both members of Telecom Canada, sought to increase the rates they charged for local service and to reduce long-distance toll charges.[3] They also wanted to adjust the revenue settlement agreements that they had with other telcos.[4] They were responding both to potential competitive forces and to technological determinism in the telecommunication field. Canada's major carriers face competition to some extent from CNCP Telecommunications and other domestic providers, such as mobile cellular telephone companies, as well as from the currently limited activity of foreign carriers in large Canadian cities such as Toronto, Montreal, and Vancouver. These U.S.-based systems are attempting to profit from the lucrative long-distance traffic by offering considerably lower rates than the Canadian telephone companies. Microwave Communications Inc. (MCI) attempted to do the same thing in the United States when American Telephone and Telegraph (AT&T) still operated as the monopoly long-distance carrier. Ironically, MCI is one of the foreign entrants in the Canadian market and it is actively marketing its services in Europe as well.

Although neither the regulator (CRTC) nor the government (DOC) have made any major public policy decisions on competition to date, it is likely, as chapter 9 discussed, that some type of reregulation leading to greater competition will emerge. The consequence of lower long-distance rates and higher local residential phone rates is yet to be thoroughly assessed, but a growing awareness that Canadian telecommunication manufacturers and service industries must become competitive on the domestic scene before they can compete internationally may make a loosening of regulation inevitable. Similarly, the decline of industrial occupations and increase in service sector jobs, particularly in high technology, make it necessary for Canada to promote a domestic information industry that compares favourably with all others.

The studies discussed earlier pointed out the long-term consequences of telecommunication on the Canadian labour force. To some extent, those consequences are now being felt and the number of success stories for Canadian telecommunication firms is rather limited. Even the once highly praised Telidon System, heavily supported by DOC funding, is now history. Another concern is that Northern Telecom, the largest company in the telecommunication field, could become fully U.S. based over time, leaving Canada in an even more weakened position as an information economy.

The current situation

In 1985, federal Minister of Communications Marcel Masse announced the intention of the government to conduct a thorough review of telecommunication policy in response to "great pressures for change—from both inside and outside the system and the country" (Masse 1985, 10). As part of the policy review, three studies have been undertaken: an examination of telecommunication pricing and universality; the impact of competition on telecommunication companies and users; and the impact of telecommunication on regional economic development. The whole review process is guided by four principles:

1. Universality must be maintained.

2. Canadian solutions must be sought.

3. The benefits of technology must be available to all Canadians.

4. Canada must remain internationally competitive.

The review involves highly sensitive, even contentious, issues, the most important of which are universal service and rate rebalancing. Universal service is the long-held tradition that universal access to telephone service is a primary goal of regulation. Universal service could be threatened by rate rebalancing, the policy that would reverse the current strategy of keeping long-distance rates artificially high in order to subsidize artificially low local rates.

Any policy proposals emerging from the telecom review will have important social, cultural, and economic ramifications for the whole nation, affecting not only governments, carriers, and business users but also individual Canadians. Despite the potential problems, the government is convinced of the need to proceed with this policy debate:

> The continued survival and prosperity of Canadian telecom-munications is far too important to jeopardize through politi-cal indifference or bureaucratic arrogance. Its significance to all Canadians is too great for it to be restructured or otherwise changed without full public debate, and there must be full public awareness of the implications and the consequences (Masse 1985, 9).

In July 1987, federal Minister of Communications Flora MacDonald issued the first comprehensive policy statement for the Canadian telecommunication sector since the early 1970s. The policy was developed to meet two fundamental objectives, economic renewal and national reconciliation. The question of national reconciliation was im-portant because of the regional disparities within Canada and several decades of relatively hostile federal–provincial negotiations over control, influence, and power in telecommunication regulation. The new policy established two classes of telecommunications carriers, Type I and Type II, to simplify the regulatory environment and promote effective competi-tion:

> Type I carriers, which *own and operate* interprovincial and in-ternational *network facilities* would include the member com-panies of Telecom Canada, as well as CNCP Tele-communications and Teleglobe Canada. This recognizes their position as national carriers providing network facilities and services in all parts of Canada, and the obligation upon them to provide service across Canada.

> Type II carriers are *service providers*, who use facilities leased from Type I carriers. They include operators of such services as mobile radio, resellers of telecommunications and enhanced service providers (Canada, DOC 1987, 1–2).

Despite the official fanfare surrounding the announcement, it was greeted with considerable scepticism. Consider the following, from the *Globe and Mail* (1987) under the lead "Critics attack 'shallow' new policy on telecommunications regulation":

Critics and some industry players are attacking Flora MacDonald's national telecommunications policy as shallow, deficient and premature. But industry groups and consumers, who have been waiting since the 70's for clear rules on competition and regulation, still must wait for the negotiation of a federal–provincial agreement on telecommunications. The policy lacks many details because it is subject to agreement with the provinces and it will require legislation to be introduced in Parliament.

That the new telecommunication policy has to be endorsed by provincial communication ministers presents a significant structural problem. The ministers held a series of meetings and will meet again before any new legislation is passed, but they and the federal ministers have not yet been able to develop a single set of rules to govern both provincial and national telecommunication, despite their lengthy negotiations. The entire question of jurisdiction is still undecided.

Many business telecommunication users have criticized the minister's policy for failing to accommodate private ownership of network facilities within the telecommunication system, to address the issue of rate rebalancing, and to resolve the entire question of competitive long-distance telephone services in Canada. Despite years of study, the federal Department of Communications presented a policy that failed to address some of the more pressing issues in Canadian telecommunication.

The Free Trade Agreement

The Free Trade Agreement (FTA) specifically covers Canada–United States trade in computer services, telecommunication, and network-based enhanced services. In general, the two countries have agreed to allow all existing treaties, regulations, and other legislation affecting telecommunication to stand. Nevertheless, the way that future rules and regulations deal with manufacturing in the telecommunication sector is governed by the FTA. Canada has reduced tariffs on imports of American telecommunication equipment. In addition, manufacturers from both nations must be treated equally in bidding processes. This is especially significant for American firms, which have been disadvantaged under the former Canadian practice of giving preferential treatment to domestic companies. The change particularly affects the enhanced services sector, in which competition will predominate.

The FTA will have almost no impact on basic telecommunication services such as local and long-distance calling. The DOC rules and conditions for basic services, which in essence protect and insulate the Canadian system from significant foreign penetration or ownership, will remain intact. Canadian negotiators deliberately avoided basic telecommunication services in FTA negotiations.

The agreement does affect computer services and data processing however. Some analysts predict that a substantial number of current and future jobs in these sectors will shift to the domestic head offices of U.S.-owned and -controlled firms currently doing business and data processing in Canada. A frequently cited example is American Motors, which does almost $800 million worth of business in Canada annually, yet employs only five data-processing employees in Canada. Clearly, the vast majority of American Motors' computer and data-handling jobs are based in the United States.

Another criticism of the FTA focusses on Northern Telecom Canada Ltd. It should be recalled that Northern Telecom is Canada's largest telecommunication firm. Moreover, it is aggressive and successful in the global telecommunication market. As a corporation, Northern Telecom strongly supported the FTA. Existing tariffs on telecommunication equipment, however, are being gradually removed under the agreement. The tariffs have protected Northern Telecom's market share in Canada and allowed it to develop superb telecommunication equipment. With the tariff reductions, U.S. firms not only gain greater access to Canadian markets, but their price can be reduced in comparison to Northern Telecom products as the tariffs are reduced. The long-standing competitive advantage of Northern Telecom in the lucrative Canadian telephone equipment market will disappear.

In the long run, the FTA may indirectly encourage Northern Telecom to consider shifting its corporate headquarters from Canada to the United States. Several factors would encourage the move. First, Northern Telecom's Canadian market for telecommunication equipment will shrink as U.S. firms take advantage of the reduction in the earlier 17.8 percent tariff on telecommunication equipment imports. Second, Northern Telecom is already the second largest telecommunication equipment supplier in the United States, and does the majority of its international business there. As Northern Telecom continues to promote it-self as a global rather than a Canadian telecommunication firm, any move to another nation will be interpreted as a corporate necessity to consolidate different parts of the company—such as research and development facilities, marketing, and senior management—in one loca-tion. Finally, the new president of Northern Telecom is himself an American. He is likely to see little advantage, either personally or profes-sionally, in maintaining substantial contact in Canada. It is probable that his primary interests are the effects of U.S. market opportunities and changes on Northern Telecom. Clearly, the Canadian loss of Northern Telecom as a corporate citizen would be a severe psychological blow to Canada's somewhat beleaguered efforts to become an information society of international calibre.

A new telecommunication act?

There may be a new telecommunication act for Canada in the 1990s. It would bring together fragmented, and in some cases, considerably anti-quated legislation in the telecommunication sector. Although certain amendments affecting telecommunication were passed by Parliament in the 1970s, no comprehensive piece of legislation has ever existed. The Railway Act, enacted at the beginning of this century, governs the telegraph system and certain ownership provisions for Canadian telcos. The Act is still the law of the land for many telecommunication firms. Ironically, cellular telephones, at the cutting edge of technology, are governed by the nineteenth-century legislation. The federal Transporta-tion Act also contains sections that pertain directly to telecommunication. In addition, several provinces have provincial telecom legislation or regulation. Yet this piecemeal approach cannot provide the various telecommunication firms with an incentive for major research and cor-porate activities. Corporations need to know the rules and laws before they will make significant investments.

The primary reason for the absence of comprehensive, modern legis-lation to this point is quite simple: there is no political momentum or will to deal with the issue. In most instances, telecommunication does not make the agenda of either the media or the politicians. The Canadian telephone system works well; compared to some foreign telephone sys-tems, it is a model of efficiency and fair pricing for consumers.

Politicians, who face many other pressing problems, therefore feel little pressure to pursue telecommunication legislation. In other words, if it's not broken, don't fix it. This attitude makes it very difficult for Canada to enact and promote the legislative revisions so vital for accommodating technological changes in the telecommunication sector.

Summary

Canada has a commendable record of studying telecommunication problems but is clearly lacking when it comes to legislative initiatives. The inadequacy has resulted in a series of disagreements among the provincial governments, the federal government, and the industry itself. Some of these conflicts have made their way into the federal courts and as a result, the courts are increasingly becoming the final arbiters of telecommunication policies. This trend, in conjunction with the growing policy role of the CRTC, has reduced the influence of the federal government on national policy. Although the government has a mandate to ensure that certain economic, social, and regional benefits are distributed equitably across Canada, it is forced into the position of observer, while others make the key policy and legal decisions that will fundamentally affect the telecommunication sector. This structural problem has placed Canada in a potentially detrimental position as it evolves into an information-based economy. Given the central role of telecommunication in the information age, severe legislative deficiencies and burdensome, anti-competitive regulations make it extremely difficult, if not impossible, for Canada to become a sufficiently progressive information economy compared to other countries.

Canada, like other Western nations, stands on the threshold of an exciting but demanding future. The dawning of the high-technology age poses many challenges, which the nation must be prepared to meet as an emerging information economy. There are vast numbers of opportunities for economic expansion through increased national productivity, regional growth, and abundant job creation. Canada's position in the twenty-first century is clearly a function of decisions that are being taken *now*. Since most other Western societies will have information economies by the year 2000, Canada must make policy decisions now that will help to place its economy on the leading edge of the competitive, international telecommunication industry.

Notes

1. This was both ironic and discouraging, particularly given the tremendous success that the Japanese government planning agency, Miti, had in the micro-electronic field. Moreover, in the face of the pervasive influence of the U.S. high-technology manufacturing industry, which clearly dominates the Canadian marketplace, it is surprising that the Canadian industry was not more interested in government assistance, encouragement, or research funding.

2. For a thorough description of the Silicon Valley phenomenon, and an in-depth analysis of the information society, see Rogers (1986).

3. As a result of these applications, the CRTC required BC Tel and Bell Canada to reduce long-distance toll rates but to maintain local service rates at current levels.

4. Because long-distance calls may involve transmitting signals across the operating territory of two or more telcos, revenue settlement agreements determine how to share the revenue that the calls generate. These agreements are negotiated between the telcos themselves, but are subject to regulatory approval.

References

Canada. Consultative Committee on Implications of Telecommunications for Canadian Sovereignty. 1979. *Telecommunications in Canada (Clyne report)*. Ottawa: Supply and Services.

Canada. Department of Communications. 1973. *Proposals for a communication policy for Canada*. Ottawa: Information Canada.

———. 1975. *Communications: Some federal proposals*. Ottawa: Information Canada.

———. 1987. News release—Flora MacDonald announces telecommunications policy for Canada. 22 July. Ottawa: DOC.

Canada. Science Council of Canada. 1982. *Planning now for an information society, Tomorrow is too late*. Ottawa: Supply and Services.

Canada. Telecommission. 1971. *Instant world, A report on telecommunications in Canada*. Ottawa: Information Canada.

Cordell, A.J. 1985. *The uneasy eighties: The transition to an information society*. Ottawa: Supply and Services.

Globe and Mail. 1987. Critics attack "shallow" new policy on telecommunications regulation. 23 July, p. B1.

MacDonald, F. 1986. Address to the Atwater Institute. 4 November. Montreal, Quebec.

Masse, M. 1985. Address to the Electrical and Electronic Equipment Manufacturers' Association of Canada. 20 June. Montebello, Quebec.

Rogers, E.M. 1986. *Communication technology: The new media in society*. New York: Free Press.

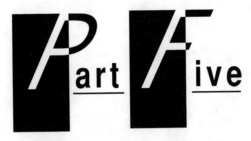

Related Media Issues

THE MEDIA
AND POLITICS

*S*ince the earliest days of Canadian mass media, politics and the press have been interrelated. From the time of the King's Printer, through the age of the openly partisan press, to the present, the relationship has sparked heated debate. It is only within the last fifty years, however, that social scientists have begun to study the phenomenon, offering various hypotheses to clarify the relationship.

Jay Blumler ([1969] 1981, 121) argues that "democracy depends uniquely on mass communication." Those who govern rely on mass media to garner public support, first for their successful election and then for the policies that they pursue. The public, on the other hand, depends on the media for information about the governors and their activities. The symbiotic nature of this relationship led Edwin Black (1982, 240–43) to conclude that the mass media can be characterized as political institutions. They play a routine and predictable role in governance over an extended period. That role includes aspects of articulating and uniting interests, making and enforcing social rules, evaluating policies, political actors and so on, and communicating political events, ideas, values, and other issues. Unlike other political institutions, however, the media do not have a unified purpose.

Other scholars, such as William Rivers (1970), see the relationship between politics and the media as adversarial. They argue that this dissension is the basis for all good coverage of government, and emphasize the media's role as "the watchdog," or the "unofficial opposition." The media function to inform the public of everything that goes on within government and conflict is therefore inevitable.

Whether one accepts the notion of a symbiotic relationship or an adversarial one, the issue of media power and influence remains. Ever since Alexis de Tocqueville ([1837] 1947, 119) asserted that "nothing but a newspaper can drop the same thought into a thousand minds at the same moment," an argument has raged on how much power the press has to create, change, and unify public opinion. That debate is still highly relevant today. Political events can be reported instantly, but even live coverage is mediated by television crews, reporters, and other gatekeepers.

Some observers believe that media are very influential. Joe McGinnis (1968, 30) argues, for example, that they can be used to sell a presidential candidate to the passive and disinterested electorate. In his cardinal rule of media politics, he paraphrases Marshall McLuhan: "Style becomes substance. The medium is the massage and the masseur gets the votes." Others, however, are more sceptical of the power of the media. They believe media to be only one of many forces that have an impact on the public's awareness of and attitudes towards politics and political leaders. Their scepticism is fuelled by a greater belief in the complex nature of public opinion.

Attitudes, opinions, and change

In order for the media to create or change public opinion, they must also create or change individual attitudes and opinions. For this reason, it is important to understand the nature of attitudes and opinions. The following pages briefly examine the social science literature on attitudes and attitude change.

Public opinion is most simply defined as opinions held by private individuals, which when taken together provide a collective point of view. It does not include the opinion of everyone; it may not even represent the opinion of the majority. It is frequently uninformed and based on emotion. Nevertheless, public opinion is often used by politicians to justify their actions and decisions, and if powerful enough can actually influence public policy decisions.[1]

Attitudes are "more or less enduring orientations toward an object or situation and predispositions to respond positively or negatively toward that object or situation" (Best 1973, 6). As such, an attitude has three distinct elements: knowledge about an object or situation; an affective evaluation of it; and a behavioural predisposition on the part of the person holding the attitude to react in a certain way. An *opinion* is merely the verbal expression of an attitude. A *belief* is an hypothesis or expectation about the relationship between two objects, ideas, or events. While an attitude always includes an affective dimension, a belief does not. For example, the statement, "The media report on politics" reflects a belief; whereas the statement, "The media are biased in their political reporting" reflects an attitude. Attitudes and beliefs are organized into a hierarchical structure known as a *value system*, which is a "collection of attitudes" (Wagner and Sherwood 1969, 3) about related events, objects, or situations, such as the political system.

To determine the likelihood of changing an attitude, we need to examine several aspects of it (Katz [1960] 1981, 41–43). In the first place, there are five dimensions to every attitude, which define its strength, or susceptibility to change:

1. Intensity refers to the strength of the affective component; the stronger the feeling, the less likely it is that a change of attitude will occur.

2. The degree of differentiation refers to the number of beliefs or known facts involved in the attitude. Attitudes based on few or simple beliefs are easier to alter than those that have developed as a result of intense, detailed examination of an object or situation.

3. The relationship of a specific attitude to the general value system is also a factor. If the link is strong and reinforced by other attitudes, the attitude will be resistant to change.

4. Closely related to this is the centrality of the attitude with respect to the value system. An attitude that rests at the core of many other attitudes or beliefs is usually more strongly held than one existing at the periphery.

5. Finally, the durability of an attitude is reflected in its relationship to action or behaviour. If the attitude is overtly exhibited in behaviour, it is more difficult to alter than one that is not.

The following example illustrates these points. Person A strongly supports programs to protect the environment. After considerable study, he or she believes that comprehensive legislation and funding are necessary to deal with environmental problems. Volunteer work with environmentalist groups has reinforced Person A's value system, thus introducing an element of peer group support. Given these characteristics, it would be very difficult to produce a change of attitude in Person A. Person B, on the other hand, is ambivalent about environmental protection. He or she doesn't really understand what the ozone layer or acid rain are, for example, and doesn't know what steps are necessary to prevent further environmental damage. While Person B finds the idea of being able to swim at the local beach appealing and is a bit uneasy about recent changes in the weather patterns, he or she is unwilling to give up driving a car on leaded gasoline and finds recycling programs too time-consuming. Given this situation, Person B is more susceptible to forces that might alter his or her attitude one way or another, especially if one salient issue, such as a new PCB incinerator near Person B's house, created a personal dilemma.

The reasons why we hold the attitudes we do also influence the susceptibility of those attitudes to change. According to Katz ([1960] 1981, 43–47), attitudes serve four functions. First, they may have an instrumental, or utilitarian, function. We tend to hold attitudes that maximize personal rewards and minimize personal punishments; they are useful or functional to our everyday behaviour. Most university and college students, for example, have positive attitudes about the value of education in their lives. Second, ego-defensive attitudes protect us from acknowledging harsh realities about ourselves or the world. Students who blame the weaknesses of the educational system for their failures, for example, hold an ego-defensive attitude. By holding negative attitudes about the professors, courses, textbooks, grading systems, and so on, students can minimize their own weaknesses and feel better about themselves. Third, attitudes help us to define our own self-images more accurately. Individuals derive satisfaction from holding and expressing attitudes appropriate to their personal value systems. A person who strongly believes in environmental protection, for example, will tend to express closely related values about a range of issues such as leaded gasoline, disposable diapers, recycling, and organic farming. All these attitudes reinforce the person's own self-image. Finally, attitudes serve a cognitive function by helping us to organize or structure reality. They do not increase our knowledge of the world but rather, enable us to understand it better by providing consistency and stability. Stereotypical attitudes fall into this category because they define certain objects, people, or situations predictably, and thereby allow us to react to those elements in a consistent manner. In general, the susceptibility of an attitude to change is determined by the value of that attitude to satisfying a personal need. The more satisfying the attitude, the less likely that it will be changed, yet as our needs change so will our attitudes.

There are two, conflicting schools of thought about how attitudes originally develop. One school argues that individuals have limited powers of reasoning but respond more readily to emotional needs, and are therefore easily influenced. The other asserts that attitudes develop through realistic and informed choices. Within the second model, there are four basic approaches to attitude development and change.[2]

The functional approach rests on the idea that attitudes develop and change in response to an individual's goals or needs. These needs are either instrumental, ego-defensive, value expressive, or cognitive, the four types just identified above. Adherents of the functional approach also assert that attitudes may develop or change as individuals attempt to comply with the demands of others (employers, for example), to identify themselves with those they admire (a peer group or mentors), or to internalize attitudes that are more consistent with their own personal value systems.

Learning theorists, on the other hand, see attitude development and change in simple stimulus/response terms. Individuals acquire or alter their attitudes in response to the stimuli with which they come in contact, according to the principles of basic learning theory. Our attitudes towards religion, for example, are learned early in life through family-directed patterns of stimulus and response.

Those who take the perceptual approach contend that perceptions are a function of people's definitions of self and their real-life situations.

Attitudes develop out of individuals' perception of objects, people, ideas, or situations, and change when the individuals redefine or reinterpret the subjects of their attitudes because their self-definitions or actual situations have changed.

The fourth approach focusses on change in an attitude rather than its initial formulation. The approach is based on the principle that individuals attempt to maintain consistency in their attitudes and value systems. If an inconsistency becomes apparent, they begin to re-examine the attitudes that conflict with one another. The concept of *cognitive dissonance* was discussed in chapter 1 but it is worth reviewing here. Individuals try to keep their attitudes, beliefs, and values consistent in order to remain psychologically comfortable. If a fact, attitude, or value is in conflict with one already held, the dissonance creates an aversive reaction. There are a number of ways in which people can reduce the discomfort. They can remove or minimize the dissonant element by using the principles of selective attention, selection, and retention; by changing one of the elements; or by increasing the number and importance of consonant elements in their attitudes. Smokers, for example, cannot easily ignore evidence that smoking leads to heart disease, but by increasing the number and importance of elements consonant with continuing to smoke, they reduce cognitive dissonance. The consonant elements might be ideas such as "It won't happen to me," "I don't smoke very much," "I can quit whenever I want," and so on. Wagner and Sherwood (1969, 59) claim that people will choose the way of reducing dissonance that requires the least effort or is least resistant to change.

All of these approaches to attitude change are relevant when one examines the power of the media to influence politics and public policy. Political attitudes and values exist at many levels. Their uniformity and strength vary with the consistency of their subject. Attitudes towards the political system in general, for example, tend to be stable; attitudes towards the government of the day will fluctuate. Political leanings are made up of attitudes towards three different phenomena (Van Loon and Whittington 1984, 109):

1. the political community—territorial concepts such as national borders, symbols such as the flag, and concepts of nationhood, Canadian identity, and the Canadian way of life

2. the political regime—the framework of government found in the Constitution, Parliament, federalism, symbols such as the crown and the parliament buildings, and concepts related to ideology

3. the authorities—the government of the day and the politicians who belong to it, symbols such as the office of prime minister, and concepts related to specific current issues

General political values underlie our attitudes towards specific political ideas and events and establish the boundaries for individual political behaviour that our particular society considers legitimate. According to Van Loon and Whittington (1984, 95–100), Canadian political values are rooted in traditional Western political thought, Judaeo-Christian traditions, and eighteenth- and nineteenth-century democratic theory. Although rarely articulated, these values depend on a positive evaluation of the following ideas:

1. popular sovereignty—the achievement of the common good through a system of government that recognizes the will of the people as opposed to that of an elite group

2. political equality—the right of every adult citizen to participate fully and on an equal footing in the political decision-making process

3. majoritarianism—the idea of majority rule in both the electoral and decision-making processes as long as it does not threaten the basic rights and freedoms of the minority

4. liberal and socialist democracy—commitment to individualism, individual rights, and capitalism, tempered by an acceptance of government intervention to promote a higher degree of social and economic equality among all Canadians

Despite a general consensus among Canada's citizens over a broad system of values, attitudes towards specific issues, concepts, or symbols are more diverse. Moreover, differences in attitude tend to be aligned along a number of identifiable dimensions, including the degree of participation in the political system, political party affiliation, and linguistic, ethnic, and regional background. Nevertheless, this diversity should not be construed as an undermining force; the cohesive nature of basic political values in Canada maintains the legitimacy of the whole political system.

To this point, we have examined the concepts of attitudes, opinions, beliefs, and values; we have reviewed the theories that attempt to explain how and why we acquire or change our attitudes; and we have discussed Canadian political attitudes and values in general. Before examining the potential of the media to create or alter attitudes, the chapter next reviews the way that the Canadian media communicate public affairs.

Mass media: Communicating public affairs

Following their study of the relationship between newspapers and politics for the Kent Commission in 1981, Frederick Fletcher and Daphne Taras (1984, 193) concluded that "the mass media have become in modern industrial societies the primary communicators of politically significant images." With that premise, it is necessary to examine just what the media do and do not do with respect to their coverage of public affairs. The following review is necessarily brief, and the reader is directed back to part 2 of this text for a more detailed analysis of the news function.

Fletcher (1981, 9–10) identified four levels within the Canadian public affairs information system, each of which plays a different role and serves a different segment of the public. The national media, including the *Globe and Mail*, the *Toronto Star*, *Le Devoir*, Canadian Press, the CBC radio and television networks, and the CTV television network, serve a large, dispersed, national audience. They disseminate most of the news about public affairs at the national or federal level. The regional media serve large but more localized audiences. They include the major daily newspapers and television stations in a particular region or province, and although they provide national political news they concentrate their energies on gathering information about provincial government affairs. The newspapers, radio, and television stations in smaller centres primarily collect and report news of local interest. They form the third level of the information system. The final level is composed of local weeklies, which supplement the local coverage of the other three media levels. These divisions are arbitrary and therefore somewhat artificial, but they do provide an analytical tool for media studies. For the purposes of the discussion here, we focus primarily on the first level, the national media, but much of the examination is relevant to the other levels as well.

As noted earlier, the Canadian media were initially very partisan and everyone knew it (Kesterton, 1967). Over time, the media have, with some exceptions, taken on a more objective posture. This change was prompted and reinforced by many factors, two of which deserve particular attention. First, the media were initially family-owned and -operated businesses, and they reflected the political leanings of their owners. As these undertakings came to be seen more as profit-making enterprises than as political platforms, their editorial purposes shifted in order to broaden their audience appeal. Demographics and income, not political partisanship, became the key elements in media management. A number of tabloids, for example, most notably the *Sun* and the *Journal de Montréal*, are aimed at commuters with an interest in sports and crime-related news. Other newspapers, such as the *Globe and Mail* and the *Financial Post*, are clearly directed towards business- and politically oriented readers.

Second, rapid public acceptance of television as a news and entertainment medium generated competition for newspapers. Because access to the electronic media is by nature limited, these media have been regulated in the public interest almost from their inception. Part of the regulatory guidelines provides for fair, balanced, and unbiased coverage of political affairs. This injunction of objectivity from the electronic media has influenced the newspaper's perception of its own news function. It has also had an effect on the operation of legislative press galleries, which have been described as "the most important instrument[s] of political communication in this country" (Task Force on Government Information 1969, 115–19, as reported in Fletcher 1981, 49).

Press galleries are made up of journalists who cover the affairs of both Parliament and the ten provincial legislatures. Originally run as clubby, partisan institutions, the galleries have become less biased with the growing professionalism of journalists and the general trend towards more objective public affairs reporting. The Parliamentary Press Gallery in Ottawa is composed of both print and broadcast journalists and representatives of the major wire services. Few individual media undertakings have correspondents in Ottawa; the vast majority rely upon the Canadian Press Parliamentary Gallery bureau for the news they disseminate (Fletcher 1981, 55). The Gallery operates as a self-governing body but is subject to the Speaker of the House of Commons on matters of management and discipline. As the primary gatekeepers who define and select newsworthy copy, the members of the Parliamentary Press Gallery are vitally important. They determine which aspects of public affairs are communicated to the public and are therefore the principle link between the governed and the governors.

In general, the Parliamentary Press Gallery focusses on the activities of Parliament and the provincial galleries emphasize the activities of the provincial legislatures, although gallery reporters may also follow stories beyond Parliament to various government departments and agencies. Question Period is the daily opportunity for MPs, particularly members of the Opposition, to place government members on the proverbial hot seat by demanding answers. It usually attracts the majority of the gallery members' attention because it is a made-to-order media event. Question Period involves public personalities, drama, and conflict, and is packaged in neat, discrete temporal units. The Gallery also covers special events such as the opening of Parliament, budget debates, federal–provincial meetings, and political crises and scandals. These, too, fit the media definition of newsworthy events. The members of the gallery are less likely, however, to provide adequate coverage of the slow, developmental processes of politics. Media preference for hard, fast-breaking news over more thorough coverage of slower processes was identified earlier as one of the major weaknesses of the news undertaking.

While most observers concede that public affairs coverage is generally accurate and objective, they also bemoan the uniformity of political news and the lack of critical investigative reporting. Allocating inadequate resources to the news function has lead to understaffing and an overdependence on Question Period, press conferences, and press secretaries for news copy. Current management philosophies and journalists' predilection for dramatic, discrete news items have encouraged pack journalism. All reporters rush to cover the same aspects of the same stories to prevent their newspapers or news programs from being scooped by competitors. Investigative reporting is also hindered by an absence of journalistic specialities. Journalists have always prided themselves on being generalists, but as the nature of the political process and the various policy fields becomes increasingly complex, no individual reporter can be expected to keep abreast of all the developments. Finally, journalists are, in some respects, captives of the political actors themselves. They must follow the agenda set by the government or the opposition if they are to keep the public accurately informed.

Moreover, government officials are often reluctant to co-operate with the press. Journalists sometimes find it difficult to get access to the information they require to give a full account of the day's events. Although political manipulation of the press is only occasionally overt, media management can and does take subtler forms. Examples range from staging photo opportunities or leaking favourable stories to friendly journalists, to situations in which political officials simply issue press releases and provide no opportunity whatsoever for questioning.

A variety of remedies has been suggested to bring more diversity into news copy: insistence on the right of reply, allowing all sides of an issue to have equal media access, using reporters who are specialists in different fields, and so on. Nevertheless, the formidable strength of traditional news-gathering and gatekeeping norms tends to inhibit successful solutions. While individual journalists or media undertakings may take the initiative to step outside the institutional mould, such action is unfortunately rare.

Media influence: Real or illusory?

Among scholars and political actors, a growing interest in the potential of the media to influence politics and public policy making rests on the assumption that the mass media in modern society operate as a powerful educative force (Best 1973, 115). Media are the primary source of information about political events but they cannot cover everything, and media gatekeepers are therefore forced to make judgments. By conferring status on certain personalities and events, and withholding it from others, gatekeepers have the capacity to distort our perception of reality. The distortion may not be intentional, but its effects can be widespread because the mass media reach very large audiences daily. As well, as discussed earlier, increasing homogenization of news coverage has left the media open to manipulation by a number of forces.

Despite the considerable potential for the media to have a political impact, relatively little can be said about the specific nature of their influence. In theoretical terms, there are two conflicting models for the role of the media in public affairs. Liberal democratic theorists describe the media as the fourth branch of government. By disseminating information and interpreting political events and personalities, the media function as a forum for public debate. This view assumes that the media operate as diverse, independent, and objective observers of the political process and provide accurate and balanced accounts of the day's events to the electorate. Neo-Marxists, on the other hand, base their approach upon very different assumptions. They describe the media as promoting the dominant ideologies of the ruling elite.[3] News gathering, interpretation, and dissemination all reinforce the status quo, preserve existing power structures, and convince the electorate that all is generally as it should be.

After examining these two approaches with reference to the Canadian newspaper industry, Fletcher and Taras (1984, 205) conclude that "there is little doubt that [all] the media present a rather similar picture of society, in general terms." Nevertheless, they argue that this tendency to preserve the status quo may simply indicate economic rationality: "The media cling to the 'extreme middle' of the political spectrum . . . because their profits depend upon attracting mass audiences to sell to advertisers, and mass values tend to be middle-of-the-road" (Fletcher and Taras 1984, 205–6).

Research into media effects not only takes different philosophical standpoints, but may also differentiate between television (electronic media) and newspapers (print media). This approach has resulted in more concrete findings than others because it is better suited to empirical methods of research. It has been shown that, in general, newspapers provide a fuller account of public affairs. Because they have greater flexibility about the size of the newshole, larger editorial staffs, and higher degrees of reviewability and audience control over content, they can provide more detailed information, specialized coverage, and more thorough analysis. Fletcher (1981, 110) argues, however, that Canadian newspapers have not for the most part exploited these advantages. While newspapers remain the primary source of news for the more politically attentive segment of the population, including the political and economic elites and opinion leaders, general readership is declining.

Television, on the other hand, is more adept at communicating the immediacy and drama of political events, and is less likely to editorialize. Despite time and space restraints, it reaches a larger audience than do newspapers. Much research indicates, however, that it is a different sort of audience. Because television is primarily an entertainment medium, it requires less active involvement on the part of its audience, many of whom watch the news simply because it is on and only incidentally assimilate its content.

Considering the characteristics of television coverage, it is interesting to note that newspapers are rigorously studied and vigorously criticized while the weaknesses of television news programs are virtually ignored. Moreover, studies indicate that television is the main source of information about public affairs for a growing segment of the population, and increasing numbers are likely to assert that television is the most believable of the media (Fletcher 1981, 105–8). These findings suggest that television research has been inadequate. There is a need for more intensive investigation of television's role in providing information about public affairs.

Prior to 1950, the one-step, "hypodermic needle" model of media influence was popular. According to this approach, the media simply had to "inject" information, ideas, and opinions into the audience for them to have influence. Subsequent research indicated that this was not so, and two-step and multi-step models were created to take other factors into account. In multi-step models, the information provided through media is affected by other variables, such as peer group, family, level of education, political affiliation, and so on. Some of these influences were discussed earlier in this chapter, in the discussion of attitudes, beliefs, and values. Researchers identified these elements as confounding variables that make it difficult to track the impact of the media on politics. Nevertheless, research on media influence has continued and some trends, and even direct effects of the media, have been uncovered.

Perhaps the most broadly accepted effect that the media have on their audiences in the area of public affairs reporting is their contribution to public knowledge. Since most of us have little direct contact with the political process, most of what we know about it we learn through the media. Some people may learn more than others because of their personal interests but in general, the greater the use of public affairs media, the higher an individual's level of political knowledge will be. Most other potential effects of the media are related to this one.

The media also play a role in political socialization, the process whereby we internalize the norms and values of our political system. While parents, educators, and peers are the primary agents of socialization, the media can and do play a secondary role. They tend to reinforce the other agents by providing an alternative source of political information (Roberts and Baclen 1981, 339). Television, because of its pervasive nature, is viewed as particularly important in both the early socialization of children and the long-term socialization of adults. Although it is widely acknowledged as a general theory that the media play a role in socialization, there is no direct, empirical evidence of the phenomenon (McQuail 1984, 201).

Closely related to the media's ability to socialize their audiences is their potential for defining and structuring political reality. By doing so, the media influence our basic value systems and may even change our behaviour. Once again, no research definitively proves that the media have such power, but several hypotheses suggest that a relationship exists between the way that media present public affairs and their audience's political perceptions. Fletcher and Taras (1984, 217) identified a number of systemic biases in media coverage of public affairs: reinforcement of the status quo, emphasis on conflict and on public rather than private sector activities, and denigration of political leaders and institutions. Some critics postulate that all of these biases *may* have significant, long-term political ramifications in terms of our overall perception of the political system.

As we have seen, some research indicates that the media can have an impact on our political knowledge, socialization, and perceptions. There is another growing body of literature, with a slightly different approach, concerning the media's ability to define our priorities and thereby structure our awareness of political issues. Agenda-setting refers to the media's role in forcing our attention to certain issues.[4] The relevant research indicates, but does not prove, that while the media cannot tell us *what* to think, it can direct us to think *about* certain objects, issues, or situations. In other words, this research suggests that although the media may influence trends in public opinion, they do not influence the content or intensity of attitudes and opinions.

There have been no studies in Canada that follow accepted methodology for studying agenda-setting (Fletcher 1981, 16), but some Canadian research does incidentally support the proposition that newspapers influence what the public regards as worthy of attention.[5] Moreover, Fletcher suggests (1981, 20) that newspapers, especially the *Globe and Mail* and *Le Devoir*, set the agenda for the other media, including the Canadian Press. It therefore appears that the mass media have some part in influencing public priorities with respect to policy issues.

There is also some indication that the media may influence governments, a phenomenon explored in chapter 5 of this text. Once again, the research poses more questions than it answers but some trends are evident. The media appears to have an indirect effect on public policy. They act as a source of information to political actors who lack expertise in a given policy field, and they function as barometers of public opinion (Fletcher 1981, 18).[6] Only occasionally, however, do the media raise issues or prompt political action independently of the other sources of power in society—government and big business. "Exposure journalism" can motivate governments to act, especially if they believe that the public will react strongly to the issues, but politicians tend to argue they are responding to public opinion and serving the needs of the electorate rather than reacting to media pressure. Finally, many critics believe that the impact of the media is felt most keenly in the general approach that they take to political affairs. By creating a win-or-lose atmosphere, and by emphasizing style over substance, media undermine the more serious and consequential nature of the entire political process.

Despite the inconclusive nature of these various hypotheses, one finding does have empirical support. The media, especially newspapers, have the most impact at the municipal level. At this level, government is less organized, more personal, has less party involvement, and lacks an official opposition. Because of the nature of municipal government, the media serve as "essential vehicle[s] for presenting alternative perspectives" (Fletcher 1981, 21). Once again, they do not necessarily create public opinion but they can operate as an unofficial opposition and encourage the municipal government to re-examine its decisions.

In general, the impact of the media is mitigated by all the factors influencing attitude acquisition and change; by the degree to which the audience pays attention to the media messages; by the level of originality in those messages, and the attention they consequently attract; and by the ability of media to shape the information they disseminate. Given the nature of these variables, it is not surprising that the literature on media effects remains inconclusive.

In 1958, Joseph Klapper encapsulated the state of social science knowledge about media effects into three generalizations:

1. Mass communication cannot, on its own, affect its audience, but in combination with other factors can have some effect.

2. Media serve primarily to reinforce existing attitudes, beliefs, and values.

3. In order for the media to effect attitudinal change, two other factors must be present: other, mediating influences must be inoperative, or must also be promoting change; and the effect of the media must be direct.

Not much has changed in the past thirty years. Research has refined Klapper's findings but it is still not possible to draw firm conclusions about the potential of media to have an impact in the political arena.

Election coverage: Media front and centre

Media coverage of election campaigns has been the focus of numerous research studies. We know that most Canadians get most of their news and information about election campaigns from the media. It is therefore not unreasonable to assume that the media may influence voting behaviour and thus the outcome of elections.

The media dedicate substantial resources to election coverage. A study of the 1984 general election by Alan Frizzell and Anthony Westell (1985, 57) found that the media devoted a significant portion of the newshole—about 8 percent for English-language newspapers—and a large segment of their staff resources to election coverage. For any election, media content includes news items, columns, background articles, and analysis. On election night itself, the media pull out all the stops. They direct all their resources towards providing immediate details and spotting voting trends. In fact, the television networks compete to be the first to predict the election outcome accurately. In some respects, this is hardly surprising. Election campaigns appear well-suited to the media's definition of news: they are possible sources of conflict, drama, and personalities, and media coverage has encouraged their potential in this respect.

During campaigns the media serve several purposes and employ a variety of techniques to bring voters the information they require.[7] At the outset, the media identify the candidates and parties. Through interviews, candidate profiles, and coverage of all-candidates meetings and debates they shape the image of candidates and party leaders. Frizzell and Westell (1985, 59–60) discovered that, among the newspapers they studied, the press often focussed on the national leaders to the exclusion of other candidates. Other research has indicated that while the media are excellent vehicles for portraying style, they are much less adept at analysing a candidate's position and past record (Comber and Mayne 1986). This weakness has been of particular concern to the American Assembly on Presidential Nominations and the Media ([1978] 1980, 421), which warned, "Candidates and the media should remain watchful, lest either coopt or manipulate the other to the detriment of the voting public. The quest for novelty should not be allowed to detract from the overwhelming need for substantial and consistently developed political information."

Televised debates are one of the most significant changes in politics brought about by the media. Ever since the debate between John Kennedy and Richard Nixon, political analysts have been convinced that televised debates can identify candidates as serious contenders for office. Two Canadian examples illustrate the important role that national election debates may play. The first is the 1984 debate between then Prime Minister John Turner and Opposition leader Brian Mulroney. Many political analysts maintain that Mulroney's forceful debating style, particularly with respect to the patronage appointments of the former government, allowed him to mount a successful campaign. Four years later, during the 1988 federal election campaign, the two leaders once again participated in a nationally televised debate. This time it was John Turner, as leader of the Opposition, who performed well. Early in the campaign, many had concluded that Turner and the Liberal Party simply did not stand a chance against the well-organized Tory electoral machine. In fact, there was even speculation that the Liberals might place third overall and lose their role as the official Opposition. Turner's performance during two national debates, particularly with respect to the Free Trade Agreement, surprised the pundits and public alike. He made such a clear and emotional plea on behalf of Canadian cultural sovereignty and identity that the party's fortunes were partially reversed. Based on the success of the debate, Turner was able to run a strong campaign that allowed the federal Liberal Party to retain its status as the official Opposition.

It now appears that nationally televised debates between political leaders will play a significant part in future election campaigns. Debates are important for uncommitted voters because they provide an opportunity to review the leaders of all the major parties and all the party positions at the same time. In fact, some voters may decide to switch allegiance from one party to another on the basis of the debates alone. Of course, debates have the potential to distort election information as well. The press will often report that one candidate "won" the debate, for example, a subjective response that members of the public can become attuned to, whether or not they saw the debate and had the opportunity to judge for themselves. Similarly, one candidate may make an attack on the policies of another that the second candidate does not have an immediate chance to rebut because of the structured nature of the debate. The delayed defence may not have the same impact as the accusation, especially if the accusation is made forcefully. In a close election, debate performance could become a crucial electoral variable.

In addition to identifying candidates through debates and other coverage, the media may choose to endorse them. Editorial endorsements were once considered to be both the right and responsibility of the media in their role as public opinion leaders. Recently, however, endorsements have lost their media appeal. A new management philosophy suggests that the media should provide full and impartial coverage and let the voters make their own decisions.[8] Moreover, research has indicated that endorsements are generally ineffective, although they may have more influence at the municipal level (Fletcher 1981, 83).

Another major function of the media is to select central campaign issues. McCombs and Shaw (1972) undertook a study of the 1968 presidential campaign in the United States to determine the ability of the media to influence the prominence of particular attitudes towards the various campaign issues. Their evidence suggests that voters share the media's composite definition of what is important. The findings lend support to the agenda-setting theory and can be generalized to the Canadian case.

One of the major criticisms of media campaign coverage, however, concerns their poor record in dealing with the substance of issues—the arguments on both sides and the details that support or detract from those positions. Frizzell and Westell (1985, 62) found that only about one-quarter of the campaign news items they analysed concentrated on policy issues or proposals, with items about the economy and national unity topping the list. Although they don't attempt to determine who sets the policy agenda or how well the media address the issues, other analysts, such as Mary Ann Comber and Robert Mayne (1986), are very critical of the media's lack of exhaustive interpretive analysis of political issues during campaigns. They argue that the media trivialize issues by emphasizing leadership style and the "horse-race" aspect of the campaign process itself.

The media's role in influencing the tone of the campaign and defining the criteria for assessing campaign activity is also subject to scrutiny. Frizzell and Westell (1985, 64) discovered that almost 40 percent of the election news items in their sample from the 1984 general election campaign dealt with party strategies and the campaign process; 5 percent concerned poll results as their primary subject; and another 5 percent discussed polls as a secondary subject. The emphasis on the process, or machinery, of elections is understandable if we review the criteria for news selection discussed in chapter 5. The drama and conflict lend themselves well to the media's definition of news, but can obscure the real substance of the campaign.

Finally, it has been noted that the media have the ability to integrate local campaigns into a national perspective, bring the national perspective to the local ridings, and link the two together. By doing so, the media can influence the electorate's outlook. Frizzell and Westell (1985, 59) found that each newspaper in their sample concentrated on news from its home province, followed by a higher proportion of items originating from Ottawa than news from other provinces. This is not surprising, since local campaigns should be of vital interest to voters and activities in Ottawa are important to the national campaign. On the other hand, the data also indicate a general lack of interest in coverage of other provinces and regions. Although Ontario (political and corporate elite headquarters), Quebec (Mulroney's home base), and British Columbia (Turner's constituency) generally received adequate coverage, the other provinces drew scant attention. No definitive conclusions can be drawn from these findings without additional research but they do lead us to question the degree to which media integrate election activities from across the country into a national perspective of the campaign. It is not possible to understand the views of other regions when we are not even aware of them.

Much of the research on media effects during election campaigns tries to identify and analyse the differences between television and newspapers. A number of findings are of interest in the Canadian case. While television is the preferred medium for most voters, newspapers are favoured by the more politically attuned segment of the population. Nevertheless, television is the preferred medium of party strategists because they believe that it reaches more uncommitted voters, who are watching television for other reasons. According to Jeffrey Simpson (1980, 256),

> A newspaper story reaches a greater percentage of committed voters than a comparable television report. The uncommitted voter, in contrast to a partisan, is less likely to have a keen interest in things political. Impressions and images are more influential than issues for the uncommitted voter, and television—which conveys images more adeptly than it does ideas, and impressions more easily than facts—is therefore the medium most likely to provide the information upon which the uncommitted voter makes up his [or her] mind.

Television is best suited for action and for communicating the national elements of the campaign. It focusses on leadership, style, drama, and on-the-spot coverage. Newspapers do a better job of covering individual constituencies, and provide more thoughtful discussion and analysis.

Based on the research to date, the media do not appear to be an important determinant of voting behaviour. They may influence voter turnout or affect the commitment of party workers by either reinforcing their convictions or introducing feelings of futility, but their influence on the individual voter seems to vary according to myriads of other factors. Since the majority of electors have made their decisions before the election is even called, and few of those change their minds during the campaign, the media tend to reinforce preferences (Lang and Lang [1959] 1980). For uncommitted voters, the media provide information to be accepted, reinterpreted, or ignored as those voters struggle to reach a decision. Perhaps the most significant impact of media election coverage is its potential for influencing the election process. When elections became media events, party strategists sat up, took notice, and began to adapt their campaigns to suit the media's criteria. One of the more widely criticized elements of election coverage is the new-found interest the media have been taking in public opinion polls.

Polls

During the last few decades, polls have increasingly been accepted as a legitimate part of the news-gathering function, especially during election campaigns.[9] During the 1984 Canadian general election more polls were conducted by the media and political parties than ever before (Frizzell and Westell 1985, 75), and polls became a controversial election issue in themselves. The Canadian record in polling, however, is modest compared to the United States and Great Britain.[10]

When evaluating the role and impact of public opinion polls it is important to understand their methodology and their purpose. Polling uses a small sample to discover the opinions of the population. Polls tell us what people are thinking at a particular time in relatively clear-cut terms, but they do not predict future attitudes or behaviour. In fact, the accuracy of polls is closely correlated with their proximity to the actual election.[11] If a poll is methodologically sound, it is possible to draw meaningful generalizations from the results. Both the media and political party strategists sometimes use polls in this way. Polls supplement normal election reporting by allowing the media to let the public know which party is ahead and why. Polls also help the media to determine what topics to cover. Political party strategists use polls to develop or adjust campaign strategies. As for the politicians themselves, Frizzell and Westell (1985, 85) claim that attitudes towards opinion polls are "highly correlated with his/her standing in them."

The most crucial aspect of the polling process is the selection of the sample. In order to generalize from the sample to the population, the sample must be similar to the population in terms of age, sex, geographic location, and other demographic factors. Although random selection, in which each person in the population has an equal chance of being included in the sample, is the best method of achieving a representative sample, it does present a number of practical difficulties that pollsters must overcome. Making a random selection by telephone, for example, automatically excludes people who have no phones and people in hospital. The method used to collect the data also influences the results. Phone surveys, in-home interviews, and mailed questionnaires are all acceptable but each has its own advantages and liabilities.

The nature of the questions asked in a poll can also present problems. All questions should be tested in advance to avoid any ambiguity in the results. Political polls should include standard questions about parties, leaders, and issues—such as Who will you vote for? and What issues are most important to you? They should also contain questions that probe intentions and strength of commitment, and questions that elicit basic demographic information.

Polling in Canada has additional difficulties (Frizzell and Westell 1985, 79–80). The widely dispersed nature of the population makes interviewing onerous. Because of differences in regional interests and attitudes, voting varies across regions and consistent national trends are less likely to occur. This also makes it difficult to translate poll results into an accurate distribution of seats in the House of Commons. Finally, because the Canadian electorate tends to be a volatile one, polls are always trying to catch up with the changes. Trends are more meaningful than any individual result.

One of the main problems with polls is the manner in which they are reported and interpreted. The media are often weak in this respect. In order to understand the implications of poll results, we need to know their technical limitations, including sample size and selection, the interview techniques used, the dates during which the poll was conducted, and the margin of error.[12] We also need to know the exact wording of the question posed, in order to determine whether it has really probed the given attitude and whether the answers have meaning. In addition, there is a danger that the media may overemphasize poll results and ignore serious analysis of trends and other election news. Because the media tend to treat an election as a race, they also tend to stress small differences in polls when in reality all the polls may be indicating similar trends.

These weaknesses make many critics fear that polls could have an undue influence on politicians and the public. Three possible effects of polls on voters have been identified: voters may not bother to exercise their franchise if they believe that their chosen candidate is sure to win or lose anyway; a "bandwagon" effect may induce voters to switch allegiance in order to be on the winning side; or voters may change their opinions and vote for the underdog out of sympathy. None of these effects have been proven, and the real impact of polls on voting behaviour remains unclear. Nevertheless, to be influenced by polls, voters not only need to know about poll results but must also both believe that they are accurate and use them as a basis for making decisions. Research indicates that people tend to distrust polls and it therefore seems likely that the effect of polls on the electorate is minimal (Frizzell and Westell 1985, 85).

Summary

A number of trends have been identified in this general examination of media coverage of public affairs, and they may be summed up as follows:

1. Television is the main source of public affairs information for most people. Television news coverage emphasizes leadership and style. It stresses the national dimensions of election campaigns and often determines the type of plans that political strategists make.

2. There is a remarkable degree of consistency in the coverage of public affairs. Homogeneity is fostered by pack journalism, reliance on similar news sources, and a tendency to emphasize national rather than regional activities.

3. Polls are increasingly viewed as a legitimate part of the news-gathering process. In reporting poll results, the media focus on leaders and conflict to the detriment of coverage of complex issues that are more difficult to report.

4. The media have tended to trivialize public affairs and the political process. The trend is evident in the media's emphasis on leaders, style, slogans, colour, conflict, and drama, and in their failure to provide sufficiently thorough analysis of serious issues and problems.

5. Public affairs coverage tends to be more cynical and confrontational than formerly. There is a growing anxiety that media cynicism and criticism may contribute to a widespread distrust of the political process.[13]

Wide-ranging criticism of public affairs coverage is based, in part, upon the suspicion that the media, because of their pervasive presence in modern society, must have some role in influencing both public perceptions and behaviour, and the political process itself. Although there exists little empirical evidence to back those claims, the media are not necessarily impotent. It may simply mean that research has failed to isolate the significant variables. What we do know, however, is that the media play a role in setting the public affairs agenda, and this alone makes them important actors in the political process. They have a responsibility to the Canadian public, which has the right to expect full and fair coverage of the day's intelligence.

Notes

1. An example of the power of public opinion to influence public policy was provided in the summer of 1987. When a boatload of illegal immigrants waded ashore in Nova Scotia and claimed refugee status, the public was outraged. This second successful attempt at immigration queue jumping created a public demand for more stringent handling of the immigrant and refugee process. The federal government responded quickly. Prime Minister Mulroney recalled Parliament from its summer recess and introduced a new immigration bill with much stricter provisions. Undoubtedly the media played major roles in bringing news of the event to the public and in apprising politicians of the public reaction. Nevertheless, without a detailed and rigorous study of the situation it is not possible to determine accurately whether or not the media coverage was a causal factor in either the development of public opinion or the reaction of the government.

2. See Wagner and Sherwood (1969) for a more detailed analysis of attitude development and change.

3. The reader is referred back to chapter 3 and the discussion of Wallace Clement.

4. See chapter 1 for more detailed discussion about agenda-setting.

5. See, for example, Fletcher and Drummond (1979).

6. See Bell and Fletcher (1979) and Munton and Clow (1979).

7. Members of the media are themselves concerned with how well they do their job. They worry about their potential impact, and the way in which they report and interpret campaigns and outcomes. Following the 1984 general election, the Centre for Investigative Journalism held two conferences to examine the manner in which the media handled campaign coverage. For details, see Frizzell and Westell (1985, 55–56).

8. Fletcher (1981, 86–87) found no correlation between the pattern of endorsements and chain-owned newspapers. Moreover, he cites only one case in which a head office set endorsement policy for its papers. Paul Desmarais, head of Power Corporation, informed his papers that editorial support for the "Oui" side in the 1980 Quebec Referendum on Sovereignty Association would not be acceptable, although a neutral stance was permissible.

9. Polls also democratize the policy process between elections by emphasizing public preferences.

10. During the 1984 Canadian election campaign, which lasted fifty-eight days, twelve polls were published by the media. In Great Britain, during the thirty days prior to the 1984 general election, forty-seven polls were published (Frizzell and Westell 1985, 75).

11. This fact is due, in part, to the many "undecided" respondents, who make it difficult for pollsters to determine what is going on.

12. Provided that no other interviewing or calculation error occurs to affect poll results, national polls with a sample of 1 060 respondents are accurate within 4 percentage points, 19 out of 20 times. This means that if the polls were repeated over and over again, the results would be almost the same, all of the time.

13. In place of their once partisan stance, the media now appear to have taken on a mantle of scepticism, an attitude reflected in most coverage regardless of the party in power. It is interesting to note that Brian Mulroney's federal Conservative administration is very critical of many of the same media practices that the Conservative Party applauded during the years of the Trudeau–Turner Liberal administration. The media's self-appointed role as watchdog or critic is now deeply entrenched and is unlikely to be affected by the political stripes of the governing party. The industry views itself as the unofficial opposition and will continue to deal with issues in that way.

References

American Assembly on Presidential Nominations and the Media. [1978] 1980. Statement. Reprinted in *Readings in mass communication*, ed. M. Emery and T.C. Smythe, 413–21. Dubuque: Brown.

Bell, D., and F.J. Fletcher. 1979. The Canadian mass media and the reporting of transportation policy. *Transportation Research Forum* 20(1): 42–47.

Best, J.J. 1973. *Public opinion, micro and macro*. Homewood, IL: Dorsey.

Black, E.R. 1982. *Politics and the news, The political function of the mass media*. Toronto: Butterworths.

Blumler, J. [1969] 1981. The press, television and democracy. In *Reader in public opinion and mass communication*. 3d ed., ed. M. Janowitz and P.M. Hirsch, 121–26. New York: Free Press.

Comber, M.A., and R. Mayne. 1986. *The newsmongers: How the media distort the political news*. Toronto: McClelland and Stewart.

de Tocqueville, A. [1837] 1947. *Democracy in America*. Vol. 2., trans. by H. Reeve. New York: Oxford.

Fletcher, F.J. 1981. *The newspaper and public affairs*. Vol. 7 of *Royal commission on newspapers research publications*. Ottawa: Supply and Services.

Fletcher, F.J., and R.J. Drummond. 1979. *Canadian attitude trends, 1960–1978*. Montreal: Institute for Research on Public Policy.

Fletcher, F.J., and D.G. Taras. 1984. The mass media and politics: An overview. In *Canadian politics in the 1980s*. 2d ed., ed. M.S. Whittington and G. Williams, 193–228. Toronto: Methuen.

Frizzell, A., and A. Westell. 1985. *The Canadian general election of 1984: Politicians, parties, press and polls*. Ottawa: Carleton University.

Katz, D. [1960] 1981. The functional approach to the study of attitudes. In *Reader in public opinion and mass communication*. 3d ed., ed. M. Janowitz and P.M. Hirsch, 38–49. New York: Free Press.

Kesterton, W.H. 1967. *A history of journalism in Canada*. Toronto: McClelland and Stewart.

Klapper, J.T. 1958. What we know about the effects of mass communication: The brink of hope. *Public Opinion Quarterly* 21: 454–74.

Lang, K., and G.E. Lang. [1959] 1980. The mass media and voting. In *Reader in public opinion and mass communication*. 3d ed., ed. M. Janowitz and P.M. Hirsch, 327–40. New York: Free Press.

McCombs, M.E., and D.L. Shaw. 1972. The agenda setting function of mass media. *Public Opinion Quarterly* 36: 176–87.

McGinnis, J. 1968. *The selling of the president*. New York: Trident.

McQuail, D. 1984. *Mass communication theory: An introduction*. Beverly Hills: Sage.

Munton, D., and M. Clow. 1979. The media, the bureaucrats and Canadian environmental policy. Paper presented at the International Studies Association annual meeting. March. Toronto, Ontario.

Rivers, W.L. 1970. *The adversaries*. Boston: Beacon.

Roberts, D.F., and C.H. Baclen. 1981. Mass communication effects. *Annual Review of Psychology* 32: 176–87.

Simpson, J. 1980. *Discipline of power*. Toronto: Personal Library.

Van Loon, R.J., and M.S. Whittington. 1984. *The Canadian political system: Environment, structure and process*. 3d rev. ed. Toronto: McGraw-Hill Ryerson.

Wagner, R.V., and J.J. Sherwood. 1969. *The study of attitude change*. Belmont, CA: Brooks/Cole.

THE MEDIA
AND ADVERTISING

*A*dvertising as a means of communicating information about goods and services is an ancient practice. Today, it is also big business, generating billions of dollars in revenue worldwide. Moreover, it is considered by many to be essential to the operation of the contemporary Western economic system. Advertising has become so omnipresent that it is difficult to imagine our lives without it: we are bombarded with advertising messages from the time that we open the morning newspaper to the time that we watch late night television shows. The mail often brings more advertising and throughout the day we are exposed to a variety of advertisements as we go about our regular business. In fact, many people become so accustomed to these messages that they no longer register them consciously.

There are four classes of actors involved in the advertising process: the advertisers who want to sell products, services, or ideas; the agencies that prepare the messages and plan the advertising campaigns; the media that disseminate the messages; and the consumers who receive the messages and sometimes act upon them. It is clear from this that advertising is *not* a medium; rather, it consists of messages distributed by various media. The distinction is important because it hints at the relationship between advertising and the media.

It can be argued that the fundamental function of any medium is to deliver an audience for advertisers but the relationship between media and advertising can also be seen in terms of symbiosis. Undoubtedly, advertisers need the media to disseminate their messages to the large number of potential consumers whom they cannot otherwise reach in such a cost-efficient manner, but the media also need the financial support of the advertisers. Advertisers are the media's largest customers, in some cases their only customers.

For the media, the relationship has both advantages and disadvantages. Advertising defrays a large portion of their costs; it has been estimated that the average daily newspaper would cost the consumer between $1.50 and $3.50 without advertiser support. At the same time, advertising brings information to the audience, both the sponsored information and the other information that the media carry. On the negative side, media dependence on advertising support can provide an opportunity for advertisers to exercise control over media content. As well, advertising sometimes results in clutter; its quantity and frequency can interfere with the audience's enjoyment or understanding of other media content.

Whether or not the media could exist without advertising is open to question. *Reader's Digest* did for over thirty years from 1922 to 1955. Public broadcasting and educational television operate without advertising, depending instead on government funding and donations. The removal of advertising revenue would probably not spell the end of all media, but it would certainly reduce the choices available.

This chapter first briefly examines advertising itself—its processes, forms, and functions, its presumed effectiveness, and the general issues surrounding its practice. It then reviews the role of media in the advertising process, the relationship between advertising and the media, and the various concerns raised about the nature of that relationship.

Advertising: The enterprise

Definitions and classifications

The word advertising comes from the Latin *advertere*, which means to turn the mind towards. Modern definitions tend to emphasize the process of advertising. It has been described as a communication process, a business process, a marketing process, a public relations process, a process of informing and persuading, and an economic and social process. Advertising also has a dual nature as both "a powerful communications force and a vital marketing tool, helping to sell goods, services, images, and ideas (or ideals) through channels of information and persuasion" (Wright et al. 1984, 8). The definition that this text uses is a composite of the many available:

1. Advertising uses the mass communication media (and the mails) to distribute its messages.

2. It communicates information.

3. It is about goods, services, or ideas.

4. The content and timing of its messages are controlled.

5. It delivers the messages repeatedly.

6. Its source and purpose are identifiable.

7. It is usually paid for by that identifiable source.

8. It is persuasive in nature and attempts to influence behaviour. It does not pretend to be unbiased.

9. It uses non-personal communication directed at specific large groups of people.

If we apply these criteria, neither publicity nor propaganda can be described as advertising. Publicity is unpaid coverage of issues, events, people, and so on, undertaken by an independent source. News coverage of a company's research and development breakthrough is an example. While publicity lacks the elements of control, persuasion, and measured reach and remuneration, propaganda attempts to obscure the true source or purpose of the message. Advertising exists in many forms and can be classified according to its predominant elements (table 12.1).

Table 12.1

Methods to classify advertising

Advertising method	Sponsor	Purpose	Type of campaign	Audience	Example
A. By sponsor or advertiser					
National	Sponsored by manufacturers or producers who do not sell directly to the public but want to convince the consumer that he or she will benefit from buying and using their products.	The manufactuers want to make their products known and create a demand for them. The message says, "Buy our brand or our product!"	Although the sponsors are national companies, their campaigns may either advertise across an entire country or pinpoint certain regions.		Coca-Cola
Retail	Sponsored by retailers who sell directly to the consumer.	The retailers want to convince consumers to shop in particular stores. The message says, "Buy here!"	Regional or national, depending on the location of the retail outlets and the likelihood of encouraging sales in any given region.		The Bay, Canadian Tire

Advertising method	Sponsor	Purpose	Type of campaign	Audience	Example
Co-operative	Sponsored jointly by a manufacturer or producer and a retailer.	The sponsors want to convince consumers to buy a particular type of product at a particular store. The message says, "Buy our brand at this store!"	The manufacturer usually provides the copy and the costs are shared.		
Government institutions, social groups	Sponsored by organizations other than those which manufacture, produce, or sell goods and services.	Usually tries to change behaviour or elicit donations.	Public service announcements, political advertisements, etc.		Canadian Cancer Society
B. By Audience					
Consumers			Generally uses the mass media.	Directed at members of the consuming public who purchase goods and services for their own use.	

Advertising method	Sponsor	Purpose	Type of campaign	Audience	Example
Business	Many types of sponsor: trade (wholesalers, industrial manufacturers, utilities, transportation); professional (doctors, architects, teachers); and agricultural.	The purchase is not for personal use.	Tends to use specialized media.	Directed at other manufacturers, or distributors.	A pharmaceutical company that advertises its drug products in magazines and trade papers for physicians
C. By purpose					
Commercial	Sponsored by organizations that manufacture, produce, or sell goods and services.	Designed to sell goods, services or ideas.	Emphasizes strength, competence, or status rather than commercial output.		
Institutional	Sponsored by corporations, institutions.	Designed to develop an image.	Usually has no direct commercial component.		
D. By appeal					
Direct	Various		Tries to get an immediate response. The message says "Buy now!"		

Advertising method	Sponsor	Purpose	Type of campaign	Audience	Example
Indirect	Various		Builds an image or seeks familiarity.		
Primary	Various		Promotes a generic product.		Automobile tires
Selective	Various		Promotes a particular brand.		Goodyear
Rational	Various		Appeals to practical needs, or logical reasoning.		
Emotional	Various		Appeals to social, psychological, or emotional needs.		
One-sided	Various	The message says, "Our product is the best!"	Provides only positive information about products or services.		The vast majority of product ads
Two-sided	Various	The message says, "There are different sides to this issue. Here is the information you need to make a choice."	Provides information about both sides of an issue or service.		Public service ads

Advertising method	Sponsor	Purpose	Type of campaign	Audience	Example
E. By strategy of presentation					
Testimonials, endorsements	Various		An individual or a group advocates a product, service, or idea.		
Demonstrations	Various		Exhibits a product's uses and value.		
Slice-of-life	Various		Describes a problem and illustrates that the product, service, or idea can solve it.		
Comparison	Various		Compares products, services, or ideas to illustrate the value of one.		
Straight	Various		Presents information in a clear and simple manner.		

Advertising method	Sponsor	Purpose	Type of campaign	Audience	Example
Lifestyle	Various		Focusses on lifestyle over product, service, or idea.		
Animation, special effects	Various		Utilizes special effects or animation to simplify the complex or build familiarity.		
Humour	Various		Uses humour to attract and hold attention.		
F. By geography					
International	Various			Aimed at foreign markets.	
National	Various			Aimed at the domestic market.	
Regional	Various			Aimed at selected domestic regions.	
Local	Various			Aimed at purely local customers.	

Advertising method	Sponsor	Purpose	Type of campaign	Audience	Example
G. By medium					
Print	Various		Uses newspapers, magazines, flyers, catalogues, etc.		
Broadcast	Various		Uses radio, television.		
Home	Various		Uses direct mail, handbills.		
Out-of-home	Various		Uses billboards, transit (buses, trucks), hot air balloons, stadium scoreboards, sky writing, etc.		

Why advertise?

Table 12.1 also suggests why advertisers advertise. Undoubtedly the primary reason is to communicate a message but advertising is really multifunctional. It meets the marketing, educational, and economic needs of the sponsors and consumers. For many sponsors, advertising is considered the most important component of the distribution process for their products, services, or ideas. The ability of advertising to expose large groups to a predetermined, controlled message at a low per prospect cost (cost per prospective consumer) makes it especially attractive (Stanley 1982, 58). By introducing, identifying, explaining, and differentiating among products, their uses, and locations of sale, advertising builds brand loyalty and increases use of products. It thereby opens new markets and expands old ones. There is no other so potentially powerful tool for sponsors to get their messages across.

Advertising can benefit consumers as well as the advertisers themselves (Wright et al. 1984, 133). It provides information about available products, services, and options, not only educating consumers but also saving them time. It can also give the consumer some assurance of quality, since brand loyalty is founded on the strength of the brand's reputation. Finally, although it is incidental to their purpose, advertisements can, and do, provide entertainment for millions of consumers. Nowhere else in the media world will one find such high expenditures on one page of copy or thirty seconds of air time.

Despite its advantages, advertising involves great uncertainty and may not be suitable for promoting all products, services, or ideas. Potential sponsors must consider: the quality, uniqueness, suitability, and price of their product; their realistic market potential given existing competitors and demand; the nature of their own production and distribution infrastructures; the cost of advertising in terms of both absolute expenditures and per prospect cost; and the availability of suitable media. Moreover, advertisers should be convinced of the efficacy of advertising as a marketing tool. An imaginary case will illustrate the point. Apex Plumbing has developed a new, high-quality widget for a dripless faucet. The potential market for the widget is very large, and includes new house construction and plumbing repairs. The widget is very expensive compared to existing faucet hardware, however, because it has a complicated production technique and is made of a rare metal alloy. Right now, Apex has a contract to sell 80 percent of its widgets to a local builder of luxury apartments. Should Apex advertise in order to sell the remainder of its existing inventory? Judging from the situation just outlined, a mass media advertising campaign is probably not the right move for Apex at this time. Despite the market potential of the widget, its very high cost would be likely to limit sales. As a result, advertising would be expensive in terms of the number of sales per advertising dollar spent. On the other hand, if the campaign were highly successful and the demand for widgets skyrocketed, production constraints would prevent Apex from satisfying its prospective customers. It therefore appears that Apex would do better to rely on personal recommendations and direct sales to sell its remaining widgets. If it could modify its production methods or find a cheaper substitute for the metal alloy, Apex could produce the widgets at a lower cost and would need to reconsider its advertising decision.

The business

As mentioned earlier, the practice of advertising dates back to ancient times, but advertising as a business is a more recent phenomenon. It developed in response to the Industrial Revolution. The capacity to manufacture mass quantities of innovative products created a need to communicate their virtues and transport them to potential markets. As the population grew and compulsory education promoted literacy, the mass media also expanded. Advertising was a natural extension of all these developments. In Canada, the first modern advertisements using the mass media were placed in the premiere edition of the Halifax *Gazette* on 23 March 1752.[1]

It was over a century later before Canada's first advertising agency was established by Anson McKim in 1889. The business of agencies grew as the media's dependency on advertising revenue increased. Ad agencies bring advertisers and the media together so that each can serve the needs of the other. Courtland Bovée and William Arens (1982, 115) define an advertising agency as an

> independent organization of creative and business people who specialize in the development and preparation of advertising plans, advertisements, and other promotional tools. The agency also arranges or contracts for the purchase of advertising space and time in communications media. It does all this on behalf of different sellers, who are referred to as clients, in an effort to find customers for their goods and services.[2]

While not all advertisers use advertising agencies, most do, because of the advantages they offer. Agencies can provide a more objective point of view about the content and influence of advertising than can in-house specialists employed by the sponsor, who are more likely to be reluctant to express a negative opinion to their senior management. In addition, agencies have the specialized personnel to design and produce advertisements and to purchase suitable media time or space. They provide a variety of other services as well—including research, monitoring, and evaluation—which would be very costly for advertisers to undertake themselves.

In Canada, more than five hundred thousand firms advertise or are affected by the advertising of others; there are also between three and five hundred advertising agencies, which employ more than ten thousand employees (Wright et al. 1984, 786). Canadian firms spend over $2 billion annually on advertising or more than $100 per capita (Bovée and Arens 1982, 30). Although both the total and per capita amounts are small relative to those in the United States, Canada's total advertising expenditures rank among the top ten in the world and our per capita expenditures rank among the top five.

Several of Canada's largest agencies are branch plants of American or European agencies. Over the past fifteen years, as the trend to rationalize the industry has prompted consolidation, the number of American-owned agencies among the top fifteen in Canada has grown from three to ten (*Globe and Mail* 1987, B3). The ranking of Canada's top agencies varies depending upon the calculations used to determine billings, revenues, and profits, and table 12.2 provides one list of the largest advertising agencies operating in Canada. Although no Canadian agencies rank among the world's top fifty, many of their parent companies do (*Advertising Age* 1987, 60).

Consolidation and multinational agencies (ones that operate in a number of countries other than their own) are part of a process of global amalgamation that is increasing agency profits and giving agency clients access to markets worldwide.[3] It involves American, European, and Japanese agencies as well as Canadian. In fact, Dentsu Inc. of Japan, the world's largest agency, is one of the few multinationals without a Canadian subsidiary. Most of the top ten American agencies generate revenues outside the United States equal to or greater than their domestic revenues (Kleppner et al. 1984, 561). The phenomenon is not altogether

Table 12.2

Canada's largest advertising agencies

Agency	1988 billings in $ millions
FCB/Ronalds-Reynolds Ltd.	182.0*
MacLaren Advertising	180.0
McKim Advertising Ltd.	175.0
J. Walter Thompson Company	170.5
Cossette Communications-Marketing**	170.3
Vickers and Benson Companies Ltd.**	166.6
Ogilvy and Mather Advertising	165.0
Saffer Advertising Inc.**	155.0
Young and Rubicam Advertising	144.5
Baker Lovick Ltd.	143.0

* Billings were calculated on the basis of all fees and commissions. Branch office billings are included, but income from subsidiary or separate satellite agencies owned wholly or in part by the agency is not.

** Canadian-owned agencies

Source: Marketing, *12 December 1988, 23.*

surprising, although it is causing international concern about how well domestic agencies will fare as foreign firms move in to compete. Black and Whitney (1983, 842) have estimated that 5 percent of the world's population generates 60 percent of its advertising. This small group of advertisers is no longer content to reach only domestic markets, and multinational agencies offer them the convenience of "one-stop shopping."

Canadian agencies have not been able to counteract this trend, and opinions of their ability to adjust to it vary. Otto Kleppner and his colleagues (1984, 561) claim that Canadian firms have been successful in maintaining and even increasing their billings, client lists, and general influence. Moreover, some Canadian firms are expanding into foreign markets as well. An October 1987 report in the *Financial Post* (1987, 11), however, warns that "Canadian advertising agencies are paying a heavy price for the increasingly global business strategies of their multinational clients." The report cites examples of large advertising accounts lost to large multinational advertising agencies. It also describes the rash of multinational amalgamations that have already occurred. *Business Week* (1988, 92) reported that six of Canada's top ten ad agencies were American owned and predicted that uniformity in advertising will increase under the Free Trade Agreement. Many Canadian agencies continue to service the large advertising accounts of the federal and provincial governments,[4] but they face difficult challenges: competition from multinationals offering a broader range of services; declining profit margins; fragmented advertising spending; and the loss of qualified creative and business talent to multinationals, which offer more perks and higher salaries. These factors led the *Financial Post* (1987, 11) to conclude that "a merger between any of the top Canadian agencies would strengthen their franchise, consolidating their client lists and making it easier to resist foreign conglomerates cherry-picking among Canadian companies."

Quebec: A special case[5]

Quebec represents a special case for advertisers in Canada, who need to consider its linguistic and cultural differences as significant variables. At one time, companies wishing to advertise in Quebec simply translated English advertisements into French. The events of the Quiet Revolution, followed by a decade of FLQ-sponsored terrorism and the rise to political power of the Parti Québécois, forced advertisers to acknowledge that Quebec was different from other Canadian provinces and that this difference might also be reflected in buying patterns and consumer behaviour.

Subsequent research did uncover certain unique characteristics. Francophone Quebeckers behave differently as consumers from their English-Canadian counterparts. They spend more, per capita, on clothing, personal care items, tobacco, alcohol, soda, candy, maple sugar, instant and decaffeinated coffees, and headache and cold remedies (Wright et al. 1984, 364–65). They buy a greater number of expensive products and use more coupons. Their media habits also indicate more frequent use of radio and television. Evidence of buying patterns helped advertisers to target their market, and further research indicated how that market could be reached. For example, Jacques Bouchard (1980) identified six themes in Québécois culture. The Québécois are "people of the soil," with an agricultural heritage and a closeness to the environment; feel that they are a minority; are North American; are Catholic but have a modified attitude towards the Church; are Latin in heritage and sentiments but subject to North American influences; and are French-speaking but feel no closeness to the people of France. Advertisers need to appeal to these characteristics if their campaigns are to be successful. During the 1988 federal election, for example, the Progressive Conservative party ran ads on Quebec television that were significantly more emotional in their appeal than those run in the rest of Canada, although the ultimate objective was the same.

Strict translation still accounts for the majority of national advertising, but it is supplemented by adaptations to reflect Quebec's tastes and by original francophone ads. A number of French-Canadian agencies have sprung up to serve sponsors' new requirements, some as branch offices of large English-Canadian firms, others as independents. Recently, two agencies have expanded from Quebec to serve English Canada, and both are among Canada's top ten agencies.

Advertising in Quebec also operates under unique legal restrictions. The most far-reaching is Bill 101, Quebec's controversial language legislation, which requires that all outdoor public signs, billboards, posters, direct mail, and advertising on vehicles be in French only. Since 1988, signs and notices indoors may use English but French must be predominant. Bill 101 also prescribes French as the language of the workplace. In addition, sales tax and lottery regulations and consumer protection legislation strictly govern the practice of advertising. Quebec and its francophone population still represent a unique case of which advertisers should be aware, even though differences between consumers in Quebec and the other provinces decreased during the 1980s.

The functions and effects of advertising

The value of advertising to society is judged in terms of its economic and social functions. As in all aspects of the advertising enterprise, however, the matter of value is subject to debate. When discussing the functions of advertising, the chapter presents both points of view and leaves readers to draw their own conclusions.

Economic functions

Advertising is said to serve several economic functions, at both the macro and micro levels. Macro-level functions can be generalized to the economy as a whole and include, among others, the following four. First, it can be argued that advertising creates general benefits for the economy. It encourages production by stimulating demand and fostering more effective distribution, an element crucial to the success of mass production. Increased production, in turn, encourages investment, creates employment, and generally raises the standard of living. On the other hand, it can also be argued that advertising as it is currently practised is simply a waste of valuable resources. It diverts significant investment from production into the non-productive and unnecessary glamour of the advertising campaigns themselves.

Second, advertising affects prices, a function related to increased production. The 1968 Prairie Provinces' Royal Commission on Consumer Problems and Inflation concluded, "One of the surprising findings is how relatively low the cost of communications through advertising seems to be in so many cases" (in Wright et al. 1984, 50). Although advertising is an expensive undertaking itself, and passes its costs along to the consumer, supporters argue that advertising may actually lower retail prices. Increased demand generates larger production runs, thereby lowering the per unit cost of the product. Combined with the more effective distribution that is induced by advertising and the price pressures of competition, this means that the consumer pays little for advertising and may, in fact, even save in the long run. The other side of the argument is that advertising causes waste by encouraging consumers to buy even if there is no need. It promotes artificial obsolescence and wastes non-renewable resources in terms of both production of goods and the advertising processes that sell the goods. Ink, for example, is a petroleum-based product used copiously in the production of advertising. Advertising, then, whether directly or indirectly, merely adds to the cost of goods and services.

Third, advertising adds value to goods and services. By providing information, explaining alternative uses for the product (new recipes in every advertisement for Velveeta cheese, for example), and creating an image, advertising enhances a product's familiarity and prestige. Advertising may also add economic value to a service or product by forcing quality controls and quality-based competition. The counter-argument, however, emphasizes the waste and potential psychological damage of perceived added value. Consumers may feel inadequate or insecure because they cannot afford the "best" car, for example, or don't look or behave like the "perfect" people in ads. As consumers, we do not need innumerable choices among almost identical products.

Finally, advertising influences the nature of competition. Some believe that advertising fosters competition by lowering the cost of information, encouraging quality control and better products, and providing the consumer with a broad array of choices. Others see advertising as a means of creating brand monopolies. Since advertising is an expensive undertaking, only larger firms can afford it; by controlling information about products, large advertisers can force their smaller competitors out of the market.

Advertising can have micro-economic functions as well. While these functions are similar to the macro-economic ones outlined above, their impact is more restricted. They are usually specific to one product, firm, class of competitors, group of customers, or local business community. The opening of a large, independent grocery store in Calgary, Alberta, provides a classic example of the micro-economic impact of advertising. The new store advertised extensively in the Calgary area prior to and following its opening in the fall of 1988. Its ads emphasized low prices and high quality. In response, the grocery chains in the area countered the new competitor's claims with ads of their own. The price of a basket of groceries then dropped, at least in the short run, and consumers benefited. While the benefits were created by the entry of a new competitor, they were enhanced by the advertising that accompanied it.

Social functions

Advertising has social functions, and these are generally more open to criticism than its economic role since they influence all of us as consumers both of goods, services, and ideas, and of mass media advertising. Advertising influences our values and lifestyles. Again, opinion varies on the result. Some argue, Richard Stanley (1982, 181) among them, that advertising merely reflects, accentuates, or accelerates trends but does not create them. Yet consumer advocacy groups and others blame advertising for creating a lifestyle based on conspicuous consumption, inconsequential or material values, greed, and envy. Moreover, advertising is particularly disruptive for low-income members of the population, who are persuaded to want things that they do not need and cannot afford.

Second, advertising supplies the public with information. It efficiently and effectively conveys the information that sponsors want consumers to have about the availability of products and services. While the information may often be incomplete, inadequate, or biased, only rarely is it actually false. Critics argue, however, that if one examines all advertising, not just that directed to one particular product or service, it usually involves conflicting or competing claims that the consumer cannot easily verify. A laundry detergent manufacturer that conducts a demonstration to prove that its detergent washes clothes cleaner than another brand does, for example, or a dish-washing detergent company that shows its product getting more dishes clean per container than other detergents do, is producing evidence that the average consumer would find difficult to confirm or disprove. The propensity that advertising has for bias increases consumers' cynicism and distrust. Moreover, to be successful, advertising is highly repetitious. It is difficult to determine how much advertising is required to produce desired results and much is therefore wasted. Despite these drawbacks, there is no other means of bringing so much consumer information to the public at equal cost.

Advertising also meets our need for information about issues, rights, obligations, and opportunities. Notices from governments, industries, companies, and political parties can inform, advise, and perhaps, persuade. Paid space is indisputably useful in assisting the public to evaluate a variety of issues. Such information is one-sided, however, and parties interested in making their points of view known do not all have equal financial ability to do so.

Fourth, advertising is credited with serving the individual's need for social status and a sense of belonging. Critics note, however, that these needs—based primarily on emotion rather than intellect—can often be satisfied only by spending beyond one's means. What advertising really does, they argue, is create artificial needs that lead to personal frustration.

Finally, advertising supports press freedom. By offering the media a variety of sources of financial independence, advertising reduces the cost to the public of media services and limits government opportunities to manipulate the press. Moreover, because advertising involves such large-scale expenditures and seeks specialized audiences, it fosters the diversification of media services that might not otherwise be affordable. A magazine especially for skiers, for example, would be too expensive to produce without advertising support because the audience is so special-ized. For ski equipment manufacturers and resort owners, however, the specialized audience for such a magazine is ideal for advertising pur-poses. On the other hand, advertisers have the potential to corrupt and distort the media for their own purposes. The two sides of the issue will be examined more closely in a review of the relationship between media and advertisers later in this chapter.

Social and psychological effects

As the discussion above illustrates, advertising is vociferously criticized by members of the public and consumer advocacy groups. This is due, in part, to the high visibility and ubiquitous nature of the enterprise. Fur-thermore, our position as consumers, confronted by a daily barrage of ad-vertisements and perhaps frequently bewildered and frustrated by what we see and hear, prompts us to react negatively to the nature and content of commercial messages, rather than positively to their potential economic benefits (Black and Whitney 1983, 343). Much of this an-tagonism is based on the assumption that advertising is effective in per-suading us to behave or think in a predetermined way. As in the case of public affairs reporting (discussed in chapter 11), ideas about the efficacy of commercial communications depend upon one's view of human nature.

Again, the literature provides two dichotomous types of theories. One set of theories emphasizes the emotional view of human nature. In this view, simple, repeated exposure to an advertisement guarantees a response even if that response is not in the consumer's best interest. Ad-vertising appeals can manipulate us into spending, buying, or using products regardless of need. In opposition to this are theories based upon the idea that the consumer is sovereign, rational, and reasonable. These approaches take the view that consumers apply cognitive skills to filter the advertising messages they receive, gathering data to make informed, reasoned decisions.

Of course, a number of theories fall somewhere between these two extremes. Some analysts rely on Abraham Maslow's seven-stage hierar-chy of needs to explain how advertising can affect the individual. Ac-cording to Maslow (1970), individual needs form a hierarchy beginning with our need for physiological satisfaction, and for safety, and sys-tematically progressing through the need to belong and be loved, to be esteemed for our competence, the need for intellectual stimulation, for aesthetic enjoyment, and finally, for self-actualization. Individuals must satisfy their first need before they can attempt to fulfil the second, and so on. If we accept this premise and relate it to the effects of advertising, several points become clear: advertising may emphasize certain basic needs but it cannot change or create them; it can create public awareness of needs and suggest ways to satisfy them but it cannot guarantee their fulfilment; and it may influence inconsequential behaviour or beliefs, such as choosing one toothpaste over another, but it cannot independently alter significant behavioural patterns or values.

For advertising to influence our decisions, certain factors other than the content or nature of the message itself are involved. Advertising is a communication process and like all communication requires that the receiver be exposed to the message, attend to it, and interpret it as intended. Because advertising is a special sort of message, it must also arouse awareness of a need for the product, service, or idea. The ability of any commercial message to do all this is mitigated by several variables, both internal and external to the receiver. All or most of the following variables must complement one another if the message is to have the intended effect:

1. the intensity, size, novelty, and context of the message

2. the credibility, suitability, or attractiveness of the source of the message

3. the degree to which the message fulfils the information requirements of the receiver

4. the degree to which the message conforms to the receiver's pre-existing attitudes, value system, and lifestyle

5. the degree to which the message is reinforced by peers, family, and people who may personally influence the receiver's opinions and decisions.

If advertisers address the right audience with a well-planned, fully researched, and effectively presented campaign that offers an honest and direct message, their chances of having an impact are maximized but not guaranteed. Moreover, while advertising may successfully persuade an individual to try a product or service, it cannot necessarily secure repeat business. Jack Engel (1980, 51) concludes that "by and large, people believe the advertising they see and hear. If they did not, they would cripple business. But there is public resistance." Black and Whitney (1983, 322) are somewhat more circumspect in their conclusions, delineating distinct parameters for the effects of advertising: "Advertising is unsurpassed as a device for exposure—to call attention to, to introduce a product, concept, idea or candidate. Once exposure is achieved, the purchase, acceptance or election are in other undetermined hands hidden in the complexities of public opinion formation and change."

The mass media and advertising

The mass media and advertising have a mutually interdependent relationship. The media distribute advertising messages about products, services, or ideas to large audiences. Advertisers provide the media with the revenue required to reach and appeal to these same large audiences. Advertising was not always an integral part of the private media; it began as an incidental, supplementary feature as space allowed. As subscription and newsstand sales proved increasingly insufficient to defray the costs of production, newspapers, then magazines, and finally the electronic media turned to advertising as a means of paying their bills.

This practice appears to serve everyone's needs. Advertising provides the media with a large source of revenue which permits them to improve their production techniques, diversify their output, and remain independent of government subsidies. The advertisers get access to large markets to which they can direct their messages at substantially lower costs than one-on-one could ever hope to achieve. The audience enjoys a plethora of media offerings, free from potential government intervention and at a fraction of their real cost. Yet the relationship between media and advertisers is a complex one, involving both the specific requirements of the sponsors and media, and the perceptions and demands of consumers and regulators. Each of these factors is considered in turn.

Factors in media selection

As indicated in table 12.1, one of the ways to categorize advertising is by the medium used to disseminate the message. Advertisers examine the following factors to assess the advantages and disadvantages of each medium:[6]

1. *Cost*. The *absolute* or basic fixed cost refers to the cost of purchasing time or space in a medium. The *relative* cost is often most im-

portant, and is calculated by dividing the absolute cost by the expected audience size. It is usually measured in cost per thousand audience members (CPM). In addition, advertisers must consider the *production* cost of preparing the message itself. Production costs in some media, such as television, can be very substantial. Finally, the advertiser identifies other costs such as residuals and various taxes.[7]

2. *Scope.* The scope of any medium involves all those factors that describe the size and quality of the potential audience. The *penetration* level describes the overall size of the audience, whereas *coverage* (or *reach*) refers to the ability of the medium to reach all members of a specific audience. A metropolitan newspaper, for example, counts within its penetration rate all the households in its normal delivery area. Its coverage refers to the actual number of readers it reaches. The degree to which coverage is determined by the geographic, demographic, or psychographic (psychological) characteristics of the target audience, and thus avoids wasted exposure, is known as *selectivity*. Finally, scope incorporates the *impact* of the medium and the *attentiveness* of the audience.

3. *Production.* Each medium has specific production characteristics that make it more or less attractive to advertisers. *Flexibility* refers to the ease with which advertisements can be inserted, withdrawn, or altered. *Timing* and *frequency* determine when and how often an ad is run. *Production quality* describes the reproduction characteristics of the medium, the fidelity of colour, sound, and visual quality. The *exposure life* of the ad refers to the ability of the receiver to retain the message. Radio advertisements are fleeting, for example, but consumers can keep magazine ads for further reference or clip out coupons.

4. *Control.* The degree to which advertisers can control the message and its *environment*, in terms of placement and timing, varies with the medium selected. Some sponsors want to advertise during family television programs, for example, while other sponsors would choose a different context, or environment. Controlling environment is easier for television advertising, where sponsors buy time in specified program slots, than it is for newspaper advertising.

5. *Creative considerations.* Different media are better suited to some purposes than to others. Print, for example, permits long, complex messages, but television is more suitable for product demonstrations. Advertisers must consider the nature of their messages when selecting an appropriate medium.

6. *Acceptability.* The *editorial content* of a medium and its *reputation* among prospective audience members are examples of acceptability; they are quality-related factors that influence an advertiser's decision to use the particular medium. Acceptability may also involve *competitive considerations* such as the reach and content of other ads using the given medium and the advertising practices of competitors.

Table 12.3 provides a brief review of the main advantages and disadvantages of each medium. It is important to recognize, however, that the table is extremely general. It does not accommodate the differences between national radio or television networks and local stations, daily newspapers and weeklies, broadsheets and tabloids, or general interest magazines and specialized ones.

Making and placing ads

A single advertisement that communicates effectively is a product of combined talents. Writers, artists, musicians, actors, photographers, typesetters, printers, and other experts pool their skills to meet the advertiser's objectives. Deriving a new idea from existing information is a creative process but it also involves a process of elimination, or screening. An advertising agency may produce many ideas before determining just which one will most effectively convey the advertiser's message.

Making advertisements is both an art and a science and so too is placing them. Obviously, a medium has to be chosen before the ad is created since the method of creation varies for each medium and the result is radically different. Often a decision will be made to use several media, capitalizing on the strengths and cost effectiveness of each. Media purchasing is becoming a more sophisticated endeavour. Specialized computer programs provide massive amounts of data about audiences and costs. As well, the number of media has multiplied in recent years, resulting in fragmentation of the audience. Not only has there been

Table 12.3

Considerations in selecting a medium

Medium	Advantages	Disadvantages
Newspaper	• high local penetration • broad audience • literate, affluent audience • flexible • immediate and current • permits complex messages	• limited selectivity • poor pictorial reproduction qualities • low paper quality • little control over environment • limited ability to evoke an emotional response
Magazine	• specialized audiences • high-quality reproduction • powerful use of colour • long exposure life • some control of environment • permits complex messages • prestigious, since magazine advertising tends to be bought by wealthier sponsors • high pass-along readership	• costs vary • lacks immediacy • limited ability to evoke an emotional response • long lead time—the amount of time required to insert, withdraw, or alter an ad before publication
Radio	• specialized audiences for particular stations • loyal audience • portable • flexible • repetitive • emotional, dramatic • low production costs	• fragmented audience across all the stations; reaching the general population is very expensive • inattentive audience • fleeting message • uses sound only • little control over environment
Television	• mass audience • high penetration • high impact • uses both sight and sound • some control of environment • effective for demonstrations • prestigious • emotional, dramatic	• expensive in terms of absolute and production costs • inattentive audience • long lead time • limited length • intrusive

Table 12.3, continued

Medium	Advantages	Disadvantages
Direct mail	• inexpensive • highly selective • high-quality reproduction • complete control of environment • personalized • measurable • permits complex messages	• no editorial content to attract or hold audience • junk mail image

a proliferation of traditional media choices, as new magazines, newspapers, and radio and television stations enter the market, but new advertising opportunities, such as giant television screens in stadiums, are constantly appearing. Compounding the already complex process of media selection are audience defences—for example, the use of VCRs to tape television programming and then delete the commercials. The processes of creating and placing ads reinforce one another. The job of the advertising agency is to marry the processes in the best interests of the advertiser.

Revenues

Table 12.4 illustrates the manner in which advertising revenues have been shared in the past thirty years among the media under discussion. Certain trends are readily apparent. Radio's share has remained relatively stable, hovering at about 10 percent. Television's share has experienced steady growth, almost doubling its percentage of the total available advertising revenue. Much of the increase has occurred at the expense of newspapers, which have lost over 6 percent. These changes are even more marked when measured in total dollars since the pool of available advertising revenue has increased substantially since 1960.

   The manner in which revenues are distributed among classes of advertisers also reveals an interesting pattern. About three-quarters of television's advertising revenues are generated by national advertisers; radio, on the other hand is primarily a local medium. Daily newspapers earn about 55 percent of their advertising revenue from local advertisers and about 25 percent more from the classifieds, which also tend to be local in nature. The pattern reflects the bias of each medium with respect to the geographic characteristics of its audience.

Table 12.4

Share of net advertising revenues (in percent)*

	1960	1970	1984**
Television	9.1	13.1	17.3
Radio	9.2	10.7	9.7
Daily newspapers	30.9	28.4	24.7
General magazines	3.8	2.5	4.4
Catalogues/direct mail	21.4	20.5	21.9

  * Columns do not total 100 percent because some categories have been omitted.
 ** 1984 figures are estimates.

Source: Task Force on Broadcasting Policy (1986, 384).

When we appreciate that advertising supplies two-thirds to three-quarters of newspapers' revenues, more than half for magazines, and almost all of the income for commercial broadcasting, the questions of control and influence of advertising over media take on considerable significance. What do advertisers expect in return for their much needed financial support?

Issues in advertising

The question of control

In general, advertiser influence is business related. Advertisers' desire to reach mass audiences with disposable incomes heightens the media's concern with circulation figures, ratings, and audience demographics.[8] In response to advertisers' priorities, the media favour entertainment over information and culture, established, centrist values over controversy, and tried-and-true formulas over innovative, experimental programming. The result is an increasing uniformity of media content.

Peter Sandman and his colleagues (1976, 129–33) argue that even if advertisers were ideologically neutral, their influence on content would be reflected in the media in at least four ways. Obviously, the advertisers have direct control of the content of the advertisements themselves, within the limits of legal proscriptions and media codes of ethics.

Second, they may also want to link advertising content to editorial content. Content that the media include to complement advertisements, and conversely, ads that are extensions of the content of programs and use the performers from those programs, both fit this category. Articles about skiing, for example, are often accompanied by ads for ski resorts or equipment. These combinations are often called advertorials. An example of extending program content is found in a series of commercials that featured the characters "Blake" and "Krystle" from the television show *Dynasty*, selling their own lines of cologne. Ads disguised as news stories also link editorial and advertising content.

Third, advertisers want media content to enhance their image or that of their products. This sort of influence is usually exhibited by a television show or movie using a company's product or service in the story line or by the media moving ads if they are inappropriate to editorial content. An example of the former is a scene from the television show *Dallas* that showed a box of Pampers diapers in the corner of the nursery. An example of the latter is the standing arrangement that most airlines have with the media that all their ads be withdrawn if the editorial content includes an air disaster, whether fact or fiction. There is a danger that this sort of influence may overstep inconsequential lines, if news stories revealing unfavourable information about advertisers are glossed over or omitted. Concern has been expressed, for example, that the large amount of oil company advertising in the media tends to encourage the media to take a soft approach to criticism of the oil industry. Some news stories about the industry even border on boosterism.

Finally, advertisers want to avoid any controversy in editorial content in order to ensure that their products or services are not linked to the debate and that the audiences of their messages are in receptive moods. This may encourage the media to offer inoffensive stories over contentious ones.

Although advertisers' influence appears to be more reactive than active, it has a direct bearing on all that we see, hear, and read in the various media. It has encouraged the practice of market-survey journalism, in which the media pinpoint advertisers' markets and gear their content to attract that audience, and has fostered the development of homogenized media. There can be no doubt that together, advertising and the media have influenced the way we live.

For the most part, advertisers are reluctant to acknowledge their ability to control or influence the media, but they are not so reticent about revealing what they see as clear examples of their absolute lack of power. Keith McKerracher, as president of the Institute of Canadian Advertising, told the Royal Commission on Newspapers (Canada 1981, 73),

> And you know, it's the view of the industry that we have absolutely no influence at all. And as a matter of fact, we often wish we did, because we believe that to a large extent, journalists in general—and I am not talking about newspaper journalists, I am talking about all journalists in all media, and most particularly younger ones—are extremely anti-business and hesitate not one whit in biting the hand that feeds them.

The debate about who has the power, influence and control may be moot, however, since media owners and advertisers often share ideological convictions.

The question of cultural impact

Advertising has been accused of altering the predominant value systems and lifestyles of those cultures in which it operates. While few would deny advertisers the right to communicate information about products, services, or ideas, many are concerned that the glossy, sophisticated, and persuasive techniques of advertising have prompted changes, not all of which are positive, in society's view of itself.[9]

Recognition of advertising's ability to "stamp... its imprint all over the world" (UNESCO, International Commission for the Study of Communication Problems 1979, 37) has fuelled the New World Information and Communication Order (NWICO) debate discussed in chapter 2. The International Commission for the Study of Communication Problems was established by UNESCO in 1976 and in its deliberations noted the increasingly important influence of advertising: "Advertising must be counted as one of the more important forces in our present world. It is becoming a factor to be reckoned with on the international level, since those few countries providing the major part of advertising in the world can have a strong commercial/cultural impact on the large majority of other countries" (UNESCO, International Commission 1979, 37).

As advertising becomes increasingly global in scope, host nations become more concerned about the potential for foreign or multinational advertising to distort domestic economic and cultural conditions. This fear is especially prevalent in less developed nations, which view advertising in the same way as they view other foreign communication content—as a mechanism to ensure their continued political, economic, and cultural domination by the developed countries of the Western world. As a form of electronic colonialism, transnational advertising is subject to four general criticisms (Kochevar 1982, 39–53):

1. Advertising can inhibit the development of indigenous industries and thereby damage overall economic development. It also tends to reduce competition in a developing industry. Large, well-financed foreign interests can afford to absorb initial losses in their efforts to secure new markets. Eventually, the smaller or infant domestic manufacturers are forced out through bankruptcy, merger, or takeover. Many nations argue that this constitutes direct interference with their sovereign right to determine their own internal economic plans, and view such intervention as totally unacceptable.

2. Multinational or foreign advertising induces developing nations to use their limited resources inefficiently. It creates an artificial demand for unnecessary goods and services and thereby encourages inappropriate consumer behaviour. Scarce resources are sometimes diverted from capital expenditures that could otherwise promote domestic economic development, to the fleeting but potentially powerful images of advertisements, which foster increased economic dependency.

3. Multinational and foreign advertising has a negative impact on domestic media systems. By encouraging the exhibition or publication of material that promotes foreign behavioural patterns and values, advertising furthers its own end. As the media realize that foreign content brings with it the financial rewards of foreign advertisers, they become corrupted. Indigenous creative talent is forced out of its own media system, heightening sociocultural dependency.

4. The economic, technological, social, and cultural dependency that multinational and foreign advertising creates is not only disruptive but also humiliating. It promotes stereotypes, insults the intelligence, presents false claims, and fosters colonialism. Under these conditions, advertising can have only negative consequences for individuals, and their societies and cultures.

As Kochevar explains, it does not matter whether or not these claims can be substantiated. Because many people believe them to be true, they distrust or even hate advertising, the multinational corporations that sponsor it, and the home nations of those firms:

> Advertising is mass communication designed to inform people about products and encourage their consumption. It is intended to return short-term competitive advantages to its sponsors. If it leads to hatred of international business and the United States (or Japan), then it is an even bigger problem than the critics claim. It may not matter whether advertising really has any negative effects. If angry people think it does, the consequences could be very important indeed (Kochevar 1982, 53).

The consequences to which Kochevar refers are diverse; terrorism, vandalism, and trade protectionism are all possible negative effects.

The question of taste

Because the question of taste is a subjective one, dependent upon each individual's political, social, cultural, religious, or moral perspective, it is highly variable, and difficult to examine in a logical manner. What one person finds offensive may be acceptable to others; what is inappropriate to one medium may be suitable for another; what appears as improper in one decade may be entirely within the bounds of propriety in the next.

Advertisers usually respect the predominant mores of their societies, since they recognize that they cannot sell their products if their messages offend their audiences. Nevertheless, advertising, and the media carrying it, frequently come under attack by groups, organizations, and individuals who find the messages offensive. Criticisms are generally directed towards four different aspects of advertising: the nature of the product itself, because of either the consequences of using the product (e.g., cigarettes), or the reasons for using it (e.g., hemorrhoid salve); the techniques or strategies used to communicate the message (e.g., use of sexual or violent images); the perpetuation of stereotypes (e.g., in race, ethnicity, and gender); and the intrusive, excessive, repetitious nature of the enterprise itself.

Most of these concerns have been addressed to varying degrees by government regulation and industry codes of ethics, but they must compete with other societal values. The right of individuals to freedom from exposure to unwanted, unacceptable, inappropriate, or offensive messages must be balanced against the personal right to information and the rights of the advertisers and the media to communicate.

The question of advertising to children

The issue of advertising directed towards children is particularly relevant to television. Those who oppose the advertising argue that it promotes unacceptable values, that children do not understand the selling purposes of advertising, and that they cannot properly evaluate advertising messages. Supporters claim that advertising to children presents no real problems since it is parents, not children, who make the purchasing decisions. (One can only assume that these people have never been subject to a child's persistent pleas for a toy or breakfast cereal advertised on Saturday morning television.)

Although the research is not conclusive, evidence indicates that children, especially those between the ages of five and twelve, show a great deal of variation in their viewing behaviour (Banks 1980, 52; United States, National Science Foundation 1977). Some children are very highly influenced by TV, a problem that may be exacerbated by two factors. First, much merchandising is really included in the children's programming itself. Cartoon characters are reincarnated as stuffed toys, dolls, and assorted accessories. This makes it difficult for children to distinguish between programs and advertising. The second factor is a relatively recent phenomenon. Interactive programming permits children to participate actively in the television show that they are watching. With the aid of computerized devices that attach to the television and its cable system, children can respond to questions, influence the action, and receive feedback. The practice not only heightens the difficulty of differentiating advertising from editorial content, but it also prevents children from participating in the programming without the advertised product.

While some critics support a total ban on advertising directed towards children, Canadian regulations vary. The CRTC requires all stations to adhere to the *Broadcast code for advertising to children* as a condition of licence. In addition, the CBC has its own regulations which prohibit all children's advertising in or adjacent to its children's programming, and Quebec has banned all advertising directed at children thirteen years of age or younger.

The *Broadcast code for advertising to children* was developed by the Canadian Advertising Advisory Board. It is administered by the Advertising Standards Council and stipulates a number of conditions. All advertising must be factual, indicate real size, note if assembly is required, and present results that children may reasonably attain by themselves. No subliminal advertising is permitted.[10] Advertisements may not minimize price, emphasize the premium over the product (e.g., the bubblegum in the cereal box), or urge children to buy the product. No well-known person, puppet, or cartoon character may endorse a product, and all claims must be substantiated. No ads for drugs, medicine, vitamins, or products not intended for children are permitted. In addition, any single product may be advertised only once per half hour and advertising must be limited to four minutes out of every thirty.

The code pertains to all advertising directed at children under twelve. It represents an acknowledgement by advertisers and the media that children are a special sort of audience since they may not be able to tell truth from fantasy. It is therefore incumbent on the media and its sponsors to refrain from exploiting children's confusion by presenting exaggerated claims and creating unreasonable expectations.

The question of regulation

The issue of regulating advertising is akin to the issue of regulating media. How much regulation is necessary? Who regulates? How? When does regulation in the public interest infringe upon the property and communication rights of advertisers and media? The issue is made even more complex by the number of governments, regulatory authorities, and industry associations that issue regulations and guidelines for advertisers in Canada. Yet regulation of advertising is considered to be necessary since abuses can have serious consequences for consumers, competitors, the media, and the advertisers themselves. False or misleading advertising tarnishes the reputation of all advertisers.

The Combines Investigation Act is the most comprehensive federal legislation with respect to advertising. It is designed to protect business from unfair competition by prohibiting misleading or false representations, providing prescriptive guidelines for content, testimonials, tests, pricing, and labels, holding advertisers liable for the content of the ads, and defining the penalties for breaching the law. In addition, the federal government has enacted several other pieces of legislation to address more specific aspects of advertising:

1. Broadcasting Act. The act concerns the nature of advertising on the broadcast media and the amount of time allotted to it.

2. Consumer Packaging and Labelling Act. The act covers both prepackaged products and packaging, labelling, selling, importing, and advertising products.

3. Criminal Code. The code deals with lotteries, contests, trademarks, prohibitions against forgery, and advertising some products and services.

4. Food and Drug Act. The act covers standards for food and drug advertising.

5. Income Tax Act. The act pertains to deductible advertising expenses.

6. Textile Labelling Act. The act refers to labelling, selling, importing, and advertising fabrics and fibres.

7. Weights and Measures Act. The act establishes requirements for use of authorized weights and measures.

This brief list is not exhaustive. Federal legislation also includes copyright and trademark protection acts; custom, tariff, and excise legislation; and laws governing election advertising, the use of both official languages, and advertising hazardous products, meat, and fertilizers.

In addition, all of the provincial governments have used their jurisdiction over property and civil rights to enact legislation governing advertising within their provinces. Quebec has perhaps the most restrictive legislation, while most other provinces have statutes similar in nature to the federal Combines Investigation Act and many have passed laws to tax various sorts of advertising. In total, there are more than a hundred federal and provincial statutes and numerous regulations governing advertising in this country. Advertisers, and the media that carry their ads, must be aware of all those that apply. A formidable task!

Advertisers and the media have also employed self-regulation in their attempts to pre-empt government intervention and adopt more flexible guidelines. The Canadian Advertisers Advisory Board was established in 1957 to develop and administer advertising codes, resolve complaints, and serve as a consultant to the industry and governments. It has developed guidelines for advertising cosmetics, toiletries, non-prescription drugs, feminine hygiene products, food, and horticultural products. The *Broadcast code for advertising to children* has been adopted by the CRTC as a legal measure, and the Board's *Canadian code of advertising standards* sets high standards for truth, accuracy, and good taste. In addition to observing direction from these self-regulatory bodies, specific groups of advertisers have also established their own guidelines for promoting their particular products. Canadian distillers, for example, have developed a code of ethics for advertising alcoholic beverages, which prohibits the encouragement of abuse.

The media, too, have attempted to regulate themselves and their advertisers. Not only do they endorse the Canadian Advertisers Advisory Board's codes and guidelines, but some media have developed their own as well. The CBC has a very extensive advertising policy which requires that all ads be previewed and approved before they are aired. The policy prohibits any advertising of a controversial or offensive nature. Representatives of the CTV, Global, and TVA networks established the Telecaster Committee in 1972. Although not as strict as the CBC, the Committee does require prior clearance of ads.

Given the number and range of legislative enactments, official regulations, and self-imposed guidelines it is difficult to understand how any advertisements could be offensive or misleading. Yet there will always be the occasional unacceptable or false ad that slips through. When this happens, the advertising associations are the first to recommend that such action be reported to them. Only then can they act upon the matter. As has already been noted, most advertisers recognize that a public that tunes them out or does not believe anything they see or hear in an ad is of no value. Moreover, they accept the scepticism of consumers as reasonable and for this reason, most adhere to the legislative and self-determined regulations. Failure to do so not only leads to legal penalties but also makes for bad business.

Summary

This chapter has examined advertising, reviewed the theories about its economic, social, and psychological impact, analysed the relationship between the media and advertising, and identified some of the issues inherent to that relationship. Four conclusions can be drawn from the discussion:

1. Advertising is generally accepted as a necessary and legitimate undertaking in modern society.

2. Although it is not a medium, advertising is a critical element in our mass media system, providing both content and financial support.

3. The financial support that advertisers offer the media has the potential to threaten media independence and subvert their cultural influence.

4. Conversely, that same financial support enables the media to remain independent of political power sources and also provides the revenues necessary to produce and distribute a rich array of media fare at relatively low cost to the consuming public.

Notes

1. Canada's entry into the modern advertising business came later than that of many Western nations. The first printed handbill dates back to England in the late fifteenth century, and the first advertisement in an English newspaper was placed in 1625.

2. Bovée and Arens (1982) base their definition on that provided by Gamble (1970, 4).

3. A vivid example of this amalgamation mania is the rise of Saatchi and Saatchi PLC from a "basement operation" in 1970 to one of the world's largest advertising-agency holding companies, with offices in eighty countries by 1987 (*Business Week* 1987, 60).

4. The federal government is the country's largest advertiser. It spent $75 million on advertising in 1986.

5. The ethnic media represent another special case. The term ethnic refers to print and broadcast media not geared to the English- or French-speaking Canadian but to, for example, Hindu, Spanish, Portuguese, and Chinese

Canadians. The ethnic media are becoming significant in Canada, as the number and variety of television, radio, and print outlets increases. The federal government, through the Secretary of State, has recognized the existence and function of these media in its attempts to reach specified audiences.

6. For a more detailed analysis, see Bovée and Arens (1982, 468–87) and Wright et al. (1984, 180–90).

7. Some provinces apply a tax to all advertising. The federal government allows businesses to deduct advertising as a legitimate business expense provided that it meets the criteria stipulated in the Income Tax Act. The exemption has not, however, applied to advertising by Canadian businesses in foreign media if it is an attempt to reach Canadian consumers. This provision was designed to encourage Canadian firms to advertise in the domestic media, a protection for the advertising base of Canadian media that has been eliminated under the Free Trade Agreement.

8. It is important to note that high ratings alone are insufficient to attract advertiser support. *The Lawrence Welk Show*, a very popular American television variety show during the 1960s and early 1970s received remarkably high and stable ratings while it was aired. It was cancelled by the network, however, because of insufficient advertiser support. Welk's large and faithful audience was composed primarily of the oldest third of the population, a group with little disposable income.

9. Critics of advertising frequently point to its tendency to debase language by ignoring the rules of grammar, punctuation, and spelling. The degree to which slogans and buzzwords have become part of our vocabulary indicates the unconscious but pervasive nature of advertising's influence.

10. Subliminal advertising consists of messages transmitted below the threshold of normal perception. As a result, the receiver is not consciously aware of the message. Examples include sexual symbols "hidden" in a photograph of ice cubes in a drink and messages flashed across the screen so quickly that they are only subconsciously noted. For more information, see Packard (1957).

References

Advertising Age. 1987. World's top 50 ad agency groups in 1986. 11 May, pp. 60, 63, 74–75.

Banks, S. 1980. Children's television viewing behaviour. *Journal of Marketing* 42(2): 48–55.

Black, J. and F.C. Whitney. 1983. *Introduction to mass communication*. Dubuque: Brown.

Bouchard, J. 1980. *Differences*. Montreal: Les Editions Heritages.

Bovée, C.L., and W.F. Arens. 1982. *Contemporary advertising*. Homewood: Irwin.

Business Week. 1987. Is the new, improved, giant economy-size Saatchi really better? 21 December, p. 60.

———. 1988. Madison Avenue is singing "O Canada." 12 September, p. 92.

Canada. Royal Commission on Newspapers. 1981. *Report*. Ottawa: Supply and Services.

Canada. Task Force on Broadcasting Policy. 1986. *Report*. Ottawa: Supply and Services.

Engel, J. 1980. *Advertising: The process and practice*. New York: McGraw-Hill.

Financial Post. 1987. Ad companies losing with trend to global marketing. 19 October, p. 11.

Gamble, F.R. 1970. *What advertising agencies are—What they do and how they do it.* 7th ed. New York: American Association of Advertising Agencies.

Globe and Mail. 1987. Global mergers transform Madison Ave. 19 September, p. B1, B3.

Kleppner, O., T. Russell, G. Verrill, and B. Collins. 1984. *Advertising procedure.* Cdn. 8th ed. Scarborough: Prentice-Hall.

Kochevar, J.J. 1982. International advertising: The American and Japanese experiences. *KEIO Communication Review* 3(March): 39–53.

Marketing. 1988. Canada's top 100. 12 December, p. 23.

Maslow, A.H. 1970. *Motivation and personality.* New York: Harper and Row.

Packard, V. 1957. *The hidden persuaders.* NY: Pocket Books.

Sandman, P.M., D.M. Rubin, and D.B. Sachsman. 1976. *Media: An introductory analysis of American communication.* 2d ed. Englewood Cliffs: Prentice-Hall.

Stanley, R.E. 1982. *Promotion: Advertising, publicity, personal selling, sales and promotion.* 2d ed. Englewood Cliffs: Prentice-Hall.

UNESCO. International Commission for the Study of Communication Problems. 1979. *Final report.* Paris: UNESCO.

United States. National Science Foundation. 1977. *Research on the effects of television advertising on children.* Washington: National Science Foundation.

Wright, J.S., W.L. Winter Jr., S.K. Zeigler, and P.N. O'Dea. 1984. *Advertising.* 1st Cdn. ed. Toronto: McGraw-Hill Ryerson.

CHAPTER *13*

THE MEDIA
AND THE LAW*

*T*o comprehend the legal regulation of mass communication in Canada, one must be aware both of the sources of Canadian law and of the branches that are particularly applicable. Like the United States, Australia, and several other former colonies of England, Canada acquired a common law system by inheritance.[1] The phrase "common law" here means a system based on the decisions of judges; this contrasts with systems based on Roman law, which usually employ a detailed, written code. Today in Canada, although sources of law other than judicial decisions have become increasingly important, the legal system continues to be described as a common law system. Judges effectively make law as they apply established, general legal principles to decide specific cases. Additional general principles may then be derived from the judicial reasoning in support of such decisions, and courts may apply these principles in future cases.

This chapter was written by Peter Mercer, Dean of the Faculty of Law at the University of Western Ontario.

Judicial decisions have been a preponderant source of law in disputes where the matters at issue involve the relationship between private individuals, whether persons or corporations. Most communication law issues, however, do not come within the domain of private law. Instead, legal regulation of mass communication in Canada is primarily a matter of public law, concerned not with the resolution of private disputes between individuals but with the relationship between the individual and the state and broader questions of social policy.

Under the broad heading of public law are the three major branches: criminal law, constitutional law, and administrative law. The first of these is of relatively minor importance to mass communication in Canada, although theft of broadcasting or telecommunication services is recognized as a separate offence in Canadian law. Constitutional law is more important to Canadian mass communication, both because it allocates regulatory power to the federal and provincial levels of government and because it establishes certain fundamental rights and freedoms accorded under the Charter of Rights. It is administrative law, however, and its concern with the relationship between the individual and the state as regulator, which is most significant. "Communication law," focussing on administrative decisions and legislation related to the regulation of broadcasting and telecommunication, is a specialized category of administrative law.

The genesis of public law is legislation, either in the form of federal or provincial statutes or in its secondary yet more significant form of rules and regulations. Rules and regulations are created by persons or bodies which have been delegated the authority to do so by statute. In Canada, the dominant institutional role in broadcasting and telecommunication regulation is played by the Canadian Radio-television and Telecommunications Commission. The CRTC has the statutory power and responsibility not only to promulgate regulations but also to investigate and prosecute their breach.

This chapter examines the division of legal control over mass communication in Canada and the application of the Charter of Rights and Freedoms in this field. It goes on to review the development of broadcasting regulation from a legal standpoint. Finally, the chapter explores the current state of communication law in Canada, with special reference to the powers of the CRTC, the Free Trade Agreement, and copyright laws.

The division of powers in mass communication

In 1930, in *Re regulation and control of radio communication in Canada (Radio reference)*, the Supreme Court of Canada had the following question referred to it by the federal Cabinet: "Has the Parliament of Canada jurisdiction to regulate and control radio communication, including the transmission and reception of signs, signals, pictures and sounds of all kinds of means of Hertzian waves, and including the right to determine the character, use and location of apparatus employed?" The resolution of this question depended on judicial interpretation of the British North America Act of 1867 (now called the Constitution Act, 1867), Canada's central constitutional document. Specifically, the Court had to decide whether such regulatory power was within the legislative authority of the Parliament of Canada under one of the headings in section 91 of the Constitution Act, 1867 or, alternatively, a subject of exclusive provincial legislation within the classes enumerated in section 92.

A majority of the Supreme Court of Canada held that radio communication was subject to federal authority. Since radio waves cannot be confined within a single province, radio could not be a "local matter" under section 92. Indeed, regulation of radio communication was found to be of sufficient national importance that it came under federal jurisdiction as necessary to "Peace, Order and Good Government," a clause in the section 91 preamble.

Two of the five Supreme Court of Canada Justices dissented in *Radio reference*, expressing the view that Parliament's jurisdiction could not be exclusive because a receiving antenna could be considered a "local work" and therefore within the jurisdiction of the provinces. Nevertheless, on final appeal to the Judicial Committee of the Privy Council, the argument was rejected unequivocally:

> The argument of the Province really depends on making . . . a sharp distinction between the transmitting and the receiving instrument. In their Lordships' opinion this cannot be done. Once it is conceded, as it must be, . . . that the transmitting instrument must be so to speak under the control of the Dominion, it follows in their Lordships' opinion that the receiving instrument must share its fate. Broadcasting as a system cannot exist without both a transmitter and a receiver. . . .

Their Lordships have therefore no doubt that the undertaking of broadcasting is an undertaking "connecting the Province with other Provinces and extending beyond the limits of the Province".... A divided control between transmitter and receiver could only lead to confusion and inefficiency.

The Judicial Committee of the Privy Council therefore affirmed the majority judgment of the Supreme Court of Canada.

The continuing importance of the *Radio* case can be seen in the 1978 Supreme Court of Canada decision in *Capital Cities Communications v. C.R.T.C.* This case began with an application by three cable television licensees to the CRTC to have their licences amended. As part of their basic service they carried American television signals and they wished to delete the commercial messages from these signals and substitute their own. A number of the American television stations affected were permitted to represent their case to the CRTC, but the Commission granted the request to delete the commercial messages after imposing a condition that only public service announcements could be substituted. The American stations ultimately appealed on a number of questions, two of which had a constitutional dimension. First, was the Broadcasting Act ultra vires, or beyond the legislative authority of, the Parliament of Canada in authorizing the CRTC to license and regulate program content carried by CATV systems located wholly within provincial boundaries? Second, did the CRTC have jurisdiction under the Act to regulate cable systems that receive and distribute television signals?

On the first question, the American television stations argued that although exclusive federal jurisdiction should apply to the reception of television signals at the antenna, any subsequent distribution within a province was a matter for that particular province. This argument, which would have limited the effect of the *Radio reference* case on the basis that the Hertzian waves end at the antenna of the cable distribution systems, was rejected outright by a majority of the Supreme Court of Canada. Speaking for the majority, Chief Justice Laskin stated:

The systems are clearly undertakings which reach out beyond the province in which their physical apparatus is located. . . .
The common sense. . . [which the Privy Council spoke of in the *Radio* case] seems to me even more applicable here to prevent a situation of a divided jurisdiction in respect of the same signals or programmes according to whether they reach

home television sets and the ultimate viewers through Hertzian waves or through coaxial cable. The fallacy in the contention ... of the appellants, is their reliance on the technology of transmission as a ground for shifting constitutional competence [to legislate in a particular case] when the entire undertaking relates to and is dependent on extra-provincial signals which the cable system receives and sends on to its subscribers.

The majority would also not accept the contention that Parliament could regulate only machinery and equipment and not program content:

To put the matter in another perspective, it would be as if an interprovincial or international carrier of goods could be licensed for such carriage but without federal control of what may be carried or of the conditions of carriage. The submission amounts to a denial of any effective federal legislative jurisdiction of what passes in interprovincial or international communication, whether by radio or television, and is in truth an invitation to this Court to recant from the *Radio* case. . . . Programme content regulation is inseparable from regulating the undertaking through which programmes are received and sent on as part of the total enterprise.

On the second question, the Supreme Court of Canada held that the CRTC had properly been delegated authority to regulate cable distribution systems under the federal Broadcasting Act. In the words of Chief Justice Laskin, "it is patent ... that a cable distribution system, at least one which receives signals from a broadcaster and sends them through the system, is a broadcasting receiving undertaking and is in that respect at least within the regulatory and licensing authority of the Commission."

The effect of such decisions has generally been to establish Parliament's undoubted jurisdiction to make laws governing the regulation, licensing, and control of television and radio communication. With respect to telecommunication, federal authority has been strengthened by the August 1989 decision of the Supreme Court of Canada in *CNCP Telecommunications v. Alberta Government Telephones*. CNCP applied to the CRTC, under the federal Railway Act, for an order directing AGT to permit interconnection of their two systems. This would have allowed

CNCP to offer telecommunication services in Alberta. The CRTC issued the order but AGT appealed to the Federal Court, claiming that, as a provincial telephone company, it was a local undertaking and did not come under federal telecommunication regulation. Both the Trial and Appellate divisions of the Federal Court rejected AGT's argument. Their decisions were based, not on the nature of the services, but on the evident operation of AGT's undertaking as an integral part of a national telecommunication system.

The Supreme Court of Canada clarified the jurisdictional question by unanimously upholding the Federal Court of Appeal ruling that AGT carries interprovincial telecommunication traffic and is therefore subject to federal laws. The effect is likely to be the standardization of telephone services across the country because the ruling authorizes the federal government to change the Railway Act, the law under which telecommunication is regulated. Currently, the Act covers some telephone services but not the provincially regulated companies in Atlantic Canada or the Prairie provinces.

The Charter of Rights and Freedoms

Freedom of expression

The Canadian Charter of Rights and Freedoms forms Part 1 of the Constitution Act, 1982. The Charter is part of the constitution of Canada and states that "anyone whose rights or freedoms, as guaranteed by this Charter, have been infringed or denied may apply to a court of competent jurisdiction to obtain such remedy as the court considers just and appropriate in the circumstances." One of those fundamental freedoms, set out in section 2(b) of the Charter, is "freedom of thought, belief, opinion and expression, including freedom of the press and other media of communication."

In Canada, there is relatively little regulation of the print media by government; with respect to broadcasting, however, there is a long-standing tradition of regulation. It is interesting to speculate whether the freedom of expression guaranteed under section 2(b) of the Charter may lead to the invalidation of certain features of broadcast regulation. So far, Canadian courts have dealt with issues of broadcast regulation under both the Canadian Bill of Rights and the more recent Charter of Rights and Freedoms but these judgments have not yet provided a proper analytical framework for determining the legal relationship between media regulation and freedom of expression.

The Charter is drafted so that a two-stage test must be applied to any question raised under it. It must first be determined whether an action infringes a section of the Charter. If so, a second test is applied, under the section 1 "saving provision," to determine whether the action, notwithstanding its infringement of the Charter, "can be demonstrably justified in a free and democratic society."[2]

Judicial interpretation of section 2(*b*) of the Charter as it relates to communication issues has been scant. Commentators have ignored many of the questions that arise under this section in this area of law. Instead, they have confined themselves to justifying any infringement of the Charter by providing section 1 "saving" arguments.[3] The first proposed justification for any CRTC infringement of the Charter is similar to the rationale for the "fairness doctrine" in the United States. The doctrine essentially balances two competing "freedom of expression" claims by recognizing that the freedom to express one's views in the marketplace is limited by the scarcity of airwaves and other media resources. Fairness may therefore require a limit on the use of such resources by the "owner," in favour of granting access to others with differing views. Although this concept has been discussed in Canada, it has not been specifically applied (Canada, Board of Broadcast Governors 1961). The second proposed justification for a Charter infringement is connected to the concept of harm. Legislators recognize that while freedom of expression is important in our society, some forms of expression are not beneficial for society as a whole. The most obvious of these are hate and obscenity messages. The question in this area is where to draw the line, on a subjective basis. Each society has its own standards, and as long as the CRTC applies community standards, its actions should be justifiable under section 1. Finally, an infringement of freedom of expression may be justified if it itself prevents an infringement of equality rights. These rights may be based on gender, religion, or race and, as in the United States, they are constitutionally protected.

Canadian content rules

One area in which arguments over freedom of expression might be raised is with respect to Canadian content rules. Under these rules, television broadcasters must carry 60 percent Canadian programming during a broadcast day; private stations must in addition carry 50 percent

Canadian programming during the prime-time evening period. The obvious challenge under section 2(*b*) of the Charter is that the Canadian content quota system restricts the freedom of expression of television broadcasters. Nevertheless, as Grace Westcott (1986) has noted, the Canadian content rules do not really regulate the content of programming since they "are defined not with reference to the intellectual or substantive content of programming, but rather to the proportion of Canadian creative elements that go into creating a program. This is a crucial distinction." Furthermore, as discussed below, the Canadian content rules are rooted in a nationalistic tradition that might in turn justify their being saved by section 1 of the Charter even if they contravened the freedom of expression guarantee under section 2(*b*).

Cable television "must carry" regulations

As set out in chapter 7, CRTC regulations prescribe the order of priority that cable licences must observe in distributing signals on basic cable television service. These "must-carry" rules have protected the position of local broadcasting stations by requiring that their signals be carried by cable operators in the same market.

In the United States, similar rules have been successfully challenged on the basis that they violate the guarantee of free speech set out in the First Amendment to the Constitution. In the 1985 case of *Quincy Cable T.V. Inc. v. Federal Communications Commission*, the U.S. Federal Appeals Court rejected the Federal Communications Commission (FCC) argument that the government interest in preserving local broadcasting was a sufficiently substantial justification for the rules. The FCC operates in the United States in a similar capacity to the CRTC in Canada. The question arises, of course, whether the same sort of challenge as the *Quincy* case could be successfully made in this country. This would depend on whether government interests and policies are sufficient to justify the must-carry rules despite the freedom of expression guarantee in the Charter. The history of broadcasting regulation in Canada suggests that the established bases of Canadian broadcast policy would permit a different result from that in the United States.

Canadian judicial decisions

Because the freedom of expression protections in the Charter and in the older Canadian Bill of Rights have not been the subject of a great deal of judicial comment, one can expect that Canadian courts will want to consider the American process of reasoning when they examine broadcast regulation in the future. The United States Supreme Court has frequently considered the extent to which the regulations of the Federal Communications Commission can be reconciled with First Amendment guarantees of free speech.[4]

Perhaps the most important pre-Charter decision in Canada is that of the Ontario Court of Appeal in *Re CFRB and Attorney General of Canada* (1973). There, a licensee for a Toronto radio station was charged with violating the Broadcasting Act, because the station broadcast a politically partisan program the day before a provincial election. The station challenged the prosecution on the grounds that section 28 of the Broadcasting Act, which prohibits partisan broadcasts on the day of or the day before an election, was ultra vires the Parliament of Canada and that it contravened the freedom of expression guarantee in the Canadian Bill of Rights. The Court of Appeal found that freedom of expression was not violated by section 28, since the restriction was limited in scope and was designed to support the democratic process by preventing last-minute statements which could neither be denied nor discredited in time before the election. Of more far-reaching importance for future Charter decisions was the Court of Appeal's consideration of the implications of the Bill of Rights. The Court was of the view that it was necessary to weigh the freedom of speech guarantee against both the requirements of the democratic electoral process and the regulatory function. The regulatory function included regulating scarce spectrum resources in order to "safeguard, enrich and strengthen the cultural, political, social and economic fabric of Canada."

The first important decision based on the Charter was rendered by the Federal Court of Appeal in the 1984 case of *New Brunswick Broadcasting Company Ltd. v. C.R.T.C.* The broadcasting company was the owner of a Saint John television station and was itself a wholly owned subsidiary of another company that published two daily newspapers in the television station's broadcasting area. In 1982, the federal Cabinet issued the *Direction to the CRTC on issue and renewal of broadcasting licences to daily newspaper proprietors*, which stipulated that the CRTC was not to issue broadcasting licences to anyone owning or controlling newspapers that were circulated in the broadcast area, unless there was an overriding public interest. The Saint John station's television licence was therefore renewed for a period only slightly in excess of two years, to allow the New Brunswick Broadcasting Company to arrange its affairs.

The company appealed to the Federal Court of Appeal, arguing first that the *Direction* itself was not authorized by the Broadcasting Act since it was really designed to regulate concentration of newspaper ownership; and second, that the *Direction* infringed the right of the company and the public to freedom of expression under section 2(*b*) of the Charter. The Federal Court of Appeal dismissed the appeal. Speaking for the Court, Chief Justice Thurlow said,

> While the policy stated in section 3 of the *Broadcasting Act* appears to govern and limit the objectives to be implemented by the CRTC, I do not think. . . that [the] policy is exhaustive of the purposes of the Act or that it limits the. . . reasons for which the powers of the Governor In Council [may be exercised] to prescribe classes of persons to whom broadcasting licences may not be granted. As I see it the power conferred . . . to issue directions precluding the issue of licences to particular classes of persons is exercisable by the Governor In Council for any valid reason of public policy, whether or not it is one expressed in section 3 [of the Broadcasting Act].

The Court actually went on to find that the *Direction* furthered the purpose of the Broadcasting Act, since the authority to decide who should be licensed to use radio frequencies, described in the Act as "public property," validly came within the meaning of "regulation and supervision" of all aspects of "the Canadian broadcasting system" (Canada 1968, s. 3(*k*)).

This line of reasoning was also applied to the company's complaint under the Charter. The Court found that the *Direction* did not amount to a denial of the freedom of expression in section 2(*b*) of the Charter, because the company's argument confused the Charter freedom with a right to use property, not itself protected in the Charter. In the words of the Court, the Charter gives "no right to anyone to use the radio frequencies which, before the enactment of the Charter, had been declared by Parliament to be and had become public property and subject to the licensing and other provisions of the Broadcasting Act."

In both the *CFRB* case and the *New Brunswick Broadcasting Company* case, the courts focussed on the need to regulate airwaves as public property as a justification for finding that the broadcast regulations did not infringe freedom of expression. Indeed, the history of Canadian broadcasting has given the public interest priority among the points that the law must consider.

The origins and development of the broadcasting system
Defensive expansionism, nationalism, and nation building

Prior to the establishment of public broadcasting by the Broadcasting Act of 1932, the Canadian broadcasting system had four major deficiencies. Interference from foreign stations resulted in a shortage of usable frequencies; many Canadians had no access to broadcasting service; programs were of poor or questic able quality; and American broadcast stations and programming dominated the Canadian broadcast environment (Beke 1970, 106–7). The concept of "defensive expansionism" (Spector 1976; Prang 1965) provided the rationale for a legislative response. Proponents of defensive expansionism contended that the state had a two-fold objective in assuming an active role in broadcasting regulation. It had to ensure the maintenance of Canadian political sovereignty and it had "to build a nation state that could assert its independence from both the mother country and the United States" (Aitken in Spector 1976, n. 3).

Although this explanation of government policy is tidy and credible, it is not the only key to understanding how the Canadian broadcasting system began and developed. The "emerging sense of national unity and purpose" (Spector 1976, n. 3) that sustained the policy of defensive expansionism is worthy of recognition in its own right. The distinction between the two concepts is alluded to in Graham Spry's description of the mood that prevailed in the 1930s: "The period in Canada after the recovery from the First World War . . . was a period not of nationalism in any narrow sense but of nationhood . . . not in opposition to or separation from others but in the realization of a national self" (Spry 1965). If the development of Canadian broadcasting is to be judged by accurate and reasonable standards, it should be recognized that early expansionist policy was not merely "defensive" but, in the broad and literal sense, "nationalistic."

A dual nationalist sentiment, cultural and economic, underlies many of the Canadian attitudes towards broadcasting. There is a traditional and almost universal agreement on the part of politicians and pundits that broadcasting holds great cultural and economic significance for

Canada's future. This is based on the assumption of inter-relationships among broadcasting, political sovereignty, economic independence, and a distinctive Canadian culture, itself seen as "a weak, fragile creature in need of stimulation from within and protection from without" (Black 1968). The choice of public over private enterprise as a vehicle for Canadian broadcasting was not a consequence of the prevailing political philosophy, therefore, but of this idea of nationalism.[5] One of the reasons elicited by Prime Minister R.B. Bennett for placing radio broadcasting under government control was to ensure that "national consciousness may be fostered and sustained and national unity still further strengthened" (Canada, House of Commons 1932, 3035). Even without analysing these nationalistic assumptions, of course, one may recognize that "national consciousness" cannot be objectively determined.

The Aird report

The history of Canadian broadcasting regulation begins with the report of the Royal Commission on Radio Broadcasting, otherwise known as the *Aird report*. The recommendations contained in the report were straightforward: in the best interests of the nation, broadcasting should be seen as a public service, and the stations providing such services should be owned and operated by a single national company. The report advised against any form of broadcasting employing direct advertising, and station time was to be made available for programs employing a limited amount of indirect advertising only until such time as broadcasting could be put on a self-supporting basis.

Although supporters of public broadcasting were heartened by the report, its recommendations met with several obstacles. The victory of the Conservatives under R.B. Bennett in the general election of 1930 raised doubts whether private commercial broadcasting, which had already existed without restriction in Canada for close to a decade, would be eradicated. After losing the election, the Liberals, who had previously been in favour of a public system, became more worried about the dangers of government control of radio. Finally, the government was reluctant to embark on new expenditures of public funds during a depression (Prang 1965).

In 1930, public-spirited professionals formed the Canadian Radio League to combat these impediments. Its success in rallying support for a public broadcasting system from diverse sectors of the Canadian public has been well-documented (Prang 1965). Not long after the inception of the League, and following on the heels of the *Radio reference* decision, the Conservative federal government enacted new legislation with the premise that government had exclusive control of radio. The 1932 Broadcasting Act created the Canadian Radio Broadcasting Commission and authorized it to acquire existing private stations, either with or without the consent of the owners. Provision was made for financing by parliamentary appropriations not to exceed the estimated revenue from receiving licences, private commercial broadcasting licences, and amateur broadcasting licences. In other words, the government would receive the licensing revenues and would give the equivalent funds to the CRBC. The Act therefore "provided a potential framework for a genuine public system" (Prang 1965).

Nevertheless, certain features of the new legislation, seemingly less important at the time, prevented this potential from being realized. Even though the Aird Commission and the Radio League "considered it indispensable to the successful functioning of a public broadcasting system" (Beke 1970), the Act did not create a public corporation with independent responsibility for the management of broadcasting; nor did it provide for the appointment of a voluntary board of governors with general responsibility for policy. The Canadian Radio Broadcasting Commission, consisting of three full-time members, was actually a department of government. It was appointed directly by the government and had responsibility for both management of the system and policy determination. Furthermore, the Act removed the $2.00 licence fee for individual radio sets, which left the system without adequate financing. This lack of financial means effectively prevented the Commission from nationalizing private broadcasters. Finally, the Act failed to abolish direct advertising, presumably in deference to manufacturers' claims (duly considered by the Aird Commission) that they would be unfairly disadvantaged if they were unable to compete with advertising carried on American stations and received in Canada.

Whether by inadvertence or design, the failure of the 1932 Act to preserve the integrity of the *Aird report* hindered the development of public broadcasting. Although some of the deficiencies were remedied in subsequent legislation, the continuing existence of internal contradictions in the law had the effect of keeping a major question alive: How might broadcasting be better regulated (Peers 1979, 76)? Private broadcasters, who were originally to be withdrawn from the system, pursued this question until they were given legitimate and equal status a quarter of a century later.

Subsequent political influence and control

Even before the appointment of the Aird Commission, the manner in which the Liberal government exercised discretionary power over broadcasting caused political controversy.[6] Fears that the medium might be sullied by partisan politics gave rise to serious reservations about the efficiency of public broadcasting, even among its proponents. The fears proved to be well founded, and a large part of the history of public broadcasting in Canada is concerned with the problem of political interference, the scope of which was succinctly outlined in the *Fowler report*: "The dilemma is between the danger of political interference with an agency of public information and communications and the need to retain sufficient supervision and control to ensure that public moneys are wisely spent . . . [T]here is danger in having it run by a department of government where partisan interests could have an influence or might be thought to have an influence" (Canada, Royal Commission on Broadcasting 1957, 88).

The principles on which the Broadcasting Act of 1932 was ostensibly based were violated almost immediately, as people who had been known for their political activity were appointed to the Canadian Radio Broadcasting Commission. A scant four years later, irregularities in the 1935 election campaign prompted the appointment of a parliamentary committee to inquire into the administration of the 1932 Act. It reported that,

> Your Committee finds that during the last election there was serious abuse of broadcasting for political purposes and that lack of a proper control by the Commission was apparent. . . .
>
> We also find that credit was issued to political parties in direct violation of the rules of the Commission, which rules prescribe that all political broadcasts must be paid for in advance. Generally speaking from the evidence presented before your Committee we are forced to the conclusion that there was a loose administration of Commission affairs (Canada, House of Commons 1936, 3077).

The committee recommended that a new act be substituted, and that the direction of broadcasting be placed in the hands of a corporation with full control over "the character of all programs, political and otherwise, broadcast by private stations, and the advertising content thereof." The ideals that had founded the Aird Commission recommendations are starkly contrasted with the parliamentary committee's paramount concern to wrest broadcasting from the control of unwarranted political influences.[7] The Canadian Broadcasting Corporation (CBC) was established under a new Broadcasting Act effective on 23 June 1936.

The new legislation was more effective than its predecessor and gave the CBC a credibility and authority that the Canadian Radio Broadcasting Commission had lacked. CBC management was protected from partisan pressure by the creation of a board of governors, which not only managed the CBC but was also able to resist ministerial pressure and thus act as a buffer between the Corporation and Parliament.

Nonetheless, there was no magic in the mere act of creating a well-insulated public corporation. The extent and effect of political pressure on the administration, no less than the vitality of the public corporate form as a whole, depended on the individuals whose ideals, efforts, and abilities formed the substance and "personality" of the CBC. In fact, the 1936 Act had more structured controls than those of the earlier legislation, which firmly invested Parliament with ultimate supervisory powers. While it might be said that these controls gave greater independence to the newly created CBC by clearly defining the ambit of its powers, the continuous close supervision of CBC operations by Parliament over subsequent years is recognized as having badly hampered its effectiveness. CBC officials spent a disproportionate amount of time responding to cumbersome and often ill-informed inquiries emanating not only from Parliament, but also from the relevant ministry, the governor-in-council, public hearings, and specially appointed royal commissions.

The first royal commission to study the CBC was the Royal Commission on National Development in the Arts, Letters and Sciences, otherwise known as the Massey Commission. As chapter 6 noted, the Commission's investigation revealed that the CBC was "performing its duty satisfactorily, sometimes even admirably, in providing appropriate and varied programs." It found the CBC less admirable, however, in exercising its responsibilities of control (Canada, Royal Commission on National Development in the Arts, Letters and Sciences 1951). In particular, the Commission had two major criticisms of CBC administration: that the CBC was doing too little to enlighten the public adequately and properly about its policies, plans, and methods of operation; and that it was not ensuring that private stations lived up to their licence obligations. The Commission's report pointed out that "the original intention to expropriate these stations was not carried out. It was thought that they could render an important service to the public in providing a medium for local broadcasting, in giving local news and in other ways, including the development of local talent" (Canada, Royal Commission 1951, cited in Peers 1969, 447). The proper function of a local station, as the Commission understood it, was "to reflect the life and interests of the community, and to use and develop the local talent available." Many of the private stations made little effort to fulfil this function or operate in accordance with regulations.

The failure of the CBC to further its own interests in these two vital respects is of great significance when compared with simultaneous developments in the private sector. In the early years, private broadcasting was relatively disorganized and lacked financial stability but by the end of 1948, the assets of private broadcasters had grown to three times that of the public sector in an increasingly lucrative commercial market. With the organization of the Canadian Association of Broadcasters (CAB), private broadcasters began to seek and gain the support of certain important elements of the community, such as the Canadian Chamber of Commerce and its local counterparts.

From its inception, the CAB complained of unfair treatment at the hands of the CBC. Twice during the Massey Commission hearings, the CAB appeared to argue that since the CBC had not taken over the private stations as had been envisioned in 1932, and since many new private stations had been licensed, it could reasonably be contended that the establishment of the CBC had resulted not in one exclusive national system but in a new public system in addition to the private one. They protested against the regulation of private stations by the CBC, which they referred to as their "commercial rival," and without any specific complaint, demanded that the Act be rewritten "to provide for the regulation of all radio broadcasting stations, whether CBC or private owned, by a separate and completely impartial authority not associated in any way with the CBC" (Weir 1965, 251).

The Massey Commission's reply to the CAB was strongly on the side of public service:

> We cannot agree with their conclusions. The principal grievance of the private broadcasters is based, it seems to us, on a false assumption that broadcasting in Canada is an industry. Broadcasting in Canada, in our view, is a public service directed and controlled in the public interest by a body responsible to Parliament.... That they may enjoy any vested right to engage in broadcasting as an industry, or that they have any status except as part of the national broadcasting system, is inadmissible (quoted in Weir 1965, 252).

The Commission report recommended that control of the national broadcasting system continue to be vested in the CBC as a single body responsible to Parliament. The CAB, however, was undeterred in its efforts to bring about the creation of a separate regulatory body.

Many important changes took place during the late 1940s and early 1950s. The Conservative and Social Credit parties abandoned the position they had adopted at the time of the 1932 Broadcasting Act, and began supporting the concept of a separate regulatory board.[8] This change in political philosophy was undoubtedly fostered in part by the Liberal government's practice of broadcasting "non-partisan messages" to the Canadian public during the war and subsequent unwillingness to extend political time to the opposition after the 1940 election. Private broadcasters also began to receive growing support from the press. Initially, newspapers feared competition from broadcasting for advertising revenues and thus had supported a non-commercial system. The idea of a public system came into disrepute, however, as newspaper interests gradually became involved in broadcasting. By 1950, they owned, in whole or in part, 41 of the 119 private radio stations in Canada.

In contrast with the private sector's expanding revenues and low programming costs, CBC revenues remained tightly controlled even though the demands on expenditures increased.[9] For example, the CBC, as the provider of public service in national broadcasting, was required to relieve the financial pressure being exerted on small community stations. Radio budgets tightened with the growth of television and this led to the development of large, regional private concerns. Because advertisers tended to patronize only the top twenty radio stations, smaller operations began to be squeezed out. The owners of the regional stations, whose interests lay in maximizing their coverage and earnings, proceeded to reap an increasing proportion of revenues that would otherwise have been used to support community stations. The CBC was left to shoulder the responsibility of local service.

Again, it is clear that the CBC allowed the irresponsibility of many of the private stations to continue unchecked. Even though some stations failed to supply statements of their proposed program content and plan of operations, their licences were renewed, subject only to a notification that their failure to co-operate would be taken into account in making recommendations for the ensuing year: "It was always the next time. Indeed for forty years all licences have invariably been renewed, until possession of licences has become synonymous with a vested interest in fixed properties, that are now bought and sold and traded. . . . If a single licence was cancelled for non-fulfillment of obligations, the fact has yet to be revealed" (Weir 1965, 246).

The election of a Conservative government in 1958 resulted in new legislation to tackle the conflict between public and private broadcasting in Canada. The Broadcasting Act of 1958 went beyond previous recommendations for dealing with the dichotomy, to the point of departing from the concept of a single, unified system.

Legitimizing the private sector

Lester Pearson, speaking before the House of Commons about the proposed new legislation, recalled how the position of the Aird Commission towards private broadcasters, subsequently established by the early legislation, had been suspended:

> We must bear in mind that an essential and clearly recognizable feature of that system was that these private stations had no special rights of their own. They had a privilege granted to them . . . [O]ver the years we have perhaps begun to lose sight of the initially accepted doctrines of public control through a national system and of the vital necessity of maintaining and strengthening that system . . . [W]hat was once a privilege for private broadcasters has gradually become a vested interest and eventually has been invoked as a right, which, of course, it was not. . . . [T]hen the position of the

CBC, the public corporation, could be attacked on the grounds that the public agency was at the same time a judge and a competitor (*Hansard* 1958, 4048–49).

By creating two separate bodies, the BBG and the CBC Board of Governors, the Broadcasting Act of 1958 marked the culmination of the evolutionary process by which the status of private broadcasting finally came to be acknowledged.

The effect of the new legislation went beyond the mere creation of a dual system. In his speech to the House of Commons, Pearson presaged one of the dangers of the new arrangement when he added, prophetically, "The new BBG, because CBC program standards will likely be above the minimum prescribed, will tend to become a regulatory body for private stations only. . . . More and more then, this board may be concerned with private systems rather than the control and regulation of a national system" (*Hansard* 1958, 4049). CBC program standards and the financial position of the private stations combined to isolate the Corporation as the relatively static element within the system. The 1958 Act gave the private broadcasters new momentum while putting the CBC on the defensive.[10] Now the private broadcasters were "to take 'the upper hand' in defining the content and character of Canadian broadcasting."

Recent developments

The broadcasting model resulting from the 1958 Act operated on a frequently competitive basis. The BBG issued licences to new private stations and granted power increases to existing private stations in significant part on the rationale of balance with the CBC. Not only did the operation of this model favour the growth of private commercial broadcasters, but susceptibility to BBG attempts at regulation could at the same time be limited by the terms of statutory authority granted to the BBG. In 1959, for example, the BBG refused to allow a stock transfer from Baton Broadcasting to ABC. The companies rearranged the transaction as a purchase of debentures, a form of transfer outside the purview of the 1958 Broadcasting Act (Feldthusen 1986, 93). By 1961, the year in which the BBG approved the formation of the private CTV network, Graham Spry took this view of the Canadian broadcasting system: "It is not a system of national public ownership with local private stations, but a system of local private stations with a lesser public sector serving and subsidizing private stations. The private advertising sector is the dominant sector. The public service sector is the subordinate" (Spry 1961, 225).

In combination with the preference of the majority of Canadian viewers for American private stations, the structure of the Canadian broadcasting system has given a pre-eminent position to commercially sponsored broadcasting. Both the report of the Federal Cultural Policy Review Committee, 1982 (the Applebaum-Hébert Report) and the report of the Task Force on Broadcasting Policy, 1986 (the Caplan-Sauvageau Report) describe this situation in considerable detail.[11] The regulatory response has been modest, largely because there is little regulatory scope for affecting either the supply of American stations or the Canadian demand for American programming. Indeed, the CRTC has under-standably responded to the phenomenon of technological availability by allowing cable television companies in Canada to carry American sta-tions. As would be expected, American stations command an appreciably greater share of the audience as a result.

Cable television provides the backdrop for several issues of regula-tion and deregulation because of the many cultural and economic factors involved. It is not always clear, however, which factors are being con-sidered in any given regulatory decision. For example, the CRTC has given cable companies only limited program production opportunities, a decision that can be attributed to regulatory concern over potential con-flicts of interest, but has also been described as arising out of desire to protect on-air broadcasters, especially local on-air broadcasters, from economic competition (Babe 1976). Other regulatory powers, such as the CRTC's power to authorize alteration of signals—an increase in signal strength, for example—can be used to further economic or cultural policies, or both.

The realities of commercial broadcasting and American program-ming are no less real on the international scene than in Canada. By 1966, over fifty countries had television systems controlled in whole or in part by private interests under state supervision and commercial advertising was carried by the vast majority of the world's ninety-five television sys-tems.[12] By 1985, this trend had become well entrenched in Western Europe:

> American and local commercial interests form a temporary al-
> liance which is well financed and relentless in its lobbying ef-
> forts. Success in one country immediately jeopardizes a state

monopoly in a bordering country. Pirate stations are financed. Satellite broadcasting, itself a part of the planned operation discussed above, is introduced. The British commercial satellite channel, Sky Channel, reaches two million viewers through 106 cable systems in Europe. It broadcasts primarily American programs, exclusively in English (Macdonald 1985).

The plethora of American programming, as compared to domestic, is one of the inevitable results of commercial broadcasting. As discussed in chapter 8, the regulatory strategy to increase the quantity and quality of domestic programming on Canadian stations has been to impose Canadian content quotas on domestic broadcasters. It is doubtful, however, that the economic impulse of private broadcasters to fill peak viewing periods with American programming can be overcome by regulatory initiatives, despite the CRTC's recent proposal to require minimum spending levels in specific program categories as a condition of renewing private broadcasting licences.

On the other hand, the CRTC appears to believe that a flourishing private broadcasting industry will generate Canadian programming. Commentators have noted the extent to which private broadcasters continue to earn excellent profits while they are protected from foreign and domestic competition. The Caplan-Sauvageau Report (Canada, Task Force 1986, 38–39) was remarkably explicit on this point:

> The CRTC protects the industry for its own sake, as an end in itself. . . . The CRTC believes that broadcasting renders a legitimate benefit to the domestic economy with respect to employment, trade balances and foreign exchange investment, benefits which would naturally end were the Canadian system destroyed in head-to-head competition with the Americans.

The "capture theory" of regulation holds that incumbent private broadcasters can be *expected* to emerge as the prime beneficiaries of commercial broadcast regulation policy, since the regulatory mechanism has certain inherent limitations (Posner 1974). A well-financed and sophisticated participant in the marketplace has both the resources and the acumen to convince a regulator (perhaps with detailed supporting documentation) to see things its way. Given the present fascination with deregulation, one must therefore ask what results a regulatory structure is capable of generating. If regulation cannot prompt high-quality

Canadian programming or an increased number of Canadian productions, can a system with less regulation achieve the ends that politicians seem to desire?

The CRTC

As a statutorily authorized tribunal, the CRTC derives its authority, mandate, and jurisdiction from the Broadcasting Act. When broadcasting licences are issued, renewed, or transferred as a result of corporate reorganization, the CRTC applies a "significant and unequivocal benefits" test before granting or refusing the application. This procedure allows for a case-by-case approach to applications, rather than a rigid, inflexible standard. The test has three prongs. An applicant must persuade the CRTC that acceptance of the application will yield significant and unequivocal benefits to the community, that the application is beneficial to the Canadian broadcasting system as a whole, and that the application is in the public interest. The onus to prove these contentions is on the applicant.

Guiding principles have emerged as to what the CRTC feels is the broadcasting policy for Canada. First, it acknowledges that Canada must house broadcasters of different sizes. Second, concentration in any particular market is not an automatic bar to any licence application, as long as the objectives of the Act are met. Finally, media cross-ownership—ownership of newspapers, television stations, and/or radio stations in one market—does not create a problem as long as consumers are allowed access to the media and different points of view are provided to the community.

The CRTC appears to have absolute control over Canadian broadcasting, but a party to a CRTC decision may "appeal" to the federal Cabinet. This body is composed of ministers, each with a portfolio defining their responsibilities. The word "appeal" is used advisedly, because it invokes connotations of judicial process and legal rules. The process is actually more similar to a review, however, and is at the complete discretion of the minister of communications.

Rather than initially appealing to the entire Cabinet, a party first petitions the minister of communications. It is the responsibility of the minister to recommend a course of action to the Cabinet. After receiving a petition, the minister will research the issues and consult officials and staff. The minister may also receive representations from other interested parties at this stage. On deciding that the petition will fail, the minister will either advise Cabinet of that fact, or notify the parties. If, on the other hand, the minister decides to undertake a course of action based on the petition, he or she will prepare a Cabinet document outlining the issues raised and containing recommendations. This document is then affirmed or denied at a meeting of a Cabinet committee, or the whole Cabinet. No part of this process requires giving notice to other interested parties or providing the opportunity to be heard. Unlike a judicial proceeding, it is totally political.

The federal government also has the power to direct the CRTC. The proposed new broadcasting legislation would enable Parliament to give a direction on any matter, insofar as it relates to CRTC policy.

The current state of broadcast and telecommunication regulation

Although several federal statutes contribute to the structure of broadcast regulation in Canada, the 1968 Broadcasting Act remains the most important by far. It sets out the powers and functions of the CRTC respecting broadcasting, the purpose and operations of the CBC, and the *Broadcasting policy for Canada*. It is unlikely that Canadian broadcast policy will change fundamentally on the regulatory side in the near future, but certain trends are evident.

In the past, much attention was paid to promoting delivery of service but we can expect to see increasing pressure for better quality programming. Indeed, this is a major thrust behind the new broadcast legislation tabled in the House of Commons in late June of 1988. In order to raise the level of Canadian content, the government has stated its intention to promote a "carrot and stick" incentive for future broadcasters (*Globe and Mail* 1988). Under this plan, private broadcasters would be encouraged to exceed Canadian content quotas and fined a certain percentage of their gross revenues if yearly content levels are not met. The other major area of concern to be faced by the new broadcast legislation is changing technology. There is now no real scarcity of broadcast "resources" and individuals have access to sophisticated receiving equipment. As the methods of bringing broadcast signals into homes increase, the rationale underlying regulation and the feasibility of some features of the regulatory system will be brought under increased scrutiny.

In the telecommunication field, the Supreme Court of Canada's decision in the *Alberta Government Telephones* case is likely to have significant effects. At present there are more than fifty telecommunication carriers in Canada and they are regulated by more than a dozen boards and commissions at both the federal and provincial levels.[13] As discussed above, the Supreme Court has upheld the decision of the Trial and Appeal divisions of the Federal Court that the federal government has constitutional jurisdiction over telecommunication, despite a long history of provincial regulation. There is now much greater incentive for co-operation between the federal government and the provinces in an attempt to build a national telecommunication policy.

The Free Trade Agreement

The Canada–U.S. Free Trade Agreement contains a sectoral annex that deals with trade in services. It sets out special undertakings with respect to enhanced telecommunication and computer services, focussing mainly on access to and use of these services. The undertakings include agreeing not to discriminate between Canadian and American lessors of local and long-distance telephone service and of public data network services. Each party is also required to maintain existing access within and across the borders of both parties and to allow for provision of enhanced services through its basic telecommunication network. The annex also confirms existing Canadian and American telecommunication regulation and does not require either party to change its policy. It is unclear, however, whether provincial telecommunication regulations are covered by the annex. If they are, the federal government will be responsible for provincial compliance. Many actions of provincial companies, such as telephone companies, would be the subject of formal consultations and possibly arbitration between Canada and the United States.

The FTA also has ramifications for the broadcasting industry. On 1 January 1990, cable companies started paying for the right to distribute distant broadcast signals. This is provided for in article 2006, which holds that both parties are to provide copyright protection to owners of programs broadcast by distant stations and retransmitted by cable companies. The article reconfirms that when the original transmission of program signals was not intended for free, over-the-air reception by the general public, retransmission is only permitted with the authorization of the copyright holder. It also goes further, however, to establish that even when the original transmission of a program signal was intended for free, over-the-air reception by the general public, any retransmission, whether in altered form or merely non-simultaneous, is only permitted with the authorization of the holder of the program copyright. A copyright owner's exclusive rights of broadcast in a distant market therefore cannot be undermined by retransmission. The only circumstance in which it is not necessary to get the permission of the copyright holder is for an unaltered simultaneous retransmission of a distant signal intended for free public reception.

The FTA affects both Canadian and American broadcasters. This, and the changing technology of the industry, will ensure that broadcasting is an exciting field for the years to come.

Copyright laws and broadcasting

Unlike the situation in the United States, copyright protection in Canada arises automatically, without formalities. As long as the work is original, presented in some "fixed" material form, and fits within one of the four basic categories of art, literature, music, or drama, it is automatically protected. A cinematographic production is also covered by copyright, if the work is fixed in writing, filmed, or otherwise graphically produced. The work must be the product of a person's labour and the expression of his or her thoughts. It is important to recognize that copyright can only exist in an "expression"; a mere idea can never be the subject of copyright.

Canadian copyright law is undergoing major reforms but portions of the Copyright Act still date from the 1920s. The reforms grow out of the report presented to the House of Commons by the Sub-Committee on the Revision of Copyright, a sub-committee of the Standing Committee on Communications and Culture. The report is entitled *A charter of rights for creators*, and was tabled in 1984. It made 137 recommendations, some of which—chiefly those involved with retransmission rights—were implemented in phase I of the copyright law reform process. Phase I, embodied in Bill C-60, was assented to in June of 1988; phase II is expected to be tabled in 1990.

Current Canadian law continues to provide copyright holders with the sole right to communicate their works by radio communication. This provision was enacted when television broadcasting was a rarity and radio communication was limited to broadcasting within a geographical area defined by the size of the station's transmitter. Questions of copyright protection are of course very different today, when it is possible to make transmissions from ground radio stations to satellites and from there to anywhere in the world.

The first category of broadcasting is transmission, which might be defined as the communication of a work from one place to a number of persons. The second category is retransmission, which refers to transmission of a broadcast signal by means different from the original transmission. As discussed above, this is how cable systems operate, and both the FTA and amendments to the Copyright Act make provision for copyright holders to be paid by cable companies who retransmit their signals.

The focus of Canada's new copyright law is clear: broadcasters only have the right to broadcast material, not to copy it. Only the author or the author's assignee has that right. Copyright owners are increasingly being given the legal protection they need to control broadcasting activities and thereby receive appropriate payment. Fundamental to the recovery of payments is the formation of copyright "societies," which will receive and distribute royalties for copyright owners in the same way that musicians' royalties are now handled.

Summary

Mass communication in Canada is affected by both constitutional and administrative law. This chapter examined those points where the law touches communication, both historically and today. The origins of Canadian communication law have shaped its present form. Yet profoundly significant developments in the communication industry have to be taken into account within the law, and the traditional regulatory structure of the Canadian industry is inevitably being re-examined. Technological globalization has, for example, rendered parts of the current copyright law obsolete and it is consequently being reformed. The Free Trade Agreement in some respects defines the environment within which enhanced services are to develop, and this too will be reflected in law.

Conversely, developments in Canadian law that are independent of communication regulation can nevertheless affect the industry. The 1982 Charter of Rights and Freedoms has been applied to various communication disputes. As can be seen, mass media and the law have a great deal to do with one another; any study of the Canadian communication industry must examine the legal environment of that industry.

Notes

1. The exceptions in North America are the Province of Quebec and the State of Louisiana, where private or civil law matters are decided according to a system of codified law such as that in France.

2. Sections 1 and 2 of the Charter provide as follows:
   1. The Canadian Charter of Rights and Freedoms guarantees the rights and freedoms set out in it subject only to such reasonable limits prescribed by law as can be demonstrably justified in a free and democratic society.

   Fundamental Freedoms

   2. Everyone has the following fundamental freedoms:
      (a) freedom of conscience and religion;
      (b) freedom of thought, belief, and opinion and expression, including freedom of the press and other media of communication;
      (c) freedom of peaceful assembly; and
      (d) freedom of association.

3. For more information on this subject see Mahoney and Martin (1986).

4. See *Red Lion Broadcasting Co. Inc. v. F.C.C.* 395 U.S. 367 (1969).

5. Note the words of Dr. Augustine Frignon, a member of the Aird Commission: "We came to this conclusion, that if you want to accept the point of view of broadcasting in the interests of the nation, it cannot be left to private enterprise" (quoted in Weir 1965, 111).

6. For example, the question of political abuse was raised by the granting of the only clear channel in Toronto to a well-known Liberal supporter whose radio station, with only one hundred watts, was the weakest in the city. Four other stations, one of which generated five thousand watts, were forced to share four channels with American stations.

7. The view that the CBC was created in order to have a politically neutralized administrative agency is supported by Hodgetts (1970, 209).

8. According to Peers (1969, 448), party support for the private broadcasters came about partly through the efforts of local stations, whose easy access to local constituents won over many MPs. Stations gave MPs both air time and favourable mention.

9. Spry (1961) makes the important point that it was at the behest of the government that the CBC withdrew from local and national spot radio advertising, leaving these two largest sources of revenue exclusively to competing radio stations. Their importance is shown by the amounts generated. The two revenue sources totalled over $113 million in the years 1956–1958, or nearly two and a half times the entire expenditure of the CBC on its own thirty-five stations, live programs, performers, and three nation-wide networks. In North America, compared with revenues generated by operating a station, network and live programming are costly and usually unprofitable. They are also the two fields to which the CBC is largely confined.

10. Although the 1958 legislation appeared to give greater autonomy to the CBC over its own planning and administration, there were underlying tighter controls tied directly to the purse strings of the Corporation. For example, an annual capital budget having the approval of the governor-in-council, on the recommendation of the ministers of transport and finance, was to be laid before Parliament and, further, a five-year capital program was to be submitted to the governor-in-council. Furthermore, money appropriated by Parliament to the CBC had to be kept in a separate account called the Proprietor's Equity Account. These stringent controls indicate a comparative loss of independence by the CBC.

11. Among English-speaking viewers, for example, the CTV network attracts 30 percent of the audience whereas the CBC attracts 18 percent. Public stations are much fewer in number, command a much smaller audience, and still carry commercial messages themselves. See the report of the Federal Cultural Policy Review Committee (1982, 273–80) and the report of the Task Force on Broadcasting Policy (1986, 99).

12. See the discussion in Schiller (1970, 94).

13. An excellent discussion on telecommunication regulation is contained in Dunbar (1986).

References

Babe, R.E. 1976. Regulation of private television broadcasting by the Canadian Radio-television and Telecommunications Commission: A critique of ends and means. *Canadian Public Administration* 19: 552–86.

Beke, J. 1970. Government regulation of broadcasting in Canada. *Canadian Communications Law Review* 2: 104–44.

Black, E.R. 1968. Canadian public policy and the mass media. *Canadian Journal of Economics* 1: 368–79.

Canada. 1968. *Broadcasting Act, 1968.* Ottawa: Supply and Services.

Canada. Board of Broadcast Governors. 1961. White paper on broadcasting.

Canada. Federal Cultural Policy Review Committee. 1982. *Report.* Ottawa: Department of Communications.

Canada. House of Commons. 1932. *Debates.* 17th Parliament.

———. 1936. *Report of the Special Committee to Inquire into the Administration of the Canadian Radio Broadcasting Act, 1932.* Vol. 3 of *Official reports of debates of the House of Commons.* Ottawa: King's Printer.

Canada. Royal Commission on Broadcasting. 1957. *Report.* Vol. 1. Ottawa: Queen's Printer.

Canada. Royal Commission on National Development in the Arts, Letters and Sciences. 1951. *Report.* Ottawa: Edmund Cloutier.

Canada. Task Force on Broadcasting Policy. 1986. *Report.* Ottawa: Supply and Services.

Capital Cities Communications v. C.R.T.C. [1978] 2 S.C.R. 141.

CNCP Telecommunications v. Alberta Government Telephones [1985] 2 F.C.R. 472 (Trial Division); [1986] 2 F.C.R. 179 (Appellate Division); S.C.C., 14 August 1989, not yet reported.

Direction to the CRTC on issue and renewal of broadcasting licences to daily newspaper proprietors. 1982. SOR/82-746; later rescinded by SOR 84/492.

Dunbar, L.J.E. 1986. Telecommunications and the Constitution: New developments. Communications Law Conference program materials. Law Society of Upper Canada.

Feldthusen, B.P. 1986. Awakening from the national broadcasting dream: Rethinking television for national cultural goals. Unpublished paper. University of Western Ontario.

Globe and Mail. 1988. 24 June. p. 1.

Hansard parliamentary debates. 1958. 1st session, 24th Parliament. Vol. 4. 25 August.

Hodgetts, J.E. 1970. The public corporation in Canada. In *Government enterprise: A comparative study*, ed. W. Friedmann and J.F. Garner, 201–26. London: Stevens.

Macdonald, D. 1985. Sky Channel and the Coca-Cola bird. *Broadcaster.* March. pp. 32–34, 66.

Mahoney, K. and S. Martin. 1986. *Broadcasting and the Canadian Charter of Rights and Freedoms: Justifications for restricting freedom of expression.* Calgary: University of Calgary.

New Brunswick Broadcasting Company Ltd. v. C.R.T.C. [1984] 2 F.C.R. 410.

Peers, F.W. 1969. *The politics of Canadian broadcasting: 1920–51.* Toronto: University of Toronto.

———. 1979. *The public eye: Television and the politics of Canadian broadcasting.* Toronto: University of Toronto.

Posner, R.A. 1974. Theories of economic regulation. *Bell Journal of Economics* 5: 335–58.

Prang, M. 1965. The origins of public broadcasting in Canada. *Canadian Historical Review* 46: 1–31.

Quincy Cable T.V. Inc. v. Federal Communications Commission. 1985. 768 F.2d 1434.

Re CFRB and Attorney General of Canada [1973] 3 O.R. 819, affirming [1973] 1 O.R. 79 (H.C.).

Re Regulation and control of radio communication in Canada (Radio reference) [1931] S.C.R. 541; appealed [1932] A.C. 304.

Red Lion Broadcasting Co. Inc. v. F.C.C. 1969. 395 U.S. 367.

Schiller, H.I. 1970. *Mass communications and American empire.* New York: Augustus M. Kelley.

Spector, N. 1976. The Canadian broadcasting system within the miniature replica economy. Paper presented at the conference on The Crisis of Canadian Broadcasting. 1975. Saint Mary's University. Halifax.

Spry, G. 1961. The decline and fall of Canadian broadcasting. *Queen's Quarterly* 68: 213–25.

———. 1965. The origins of public broadcasting in Canada: A comment. *Canadian Historical Review* 46: 134–41.

Weir, E.A. 1965. *The struggle for national broadcasting in Canada.* Toronto: McClelland and Stewart.

Westcott, G. 1986. Broadcasting regulation and the Canadian Charter of Rights. Communications Law Conference program materials. Law Society of Upper Canada.

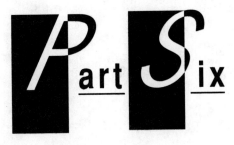

Conclusion

CANADA AS A
COMMUNICATION LABORATORY

*I*t is difficult to conclude a book on communication policy in Canada. Almost every month, and certainly every year, new policy statements are made; and somewhat less frequently, new legislation is developed for one or more aspects of the communication environment, whether for film, television, cable, TVROs, VCRs, or telecommunication. Technological advances fuel further changes, often to the chagrin of both regulators and Canadian cultural nationalists. This chapter is therefore not so much a conclusion as a transition. Readers are encouraged to be alert to new and unexpected events in the communication field, and to continue updating the issues raised in previous chapters accordingly. What follows is a summary of the primary themes addressed in this book and some speculation about the parameters of issues that Canadians will be confronting in the next decades.

The Canadian communication environment, created by the accidents of geography and demographics, has historically been considered unique. Rapid changes in the entire communication field have clearly made the Canadian situation less uncommon. The development of sophisticated telecommunication delivery systems and a plethora of new or enhanced receiving systems are forcing once solely Canadian problems onto the international stage. Many other nations, aware of the potential benefits and dangers of the new technologies, are now hoping to learn from Canada's lengthy experience with similar challenges. The breadth and scope of Canadian experiences make the country an attractive communication policy laboratory, or case study.

Themes in Canadian communication

Seemingly disparate issues presented throughout this text do tend to coalesce into a few major themes: the relationship of cultural, political, and economic sovereignty to mass communication; the impact of new communication technology; and the social effects of mass media. Part 1 of the book introduced the Canadian cultural policy dilemma. The small, dispersed, bilingual, and multicultural nature of the Canadian population, set beside the large, unilingual, well-financed, and highly productive cultural industries of the United States, make Canada's crisis with its own cultural identity understandable. The situation has motivated both nationalistic cultural leaders and concerned policy makers to seek ways to safeguard the nation's cultural integrity. It has also been suggested that their sensitivity to Canada's cultural ambiguity propelled both Harold Innis and Marshall McLuhan into the ground-breaking theoretical work that dominated their academic careers. Both scholars offered intriguing insights into the relationship between culture and communication.

Discussion of these theoretical treatises was accompanied in part 1 by an introduction to a broad range of approaches to communication study. There is a growing interest in mass communication and its potential impact on its audiences. Most of the research is still tentative but is supported by an almost intuitive sense that any institution as ubiquitous as the mass media must also be powerful and persuasive. This concept also motivates policy makers, especially Canadian policy makers, most of whom readily acknowledge their uneasiness about the nation's proclivity for importing, almost in its entirety, another nation's culture.

Part 2 dealt extensively with the print media. It examined Canada's main newspaper chains, magazine publishing industry, and domestic and international wire services. The section emphasized current concern about increasingly concentrated newspaper ownership and the tendency to treat newspapers first and foremost as business enterprises. Such practices pose potential dangers for freedom of the press and modern ideas of democracy. In some respects, however, the current state of the Canadian industry gives more cause for optimism than in the past. Although many large American cities are experiencing difficulties with the viability of their competing daily papers, the same is no longer the case in Canada. Not only are the chains themselves quite profitable, but recent activities in Ottawa, Montreal, and Toronto, where new dailies have entered the market, indicate the vibrancy and profitability that the daily press enjoys in Canada's major cities.

As a conclusion to its review of the print media, part 2 examined the future of the daily newspaper. Some anxiety was expressed over the possibility that several aspects of the traditional daily, notably the financial, sports, and classified sections, will become available in video format via cable television. In May 1989, for example, the *Hamilton Spectator* instituted a new service, called Spec-Tel. Anyone with a touchtone telephone can ring up Spec-Tel. Once users are connected, a four-digit code will give them access to local, national, or international news, sports, the weather, and so on. Taped news messages come complete with advertisements. This represents a novel newspaper service, perhaps the first step in electronic news delivery. At some point, electronic information services will find their niche in the overall information marketplace, and they may lure customers in significant numbers from traditional print formats. The change is not inherently negative but it will force policy makers to rethink traditional ideas about press regulation and the role of the press in the Canadian environment.

This discussion was followed by an examination of the electronic media in Canada. Part 3 of the text described the development of the Canadian broadcasting and distribution systems, both public and private, focussing on the various royal commissions and investigations into broadcasting from the early development of radio through to the framework of the system today. Aspects of both English- and French-language broadcasting were outlined, with their systemic differences. The section also identified Telefilm Canada as the main cultural financial agency to support and encourage Canadian productions suitable for television and feature films. Because of their substantial impact and importance, cable, satellite, and pay television services—and some of their major structural difficulties—were also examined. Finally, part 3 covered the issues of regulation and Canadianization of the airwaves, in the form of Canadian content rules, quotas, and other cultural imperatives. The Caplan/Sauvageau Task Force and the Standing Committee on Communications and Culture, the most recent public examinations of the Canadian broadcasting system, received considerable attention.

Throughout the discussion, the section emphasized the position of broadcasting as Canada's cultural beast of burden; no other policy arena is so closely involved with the Canadian cultural dilemma. Broadcasting policy debates revolve around three challenges that the system faces. First, the traditional role of broadcasting as the medium primarily responsible for communicating and consolidating a national identity has to compete against the lavishly produced and highly popular broadcast programming of the United States. Second, the broadcasting sector confronts many economic difficulties. Finally, the Canadian system must continually adjust to technology that, more and more, oversteps international boundaries. This last factor has transformed a problem once uniquely Canadian into an international one. Part 3 thoroughly explored all three factors in the broadcasting policy debate.

Technology is also forcing a reconsideration of the telecommunication infrastructure and policy, as outlined in chapters 9 and 10. Although the telecommunication sector is less visible than broadcasting and clearly less dramatic in terms of media interest, this book devoted much space and attention to it. Telecommunication is an important component of two of Canada's evolving roles—as an information society and as a model of high-technology applications for other countries to study. Modern banking, tourism, education, and other industries of all types now rely on complex and sophisticated telecommunication networks. Although many people still consider "telecommunication" synonymous with "telephone," the telephone is only one small segment of a vast range of technologies and services that encompasses everything from optic fibres and satellites to high-speed, high-storage computers, robotics, and "smart" buildings. Part 4 followed the evolution of telecommunication policy in Canada and described crucial contemporary issues such as rate rebalancing. As in the broadcasting arena, Canada leads the international community in examining its own telecommunication sector. Although the frequent and innovative studies have rarely resulted in legislation, the

Canadian telecommunication industry has moved forward at a reasonable pace. With the 1989 Supreme Court decision awarding the federal government almost total control of telecommunication, there is now some hope that the pace will quicken. In particular, a new telecommunication act would provide needed direction for the industry.

Experts are now predicting that as much as 75 percent of the future work force will be involved in information-related jobs. In the years to come, a modern nation such as Canada will clearly need not only large information-technology manufacturers and service-sector firms, but also enlightened legislation and federal fiscal policies to promote our information economy in a competitive international environment. One has only to look to the European Community, which recently issued a green paper as its guide for encouraging worldwide distribution of European information technology, to see that the competition is very determined. When one takes the United States and Japan into account as well, it becomes clear that Canada's future as an information society may be tenuous unless sufficient attention and funding are devoted to progressive Canadian information policies and industries.

Discussion in this section reflected, once again, the recurring themes of the book. Canada's national independence is closely linked to its position on communication policy. The mass media arouse issues of cultural and political sovereignty; the telecommunication arena provokes questions about economic sovereignty. Nationalism, economics, and technology all resurface as vital elements in the future of Canadian mass communication.

Part 5 examined three communication-related topics: politics, advertising, and law. Although they are not media of communication in their own right, all three are directly related to the influence and role of the mass media in Canadian society. The omnipotence often ascribed to the media makes it essential to examine their methods of reporting public affairs and of conveying advertising. Research on the impact of media in these areas, though inconclusive, is evidence of much concern.

Television has replaced newspapers as the primary source of news and political information, and the first chapter in the section examined both the impact of television in the political arena and the rise of public opinion polling. The chapter on advertising concentrated on media content and the financial support that the media receive from advertising. It outlined the role, strategies, and potential effects of advertising, as well as some of the organizational dimensions of advertising agencies in Canada.

The contribution of advertising to the success of different media merited some attention in the chapter as well. Because Canadian advertising resources are limited and the mass media are moving towards deregulation, it will be interesting to see what effect the competition for advertising dollars among different media will have both on the future commercial success of those media and on the actual existence of traditional media.

The final chapter in this trio dealt with communication law. It set forth the division of powers in the field of mass communication, in terms of legislative authority and regulation. Canada has a long history of dispute between federal and provincial governments over communication jurisdiction.

The Charter of Rights and Freedoms is also a fundamental consideration in communication law today. The chapter looked at various Canadian judicial decisions that have dealt with the application of the Charter, and the Bill of Rights, to communication. The issues of freedom of expression, regulation of media content, and regulation that prescribes priorities for carrying signals over cable all have relevance here. Does regulation contravene freedom of expression as set out in the Charter? The way in which Canadian broadcasting developed has lent support to a policy of active government involvement in the broadcasting system.

The chapter therefore outlined the historical development of the system from a legal perspective. The implications of a chain of statutes and studies, stretching over the past sixty years, were examined. Canadian communication policy arose out of the unique Canadian broadcasting environment. Nevertheless, the communication infrastructure is now in place and we are likely to see a shift in policy from delivery of service to quality of programming. What is more, changes in technology are rapidly necessitating changes in the law. Copyright law, in fact, has changed recently. Current broadcast practices, such as retransmission of signals, and new technology, such as VCRs, have raised many issues that the former Act did not address. The final section of the chapter discussed this important area of law.

Diverse in scope, the media topics in part 5 tend to unify around two related themes: that the media are powerful instruments for communicating messages and influencing public perception, and that some control of the media is therefore justified in a liberal democratic society. Canadian policy makers define "public good" or "public interest" more broadly than do their neighbours in the United States and many other nations are beginning to look to Canada for guidance in this respect. Our strengths and weaknesses, successes and failures, are being scrutinized internationally in an attempt to find the right formula for ensuring cultural sovereignty through enhanced cultural diversity. As McLuhan's global village materializes, the nations of the world search more desperately for a way to maintain their cultural uniqueness.

Diverse origins

To date, Canada has been fortunate in its communication scholarship although it has relied more on good luck than on any sort of systematic inquiry. The materials presented in this book make it clear that Canadian scholarship in this field developed from very diverse disciplines, ranging from anthropology to political science. Indeed, it was not until the mid-1960s that the first university-based communication department was established in Canada, at Loyola College, although there were of course schools of journalism prior to this, most notably at Carleton University and the University of Western Ontario.

The interdisciplinary nature of communication itself suggests that interdisciplinary study is absolutely necessary to a thorough understanding of the concept. On the other hand, fragmented and dislocated scholarship has not helped communication studies to become a unified discipline in Canada. As for the future, the explosion of interest in communication at all levels and in all disciplines that we are now experiencing may lead to a rapid increase in the number and strength of communication departments at Canadian universities. It is also to be hoped that the current paucity of related doctoral studies will give way to many strong new communication degrees by the year 2000. (At present even Ontario, with its sixteen universities, does not offer a Ph.D. program in communication.) Such a trend would necessarily help to codify and expand the body of knowledge so important to students of communication, particularly with reference to some of the policy and theoretical questions.

Nevertheless, academic study is not the sole source or, in some cases, even the main source of information on Canadian broadcasting, telecommunication, and cultural concerns. Several royal commissions and other investigative bodies have also provided a wide array of research with a perhaps more practical bent, especially in terms of understanding the various forces and actors involved in this policy arena. In addition, authors outside of the academic environment such as J.P. L'Allier and Bernard Ostry have offered thoughtful analysis of the role of, and forces affecting, communication in Canada.

When one considers the diversity of these contributions, the durability of certain issues is striking. Regardless of interest, approach, or even conclusion, much Canadian communication scholarship is preoccupied with the cultural challenges facing the nation. There is no consensus on either the consequences of cultural domination or the best approach to take towards it in our public policy but one thing is clear. If it is to deal with the complexity and sophistication of communication technologies and industry infrastructures, Canada can ill afford to rely on its past good fortune to identify appropriate public policy mechanisms.

The new internationalism of Canadian communication issues

The history of Canadian communication and the foundation of much of the original Canadian theoretical work in the field is closely intertwined with the geographic, demographic, and cultural proximity of the United States. This is true of radio, film, television, magazines, and other types of printed and electronic materials. Scholars and policy makers have concerns not only about American content in Canadian media but also about the related, more indirect impact of that content on the standards against which Canadian productions are judged. The effect of the American media on Canadians and their media began in the first quarter of this century with the importation of U.S. radio broadcasts. It continued with the development of content regulations to prop up a Canadian presence on the television screens of the 1960s, 70s, and 80s, and is still with us as contemporary concerns force us to re-examine our media and cultural industries.

The issues that Canadian citizens, broadcasters, planners, regulators, and policy makers have grappled with for the last seventy years are now confronting other nations, particularly European ones, in a more dramatic fashion. A proliferation of cable- and satellite-delivered broadcast signals, and alternative delivery systems such as VCRs and high-definition television, is compelling other countries to acknowledge some familiar problems. The Canadian communication story, as described in the preceding chapters, is instructive for students of communication from Australia to the United Kingdom.

Developments in communication technology that have transformed Canadian challenges into international ones now offer Canada two related opportunities. On the one hand, it can share its communication history with the international community so that other nations can benefit from Canadian experience. On the other hand, Canada can now learn from the policies put forward by these nations, for it must be acknowledged that the Canadian experience has not always been positive. Our prime-time television fare is still dominated by the three major American networks, while competing Canadian television programming remains essentially pedestrian, motivating the Canadian audience to abandon it in droves. Despite substantial government investment in the feature film industry, via various agencies, the 1987 Cinema Bill has been watered down. It was initially aimed at guaranteeing a strong Canadian presence in the distribution of films in Canada. Finally, although Canadians have been instrumental in developing several important types of communication hardware, parallel dedication in establishing a Canadian software industry of international size, scope, or influence has been lacking.

There is still some hope, however, that lessons have been learned and appropriate models and mechanisms identified in order to establish a place for Canada in a world where communication is an ever-expanding part of daily life. These attempts may prove instructive for other nations who are just now beginning to confront the realities of globalization.

Canada as an information society

As Western nations transform themselves from industrial to information societies, it becomes evident that telecommunication, information technologies, and a renewed emphasis on research and development are central to the transition, and will create new employment opportunities. Canada has a mixed record as an information society. The success of firms such as Northern Telecom Canada Ltd., Rogers Communications Inc., and Novatel Communications Ltd. provides Canada with tremendous opportunities and resources. The domestic satellite system, called Anik, is also able to hold its own internationally. The number and quality of policy studies in the area have also helped to generate a positive image for Canada abroad.

Yet there have been noticeable weaknesses. The failure of Telidon to capture the videotex market, for example, is not encouraging. Lack of funding is a significant problem for Canadian industry and research institutions. As recently as 1986, Canada invested only 1.4 percent of its gross national product (GNP) on research and development, compared to 2.9 percent in the United States and 2.8 percent in Japan. Even nations with more modest patterns of investment, such as Sweden, France, Britain, West Germany, and the Netherlands, put more than 2 percent of their GNP into research. The long-term consequences of this lack of commitment by government and industry to high-tech research are serious.

There is little doubt that Canadians will continue to purchase all kinds of modern communication technology, from personal computers to video cassette recorders, but they will have to import it. The state of our industries will not permit otherwise. Fewer and fewer technical breakthroughs will be made in Canadian labs or at Canadian universities. Canada could be forced back into a role as a net exporter of natural resources and net importer of high technologies, primarily from the United States and Japan, if it does not make aggressive public policy decisions in the near future.

A final note

Canada's problems with communication are not a solely twentieth-century phenomenon. Confederation, in 1867, arose as much from the desire to solve communication-related dilemmas as from a need to resolve political difficulties. Once elected, the new federal Parliament acted rapidly to build a railway joining provinces from the Atlantic to the Pacific. Not even the monumental barrier of the Rocky Mountains could dissuade the government from its national dream of an east–west axis to counterbalance the strong, natural north–south influences. Successive federal governments realized, almost instinctively, that effective communication was the only hope for coping with the enormous problems created by the country's size. They also recognized that the essential ideas of nationhood—sovereignty, cultural identity, nationalism, and patriotism—were crucially affected by the presence and sophistication of communication infrastructures. Yet in spite of this insight, policy makers have never mastered the practicalities of promoting communication as a vital part of the national destiny. The pieces of the puzzle don't seem to fit properly. Why hasn't the mosaic come together?

The dilemma is even more perplexing when one examines the technological and institutional base upon which the system is founded. The completion of the trans-Canada railroad was accompanied by telegraph links from coast to coast, which allowed faster transmission of news. The telegraph system was followed by a string of radio stations, movie theatres, and television stations. As technology advanced, so did the manner in which the nation used it, and today Canada is one of the best-served nations in the world with respect to communication and telecommuncation services and opportunities. The system consists of both public and private undertakings, which should, at least theoretically, give Canadians the best that both approaches have to offer. Government involvement takes the form of exhortation, financial subsidies, and regulation, all undertaken in the public interest to ensure that Canadians are well served. And yet the challenges persist!

There are clear reasons for this. Our demographic and cultural similarity to the United States, and the strength and quality of American media vis-à-vis our own, make domination natural. Second, our small market base and limited resources make equal competition impossible. We simply cannot afford to produce the quality and quantity of cultural products that our neighbours to the South do. A third reason, though more complex and more difficult to prove than the previous two, also deserves some attention.

A sense of nationhood always comes with some difficulty. This is particularly true for colonies that achieved their independent status through peaceful political means. They have few exciting heroes and even fewer dramatic events to commemorate. An evolutionary process of independence may be a source of pride in and of itself, but it makes it difficult for the people of these new nations to identify significant symbols of independence around which they can unite. This is especially true for Canada and Canadians.

Canadian independence from Britain came slowly indeed. It was not until after World War II that Canada tentatively began to test its real power as an independent nation. By this time, other factors were undermining its sense of national identity. Canada was a nation of "two solitudes," a division that had been exacerbated by the conscription crisis during World War I. The non-francophone majority still maintained ties with Europe, but the Québécois, who had been deserted by France centuries before, held no similar allegiances. They had their own heroes, language, and culture, which eventually propelled them into serious conflict with the nation as a whole. The majority of Canadians, however, lacked the identifying and unifying features of the Québécois. Many were recent immigrants who came to populate the vast open spaces of the country. Their cultural identities were more closely linked to the countries they had left than to their adopted home. Developing Canadian policies of bilingualism and multiculturalism promoted diversity rather than conformity. In addition, by the time Canada finally achieved independence from Great Britain, its dependence on the United States was increasing. Moreover, Canadians were experiencing the beginning of the age of the electronic media. Before they had a real opportunity to know themselves, Canadians were inundated by the stories and images of their powerful and attractive neighbour. It should therefore not be surprising that the nation has not yet provided itself and its people with a concrete conception of its identity. But the key word here is "yet."

During the past century, Canadians have exhibited thoughtful insight when analysing communication issues. Even so, they have apparently failed to provide solutions, other than occasionally suggesting that we separate our communication channels from those in the U.S. with an electronic Berlin Wall. The idea is, of course, not only contrary to our notions of liberal democracy but also doomed to failure by the technology that Canadians have themselves helped to create. Canada's cultural future does, however, contain cause for optimism. There are clear and encouraging signs that Canadian literature, certain segments of the Canadian feature film sector, and various other cultural industries are receiving national and international recognition. (Sales of Canadian television programming abroad, for example, are doing well.) It appears that Canadian culture is about to take off, if it receives appropriate national support.

Perhaps the old adage that you can't find the right answer until you ask the right question will ring true in this case. Canadian policy makers have tirelessly pursued the answers to a number of relevant cultural questions, but they have not specifically asked what images and ideas the complex and sophisticated communication infrastructure should distribute. This has been left up to individual Canadians, and rightly so. With our cultural disadvantages, it should not be so very surprising that it has taken a hundred years or so for Canadian writers and artists to begin to articulate the uniqueness of the Canadian experience. The growing strength of cultural self-awareness in Canada lends support to our optimistic belief that the potential for Canadian self-expression lies just beyond the horizon.

Index

1 2 3 4 5   4685-2   94 93 92 91 90